THE POLITICS OF
CONFLICT

A SURVEY

T0347235

THE POLITICS OF
CONFLICT

A SURVEY

FIRST EDITION

Edited by Vassilis K. Fouskas

Routledge
Taylor & Francis Group

LONDON AND NEW YORK

First Edition 2007
This edition published in paperback 2011
Routledge
2 Park Square, Milton Park, Abingdon, Oxon OX14 4RN
711 Third Avenue, New York, NY 10017, USA

Routledge is an imprint of the Taylor & Francis Group, an informa business

ISBN 978-1-85743-405-7 (hbk)
ISBN 978-1-85743-581-8 (pbk)
ISBN 978-0-203-83204-2 (ebk)

Editor Europa New Projects: Cathy Hartley

Typeset in Times New Roman 10.5/12

The publishers make no representation, express or implied, with regard to the accuracy of the information contained in this book and cannot accept any legal responsibility for any errors or omissions that may take place.

Typeset by AJS Solutions, Huddersfield – Dundee

In memoriam: Vassiliki Boudouki

Foreword

The contributors to *The Politics of Conflict* make a single, real, albeit depressing, case: that conflicts and wars in the world are *politically* mediated and ramified, for without politics, the end-aim of war itself, conflict is meaningless. But the political, in this respect, is both 'national' and 'international', both of which they mingle in inextricable and complicated ways.

The book is divided into sections. The first, Essays, begins with a comprehensive Introduction by the Editor, summarizing the main arguments put forward by the contributors. Next, a theoretical and speculative essay by Andrew Wheatcroft maps out and contextualizes the theme of 'evil' in the contemporary discourses of the US 'Empire'.

The following five chapters deal with conflicts in the most conflict-ridden regions/continents of the world. Jairo Lugo and Phia Steyn analyse conflicts in Latin America and Africa respectively. The chapter by Emmanuel Karagiannis focuses on the Caucasus and Central Asia, a most interesting and under-examined area of the post-Soviet region. Rajat Ganguly examines the conflict cases of Kashmir and Sri Lanka, whose significance is paramount for the security and stability of the entire Asian region. Yoke-Lian Lee and Roger Buckley make a comprehensive reading of the situation in South-East Asia, viewing it through such analytical categories as 'decolonization, modernization, nationalism and state-building'.

The focus of the next five chapters is on four individual case studies, precisely because of their contemporary and historical prominence. Rory Miller tackles the Arab–Israeli conflict and John Doyle the case of Northern Ireland. Then there are two chapters on the issue of Yugoslavia's collapse, summarizing the two main viewpoints in the contemporary debates on the issue: which factors are more important in explaining the collapse of the country, domestic/ethnic nationalism or external agencies? Finally, the chapter by Vassilis K. Fouskas deals with the case of Iraq in a theoretically and historically informed way.

The A–Z Glossary on conflicts in the world is composed by Vassilis K. Fouskas with the assistance of Hazel Cameron.

A section of maps follows for reference, including clear maps of the Aegean, South and South-East Asia, Iraq, Africa, South America, and other countries and regions.

A comprehensive Bibliography section concludes the book.

Vassilis K. Fouskas
Senior Lecturer in International Relations
University of Stirling
May 2007

Acknowledgements

I am immensely indebted to Cathy Hartley, Development Editor at Routledge, for her constant support and encouragement from the beginning to the very end of this book. Without Cathy, this project would not have materialized.

I am also very grateful to Gareth Wyn Jones for his enviable editing skills and accurate comments on South-East Asia, particularly the ongoing conflict in the Fiji islands.

I wish to thank all the contributors to this volume, from whom I have gained a tremendous amount of knowledge and information. I am grateful that they all delivered their manuscripts on time and dealt with editorial comments in the most professional and prompt way. It has been a great pleasure working with them all. Thanks are also due to Hazel Cameron, a PhD student, who volunteered to help me with the A–Z Glossary, particularly with the entries on Africa, of which her knowledge must be acknowledged and praised.

Last but not least, I am grateful to my colleague at Stirling, Andrew Wheatcroft, who was a constant source of support and encouragement to me throughout the difficult winter of 2006/07. Andy read and commented on both my Introduction and the chapter on Iraq, and I can only hope that the published version meets his high expectations.

The Politics of Conflict: A Survey is dedicated to the memory of my beloved grandmother, Vassiliki Boudouki. She was born in Asia Minor in 1909 (no record of her exact birth date has ever been found) and died in Petra-Lesvos, Greece, on 20 February 2001. She, like the hundreds of millions of other people of every religion, nationality or creed in the modern era, was a refugee, the most innocent victim of the *politics* of conflict and war, who could never return to the land where she was born: Μοσχονήσια (Moschonisia), today's Cunda (Ayvalik), Turkey. Old and incapable of travel, she had scribbled down on paper countless times where her house was, so that I could go and find it and bring back photographs. I failed, the land had changed. Vassiliki was very happy that some of my best friends are Turkish, because she believed that 'all people on earth have the same human needs and it is politics that divides them'. To Vassiliki Boudouki and, therefore, to the unknown refugee and the displaced of the world, this book is dedicated with affection and respect.

Vassilis K. Fouskas

Contents

Acknowledgements viii
The Contributors x
Abbreviations xii

ESSAYS
Introduction: A World in Conflict – Vassilis K. Fouskas 3
Articulating Evil – Andrew Wheatcroft 11
Modern Conflicts in Latin America – Jairo Lugo 22
Conflicts in Africa – Phia Steyn 44
Ethnic Conflicts in the Caucasus and Central Asia –
    Emmanuel Karagiannis 59
Conflicts in South Asia: Kashmir and Sri Lanka – Rajat Ganguly 74
Conflicts in South-East Asia: Decolonization, Modernization,
    Nationalism and State-Building – Yoke-Lian Lee and Roger Buckley 101
The Arab–Israeli Conflict – Rory Miller 118
Re-examining the Northern Ireland Conflict – John Doyle 132
Yugoslavia: Why Did it Collapse? – Stevan K. Pavlowitch 147
Placing Serbia in Context – Peter Gowan 155
Iraq and Meta-Conflict – Vassilis K. Fouskas 166

A–Z GLOSSARY: CONFLICTS IN THE WORLD
    by Vassilis K. Fouskas with the assistance of Hazel Cameron 185

MAPS
Map 1: The Aegean 235
Map 2: The Caucasus and Central Asia 236
Map 3: Latin America 237
Map 4: East and South-East Asia 238
Map 5: Africa 239
Map 6: South Asia 240
Map 7: Ireland 241
Map 8: Israel-Palestine 242
Map 9: Iraq 243
Map 10: Yugoslavia 244

BIBLIOGRAPHY 245

The Contributors

Vassilis K. Fouskas is the Director of the MSc in International Conflict and Co-operation at the University of Stirling (United Kingdom). His work includes: *The New American Imperialism* (2005—with Bülent Gökay), *Zones of Conflict: US Foreign Policy in the Balkans and the Greater Middle East* (2003) and *Italy, Europe and the Left* (1998). He is the founding Editor of the *Journal of Southern Europe and the Balkans*.

Roger Buckley is Professor of International Relations at the Japan campus (Tokyo) of the USA's Temple University, and a Research Associate at the Rothermere American Institute, Oxford (United Kingdom). He is the author of *The United States in the Asia-Pacific since 1945* (2002).

John Doyle is a Lecturer in International Relations at Dublin City University, Ireland, and Director of the MA Programme in International Relations. He has published widely in the fields of comparative nationalism and conflict and of international security and foreign policy.

Rajat Ganguly is a Fellow of the Asia Research Centre at Murdoch University, Western Australia. He was previously a Senior Lecturer at the School of Social Sciences and Humanities, University of East Anglia (United Kingdom). He has written widely on ethnic conflict and South Asian politics and security. He is the author of *Kin State Intervention in Ethnic Conflicts: Lessons from South Asia* (1998), *Understanding Ethnic Conflict: The International Dimension* (2005, third edition—with Ray Taras) and *Ethnicity and Nation-Building in South Asia* (2001, revised edition—with Urmila Phadnis). He also serves as the Editor of the *Journal of South Asian Development*.

Peter Gowan is an Editor of *New Left Review* and the author, among others, of the prize-winning *The Global Gamble: Washington's Faustian Bid for World Dominance* (1999). He is a Professor of International Relations at London Metropolitan University (United Kingdom).

Emmanuel Karagiannis is a Lecturer in International Relations at the University of Macedonia in Thessaloníki (Greece). He has a PhD in Politics from the University of Hull (United Kingdom) and an MA in International Security Studies from the University of Reading (United Kingdom).

Yoke-Lian Lee teaches and researches at Keele University (United Kingdom) in the areas of international law, international relations and feminist political theory.

Her recent research is on the relationship between sovereignty, gender and human rights and she is the author (with John Horton) of 'Iraq, Political Reconstruction and Liberal Theory', in *The Iraq War and Democratic Politics* (2004, edited by A. Danchev and J. MacMillan). She is now workling with Glen Newey on a project on the themes of 'After Politics' funded by Keele University's Roberts Fund.

Jairo Lugo holds a BA in Media and Communication Studies from the University of Zulia, based in Maracaibo (Venezuela), an MA in Defence and Security Analysis from Lancaster University (United Kingdom) and a PhD from the University of Sussex (United Kingdom). He has worked as a correspondent, staff writer and editor for several newspapers, magazines and radio stations in Colombia, the USA and Venezuela. He is an associate member of the Centre for Defence and International Security Studies (CDISS) in Henley-on-Thames (United Kingdom).

Rory Miller is Senior Lecturer in Mediterranean Studies, King's College, University of London (United Kingdom), where he teaches courses on the European Union and US involvement in the Middle East. Among his publications are *Divided Against Zion: Anti-Zionist Opposition to a Jewish State in Palestine, 1945–48* (2000) and *Ireland and the Palestine Question, 1948–2004* (2005). He is Associate Editor of the academic journal, *Israel Affairs*.

Stevan K. Pavlowitch is Professor Emeritus of Balkan History at the University of Southampton (United Kingdom). He is the author of, among others, *Tito. Yugoslavia's Great Dictator: A Reassessment* (1992), *A History of the Balkans, 1804–1945* (1999) and *Serbia: The History behind the Name* (2002).

Phia Steyn teaches African Political and Environmental History at the University of Stirling in Scotland (United Kingdom). Her research and publications have focused mainly on petroleum-related struggles in the West African and Latin American tropics, multinational resource exploitation in Africa and the history of environmentalism in South Africa. She is currently writing an environmental history of apartheid in South Africa.

Andrew Wheatcroft is the Director of the Centre for Publishing Studies in the University of Stirling (United Kingdom) and a widely published cultural historian, his emphasis being on war and society. His most recent book is *Infidels: The Conflict between Christendom and Islam* (2005). His earlier work includes *The World Atlas of Revolutions* (1983), *Zones of Conflict: An Atlas of Future Wars* (1986—with John Keegan) and *The Road to War* (1989—with Richard Overy). His books have been translated into 11 languages.

Abbreviations

AA	anti-aircraft
Adm.	Admiral
ASEAN	Association of South-East Asian Nations
AU	African Union
Brig.	Brigadier
c.	*circa*
CIA	Central Intelligence Agency
Co	Company
Col	Colonel
DC	District of Columbia
Dr	Doctor
DRC	Democratic Republic of the Congo
Ed.	Editor
edn	Edition
et al.	*et alii* (and others)
EU	European Union
Gen.	General
ha	hectare(s)
ibid.	*ibidem* (in the same place)
Inc	Incorporated
km	kilometre
Ltd	Limited
m.	million
Maj.	Major
MIT	Massachusetts Institute of Technology
NATO	North Atlantic Treaty Organization
OAS	Organization of American States
OECD	Organisation for Economic Co-operation and Development
Publrs	Publishers
Publs	Publications
Ref.	reference
Sgt	Sergeant
St	Saint
Trans.	translated
UK	United Kingdom
UN	United Nations
US	United States
USA	United States of America
USSR	Union of Soviet Socialist Republics

Note: in the text, 9/11 refers to 11 September 2001, the date of the al-Qa'ida attacks on New York and Washington, DC, USA.

Essays

Introduction: A World in Conflict

VASSILIS K. FOUSKAS

One reason why Fascism has a chance is that in the name of progress its opponents treat it as a historical norm. Walter Benjamin, 'Theses on the Philosophy of History', 1939.

CONFLICT STUDIES

'Conflict studies' in the higher education institutions of the West is a relatively recent phenomenon. The subject stormed out of our military academies, to see itself assume pride of place in the list of postgraduate taught courses, especially in the United Kingdom. What generated this interest, of course, and sensitized the most alert members of the academic community in the field of international relations, was the end of the Cold War coupled, some 10 years later, with the terrorist attacks on the USA on 9/11, 11 September 2001. The clash, now, people like to say, is no longer between opposing states and power blocs, but rather between 'civilizations', religions and nationalisms. Conflict is also attributed to 'rogue' or 'failed' states and regions and can thus be 'asymmetric' in cases where a great power intrudes, attempting to impose 'order and justice' upon disobedient societal actors.

True, American academics and practitioners had pioneered the field well before the collapse of 'really existing socialism', particularly with their work in Ivy League institutions and specialized think-tanks: peace and conflict studies, conflict management and resolution, peace-making and peace-building, mediation and conflict—the list is endless. In fact, 'conflict' seems to have become the buzzword in the relatively new discipline of international relations. It is understood as an independent and neutral category in social sciences, a category that is not reducible to the classic concepts of sociology and political science, those of class, status and security. Thus, conflict-resolution frameworks in the field of conflict studies resort to technical instruments drawn from legal codes and the practices of industrial disputes: informal negotiation and arbitration first; then good offices, judicial settlement, reconciliation and problem-solving workshops; and, if need be, healing practices.

Despite the merits of this approach and its immense contribution to the study of conflict, in this book we have chosen not to engage directly with and/or problematize this analytical framework. The essays presented here have a much more modest aim, which is to describe, inform and dispose of issues relevant to the specificities of the regional conflicts that each contributor examines. We do not talk about conflict in general, nor have we thematicized the variety of conflicts, such as according to gender, environment, etc; also, we do not make reference to low intensity conflicts (such as drugs trafficking, small weapons trafficking, etc.). Instead, we offer an informed discussion about high intensity conflicts across the globe, actual or latent, conflicts that pertain to the classic analytical matrices of class, state and security, and thus of power. *The Politics of Conflict: A Survey* has to be understood, and judged, from this idiosyncratic perspective.

Obviously, not everything can be reduced to the concepts of class, state, security and power. Identity, perceptions, the environment and cultural and ideological issues are determined neither in the last nor in the first instance by class or security. Identities and ideologies would not disappear in a hypothetical classless and stateless global society, although they may very well be interacting with each other under capitalism. To paraphrase Max Weber, it is not the Church that created Christianity as an ideological and identity theme of Western publics, but rather the other way around. Thus, conflict, in one form or another, will always be present, not because capitalism might last a long time but because *the future* will last longer than capitalism.

However, all sorts of religions, cultures, psychologies and identities can be referential to class by virtue of links—and access—to education, economic standards, anxieties about lack of money and so on. They can also be referential to security, broadly understood; for instance religious-based militias or the need of individuals to find spiritual refuge and shelter in a direct communication with transcendent powers, thus addressing problems of individual insecurity, health concerns, etc. In other words, constructivists and post-structuralists have one or two things to say to enrich our understanding about the antagonisms of con-temporary international relations. None the less, at the end of the day, one has to ask the crucial question: what is the driving force of antagonisms in this world? How can we untangle this skein of different strands, class, power, security, identities and so on? The answer is that all these are large themes constituting the actual ingredients of most conflict situations, although I should make clear, in order to avoid misunderstandings and as I implied earlier, that my methodological preference is to privilege class, state power and security in the shaping of the actual politics of conflict. This is in preference to ideological or cultural themes, or to themes related to Michel Foucault's relational and relativized concepts of the microphysics of power and panoptism (Foucault, 1975; and Negri and Hardt, 2000—see Bibliography).

These methodological and epistemological preferences have not been imposed on any of the contributors to this book—quite the opposite. The interesting thing to note is that the empirical findings of all the essays uphold this combination of 'neo-realist' and 'neo-Marxist' methodological standpoints. Let us now focus on the contributions and the empirical case studies with which the authors in this book have engaged.

THE BOOK

The first essay, by Andrew Wheatcroft, makes out a reflective argument on 'evil'. He tries to understand how a world that before 1945 and the Nuremberg trials came out of the mouths of priests and theologians has since become a term used by politicians, military analysts and political scientists—even more so after 9/11. 'Evil' and the 'war on terror' have indeed become the ideological organizing principles around which the USA has been thematicizing its global hegemonic politics since 9/11. If the enemy is evil, then the enemy is criminal, and should be treated as such. Using works by David Frankfurter and Roy F. Baumeister, Wheatcroft goes on to argue that evil is a theme that has great mobilization potential, as the history of conspiracies and pogroms for more than 1,000 years has shown. The theme of evil, therefore, is a very powerful tool and the USA is using it in order to achieve concrete material outcomes. Wheatcroft then connects this analysis with the theme of Christendom, as this concept of evil has originated not in the Islamic East but in the Christian West. In this context, 'evil' may be seen as consubstantial to wars led by the war departments of the US 'Empire'. That Empire—defined as an articulate organizer of imperialism (global projections of power, strategies of domination and economic exploitation, etc.)— converts the theme of evil from ideology into the practical terrain of material violence[1]. In this sense, 'evil' is the post-9/11 code of organized global violence. Furthermore, 'evil' is here to stay, Wheatcroft warns, not least because the war on terror, as President George W. Bush and the Pentagon have said explicitly, might last forever. Wheatcroft's contribution is a splendid exposure and criticism of the way in which the USA has been using the theme of evil in order to achieve power-politics ends.

As noted earlier, a common sense view is that post-Cold War conflicts are mainly intra-state and dominated by nationalistic and religious wars. Jairo Lugo tells us that this is not exactly the case in Latin America, inasmuch as civil and other forms of conflict there are still dominated by class and ideological issues, together with the left–right divide. Lugo, moreover, exemplifies a point made by virtually all the contributors: that 'imperial' or external interventions, whether by means of an open invasion or by means of CIA machinations, for instance, have characterized and defined the region's conflicts throughout its modern history. We are, therefore, already becoming aware of the fact that imperial undertakings are both constituting and instituting agents of conflicts, not neutral arbiters, impartial mediators or 'good will' negotiators.

In examining the nature of conflicts in independent Africa, Phia Steyn mentions the arbitrary drawing of borders between the colonial powers, seldom reflecting the political, economic, ethnic and geographical realities of African regions. This was also the case in the Middle East and to an extent in the Balkans and east-central Europe, but Africa has seen all sort of colonists coming and going, be they British, French, Portuguese, Belgian, Spanish, Dutch, German or Italian. This legacy left an indelible mark on Africa and exacerbated its ethnic, tribal and religious problems; Steyn does not fail to point out as well the colonial policies of 'divide and rule'. Her sober analysis is driving her to conclude that, owing to the complexity of African conflicts, no 'quick fix' or easy solution can be found.

Emmanuel Karagiannis's essay on the issue of ethnic conflicts in the Caucasus and Central Asia corroborates further the hypothesis that ethnic conflicts in the region are related to material or class and strategic interests (petroleum and gas pipeline routes, the control of resources and of strategic passages, etc.), as well as to greater schemes of security and power politics driven by neo-imperial and/or external interference (from Russia, Turkey or the USA, for example). In this respect—although the internal dynamics of ethnic conflicts as such should not be underestimated—ethnic and religious minorities can be used by external agents as vehicles to fulfil their state agendas and class objectives.

Rajat Ganguly examines two of the most important—from the standpoint of regional and international security—conflicts in South Asia: the Indian–Pakistani conflict over Kashmir; and the Tamil–Sinhalese conflict in Sri Lanka. None of these seemingly ethnic and religious conflicts is dissociated from imperial and/or external interference. With Kashmir, India and Pakistan are obviously involved, but so is the People's Republic of China, by virtue of its border dispute with India. The United Kingdom, the former colonial power in the region—as in Sri Lanka— has withdrawn to the background, but still plays a role in both conflicts. India (which supports the Hindu Tamils of Sri Lanka) and even Pakistan and Israel (which support the Sinhalese-majority Government) are also involved in the island. Ganguly is outspoken about US training of *mujahideen* (freedom fighters) during Afghanistan's occupation by the USSR, a point that corroborates our generic principles: first, that modern imperial interests are a fundamental con- stituting factor generating conflict situations; and, second, that domestic (ethnic and religious) types of conflict are used by imperial and external powers either for power-politics ends or to address their security concerns.

Yoke-Lian Lee and Roger Buckley comprehensively present a wide range of conflicts in South-East Asia, underlining issues of legitimacy and institutional weakness in the South-East Asian state. They point out the negative legacy of colonialism in the shaping and transformation of the regional conflicts and raise concerns about how the South-East Asian state can provide a conflict-resolution framework in a region dominated by the often competing agendas of far more powerful states, such as China, India, Japan, the United Kingdom and the USA— and, more recently, Australia.

The focus of the book then switches to four single case studies, on: the former Yugoslavia; Iraq; Northern Ireland; and the Arab–Israeli conflict. This has not been an arbitrary choice. Northern Ireland and Palestine have been defining regional—even international—security relations since the First World War, whereas Yugoslavia and Iraq have risen to prominence, from the point of view of conflict studies, in the wake of the collapse of 'really existing socialism'. Furthermore, the comprehensive analysis provided by the authors exemplifies the realist linkages between exogenous and endogenous actors in the origination, shaping and transformation of conflict. The best summaries available on the issue of linkages are the essays by Stevan K. Pavlowitch and Peter Gowan, first published in late 1999 in the *Journal of Southern Europe and the Balkans*. Whereas Pavlowitch seems to suggest that the West bears minimal responsibil- ities for the dissolution of Yugoslavia, making the internal complexities of the country a key to understanding its case, for Gowan the articulation of domestic and external agents amounts to an explanation of the crisis. From this perspective, the next three cases need the least explanation of all; Iraq, Palestine-Israel and Northern Ireland have been and are the most mediated—thus, politicized and internationalized—conflicts ever. All three contributors, Rory Miller (Arab-Israeli conflict), John Doyle (Northern Ireland) and Vassilis K. Fouskas (Iraq), offer original and highly informative analyses of the conflicts with which they deal.

A REALIST WORLD IN CONFLICT?

This, therefore, seems to be a *realist* world in conflict, which persistently and tenaciously refuses to fit into preconceived technical frameworks of conflict prevention, management and resolution, which at times are operated, after all, by 'impartial' agencies of which we might have some suspicions. The failure of the UN, NATO, the Organisation for Security and Co-operation in Europe (OSCE) and other inter-governmental or 'non-governmental' organizations to achieve comprehensive peace in areas in which they have been engaged, either as aggressors or as mediators and peacemakers, is colossal. Successful diplomatic or military missions led by them are few, or the conflict in question is unresolved, temporarily fixed and/or still lurking (see, for example, the case of Cyprus and other cases in the A–Z Glossary). This might be because, as Georg Simmel mentioned a long time ago, 'Conflict itself constitutes a resolution of the tension between the contraries' (his 1904 essay can be found in a 1963 publication cited in the Bibliography). However, for a 'duel' to be held in international and social relations would be but an ideal; there are no gladiators in international politics. In reality, this sort of duel does not exist because conflict is always mediated by a variety of other agents, sites and structures. In this respect, this volume establishes and offers an answer for two major issues in the field of international relations and conflict:

First, there has never existed an ethnic, religious or whatever conflict in the first place, and an international (or third party) intervention that followed, in order to bring about 'peace', 'war', 'a settlement', 'transformation' or whatever to that ('domestic') conflict.

Second, ethnic, religious (let alone inter-state) and other non-individualistic forms of conflict are deeply political and international, which is to say, consubstantial with the issues of class and security.

Needless to say, both the themes established here are very much inter-linked. Let us shed some light on them.

To begin with, modernity is consubstantial with internationalization and, first and foremost, with the internationalization of both capital and labour as forms of antagonistic social relations[2]. Every form of ethnic and religious conflict is profoundly international, because all examples that we possess from modern history indicate that imperial/external powers and domestic agents are both and

7

simultaneously responsible for the conflict in question, or that conflict was caused and/or exacerbated/transformed by external/imperial intervention. Obviously, this thesis turns theory and the theoreticians of conflict resolutions and mediations on their head. What kind of impartial mediation could, for example, have been offered by a British negotiator in the Cyprus dispute, since it was primarily the United Kingdom itself that exacerbated the problem there? What kind of impartial service could conceivably be undertaken by Michael Levy in his position as the United Kingdom's special envoy for Israel-Palestine, when he was a former Chairman of the Jewish Appeal Board and former board member of the Jewish Agency, has business and a house in Israel and has a son working for the Israeli justice ministry (Pilger, 2002)?

Secondly, we should remember that when great powers intervene, in whatever way, in the domestic affairs of a smaller state, they do so via their own state or state agents. What realist theoreticians call national interest is, in fact, an amalgam—albeit contradictory and, at times, even deficient (see Fouskas's essay on Iraq)—of the class and security interests of the imperial power in question. If we look at the US 'Empire' and the way in which it expresses discourses on and strategies for power, as Wheatcroft's essay suggests, can we then consider it to be a *conflict organizer*, rather than a conflict appeaser or even a conflict manager? I think we can.

The post-1945 'Empire-State' is aiming to provide a structured system of global governance, built on a 'pecking order' of lesser powers, defined and regulated by it and according to the security and class interests of the grand Empire-State. This is what neo-Marxists (Fouskas and Gökay, 2005) and others, such as Josef Joffe (2005), have called the 'hub and spoke' system of global governance, led by the USA (also see footnote 1 at the end of this Introduction). The essays in this book, without necessarily employing a similar theoretical framework on the issue of Empire/imperialism, suggest that the USSR and the USA each organized conflicts in order to undermine and upset the global security and class orders of the other, as both perceived the other to be its chief competitor Empire-State. Smaller competitor states have done and are doing the same to each other, the difference being that they often either have to report their actions beforehand to their master, to ask for authorization, or are actually doing it following instructions from their master.

If this all is true, then can we move a step further and assume that the US Empire-State today actively and consciously employs political strategies of conflict proliferation, instead of launching a comprehensive and global diplomatic initiative that would create viable conditions for conflict resolution, upholding human security and rights? We cannot answer this question. However, if we draw on the findings of the last work by Christopher Layne, *A Peace of Illusions* (2006), then we can answer why the USA launches its wars of aggression, eventually disregarding human security and humanistic considerations. Layne convincingly argues, following the pioneering work of William Appleman Williams, that the USA sincerely believes that exporting the liberal values of liberty, justice and free market capitalism across the globe is a good and progressive thing. Tony Blair seemed to believe the same. Upon announcing the withdrawal of some 1,600 British troops from Iraq in February 2007, he argued that what was happening in Iraq was 'part of a wider struggle taking place across the region. . .an epochal struggle between the forces of progress and the forces of reaction.'[3] Simultaneously, this idealism fits into the transforming social orders of the Empire's global class and security interests. In other words, the 'American Emperor' is an 'idealist-realist' at heart—both an idealist and a realist at the same time. Apart from this being very telling, it is also very helpful in understanding the normative features of the American Empire, as well as the very meaning(s) of the USA's definition of 'progress'. 'Realism' can choose and impose an authoritarian state of emergency over poor and deprived populations as long as the national interest of the American Empire is served. 'Idealism', with its immense liberal powers of conviction, donations and generosity towards those populations, accompanies every single step taken by 'realism'. That is what US policy-makers call democratization of the greater Middle East or the spreading of the values of freedom across the globe—what they call progress. However, if this is the case, then we must observe Walter Benjamin's concern and avoid treating such progress as a 'historical norm'.

NOTES

1. I would define 'Empire' as a structured system of global governance and 'imperialism' as the expansionist manifestations of Empire, present in the articulations of an empire's foreign policy, be it predominately, but not exclusively, economic (appropriation of international value), cultural-political (such as the imposition of Western forms of liberal democracy) or purely political (projection of power). The US Empire, therefore, has since 1945 tried to build a global system of governance that is radically different from the classic imperialism of the British, the Portuguese, the French, etc. Whereas all pre-1945 modern European Empires divided the world among them, which had led to inter-imperialist wars of Empire-contraction, the post-1945 American Empire has put to work 'hub and spoke' arrangements, with the US capital of Washington, DC, being the 'hub' and all other developed metropolitan centres (principally the European and Japanese ones) at the end of its dependent 'spokes'. This Empire-State system, as I have shown elsewhere (Fouskas and Gökay, 2005) and as opposed to pre-1945 imperialisms, is consubstantial with neo-imperialist wars of Empire-expansion. Whereas all pre-1945 imperialisms contracted (hence Lenin's erroneous prediction that 'imperialism is the highest stage of capitalism'), the nature of US post-1945 neo-imperialism is inherently expansive ('America, the World is Yours'). I am thankful to Andrew Wheatcroft for discussing with me these important issues. It would be unfair, however, to assume that Wheatcroft's text uses the term 'Empire' precisely in the way that I have defined it here, or that he necessarily espouses my discourse on the subject of 'Empire' and 'imperialism'.

2. This is the framework, for example, in which one should place and examine the 'low intensity conflict' caused by immigration and emigration.
3. Chris Marsden, 'Blair Announces Partial Troop Withdrawal from Iraq', from World Socialist Website (WSWS) of 22 February 2007.

Articulating Evil

ANDREW WHEATCROFT

A new term—or, rather, an old term reincarnated—has again entered the profes-sional discourse of conflict. 'Evil' was a word that once came more easily to the lips of a theologian than to those of a political scientist or a military analyst. Now we have to take serious note of 'the war on evil', 'the axis of evil' and the 'evil enemy'.

The modern context of evil has developed since the trials before the Interna-tional Military Tribunal in Nuremberg from 1945. At the Nuremberg sessions (and the successor tribunals) the language of evil and wickedness appeared sporadically in the oral testimony, but the intention of the court was to move towards a new framework of criminality, a standard embodied in the Principles of International Law Recognized in the Charter of the Nuremberg Tribunal and in the Judgment of the Tribunal, which were adopted by the International Law Commission of the United Nations in 1950 (see the Bibliography) Three general categories of crime under international law were proposed.

> Crimes against peace: Planning, preparation, initiation or waging of a war of aggression or a war in violation of international treaties, agreements or assurances; participation in a common plan or conspiracy.

> War crimes: Violations of the laws or customs of war, which include, but are not limited to, the murder, ill-treatment or deportation to slave-labour or for any other purpose of civilian populations of or in occupied territory, the murder or ill-treatment of prisoners of war or of persons on the seas, the killing of hostages, the plunder of public or private property, the wanton destruction of cities, towns or villages, or devastation not justified by military necessity.

> Crimes against humanity: Murder, extermination, enslavement, deportation and other inhuman acts done against any civilian population, or persecutions on political, racial or religious grounds, when such acts are done or such persecutions are carried on in execution of or in connection with any crime against peace or any war crime.

Thus, acts once often described as evil were now formally proscribed as criminal.

The publication of Hannah Arendt's book, *Eichmann in Jerusalem: A Report on the Banality of Evil*, reinterpreted the concept of evil and, in the process, diminished its potency (Arendt, 1963—see Bibliography). In a later work Arendt observed:

> 'It is indeed my opinion now that evil is never "radical", that it is only extreme, and that it possesses neither depth nor any demonic dimension. It

can overgrow and lay waste the whole world precisely because it spreads like a fungus on the surface. It is "thought-defying", as I said, because thought tries to reach some depth, to go to roots, and the moment it concerns itself with evil, it is frustrated because there is nothing. That is its "banality".' (p. 251, in Arendt, 1978.)

It was not until 1983, when US President Ronald Reagan designated the USSR as the 'evil empire', before a gathering of the American National Association of Evangelicals, that the notion of evil began to reassert its previous position in political discourse. It now appears that, in formulating these ideas, he and his speechwriter drew upon Alexander Solzhenitsyn, who in 1975 had talked publicly of the USSR as 'the concentration of World Evil', and on Gen. Alexandre de Marenches, the head of French intelligence, who briefed Reagan personally in 1980 about *l'empire du mal* (p. 472, in Morris, 1999). After Reagan's presidency and the end of the USSR, the atrocious events of the 1990s in the Balkans and in Africa strengthened the idea in the popular mind and in the media. They rendered the idea of 'banal' evil nugatory. Even before the dramatic use of the terminology of evil by US President George W. Bush in September 2001, and subsequently, there was a desire to find a language more potent than the dry legalism of the post-Nuremberg environment. Law, it seemed, had failed to respond adequately to new horrors, while a Western culture formed around the concepts of enlightenment and reason had also failed to accommodate or explain what appeared to be mindless unreason. The idea of evil had never ceased to be potent among religious believers, but now it re-emerged as a response to the new experiences of many non-believers as well. In the process, it has been secularized and normalized.

Evil exists in our lexicon. However, what does the word now mean in Western cultures? How has its meaning and usage changed over time? In the following, I have preferred to let the writers speak for themselves, since my paraphrase would inevitably lose the tone and register of what they say. Roy F. Baumeister, Eppes Professor of Psychology at Florida State University, in the USA, sees evil all around us and charts how it has entered the repertoire of modern social psychology (Baumeister, 1997). What evil might mean as a concept is, for him, a philosopher's task, but as a social scientist he knows that it exists and is self-evidently potent in the world. Lack of definition is not a problem, since 'science can work with fuzzy sets and grey areas'. Moreover, this particular fuzzy set is useful. Baumeister uses 'evil' because it is the 'traditional term' and it is important to connect it with 'ancient and fundamental questions about human life'. The term is flexible, highly adaptable and turns up everywhere. Baumeister's idea of evil extends beyond great crimes and horrendous acts 'to the petty cruelties and minor transgressions of everyday life'. Thus, we can find evil everywhere, and its consequences ramify quite naturally.

Baumeister charts new kinds of evil growing and expanding in the real world of conflict. He speculated: 'Indeed, as we move into the twenty-first century it may be necessary to have two sets of rules of war: one for ordinary wars and another for holy wars' (p. 174, in Baumeister, 1997). What would happen, as he sees it, is straightforward. First, 'Declaring a holy war seems to mean that the ordinary rules, such as the Geneva Convention, are suspended.' Moreover, there are no politics in a holy war, so, second, 'If two countries are fighting over territory they may well make some kind of deal . . . But it is much harder to make a deal with the forces of evil . . . You can't sell half your soul to the devil.' This is an attempt to come to terms with the concept of evil, post-Arendt. In Baumeister's view we need to recognize this omnipresent evil (and its consequences) and that it is useful to possess such a broad descriptive category. Evil is easy to understand, with just four simple basic causes: desire for material gain; threatened egotism; idealism; and the pursuit of sadistic pleasure (pp. 376–77, in Baumeister, 1997). However, with the exception of the last element, his categories do nothing to encompass the long history that saturates the concept.

Scrutinize Baumeister's 1997 book, *Evil: Inside Human Violence and Cruelty*, carefully and it becomes apparent that the creation of such categories as 'instrumental evil' or 'idealistic evil' is an authorial strategy gratuitously to import the vocabulary of evil into the narrative. It is redundant, as is evident, for example, in the central chapter, 'True Believers and Idealists.' Baumeister asks the essential question, 'How can virtue and idealism lead to cruel, violent, or oppressive acts?' He answers it comprehensively (pp. 169–202), but as we read it what becomes evident is that 'Evil' is just a metaphoric appendage to his main theme. The book is unambiguously *about* cruelty and violence in historical contexts and calling them evil is a stylistic option. As he explains (p. vi), 'If I am successful at formulating an insider's view of cruelty and violence, the results are likely to be upsetting. As you will see, our culturally-dominant view of evil is very different from the actual psychology of the perpetrators.' There is, of course, now no 'culturally-dominant view' of evil, as he demonstrates; the book's purpose is to create (or revive) it. Baumeister later remarks (p. 7), 'The term [evil] has an air of anachronism . . . According to the *Oxford English Dictionary*, people hardly use the word evil anymore in everyday conversation.' Evil certainly runs through the text, but only as a leitmotif clumsily superimposed upon it.

What might be the significance of bringing the notion of Evil back into common usage? The powerful alternative position to Baumeister is that evil should not be normalized. Even using this resurgent terminology of evil, in the view of David Frankfurter, Professor of Religious Studies and History at the University of New Hampshire, also in the USA, comes at a price. He wrote recently:

'The fundamental humanistic stance [is] that evil is a discourse, a way of representing things and shaping our experience of things, not some force in itself. The most horrible atrocities—and those of us who have studied religion under the shadow of Auschwitz, Jedwabne, Srbenica, and Kigali can hardly ignore their significance—can and must be rendered sensible as human actions with proper contexts. The application of the term "evil" to some horrible act or event renders it outside the realm of human comprehension and identification ... This observation, that applying the word "evil" amounts to a strategy for setting things apart from comprehension, is not in any way original. Dividing deviant acts between human and monstrous—setting an implicit boundary beyond which acts are no longer worthy of context or empathy—is a common phenomenon of cultures. The word "evil" may have a distinctly modern absoluteness but such moral divisions, such zones beyond which is only monstrosity, are the habits of national leaders and small groups equally. Still, I start this book from the position that for the interpreter of cultures, the critic, or historian, or social scientist, the use of the term "evil" amounts to intellectual laziness, shutting off inquiry and the proper search for context. ... evil should be scrutinized as a way of thinking rather than held up as a reality for our time.'

He concludes:

'in every one of the historical cases I address, it was the myth of evil conspiracy that mobilized people in large numbers to astounding acts of brutality against accused conspirators. That is, the real atrocities of history seem to take place not in the perverse ceremonies of some evil cult but rather in the course of purging such cults from the world. Real evil happens when people speak of evil.' (pp. 11–12, in Frankfurter, 2006.)

At roughly the same time, Niall Ferguson, Laurence A. Tisch Professor of History at Harvard University, in Massachusetts, USA, writing of the 20th and early 21st centuries as 'History's age of hatred' suggested three principal factors:

'Time and again it has been in the wake of the decline of empires, in contested borderlands or in power vacuums that the opportunities have arisen for genocidal regimes and policies. Ethnic confluence, economic volatility, and empires on the wane; such was and remains the fatal formula for the generation of what others have described as "evil".'

He concludes:

'We shall avoid another century of conflict only if we understand the forces that caused the last one—the dark forces that conjure up ethnic conflict and imperial rivalry out of economic crisis and in doing so negate our common humanity. They are forces that stir within us still.' (p. 646, in Ferguson, 2006.)

It would have been easy for Ferguson to have inserted the traditional adjective 'evil' before 'forces', a temptation that others have found less easy to resist. Writing in the same year as Ferguson, Gordon G. Chang, a lawyer and analyst of current Asian economics and politics, saw not the history of the term but, like Baumeister, only its powerful instrumentality:

'We remember phrases like an "evil empire" and "axis of evil" because they first tar despotic regimes and then set us in motion. They mark turning points, defining the times in which they are uttered. People do not forget the leaders who charge them with great responsibilities.' (pp. 174–75, in Chang, 2006.)

In essence, both Frankfurter and Chang see the terminology of evil as being immensely effective, but Frankfurter concludes that it is so dangerous that it should not be used, while Chang avers that it is so effective that it must be used, but only, of course, in a good cause. Ferguson avoids the word altogether.

The reintroduction of the political concept of Evil is most easily understood not socially but syntactically. Evil had for centuries been used not as a noun but adjectivally, as a descriptor or an intensifier. An *evil* Empire is a special kind of Empire. However, we should consider its etymology. From its origins in Old English, 'evil' was the 'most comprehensive adjectival expression of disapproval, dislike or disparagement' (Bosworth and Toller, 1898). Over time, like all extreme terms of negation, it softened. In reverse youth argot, 'evil', like 'wicked', has even became a solid term of approbation. Nevertheless, hiding behind the adjective is the noun, and here we have seen a pronounced shift in recent times. Professor Peter Singer, of Princeton University in New Jersey, USA, has observed, 'George W. Bush is not only America's president, but also its most prominent moralist.' This is not an ironic statement, as he goes on to chart the shift from evil as adjective to evil as noun, which was calculated from analysing all the President's speeches, as recorded on the White House website:

> 'Bush has spoken about evil in 319 separate speeches, or about 30 percent of all the speeches he gave between the time he took office and June 16, 2003. In these speeches he uses the word "evil" as a noun far more often than he uses it as an adjective—914 noun uses as against 182 adjectival uses. Only 24 times, in all these occasions on which Bush talks of evil, does he use it as an adjective to describe what people do, that is, acts or deeds. This means that Bush is not thinking about evil deeds, or even evil people, nearly as often as he is thinking about evil as a thing, or a force, something that has a real existence apart from the cruel, callous, brutal and selfish acts of which human beings are capable. His readiness to talk about evil in this manner raises the question of what meaning evil can have in a secular modern world.' (p. 2, in Singer, 2004.)

President George W. Bush is Baumeisterian Man. This foregrounding of Evil-as-noun in the public arena, from the mouth of a powerful political actor, is of real significance. Political language is undergoing a dramatic manipulation.

CAPTURING LANGUAGE

The best entry point to this topic is not an academic study but George Orwell's appendix to his novel *1984* on 'The Principles of Newspeak' (Orwell, 1949). However, Orwell's Newspeak is fanciful, based on a kind of satirical reversal. Thus, the novel's Ministry of Love, in the real world would have been called a Ministry of War. A real-world observation of the texture of language in a time of tribulation may be found in Victor Klemperer's 1947 *Language of the Third Reich: A Philologist's Notebook*, a diary and notebook of life under the Third Reich. A professor of French literature at the University of Dresden, in Germany, until 1935, Klemperer recorded the transformation of German into a new Nazi idiom, as words altered their meaning or new words and acronyms came to dominate everyday speech.

The renaissance of Evil (the noun) is illustrative of a similar process. Professor Anna Wierzbicka, Professor of Linguistics at the Australian National University, describes how 'There is a very close link between the life of a society and the lexicon of the language spoken by it ... [which] is the clearest possible guide to everyday cognition and to the patterning of everyday discourse' (p. 1, in Wierzbicka, 1996). Her starting point is Edward Sapir's 'fundamental insight' in his *Selected Writing* that vocabulary is 'a very sensitive index of the culture of a people' (p. 27, in Sapir, 1986). In every culture there are certain key words that correspond to core values (p. 31, in Wierzbicka, 1996). For example, Wierzbicka contrasts the resonance of the different meanings of 'freedom', in Latin, English, Russian, and Polish. Words encode concepts. She observes:

> 'Freedom does not stand for a universal human ideal. In fact, it doesn't even stand for a common European ideal, although European languages contain a family of related concepts ... Words such as freedom [English], libertas [Latin], svoboda [Russian] and wolność [Polish] ... embody different concepts which reflect different cultural ideals. The emergence of such concepts in a given language can be understood only against the background of the culture to which this language belongs and they can provide precious clues to the understanding of that culture.' (pp. 152–53, in Wierzbicka, 1996.)

Her formulation that 'key words embody core cultural values' helps us to articulate the position that the word 'Evil' occupies in our current discourse of conflict.

Evil-as-discourse lies firmly embedded in the languages and literatures of those European cultures that have their roots in Christianity. Much of Europe was once called Christendom, the Christian domain, originally signifying an ideal of a religious and a political polity. Notions of Evil have carried over into its diasporas. It is normally believed that the 16th-century Protestant and Roman Catholic Reformations and Counter-Reformations in effect destroyed Christendom as an active entity, although there were constant efforts to restore that earlier sense of common activity and purpose. Rationalism and secularism supposedly provided the *coup de grace*. The Czech philosopher Jan Patočka succinctly located the roots of Europe in its antecedent, Christendom, in his third Heretical Essay:

> 'European humanity has become so accustomed to this Christian conception of the meaning of history and of the universe that it cannot let go of some of its substantive traits even where fundamental Christian concepts ... have to be significant for it and it continues to seek meaning in a secularized Christian conception.' (p. 69, in Patočka, 1996.)

Evil is a concept, Frankfurter suggests, most powerfully (but not exclusively) resonant within a Christian community. Its current use as a political term involves subverting the post-Renaissance vocabulary of politics with a radically simplified bitonal dualism of good and evil. The implications of this radical reversion are considerable. It undermines the assumptions of post-Nuremberg legal structures. Crimes against humanity and war crimes are then contextualized by the a priori condition of the actors: if they are designated Good, one rule applies; if they are designated Evil, another. There are gradations of Evil; for example, those held in the US facility at the Guantanamo Bay enclave on Cuba have been defined as 'the worst of the worst' (Lewis and Schmitt, 2004). It is not just their treatment that is in question. Their status is defined by categories that antedate the 18th-century Enlightenment. In 1764 Cesare Beccaria wrote, in *On Crimes and Punishments*:

> 'In proportion as punishments become more cruel, the minds of men, as a fluid rises to the same height with that which surrounds it, grow hardened and insensible; and the force of the passions still continuing in the space of an hundred years the wheel terrifies no more than formerly the prison. That a punishment may produce the effect required, it is sufficient that the evil it occasions should exceed the good expected from the crime, including in the calculation the certainty of the punishment, and the privation of the expected advantage. All severity beyond this is superfluous, and therefore tyrannical.' (Beccaria, 1963.)

This cruel pragmatism is set within a framework of known boundaries. A war on evil, or its surrogate, 'a war on terror', has no boundaries and no limits.

My central proposition can be simply stated. We may observe a pattern in Western culture since the Enlightenment based upon setting boundaries. The normal pattern of change since the mid-18th century has been quite slow moving but, gradually, over time social boundaries and conventions have shifted. Central issues have evolved over a period of 200 years, as have the questions: who ruled; how were they to be chosen; how could they be replaced? The process has ultimately resulted in a set of political and social conventions, now commonly described as democratic. Similarly, ideas of a common humanity and 'human rights' have grown very gradually over time, but they are now enshrined in social conventions written into international law. Periods of aberration, such as the Revolutionary Terror in France (1793–94) or the Nazi period in Germany (1933–45), were marked by rupturing or replacing those limits. However, the breaches were short-lived: the Terror ended after 11 months; the Thousand Year Reich was destroyed within 12 years; and even the one that lasted longest, the USSR, created through revolution in 1917–22, was over by the 1990s.

These boundaries or conventions-in-law of modern Western society have replaced the boundlessness both of previous social conventions and of the post-1750 aberrations. For example, there were no limits as to who might be declared a heretic or a witch, nor more recently, in the Soviet or Nazi case, who might be declared a criminal, a 'degenerate' or otherwise outside the limits of humanity. These anterior categories were often defined circumstantially, on the fly, by the monarch, the Church, the Party or the Great Leader. There were, it is true, elaborate tests and rules that supposedly defined those categories, but in reality they were mutable and could be altered without difficulty. Evil belongs firmly within this earlier, unbounded stage of social evolution.

Evil is a monocausal, self-referential explanation of how the world works, in the sense that, to believers, Evil has to be the cause of all evil. They might be right; we should remember Robert Carneiro's robust caveat about causality. He dislikes the idea that simply because there is a complex network of interrelationships within social systems, theorists steer clear of assigning 'causal primacy'. He thinks otherwise:

> 'There is nothing wrong with a monocausal theory if it works. Ideally, as scientists, we want to make our explanations as simple and economical as possible. We want to reduce the causal elements to the fewest number that will do the job. If a single cause can explain a phenomenon, so much the better. Of course, if one factor is not enough, then we increase the number of causal factors in our theory until our explanation becomes satisfactory. We may well end with multiple causation, but a multiplicity of causes, if it comes to that, should be thought of as a necessity, not a virtue.' (Carneiro, 1981.)

The process of gaining knowledge and understanding often tends towards an interior monocausality in the scholar's mind; if not a sole cause, then the strong sense of a prime cause starts to emerge. Carneiro suggests that it is the scholar's task to 'tease out' of a variety of conditions a few factors that exist in common, thus providing us with, as I would see it, *sancta simplicitas*. As he says, 'I will entertain alternative or subsidiary theories, not as a desideratum, but only as I am forced to by the facts' (pp. 54–55, in Carneiro, 1981).

The facts in the field of complex conflicts, however, lead elsewhere. I do not believe that monocausality can ever work; there are simply too many factors in play. Let me take a particular case. In the last 15 years, there have been many practical and doctrinal developments in operational art and what is usually called irregular or asymmetric warfare. The profusion of new ideas, theories and professional accounts of conflict continues to proliferate; many feed on the conduct of current struggles. The concept of fourth-generation warfare has exerted a powerful influence (Lind, 2004). There have been attempts to undermine that approach, most recently by Antulio J. Echevarria, II, Director of Research at the US Strategic Studies Institute. However, while his critique scores some hits on the fourth-generation interpretation of military history, he fails entirely to engage with the central issues concerning current warfare that its theorists advance (Echevarria, 2005). His attack was directed at a private group of military officers convened by William S. Lind, which in 2005 produced a draft fighting manual for *Fourth Generation War*. The unofficial and speculative nature of the work is indicated by the ironic name of its 'publisher', the Imperial and Royal Austro-Hungarian Marine Corps. In fact, Lind's group was dominated by retired and disenchanted US Marines officers, who contrasted the reality of war as they had experienced it with the official, authorized version. The manual describes how new ideas and practices of war are evolving, of which one was the wildly ramifying concept of collateral damage.

The USAF *Intelligence Targeting Guide* of 1998 defined collateral damage as:

> 'unintentional damage or incidental damage affecting facilities, equipment or personnel occurring as a result of military actions directed against targeted enemy forces or facilities. Such damage can occur to friendly, neutral, and even enemy forces.'

The phrase has now, through circumstance, turned from a technical definition into a euphemism. I have discussed erosion of boundaries, and these occur in current situations of conflict. Formerly, in both law and practice, there were combatants and non-combatants—military personnel and civilians—the former 'fair game' and the latter 'off limits'. This is still the position in international law. However, pragmatically, the boundary is becoming increasingly blurred. Now the language of war increasingly includes a third element: collateral damage to people, occupying a space between the two categories.

'Collateral damage' is the equivalent of the bystander being hit by a bullet labelled 'to whom it may concern'. *Fourth Generation War* does not see it as an inescapable consequence of modern warfare, but as a direct result of the wrong choices being made: 'Excessive firepower not only hurts our mobility but also is more likely to cause collateral damage and alienate the local population. We need to rethink and retool to fight a very different enemy.' The manual's authors go on to say that many aspects of high-technology warfare turn 'physical success into moral disaster'. The avoidance of collateral damage is not merely desirable on moral grounds—sustaining the inviolability of the non-combatant required by international law—but becomes the pragmatic grounds for winning a war.

That collateral damage has been transmogrified from a technical definition into weasel words shows a lack of attention to necessary and useful boundaries. The too-easy acceptance that the status of civilian non-combatant will be progressively eroded is a measure of incompetence. This language of euphemism is still being elaborated, as for instance during the Israeli intervention in Lebanon on 14 July 2006, when the US President's spokesman, Tony Snow, said: 'We think it's important that . . . they try to limit as much as possible the so-called collateral damage, not only on civilians but also on human lives' (Raum, 2006). The vacuity is studied: collateral damage has become essentially a notion, like Evil, without boundaries or limits.

FIRE AND BRIMSTONE

President George W. Bush has talked often of the 'war on terror', in terms that define it as a long war, extending perhaps over a generation. On 19 March 2004 he spoke of Operation Iraqi Freedom and Operation Enduring Freedom:

> 'The war on terror is not a figure of speech. It is an inescapable calling of our generation. The terrorists are offended not merely by our policies—they are

offended by our existence as free nations. No concession will appease their hatred. No accommodation will satisfy their endless demands. . . . There can be no separate peace with the terrorist enemy.' (White House, 2004.)

Enduring Freedom had originally been named Infinite Justice, but the name was changed on 25 October 2001, after Muslim groups had informed the US Government that God alone could be the source of infinite justice.

We have entered a new era in the history of conflict, but not one without antecedents. In Orwell's *1984*, the hero Winston Smith finds a book:

'A heavy black volume, amateurishly bound, with no name or title on the cover. The print also looked slightly irregular. The pages were worn at the edges, and fell apart, easily, as though the book had passed through many hands.'

That book was written by the Emmanuel Goldstein, the hated arch-enemy. In it, Goldstein talks at length about the new kind of war, and concludes:

'The very word "war", therefore, has become misleading. It would probably be accurate to say that by becoming continuous war has ceased to exist.'

When the French philosopher Jean Baudrillard argued that the Gulf War of 1991 did not take place, it was to suggest that it was a new kind of war, 'a masquerade of information', where the image of what happened was more significant than what actually happened (Baudrillard, 1995). The subsequent Gulf War beginning in 2003 confirmed this perception. In that second war many efforts were made by the USA to take control of how the war was perceived. Journalists were 'embedded' in military units and it was hoped that an acquired sense of *esprit de corps* would colour their perceptions. To a degree this was successful during the conventional phase of the war, but it has proved entirely and catastrophically unsuccessful in the post-war phase of pacification and reconstruction. The fault lies in basing a war upon a false assumption—that terrorism is the enemy's objective, rather than merely a means towards an objective. This belief grows out of another belief, that an evil enemy can and will only behave in such a fashion. The preoccupation with the extraordinary nature of the struggle—a war of a generation, an elemental struggle without any political dimension, against an enemy who resents the very existence of the USA—is to adopt a mindset like that of earlier generations, which once pursued witches and heretics.

However, this war may even last more than a generation; indeed, it may be endless. In the *National Strategy for Combating Terrorism* (State Department, 2003), we read:

'We live in an age with tremendous opportunities to foster a world consistent with interests and values embraced by the United States and freedom-loving people around the world. And we will seize these opportunities ... By striking constantly and ensuring that terrorists have no place to hide, we will compress their scope and reduce the capability of terrorist organisations ... We will never forget what we are ultimately fighting for—our fundamental democratic values and way of life. In leading the campaign against terrorism, we are forging new international relationships and redefining existing ones in terms suited to the transnational challenges of the 21st century ... The campaign ahead will be long and arduous. In this different kind of war, we cannot expect an easy or definitive end to the conflict.'

If this speechmaking is only propaganda, a cynical ploy and a spurious rallying cry to the free nations of the world, that too is a dangerous misreading of the situation. However, I do not believe this to be the case. The belief in Evil is honest, and the assumptions about the nature of an endless war on Terror flow directly from it.

From this emerges a much broader conclusion. Monolithic belief systems (of whatever kind) cannot produce effective solutions in a varied and complex world: they have and are proving unworkable, especially where such systems are ancient atavisms. There are no bad angels, no Princes of Darkness, merely some repellent crimes and many vicious criminals. We do not need to be driven towards a 21st-century version of John Milton's vision in Book 1 of *Paradise Lost*:

'So numberless were those bad Angels seen
Hovering on wing under the cope of Hell,
Twixt upper, nether, and surrounding fires;
Till, as a signal given, the uplifted spear
Of their great Sultan waving to direct
Their course, in even balance down they light.'

Modern Conflicts in Latin America

JAIRO LUGO

INTRODUCTION

Latin America is arguably the only region in the world that has not been massively involved in high intensity conflicts since the middle of the 20th century and that has not seen a grand-scale inter-state war since the 1982 Falklands (Malvinas) conflict. Although the countries of the region present a series of unresolved border disputes, these have been mainly dealt with by diplomatic means, with the exception of short-lived but very intensive military confrontations such as the three main military conflicts between Ecuador and Peru (1859, 1941 and 1995) and the 1969 war between El Salvador and Honduras. This is not to say that there are not increasing tensions among countries, but is to argue that the region has not been characterized by traditional warfare since the second half of the 20th century. Indeed, most conflicts, or at least those that have left the highest death toll in that period, can be categorized as low-intensity intra-state conflicts. Latin America has been a battle ground for guerrilla warfare and political and social uprisings that have left hundreds of thousands dead and millions displaced from their homes. Some of these conflicts date from the early 1900s and, contrary to common wisdom, they were not all a consequence of the Cold War era, which explains why many of them still take place across the region, especially in countries such as Colombia, where the insurgents keep important strongholds. This chapter does not pretend to provide a full account of all the conflicts in Latin America since 1945, nor does it claim to give full details of each one, for which more focused literature is recommended (see Bibliography: Levine, 1986; Martinez, 2000; Philip, 2003; United Nations, 2005; and Ward, 1997). Instead, the aim is to present an overview of the main conflicts, the significance of the conflict in terms of world geopolitics and its current state of affairs and perspectives. This account of conflict is, therefore, mainly referential for those who want to start understanding a significant part of the history of this region.

COLOMBIAN CONFLICT

Colombia figures as the battlefield of one of the oldest and bloodiest conflicts in the region. It is an intra-national, low-intensity conflict in which three different left-wing guerrilla groups, a broad coalition of right-wing paramilitary groups, several drugs cartels and the regular Armed Forces of the Government fight each other. Although now all major cities are in the hands of government forces, guerrillas, paramilitaries and drugs traffickers manage to keep their presence and exert control in some areas. The conflict itself is fuelled by drugs trafficking and kidnapping as a steady source of income for the insurgents and the paramilitaries, while government forces receive an important amount of military foreign aid. Nevertheless, the Colombian conflict does present highly contrasting ideological positions due to the very sharp inequalities in wealth distribution in the country. Guerrilla groups have a long tradition in Colombia, where political polarization and land conflicts that spread during the 1920s led to turmoil and generalized partisan violence in the 1930s, 1940s and the beginning of the 1950s—the times of 'La Violencia'. The most symbolic event of that era was the assassination of the left-wing political leader of the Liberal Party, Jorge Eliécer Gaitán, which in 1948 set off the Bogotazo, an event characterized by widespread riots across the capital, Bogotá, and attempts to organize 'popular governments' that ultimately failed. Some Colombian historians highlight the presence in Bogotá at the time of the now Cuban leader, Fidel Castro, the president of the Cuban University Student Federation (FEU), Enrique Ovares, and the Mexican communist leader, Jorge Menvielle Porte-Petit, depicting them as main agitators during these riots. Gaitan's assassination marked the beginning of the organization of small guerrilla groups in some areas of the country.

The main and oldest confrontation takes place between the left-wing guerrilla groups and the Colombian Armed Forces. The largest and oldest group is the Revolutionary Armed Forces of Colombia/Popular Army (FARC-EP), commonly known as FARC, which is self-described as a Marxist-Leninist group. It operates across the country in both rural and urban areas. The FARC was formally established in 1964 to defend what were then autonomous Communist Party-controlled rural areas. It is Latin America's oldest, largest, most capable and best-equipped insurgency. According to different observers, they have approximately 17,000 armed combatants and several thousand more supporters, mostly in rural areas. FARC is governed by a general secretariat led by long time leader Manuel Marulanda (known as Tirofijo) and six others, including senior military commander Jorge Briceño (known as Mono Jojoy). This is a very sophisticated group that manages itself through a complex network that extends nationally and abroad. It operates using five-year planning budgets and some of its top commanders are US Ivy League graduates, such as the recently captured financial head of the FARC, Simón Trinidad, who previously had been a bank manager and an academic. The FARC's income comes mainly from taxing drug cartels and peasant coca-growers in exchange for protection, from kidnapping and extortion of wealthy ranchers in Colombia, Venezuela and Ecuador and from other more obscure and complex activities. For example, in 1999 the FARC admitted murdering three Indian (Amerindian) rights activists on the Venezuelan border who were working with the indigenous U'wa people to stop Occidental Petroleum and Shell Oil exploring and drilling in their ancestral homelands. The FARC held peace negotiations with the Colombian Government in 1982–87 and in 1998—2002; both times failed. During the negotiations in the 1980s the FARC created a political party, Union Patriotica (UP), which was targeted by para-military and other right-wing groups, killing approximately 3,000 of its members or sympathizers.

The second largest group is the National Liberation Army (ELN), also self-described as Marxist, which was created in 1965 by urban intellectuals inspired by Fidel Castro and Ernesto 'Che' Guevara. It operates mostly in the rural and mountainous areas of north, north-east, and south-west Colombia and the Venezuela border regions and has approximately 3,000 armed combatants and an unknown number of active supporters. The ELN was the first guerrilla organization to count Roman Catholic priests as fighters in its ranks, among them Camilo Torres, Domingo Laín, Antonio Jiménez, Diego Cristóbal Uribe and Manuel Pérez, the last becoming the commander-in-chief until his death in 1998. Less involved in drugs trafficking, the ELN also uses ransom kidnappings of wealthy ranchers in Colombia and Venezuela as a source of income. In addition to this it taxes oil companies to stop kidnappings of their executives or attacks infrastructure such as the British Petroleum (BP)-owned Caño Limón-Coveñas oil pipeline; this tax is called the vacuna (vaccine). FARC-ELN relations are complex. While they have carried out several joint operations over the years, tensions for territorial control have led to open 'wars' in some areas. In Arauca, for example, a former ELN stronghold, this group was severely hit by FARC, now the main illegal force in the zone. Nevertheless, the ELN has operated jointly with the FARC-EP in the past, including targeting civilian populations said to be collaborating with the army or the paramilitaries, as pointed out by a report by the UN's High Commissioner for Human Rights in 2005.

The two other main left-wing guerrilla groups are nowadays largely demobi-lized. The Popular Liberation Army (EPL) of Marxist-Maoist orientation, and the political reformist M-19. The EPL was created in 1965, although it only initiated military operations in 1968, mainly in the regions of Antioquia (Urabá y Bajo Cauca), Córdoba, Sucre and the Middle Magdalena. In 1980 the EPL participated in the so-called National Dialogue Peace Initiative launched by the then Pre-sident, Belisario Betancur, a period during which it's the EPL commander-in-chief, Ernesto Rojas, was assassinated. In the early 1990s almost all its members demobilized and went back to civil life, but several of them who stayed in arms were killed by FARC in a struggle to control strategic areas, namely the banana-producing region of Urabá, where the massacre of La Chinita took place in 1994. Years later, some EPL rank-and-file members took up arms again, fighting on the side of paramilitary organizations that were blossoming at the time.

The M-19 was the only non-Marxist group, emerging to resist the alleged fraud in the presidential election of 1970. Although the group had political support from the Sandinistas in Nicaragua and from the Cuban regime, its leadership was reluctant to have any permanent foreign ties. At the peak of its activities in the mid-1980s, the number of active members of the M-19 was estimated at between 1,500 and 2,000, making it one of the largest armed groups in Colombia. By that time the M-19 had eclipsed all other guerrilla organizations in urban operations and had established columns (units) in almost every major Colombian city.

Although the group never controlled large portions of Colombian territory as the FARC and the ELN did, it achieved spectacular notoriety by mean of its activities, such as: the 1974 theft of Simón Bolívar's sword and spurs from the exhibit in the Liberator's villa; the 1980 seizure of the Dominican Republic embassy in Bogotá, when they took 15 diplomats as hostages; the seizure of the Palace of Justice on 6 November 1985, which left 106 people dead, including 11 Supreme Court judges; and the kidnapping of the Conservative presidential candidate, Alvaro Gómez-Hurtado, in 1988. The group disbanded along with two other minor rebel organizations after the National Assembly approved the new Constitution of 1991, leading to political reforms demanded by the M-19, which included non-extradition for Colombian nationals. Some of its surviving leaders are now important political figures, especially in the leftist Polo Democratico Alternativo, the main opposition force in 2006's presidential election.

Despite deep ideological differences and leadership tensions between them, the remaining active left-wing groups in Colombia have a joint task force called the Simón Bolívar Guerrilla Co-ordinator (CGSB), to provide command and control to their activities against the Colombian Army and the paramilitary United Self-Defence Forces of Colombia (AUC—see below). Originally known as the National Guerrilla Co-ordination (CNG), the CGSB was initially set up by the M-19 with Peru's Shining Path (Sendero Luminoso) and Túpac Amaru Revolutionary Movement, and with Ecuador's Alfaro is Alive, Damn It! (¡Alfaro Vive, Carajo!) group. Today the CGSB also has a political presence in Bolivia and Venezuela. This joint task force contemplates financial assistance, political collaboration and, in theory, joint military operations, although this last has not yet been the case.

On the other side of the political spectrum we find an umbrella organization formed in April 1997, which encompasses several right-wing groups, still proclaiming to be counter-insurgency, which in the past have collaborated with the regular Army in operations against the FARC and the ELN (Loingsigh, 2002—see Bibliography). The members of the United Self-Defence Forces of Colombia or AUC are commonly referred to as los paramilitares. The AUC co-ordinates the activities of local paramilitary groups and develops a cohesive paramilitary effort to combat insurgents. It is alleged that the AUC is supported by economic elites, drugs traffickers and local communities lacking effective government security. It claims its primary objective is to protect its sponsors from Marxist insurgents, although nowadays has also become actively involved in drugs trafficking, in some areas even dividing territories with the FARC. Although it is commonly stated that the right-wing paramilitaries are a recent phenomenon in Colombia, a study of the Centro de Investigación y Educación Popular (CINEP) in Colombia suggests that they have been operating since the early 1960s with foreign assistance, although not as co-ordinated and widely spread as today.

The demobilization of the AUC, which began in 2003 as the result of negotiations between the Government and the armed groups, involved over 30,000 men up to mid-2006, including not only fighters but also support structures. New paramilitary groups, however, emerged in several—although not all—of the former AUC territories. AUC operations vary from assassinating suspected insurgent supporters to engaging guerrilla combat units. As much as 70% of the AUC's operational costs are financed with drugs-related earnings, with the rest coming from 'donations' from its sponsors. The AUC generally avoids actions against foreign personnel or business interests in general and has been accused by human rights groups of co-ordinating actions with the Colombian Army against the left-wing guerrilla groups. The AUC controlled the main petroleum areas of the country (including the province of Casanare, where BP operates) since the 1990s (Loingsigh, 2002) until recently. Its main leader and founder, Carlos Castaño-Gil, has been indicted by the US Department of Justice for drugs trafficking and has publicly admitted responsibility for massacres and assassinations. Castaño disappeared in 2004, after losing control of the group to a new group of commanders more openly associated with drugs trafficking. Although the US Department of State has labelled the AUC as a foreign terrorist organization, the Colombian Government held peace talks with the outfit. Some have accused top political leaders, including President Alvaro Uribe, whose father and brother were killed by the FARC, of having links to the AUC, although this has been denied categorically by the President himself.

The other two main actors in the Colombian conflict are the regular Colombian Armed Forces and the drugs cartels. The Armed Forces are composed of the Army, Navy (including naval aviation, marines and the coast guard) and the Air Force, amounting to some 333,000 uniformed personnel (213,000 military and 120,000 police). The police play a major role in the counter-insurgency activities and have a military structure and ethos. Colombia assigns some 4% of its GDP to defence, which amounts to some US $4,000m., one of the highest military expenditures in the region. Many Colombian military personnel have received training in the USA, which in 1999 set up the Plan Colombia. By means of this US legislation, the Colombian Government initially received $1,300m. to fight drugs trafficking, which turned into some $600m. per year thereafter. Although this aid package helped the current President, Alvaro Uribe, to achieve sound military victories against the guerrillas, it has also been widely criticized by neighbouring countries such as Venezuela and Brazil for affecting the military balance in the region.

The fourth factor in the Colombian conflict is the so-called drugs cartels. Colombia is the world's largest cocaine producer and is believed to be the main source of the cocaine consumed in the USA (Associated Press, 2006). According to a report from the US Government Accountability Office, Colombia supplies an estimated 90% of the world's cocaine, with an estimated US $65,000m. in illegal drugs to the US market (Schexnayder, 2005). From the 1970s until the 1990s drugs trafficking was mainly dominated by two cartels—the Medellín cartel and the Cali cartel—although two others were also very active in money laundering and in smuggling—the Bogotá cartel and the cartel of the Guajira. The most violent of these was the Medellín cartel, the main leader of which, Pablo Escobar, led a terrorist campaign in the 1980s against Colombian politicians, police and magistrates who were supporting legislation to extradite drugs barons to the USA.

Escobar was listed in 1989 by *Forbes* magazine as the seventh richest man in the world and he controlled a vast drugs-trafficking operation, including a private army. The Colombian authorities blamed him for an intensive terrorist campaign that involved hundreds of street bombs, thousands of dead, the killing of three presidential candidates and the bombing of Avianca flight 203 and of a Bogotá security building in 1989, among other terrorist acts. Escobar was finally killed by a joint operation between US and Colombian forces in 1993, after which the Medellín cartel dissolved into smaller groups, allowing its rival from Cali to dominate the market until the mid-1990s, when its leaders, too, were either killed or captured by the Government.

The Colombian drugs market today is controlled by smaller groups, which have compartmentalized their responsibilities in terms of production, smuggling, transportation and money laundering. The US Drug Enforcement Administration (DEA) and the Colombian national police believe that there are more than 300 active drugs-smuggling organizations in Colombia today, which ship to every industrialized nation in the world. After the demise of the big drugs cartels, the guerrilla and paramilitary groups took over the cocaine trade, making it their main source of income. Guerrillas and paramilitary groups protect the coca fields and the laboratories in exchange for a large tax that both peasants cultivating coca and the traffickers pay to these organizations.

The Colombian conflict since 1950 has left hundreds of thousands of people dead and wounded, since attacking civilians is not a side-effect, but a common practice for all the groups involved, in order to obtain obedience through fear. According to the UN High Commissioner for Refugees (UNHCR), it has also displaced at least 2.5m. people from their homes, making it one of the worst humanitarian crises of the western hemisphere (according to *The Economist* in 2006). Despite several initiatives and the end of the Cold War, there seems to be no prospect of peace in the near future.

THE GUATEMALAN CIVIL WAR

As in many other countries under US influence during the Cold War, such as Italy, Turkey, Greece and Iran, modern Guatemalan history is marked by the Cold War and interference by the US Central Intelligence Agency (CIA). Together with a small group of Guatemalans, the CIA overthrew the Guatemalan elected left-wing Government of Jacobo Arbenz in 1954, after his administration expropriated unused land owned by the United Fruit Company (for such events was the term 'banana republic' coined). Arbenz was classified as a communist threat in an operation similar to the one that overthrew Mohammed Mossadegh's Government in Iran the previous year. The CIA codename for the coup was Operation PBSUCCESS, and it would become the second successful overthrow of a foreign government by the Eisenhower Administration. Military rule started with the dictator Carlos Castillo Armas, but led to 30 years of civil war and some 200,000 Guatemalan civilian deaths. According to the UN-sponsored Truth Commission, government forces and paramilitaries were responsible for over 90% of the human rights violations during the war. During the first 10 years the victims of the state-sponsored terror were primarily students, workers, professionals and opposition figures of all political tendencies, but in the last years they were thousands of mostly rural Mayan farmers and non-combatants. More than 450 Mayan villages were destroyed and over one million people became refugees in what is now widely acknowledged as genocide. The Truth Commission report also points out that during this period the Guatemalan state engaged in an intentional policy of genocide against particular ethnic groups, which is considered one of the worst ethnic cleansings in modern Latin America.

Between the 1950s to the 1990s the US Government directly supported Guatemala's Army with training, weapons and money. The United Green Berets helped to transform the Guatemalan Army into a modern counter-insurgency force, making it one of the most sophisticated and effective in counter-insurgency. US and Guatemalan authorities often shared intelligence and it is documented that US secret services provided the military regime with satellite surveillance of areas where the guerrillas operated. In 1999 the then US President, Bill Clinton, admitted that the USA was wrong to have supported the Guatemalan military forces.

The origins of the Guatemalan insurgency dates back to the early 1940s, but it was in 1982 that four Marxist groups formed a guerrilla organization, the Guatemalan National Revolutionary Unity (URNG). It acted as an umbrella organization for the Guerrilla Army of the Poor (EGP), the Revolutionary Organization of Armed People (ORPA), the Rebel Armed Forces (FAR) and the Guatemalan Labour Party (PGT)/National Directing Nucleus of PGT (PGT-NDN). These movements had their origin in the 1960 revolt of junior military officers against the de facto president, Gen. Ydígoras Fuentes. When it failed, several of those officers went into hiding and established close ties with Cuba, becoming the nucleus of the forces that were in armed insurrection against the Government for the next 36 years. Shortly after President Julio César Méndez Montenegro took office in 1966, the Army launched a major counter-insurgency campaign that largely broke up the guerrilla movement in rural areas. Then the guerrillas concentrated their attacks on Guatemala City, where they assassinated many leading figures, including US Ambassador John Gordon Mein in 1968. Between 1966 and 1982 there was a series of military or military-dominated Governments. At the same time extreme right-wing groups of self-appointed vigilantes, including the Secret Anti-Communist Army (ESA) and the White Hand, tortured and murdered students, professionals and peasants suspected of involvement in leftist activities.

In 1982 a *coup d'état* brought to power Gen. Efraín Ríos-Montt, who had the backing of the US Administration of President Ronald Reagan. Ríos-Montt formed a three-member military junta that annulled the 1965 Constitution, dissolved Congress, suspended political parties and cancelled the electoral law. However, after a few months Ríos-Montt dismissed his junta colleagues and assumed absolute power. The Government began to form local civilian defence patrols (PACs). Participation was in theory voluntary, but in practice most people had no choice but to join either the PACs or the guerrillas. Ríos-Montt's conscript Army and PACs recaptured quickly most guerrilla territory. Guerrilla activity declined and was largely limited to hit-and-run operations. However, this partial victory was won only at an enormous cost in terms of civilian lives and on 8 August 1983 Ríos-Montt was deposed by his own Minister of Defence, Gen. Óscar Humberto Mejía Victores.

Gen. Mejía arranged an election in 1984 to select a Constituent Assembly to draft a democratic constitution. On 30 May 1985, after nine months of debate, a new Constitution was finally agreed and implemented. Vinicio Cerezo, a civilian politician and the presidential candidate of the Christian Democratic Party, won the first election held under the new Constitution with almost 70% of the votes cast and took office on 14 January 1986. It took, however, another 10 years of massacres and political assassinations by the security forces and right-wing paramilitary groups before there was an end to the violence.

UN-sponsored peace accords were signed between the URNG and the military in 1996, during the Government of President Álvaro Arzú. Both sides made major concessions to end the 36-year civil war. The Army controlled urban centres, while the URNG maintained a strong presence in the countryside. The Inter-American Human Rights Court ordered the Guatemalan Government to apologize to the victims and to pay survivors and relatives US \$7.9m. in damages. However, the main perpetrators of human rights violations have never been brought to justice.

FALKLANDS WAR

The Falklands or Malvinas (in Spanish) conflict was effectively a war in 1982 between Argentina and the United Kingdom over the Falkland Islands and South Georgia and the South Sandwich Islands. The Falklands consist of two large and many small islands, in the South Atlantic Ocean east of Argentina, the sovereignty of which has been disputed since the 18th century. However, they have been a British colony since 1842. In 1965 the UN passed Resolution 2065 specifying the Falklands/Malvinas as a colonial problem, and calling on the United Kingdom and Argentina 'to find a peaceful solution'. Talks continued for the next 17 years under different governments on both sides. However, by the 1980s the position had hardened, with neither the Argentine willing to accept anything less than full sovereignty nor the Falkland islanders willing to accept a fix-time lease compromise. The Argentine military junta was also facing growing discontent and economic crisis, so it is often argued that the invasion was politically motivated to distract public opinion from the internal crisis and to allow the dictatorship to recover some support. Indeed, Argentina was in the midst of a devastating economic crisis and large-scale civil unrest against the repressive military junta that was governing the country in the period leading up to the war. The Argentine military Government, headed by Gen. Leopoldo Galtieri, decided to launch what it thought would be a quick and easy war to reclaim the Falkland Islands. War was not declared officially by either side, and there was no military activity outside the islands' perimeter; the conflict was considered by Argentina as reoccupation of its own territory and by the United Kingdom as an invasion of a British dependency.

The Argentine planned invasion had two phases. The first one started with the so-called Alpha Operation in which the military used a private entrepreneur called Constantin Davidoff to smuggle special forces into the islands by disguising them as workers. On 19 March 1982 50-strong detachment of the Argentine special forces raised their national flag on the British dependency of South Georgia. Despite calls from the United Kingdom through the USA to stop the action at this point, the second phase started on 2 April 1982, with the so-called Operation Rosario. This consisted in a full-scale invasion of 5,000 Argentine troops, which duly occupied the islands.

British intelligence services were not taken totally by surprise by the Argentine attack as is commonly stated. In fact, the Foreign and Commonwealth Office had time to warn Rex Masterman Hunt, the Governor of the Falkland Islands, of a possible Argentine invasion on 31 March 1982. The United Kingdom launched a naval task force to engage the Argentine naval and air forces, and to retake the islands by amphibious assault. The British called their counter-invasion Operation Corporate on 21 May and were heavily relying on a naval task force for military action. The force was commanded by Rear Adm. John 'Sandy' Woodward and was centred on the aircraft carriers HMS *Hermes* and the newly commissioned HMS *Invincible*, carrying only 20 Fleet Air Arm (FAA) Sea Harriers between them for defence against the combined Argentinean Air Force and naval air arm. A second component was the amphibious group commanded by Commodore M. C. Clapp. The embarked force comprised 3 Commando Brigade Royal Marines (including units from the Parachute Regiment). The United Kingdom declared a 'total exclusion zone' of 200 nautical miles (370 km) around the Falklands before commencing operations, excluding all neutral and Argentine vessels. This exclusion zone was also crucial in managing the media, since access was strictly controlled by the military. Similar tactics would be later used by the USA in Grenada and in the Gulf War of 1991. Throughout the operation 43 requisitioned British merchant ships (ships taken up from trade—STUFT) served with or supplied the task force. Cargo vessels and tankers for fuel and water formed an 8,000-mile logistical chain between the United Kingdom and the South Atlantic. During the journey and up to the fighting, which began on 1 May, the task force was shadowed by Boeing 707 aircraft of the Argentine Air Force.

By mid-April 1982 the Royal Air Force (RAF) had set up an airbase at Wideawake on Ascension Island in the mid-Atlantic, including a sizable force of Vulcan bombers and F-4 Phantom fighters to protect them. Meanwhile the main British naval task force arrived at Ascension to prepare for war. A small force had already been sent south to recapture South Georgia. On 1 May operations against the Falklands opened with the Black Buck 1 attack by RAF Avro Vulcan V bombers on the Falklands' airfield at Port Stanley from Wideawake airbase. On 2 May the Second World War-vintage Argentine light cruiser ARA *General Belgrano* (formerly the USS *Phoenix*), a survivor of the 1941 Pearl Harbor attacks, was sunk by the nuclear-powered submarine HMS *Conqueror*. Two days after the sinking of the *General Belgrano*, on 4 May, the British lost the Type-42 destroyer HMS *Sheffield* to fire following an Exocet missile strike. On 21 May the British landed on beaches around San Carlos Water, on the northern coast of East Falkland, putting the 4,000 men ashore from amphibious ships and establishing by the dawn of the next day a secure beach-head from which to conduct offensive operations. By 1 June, with the arrival of a further 5,000 British troops of the 5th Infantry Brigade, the new British divisional commander, Maj.-Gen. J. J. Moore, had sufficient force to start planning an offensive against Port Stanley, on the other side of East Falkland. On 11 June, after several days of painstaking reconnaissance and logistical build-up, British forces launched a brigade-sized night attack against the heavily defended ring of high ground surrounding Stanley. On 14 June the commander of the Argentine garrison in Stanley, Mario Menendez, surrendered to Maj.-Gen. Moore. Some 9,800 Argentine troops were made prisoners of war and repatriated to Argentina on the liner *Canberra*. On 20 June the British retook the South Sandwich Islands and declared the hostilities at an end. By then the war of 74 days had taken the lives of 255 British and 649 Argentine soldiers and of three civilian Falkland islanders.

The Falklands conflict had important political repercussions: it strengthened Margaret Thatcher in government in the United Kingdom and played a significant role in her re-election as Prime Minister in 1983; it catalysed the fall of the military junta and the restoration of democracy in Argentina; and it tore apart the Inter-American system of mutual defence (TIAR). According to some recently disclosed documents, Thatcher had threatened the French President, François Mitterrand, with using nuclear weapons against Argentina if France did not provide the codes to disable the French-made anti-ship missile Exocet (Henley, 2005). The British Government has said that it will only disclose all documents on the war in 2082. Full diplomatic relations between Argentina and the United Kingdom were restored in 1990, although Argentina was still maintaining its claim to the Falklands. Meanwhile, the British introduced a new constitution for the Falkland Islands, which grants self-determination. The Argentine President, Nestor Kirchner, sworn in 2003, has again hardened his country's position, giving a warning of 'a drastic change' in its quest for sovereignty over the Falklands (McCann, 2006). The policy shift by Kirchner's Government comes as campaigning kicks off for the 2007 presidential election.

THE EL SALVADOR CIVIL WAR

This was a low intensity intra-national conflict fought between the Salvadoran regular Armed Forces and guerrilla groups operating under the umbrella movement known as the Farabundo Martí National Liberation Front (FMLN) between 1980 and 1992. The conflict left over 75,000 civilian killed, 8,000 missing, over 1m. homeless with another 1m. exiled. The origins of the war lie in the early

1970s, although they rooted in sharp economic inequalities and static socio-political structures. Since the early 20th century El Salvador had been ruled by an economic elite, often known as the Fourteen Families, in conjunction with the military. From 1931 until 1944 the country was governed by the iron grip of Gen. Maximiliano Hernández-Martínez. It was during this period that indigenous groups and peasants started organizing themselves under the leadership of Farabundo Martí, a self-proclaimed communist who had worked with Nicaraguan revolutionary leader Augusto César Sandino. The repression from the Hernández-Martínez's Government against these initial movements left thousands of people dead. Martí himself was executed by the US-trained National Guard of El Salvador.

Since then military governments have been in power most of the time, often responding to political unrest with violent repression. Political violence increased sharply after the 1977 election, at which Gen. Carlos H. Romero became President. Although Romero was deposed in October 1979, the military-civilian junta that replaced him was unable to stop the civil war. As a concession to the left, the junta proposed a limited land reform that affected about 25% of the land. At the same time the junta, which was closely linked to the right through the army, did little to control the rightist paramilitary National Guard. Under pressure from the USA to undertake economic and human rights reform, the military junta named José Napoleón Duarte, leader of the moderate Christian Democratic Party, as President in December 1980. However, executions of farmers, peasants and workers continued on a wide scale. El Salvador rapidly became a battleground in the Cold War, in which factions were supported by either the USA or the USSR and hundreds of thousands of people were killed, wounded or displaced.

By 1981 Mexico and France had politically recognized the FMLN and called for settlement between the Government and the guerrillas. However, the conflict intensified after the 1980 election in the USA of Ronald Reagan, whose Administration (1981–89) denounced the two main leftist groups, the FMLN and the Revolutionary Democracy Front (FDR), saying that they were being helped by Nicaragua, Cuba and the USSR. During this period the USA substantially increased its aid to the Salvadoran Armed Forces, despite widespread accusations of human rights violations. In March 1981 it provided US $20m. in emergency funds and $5m. in the special government-to-government arms sales programme (FMS) credits to supply the Salvadoran Army. A five-member US advisory team helped the Salvadoran Army to reorganize its command structure and sent an additional 40 special forces trainers-advisers to tutor the 'rapid reaction' battalions, a key element in the counter-insurgency strategy. The USA provided both indirect and direct war-related assistance against the FMLN. The indirect aid accounted for about 44% of the total US assistance programme up to the mid-1980s.

It was during this same period that some of the worst human rights violations occurred. Among them was the assassination of the Roman Catholic Archbishop of San Salvador, Oscar Arnulfo Romero, while he was consecrating the Eucharist during mass. Romero had been nominated for the Nobel Peace Prize in 1979, for having become an outspoken critic of the poverty, social injustice, assassinations and torture taking place in El Salvador. He had passed from being a conservative cleric to an outspoken critic of the right-wing groups and the Government. It is believed that his assassins were members of Salvadoran death squads, including two graduates of the US-run School of the Americas. This view was supported in 1993 by an official UN report, which identified the man who ordered the killing as Maj. Roberto D'Aubuisson, who later founded the Nationalist Republican Alliance (ARENA).

Duarte was succeeded as President on 1 June 1989 by Alfredo Cristiani of ARENA. Despite having little political credentials, Cristiani turned out to be an effective operator and on 13 September 1989 his Government began negotiations with the FMLN. These talks suffered a reverse when the FMLN launched a major attack on the capital on 11 November in which hundreds of people died. The army and ARENA-supported death squads responded by intensifying their war against the guerrillas. Four days later six high-ranking Jesuit priests, a cook and her daughter were murdered in the University of Central America, provoking an international outcry. Cristiani set up a special commission to investigate and that led to the arrest of four officers, three non-commissioned officers and two soldiers. However, no link to higher commands was ever established by this commission, despite mounting evidence to the contrary. In July 1990, after mounting international pressure and in the context of the end of the Cold War, an agreement was reached in which the UN would monitor rights violations after a cease-fire between the parties concerned. UN-sponsored negotiations continued and on, 16 January 1992, a peace accord was signed between the Government and the FMLN guerrilla groups, with a cease-fire from 1 February. Under the agreement the Salvadoran army was to be sharply reduced in number, the guerrilla forces were to be absorbed into Salvadoran society, a new national police force was to be created and land reform measures enacted. In 1992 reconstruction began under which the guerrillas returned to civilian life in return for economic, social and political reforms. Nowadays the FMLN has become a political party and been elected to office in several regions, including the capital. Despite such developments, sharp economic inequality still characterizes urban and rural life in El Salvador and common crime kills as many people as the armed conflict did during the civil war. A study by the Inter-American Development Bank revealed that more than 12% of the national income of El Salvador is spent on dealing with violence (Londoño and Guerrero, 1999; Romano, 1997).

CONTRA-REVOLUTION IN NICARAGUA

The overthrow of the Nicaraguan military dictator Anastasio Somoza on July 1979 by the pro-Marxist Sandinist Front of National Liberation (FSLN) preceded the arrival in power of the Reagan Administration in the USA by about six months. It was the second left-wing group to come to power by revolutionary means in Latin America since the Cuban Revolution of 1959 and the Reagan Administration perceived them as a threat in the strategic game against the USSR.

The new US Government accused the Sandinistas almost immediately after assuming power of importing Cuban-style socialism and representing a clear and present danger for US geopolitical interests in the area through their support for leftist guerrillas in El Salvador, Honduras and Guatemala.

By 1980 various disaffected guerrilla and political groups that had participated in the overthrow of Somoza, such as the Anti-Sandinistas Popular Militias (MILPAS), the indigenous peoples group YATAMA and the Democratic Nicaraguan Force (FD), had taken up arms against the new Sandinista regime (Vanolli et al., 1998). The US Administration then decided to support the activities of these groups. On 23 November 1981 President Reagan signed National Security Decision Directive 17 (NSDD-17), giving the CIA the authority to recruit and support the so-called Contras with US $19m. in military aid. Although the insurgent groups had little or no ideological unity, they started to co-ordinate actions under the name of the Nicaraguan Resistance, although the international media very quickly labelled them as Contras, which means 'against' or 'counter' in Spanish. The effort to support the Contras was one component of the Reagan doctrine, which gave military support to movements opposing Soviet-backed, communist governments. These measures were accompanied by economic embargo and a belligerent US diplomatic strategy against Nicaragua. The Contras also received financial support and military assistance from the military juntas in Argentina and Chile, while Honduras and, to a lesser extent, Costa Rica allowed them to conduct military operations from bases in their territories. With US assistance, the Contra factions united on June 1985, under the joint task force of the Nicaraguan Resistance (RN).

Although the Contra army was much larger and more effective and influential than the Sandinistas ever acknowledged, they did not have the force or the popular support needed to overthrow the Sandinista Government, despite being able to control large parts of Nicaraguan territory during certain periods of conflict, as well as creating havoc and significant human losses. Indeed, the war was devastating for Nicaragua's fragile economy and institutional life. Between 1980 and 1988 nearly 31,000 people died, 20,000 were wounded, 10,000 kidnapped or captured, 350,000 displaced from their homes and almost 200,000 fled the country. By the end of this war, Nicaragua's debt had grown dramatically and it had an inflation of 1,000% annually, leaving 75% of the population in poverty and with the living standard equivalent to that in 1950 (p. 19; Vanolli et al.).

By the mid-1980s US funding to the Contra groups had become very problematic for the Reagan Administration. In 1986 the International Court of Justice (ICJ) ruled against the USA, calling on it to 'cease and refrain' from the 'unlawful use of force' against Nicaragua, stating that the USA was 'in breach of its obligation under customary international law not to use force against another state' and ordering the USA to pay US $12,000m. in reparations. Although the Reagan Administration ignored this decision, claiming that ICJ jurisdiction could not be above the US Constitution, Congress ordered financial support to the Contras to stop by 1984. Nevertheless, administration officials arranged illegal funding and military supplies to the Contras by means of third parties, selling arms to Iran and using the proceeds to fund the Contras. The case was uncovered in 1986 by the Lebanese magazine *Ash-Shiraa* and became known as the Iran-Contra Affair, one of the most serious US political scandals of the 1980s.

Mediation by other Central and South American governments led to a cease-fire agreement on 23 March 1988, which, along with additional agreements in February and August of 1989, provided for the Contras' disarmament and reintegration into Nicaraguan society and politics. The agreements called for internationally monitored elections, which were subsequently held on 25 February 1990. Violeta Chamorro, former Sandinista and widow of anti-Somoza journalist Pedro J. Chamorro, defeated Sandinista leader Daniel Ortega and became President with the backing of the centre-right National Opposition Union (UNO). Some Contra elements and disaffected Sandinistas would return briefly to armed opposition in the 1990s, but these groups were subsequently persuaded to disarm.

Despite winning the presidency, Violeta Chamorro and the UNO had to negotiate an agreement whereby the Sandinistas remained in control of the armed forces. Humberto Ortega, brother of the former Sandinista President, stayed as defence minister until 1995, when he retired and was substituted by his protégé, Joaquín Cuadra (Ruhl, 2003). Cuadra has stated more recently that the success of the Nicaraguan peace process 'is mostly due to the significant integration of the different actors into civil life and the institutionalization of the Army and the police' (Cuadra, 2005). Indeed, despite being the second poorest country in Latin America, Nicaragua is nevertheless one of the safest countries on the continent; the murder rate is about 3.4 per 100,000 inhabitants, a lower rate than that of any large city in the USA, and this is a level of public safety superior to that of the majority of other countries in the region. In spite of the instability that still exists, which is a product of infighting between local leaders, political violence manifested in armed groups is almost non-existent.

THE PERU–ECUADOR WAR OF 1995

This conflict, which broke out on 26 January 1995, was the result of a long-standing territorial dispute between Ecuador and Peru. The conflict, often referred to as the Cenepa War or Alto Cenepa War, lasted less than a month (26 January–28 February) and involved the armed forces of both countries. The fighting erupted in the remote jungle mountains of the Cordillera del Condor, where a stretch of border had never been clearly marked and where there are deposits of gold, uranium and petroleum. Peru claimed that the approximately 1,000-mile border between the two countries had been set by the 1942 Rio de Janeiro Protocol, which had confirmed its victory over Ecuador in a 10-day territorial war in 1941. However, Ecuador declared the protocol null in 1960, before the last 48 miles (78 km) of the border had been marked. The Cenepa conflict was preceded by two previous military confrontations in modern times: the full-scale war in 1941; and a brief clash in 1981 (also known as the Paquisha Incident). Both encounters had seen the Peruvian forces prevail over the Ecuadorian military.

Peru's President, Alberto Fujimori, sent troops and warplanes into the region (between the Santiago and Zamora rivers), although each side accused the other of being the aggressor, and deployed naval ships along the coasts. Most of the fighting, which began on 26 January 1995, took place inside the 78-km strip of disputed territory. In contrast to a similar but shorter clash that had occurred in 1981, also inside the disputed border area, the Ecuadorian Army and Air Force managed to come out of the conflict with what Ecuador considered a limited but emotionally significant tactical success, mainly because of better preparations during the rising tensions in 1994. By the end of that year, profiting from its internal lines of communications, the Ecuadorian Army had managed to strengthen considerably its presence in the area, having deployed a number of units, foremost among them several special forces formations, as well as fixed and mobile artillery on the heights of the Cordillera del Cóndor, including anti-aircraft batteries to cover the entire Ecuadorian perimeter. Meanwhile, the Ecuadorian Air Force was hastily preparing its aircraft to be ready for action and adapting existing airfields in south-eastern Ecuador to function as forward-deployment bases. For the Peruvian military, the mobilization process was somewhat more problematic, as on their side the Cenepa valley area was devoid of any major roads, population centres or helicopter bases; the Army and Air Force had to organize a veritable air-bridge to get reinforcements to the zone. Troops, heavy weapons, ammunitions and supplies had to be flown in first from the Peruvian hinterland and Lima to Bagua airbase, where they were transferred to light transport aircraft for the flight to the Ciro Alegría base. From there the final flight to the Peruvian forward bases in the Cenepa valley, mainly the one called Observation Post 1 (PV-1), was made using Peru's helicopter fleet, often in poor weather conditions (Cooper, 2003).

Figures given for losses during the Cenepa War vary widely. Although official Ecuadorian military sources put casualties at 34 killed and 89 wounded and the Peruvian authorities reported 50 soldiers lost and more than 400 wounded, the casualties on both sides were most likely greater. Furthermore, the conflict had a serious impact on the local communities. At least 28 civilians were killed during the conflict. These were never reported on the lists of casualties and their families have not yet received compensation. Of the 350 Indian communities on the Ecuadorian side of the border, 20,000 people were directly affected by the fighting, 8,000 of them permanently displaced and their habitations destroyed. Most analysts agree that the conflict had no conclusive outcome in military terms, but diplomatically it was significant. A cease-fire and truce took effect on 1 March 1995, after tense peace talks, urging demilitarization of the disputed jungle border.

Thanks to Argentine, Brazilian, Chilean and US arbitration, the two disputing countries signed a peace treaty defining the 78-km stretch of border on 26 October 1998, creating a committee to resolve border issues peacefully and setting down terms for bilateral trade and navigation rights. The USA pledged US $40m. to the Peru-Ecuador border integration project and another $4m. to support Peruvian and Ecuadorian de-mining efforts along the border. Both countries now have diplomatic relations and have increased their commercial ties.

HONDURAS AND EL SALVADOR: FOOTBALL WAR?

The five-day conflict between El Salvador and Honduras in 1969 is often referred to as the Football War, since existing tensions between the two countries were inflamed by rioting during the second North American qualifying round for the 1970 football (soccer) World Cup. It is often claimed that the attack, launched by the Salvadoran army on 14 July 1969 against Honduras, was motivated by this game, but this is a caricature of the events. Tensions between both countries were caused by political differences between Hondurans and Salvadorans, including border delimitation, land reform and immigration from El Salvador to Honduras.

By 1968 the Oswaldo López Arellano Administration was confronting a gloomy economic crisis in Honduras and political unrest continued in 1969 with widespread strikes. As the political situation deteriorated, the Honduran Government and some private groups came increasingly to attribute the nation's economic problems to the approximately 300,000 illegal Salvadoran immigrants in Honduras. The Honduran Government refused to renew the 1967 Bilateral Treaty on Immigration with El Salvador, which had been designed to regulate the flow of individuals across their common border, and started expelling Salvadorans from their lands even if they had acquired them legally. By late May 1969 Salvadorans were beginning to stream out of Honduras back to an overpopulated El Salvador. Tensions continued to mount during June. The football teams of the two nations were engaged that month in a three-game elimination match as a preliminary to the World Cup contest. Disturbances broke out during the first game in the capital of Honduras, Tegucigalpa, but the situation got considerably worse during the second match in San Salvador, the capital of El Salvador. There were clashes between fans and emotions of both nations became considerably agitated. Violent actions against Salvadoran residents in Honduras, including an attack on the vice-consuls, increased tensions, while an unknown number of Salvadorans were killed and tens of thousands began fleeing the country. The press of both nations contributed to a growing climate of near-hysteria and, on 27 June , Honduras broke diplomatic relations with El Salvador. Early on the morning of 14 July , concerted military action began in what came to be known as the Football War. The Salvadoran Air Force attacked targets inside Honduras and the Salvadoran Army launched major offensives along the main road connecting the two nations and against the Honduran islands in the Fonseca Gulf. At first the Salvadorans made fairly rapid progress. By the evening of 15 July the Salvadoran army, which was considerably larger and better equipped than its Honduran opponent, had pushed the Honduran army back over eight kilometres and captured the departmental capital of Nueva Ocotepeque. However, Salvadoran forces began to experience fuel and ammunition shortages, since the Honduran Air Force had severely damaged El Salvador's petroleum storage facilities.

The day after the fighting had begun the Organization of American States (OAS) met in urgent session and called for an immediate cease-fire and a withdrawal of El Salvador's forces from Honduras. El Salvador resisted the pressures from the OAS for several days, demanding that Honduras first agree to pay reparations for the attacks on Salvadoran citizens and guarantee the safety of those Salvadorans remaining in Honduras. A cease-fire was arranged on the night of 18 July; it took full effect only on 20 July. El Salvador continued to resist pressures to withdraw its troops for a further nine days. Then a combination of factors led El Salvador to agree to a withdrawal in the first days of August. Those persuasive pressures included the possibility of OAS economic sanctions against El Salvador and the dispatch of OAS observers to Honduras to oversee the security of Salvadorans remaining in that country. The actual war had lasted just over four days, but it would take more than a decade to arrive at a final peace settlement. The war produced only losses for both sides. Between 60,000 and 130,000 Salvadorans had been forcibly expelled or had fled from Honduras, producing serious economic problems in some areas. Trade between the two nations had been totally disrupted and the border closed, damaging the economies of both nations and threatening the future of the Central American Common Market, which had been what first allowed Salvadorans to move and buy land in Honduras. The conflict left over 2,000 people dead and thousands displaced and homeless.

The two countries formally signed a peace treaty on 30 October 1980, agreeing to solve all border disputes in the ICJ. In 1992 the ICJ awarded much of the disputed land to Honduras and the two countries have worked to maintain stable relations. El Salvador and Honduras nowadays enjoy normal diplomatic and trade relations and are currently working towards a common market in the region.

THE CUBAN REVOLUTION

This class conflict consisted of guerrilla warfare efforts between 1953 and 1959, culminating in the overthrow of the military dictator Fulgencio Batista by what became known as the 26 July Movement. The revolution began with the assault on the Moncada Barracks on 26 July 1953 and ended on 1 January 1959, when Batista was driven from the country and the cities of Santa Clara and Santiago de Cuba were seized by the rebels, led by Ernesto Che Guevara and Fidel Castro. Castro himself arrived in Havana, the Cuban capital, on 6 January after a long victory march. In military terms it was one of the most classic examples of effective guerrilla warfare as, despite the insurgents being widely outnumbered by the regular forces, the guerrillas nevertheless managed to inflict a decisive military defeat upon their enemy.

After the revolution the USA made several attempts to overthrow Castro's Government. One of the most notorious of these attempts was the failed Bay of Pigs invasion (April 1961), in which Cuban dissidents were armed and supported by the US Government. The USA saw Cuba as a strategic threat that could be used by the USSR as a launching pad, and planned to invade to overthrow Castro. The US armed forces also staged a mock invasion of a Caribbean island in 1962 called Operation Ortsac (Castro spelt backwards). Meanwhile, Castro, upon the advice of Guevara, allowed the USSR to set up nine missile sites with nuclear warheads. The highpoint of the US–Cuban tension came on 16 October 1962, when US reconnaissance showed the Soviet nuclear missile installations on the island. US President John F. Kennedy ordered an international quarantine of the island, but Soviet ships under Kremlin orders ignored it and reached Cuba. On 27 October a US U-2 spy plane was shot down by a surface-to-air missile. This increased tensions between the USA and the USSR. However, the Soviets had not authorized Castro to use that weapon system, and then decided to pull back. The crisis ended on 28 October 1962, when Soviet leader Nikita Khrushchev announced that the installations would be dismantled. A secret agreement had been reached with Kennedy, whereby the USA would not invade Cuba and US Jupiter nuclear missiles warheads would be withdrawn from Turkey. The Cuban Missile Crisis spurred the creation of a direct communications link between the President of the USA and the Soviet leader in order to avert in any future crisis the possibility of a nuclear war.

The Cuban revolution has made two of the most distinctive and important contributions towards military doctrine. Perhaps the most important is that the concern of guerrilla warfare (expressed in Guevara's book *Guerrilla Warfare*, 1960) is now key reading in most military academies in the world. The second great contribution of the Cuban revolution was the idea of collective defence responsibility, which means the incorporation of all members of society—including women and children—into resistance of powerful foreign invasions. The idea was to make the scenario of such an invasion so painful to the enemy that they would be deterred. Although the roots of the second thesis can be traced back to the Boer wars of the late 19th century, it was the Cubans who elaborated it as a structured military doctrine—a 'War of All the People' was the sole operating doctrine on the island. This strategy envisaged an armed populace willing to fight for the defence of the homeland, and mass mobilization in order to assist conventional forces in the case of an overwhelming invasion. Some have recently drawn parallels to the role of Iran nowadays, supporting insurgency in Iraq in the aftermath of the US-led invasion of 2003 (see Fouskas's chapter on Iraq below).

RISE AND FALL OF THE PERUVIAN INSURGENCY

Since the second half of the 20th century Peru's history has been marked by military coups. However, the most recent period of military rule (1968–80), which started with Gen. Juan Velasco-Alvarado, who overthrew elected President Fernando Belaúnde Terry of the Popular Action Party (AP), was marked by nationalist and left-wing policies that launched the first agrarian reform and nationalization of the fishmeal industry, some petroleum companies and several banks and mining firms. However, Velasco Alvarado was overthrown by the more right-wing Gen. Francisco Morales-Bermúdez in 1975. Some of the insurgent groups emerged during this period of dictatorship, among the best known being the so-called Shining Path, although the group never refers to itself as such but as the Communist Party of Peru.

After internal struggles and political unrest, Morales-Bermúdez had to convene a Constitutional Assembly in 1979, which was led by the leader of the main left-wing party, Víctor Raúl Haya de la Torre. Morales-Bermúdez gave up power that same year. However, civil unrest did not stop and in some rural areas it intensified to the point that not only guerrilla groups such as Shining Path became more active and openly announced armed struggle as a means of achieving political power, but other very active movements emerged, such as the Túpac Amaru Revolutionary Movement (MRTA). Although both groups declared themselves adherents of Marxism-Leninism, in practice they had very different approaches and theses.

Shining Path's founder, Manuel Abimael-Guzmán, was heavily influenced by *Seven Essays on the Interpretation of the Peruvian Reality*, a 1928 book by José Carlos Mariátegui, the founder of the Communist Party of Peru and one of the leading socialist thinkers in Latin America in the 20th century. The name Shining Path is in fact taken from Mariátegui's book. Abimael-Guzmán was also convinced that since Peru was mainly a rural economy, the method of struggle should be based on guerrilla warfare by the peasantry, adopting similar tactics to that of the Communist Party of Nepal (which was also Maoist). The Shining Path eventually grew to control vast rural territories in central and southern Peru and achieved a presence even in the outskirts of Lima, where it staged numerous attacks. The movement not only targeted government forces and the civilian population, but also members of other guerrilla groups such as the MRTA. The Peruvian Commission of Truth and Reconciliation estimates that half of the 70.000 deaths during this period were at the hands of this movement. On 12 September 1992 Peruvian police captured Guzmán ('Chairman Gonzalo') and several other leaders of the Shining Path. Guzmán's role as the leader of the Shining Path was taken over by Óscar Ramírez ('Comrade Feliciano'), who himself was captured by the Peruvian authorities in 1999. After Ramírez's capture, the group splintered, guerrilla activity diminished sharply and peace returned to the areas where the Shining Path had been active.

The MRTA was formed in 1983 from remnants of the Movement of the Revolutionary Left, an insurgent group active in Peru in the 1960s. The MRTA was active from 1984 to 1997. The group took its name from Túpac Amaru II, who led an unsuccessful indigenous revolt against the Spaniards in 1780. The last major action of the MRTA group was the 1997 Japanese embassy hostage crisis, which ended when government forces, assisted by US intelligence, stormed the embassy and rescued all but one of the hostages. However, several of the hostage takers were summarily executed after they had surrendered.

Indeed, the counter-insurgency operations of the Peruvian Armed Forces are credited for being as effective as they were bloody, especially during the presidency of Alberto Fujimori (1990–2000). Critics charge that, to achieve the defeat of terrorist cells in various towns and cities, the Peruvian military indulged in widespread human rights abuses. However, many others credited Fujimori for ending the 15-year reign of terror. The Shining Path continues to operate in Peru, although no longer posing a significant threat to the Government, although on 23 December 2005 the Shining Path ambushed a police patrol in the Huánuco region, killing eight and wounding two others. The Government declared a state of emergency in Huánuco. On 19 February 2006 the Peruvian forces killed Héctor Aponte, who was believed to be the chief military commander of the Shining Path.

INSURGENCY, INVASIONS AND OTHER CONFLICTS

Several other conflicts have taken place across the region. They were dominated by radical groups, such as the Tupamaros in Uruguay, the Armed Forces of National Liberation (FALN) in Venezuela and the Alfaro is Alive, Damn It! group in Ecuador. The FALN led armed struggles in Venezuela between 1962 and 1967, and consisted mainly of disaffected communist and left-wing leaders who split from the main ruling party, Democratic Action (AD). This proved a disaster for the left in Venezuela. Along with the targeted repression of the Betancourt Government, this strategy further marginalized the left and contributed to strengthen the political and ideological grip of the mainstream parties, the AD and the Christian Democratic COPEI (Committee of Independent Electoral Political Organization). By 1965 the Communist Party of Venezuela had already decided to pull back from the guerrilla struggle, leaving its left wing out in the cold (Levine, 1973). After effective US-assisted counter-insurgency operations, most members undertook peace talks and deposited their arms. Some urban groups still operate in Venezuela and have resurfaced into political life during Hugo Chavez's presidency (from 1998).

Another leading movement in Latin America was the so-called Tupamaros, also known as the National Liberation Movement (MLN) of Uruguay. This movement operated mostly in urban areas in the 1960s and 1970s. The Uruguayan Government unleashed a counter-insurgency campaign that led to mass arrests and selected disappearances. Torture tactics were very effective and, by 1972, the MLN had been severely weakened and its main leaders imprisoned. After democracy was restored to Uruguay in 1985 the Tupamaros returned to public life as a legal political party, the Movement of Popular Participation. Today the party comprises the largest single group within the ruling left-wing Broad Front coalition.

A lesser conflict, in Ecuador, had as protagonist the group Alfaro is Alive, Damn It! between 1983 and 1991. During its more active militant period, the organization was known to operate with similar groups from neighbouring countries. However, since then Alfaro is Alive, Damn It! has operated as a political party. Although the country has suffered from political unrest and coup attempts, it has not seen a resurgence of armed groups.

Another well-known struggle is led in Mexico by the Zapatista National Liberation Army (EZLN), also known simply as the Zapatistas, whose first uprising occurred on 1 January 1994, when seven towns in Chiapas, one of the poorest states of Mexico, were seized by the insurgency. The Zapatistas social base is mostly indigenous Indian, but they have supporters in urban areas, as well as an international web of support. It was said at the time to be one of the first struggles in 'cyberspace', since the groups and its supporters incorporated the use of satellite telephones and the internet as a way to obtain support domestically and abroad. The uprising of the EZLN was a shock to the world, since it came at a time when Mexico had just signed and implemented the North American Free Trade Agreement (NAFTA), creating a common market between Mexico, the USA and Canada. The armed clashes in Chiapas, however, were short-lived and ended on 12 January. Indeed, after just a few days of localized fighting in the jungle, President Carlos Salinas de Gortari of Mexico, then in his last year of office, offered a cease-fire agreement and opened dialogue with the rebels. There have been no full-scale confrontations since then. Government talks with the EZLN culminated in the San Andrés Accords in 1996, which granted semi-autonomy and special rights to the indigenous population. However, President Ernest Zedillo, who succeeded Salinas, ignored the agreements and increased the military presence in the region. In 2000 the newly elected Mexican President, Vicente Fox, offered renewed peace talks and the following year the Zapatistas marched to Mexico City to present their case to the Congress. The group has become increasingly more of a political movement than an armed group. 'Sub-comandante Marcos', a well-known spokesman for the EZLN, has become a symbol for resistance movements all over the world.

There have been other cases in which Latin American countries experienced conflict, such as the Paraguayan Civil War (1947), in which the Colorado Party defeated the Febreristas and the Communist Party, leading to almost 40 years of military rule. The clashes surrounding the military coups in the 1970s in Argentina, Brazil, Chile and Uruguay can also be considered as conflicts since, in some cases, they involved the confrontation of armed groups. Some countries in the region have also been on the brink of international war, such as the Beagle conflict between Argentina and Chile, stopped at the last minute by the direct mediation of the Pope John Paul II in 1984, or the Caldas incident between Colombia and Venezuela, created by the presence of a Colombian destroyer in the Gulf of Venezuela in 1987. However, US-orchestrated invasions have been the occasion of conflicts where different armies fight each other, such in Grenada (1983) and Panama (1989).

In 1983 the USA invaded the Caribbean island of Grenada and overthrew the communist-led Government in favour of a pro-Western one. A coup in Grenada, along with a perceived threat to American students on the island provided the USA with an argument for eliminating a Marxist regime allied to Fidel Castro's Cuba. During the fighting the USA suffered from insufficient intelligence data, which made it difficult to find the medical students who needed to be rescued. The Grenadan army and its Cuban allies also offered greater resistance than the Americans expected. The small Grenadan force, assisted by Cuban soldiers, put up fierce resistance for several days, but were eventually overwhelmed by the invaders, who had grown in number from about 1,200 to over 7,000. Numerous rebels fled to the jungles and kept fighting; within a month the leaders of the military Government were arrested, and Cubans, Russians, North Koreans, Libyans, East Germans, Bulgarians and suspected Grenadan communists had been rounded up and put in a detention camp. By mid-December 1983 all US combat forces had left Grenada.

The US invasion of Panama, codenamed Operation Just Cause, deposed the general and de facto military leader Manuel Noriega in December 1989, during the Administration of US President George Bush (1989–93). The USA justified the invasion by claiming that CIA-trained Gen. Noriega had turned Panama into the centre for drugs cartels activities. Many analysts point instead at the imminence of the date on which, according to the 1977 Carter-Torrijos treaties, the USA was to give back control of the canal to Panama. The numbers killed in the invasion were estimated at 200–300 Panamian combatants (soldiers and paramilitaries), 23 US soldiers and some 300 civilians. However, human rights groups still claim today that this last number was much higher. After the invasion, the Panamanian Armed Forces were disbanded and substituted by the civilian National Guard Services.

CONCLUSION

The second half of the 20th century in Latin America was marked by US and Soviet interventionism in both civil wars and military coups. As a result of the Cold War, the USA sponsored many military coups, while the USSR supported many armed groups' struggle for power. However, many of the insurgencies and conflicts in general had much deeper historical roots and, because of this, many of these struggles are still present or latent. Despite most countries adopting constitutional democracies from the 1980s, Latin America suffers widespread political unrest. The rise of left-wing governments, especially in Venezuela, Argentina and Bolivia, has created turmoil for US interests in the area and it is likely that some form of armed struggle will resurface in the short term.

By contrast, it must be acknowledged that because of these historical conflicts, Latin American military commanders, guerrilla fighters and academics have made important contributions towards modern warfare doctrine in areas such as guerrilla warfare, counter-insurgency and civic-military relations. Among them is the Argentine Ernesto Che Guevara, whose book *Guerrilla Warfare* is nowadays considered a classic. No less important are the contributions made by Latin American scholars in terms of civic-military relations and democratic institutions, as well as the role of the armed forces in popular struggle and insurgency. While the USA seems to have militarily retreated from the region, it is still the dominant geopolitical presence. The emerging power of Brazil and a more proactive role for the People's Republic of China, which has become the second economic partner of the region, will certainly create new scenarios in which Latin Americans will have the opportunity to offer new contributions towards the theory of conflict and military warfare.

Conflicts in Africa

PHIA STEYN

INTRODUCTION

The history of independent Africa is characterized by high levels of conflict that have ranged from low-intensity ethno-religious and political conflicts to protracted civil wars and from conventional inter-state conflicts to regional conflicts. In this process millions of Africans have been killed, of which an estimated 90% were civilian non-combatants. Apart from the large-scale loss of human life and associated human rights abuses, conflict has also led to the reversal of decades of development efforts, the disruption of livelihoods, the destruction of infrastructure, the loss of investment opportunities, the diversion of resources from social programmes to the military, increased debt and massive internal displacement of people who are uprooted and forced to become refugees. The causes of conflict in Africa are numerous and include the colonial legacy, the weak post-colonial African state, *coups d'état*, military intervention in political processes, regional and international political and economic systems, fundamental social cleavages (e.g. ethnic, religious and regional), weak economies, competition over scarce resources, arbitrary and repressive governance, political intolerance and the refusal of political elites to co-operate and compromise. What follows is a survey of conflicts in independent Africa that focuses on some of the main conflicts fought on the continent since the about the 1950s and on attempts at making and keeping the peace in Africa.

I have separated this chapter into three main sections. In the first I look at the causes of conflict in sub-Saharan Africa, mainly during the Cold War but also beyond that. In the second I pay attention to conflicts in Africa in the 21st century. Finally, I try to outline ways of 'making and keeping the peace in Africa'.

CONFLICTS IN INDEPENDENT AFRICA: THE 20TH CENTURY

The euphoria created by the independence process in Africa in the 1950s and 1960s was short-lived, and soon made way for political instability, repression, conflict and massive human rights abuses. In some countries conflict predated actual independence, as groups fought wars of independence, while in others, such as the former Belgium Congo (subsequently Zaire, now the Democratic Republic of the Congo—DRC), conflict followed soon after the official departure of the colonial authorities. According to David Francis et al., in *Dangers of Co-deployment: UN Co-operative Peacekeeping in Africa* (pp. 76–82; 2005—see Bibliography), conflicts in independent Africa can be divided into six categories, namely wars of national liberation, Cold War proxy wars, secessionist wars, inter-state or conventional wars, identity-based wars and resource based wars.

Wars of National Liberation

Wars of national liberation were typically anti-colonial wars that sought the removal of colonial rule and the establishment of independent, locally controlled states. These wars included those in Morocco (1953–56), Tunisia (1954–56), Algeria (1954–62), Angola (1961–75), Guinea-Bissau (1962–74), Mozambique (1964–75), Zimbabwe (1965–80) and Namibia (1966–89). Opposition to 'foreign' rule was not only confined to European colonial rule, but also found expression in Eritrean opposition to Ethiopian rule and Sahrawi opposition to Moroccan control (since 1975), and in the unique war of national liberation fought in South Africa against white domination (1976, 1983–94) (pp. 76–77, in Francis et al., 2005; and pp. 9–71, Clayton, 1999).

The Eritrean war of liberation lasted from 1962 until the Eritrean People's Liberation Front secured de facto independence for Eritrea in 1991. Following a referendum in April 1993, Ethiopia conceded independence to the territory, thereby making this liberation struggle the only one to succeed in breaking the African and international consensus to maintain post-colonial African boundaries. The origin of this struggle lies in the colonial era. Eritrea was an Italian colony between 1889 and 1941, but then came under the military administration of the British, who federated the territory with Ethiopia in 1952. In 1962 Emperor Haile Selassie abolished Eritrea's autonomy and annexed the region as a province of Ethiopia. This action led to the launching of a liberation struggle by the pre-dominantly Muslim-based Eritrean Liberation Front (ELF). Internal dissent within the ELF resulted in the founding of splinter groups, of which the most significant was the founding of two people's liberation groups, which merged in September 1973 to form the Eritrean People's Liberation Front (EPLF). Civil war broke out between the ELF and EPLF, although the two groups also occasionally co-operated against Ethiopian forces, until the EPFL succeeded in pushing the ELF across the border into Sudan by the late 1970s. The EPLF continued the struggle against the Ethiopian forces during the course of the 1980s, profiting in particular from the Soviet-supplied weapons and military equipment captured from the Ethiopians. This enabled the movement to sustain its policy of self-reliance and the non-involvement of foreign powers in its struggle. With the help of the Ethiopian Peoples' Revolutionary Democratic Front, the EPLF succeeded in 1991 in breaking through the southern front and capturing the Eritrean capital of Asmara from the Ethiopian forces (Pool, 1998; and pp. 157–59, in Clayton, 1999).

Cold War Proxy Wars

Africa's independence coincided with the intensification of Cold War rivalries. The newly independent African states soon became embroiled in the East–West struggle. The world powers were lured to Africa for a number of reasons, including vast untapped mineral resources, the continent's strategic location on the world's major shipping routes, its political strength as a bloc within the UN and its growing markets. Ideology also played a key role as the West sought to contain the 'threat of communism', whilst the USSR was eager to export its revolution abroad. Owing to their strategic importance, the East–West rivalry was most intense in the Horn of Africa and in southern Africa, where the world powers became involved in a series of Cold War proxy wars in Angola (1975–90), in Mozambique (1981–92) and in Somalia and Ethiopia in the 1970s and 1980s (pp. 77–78; Francis et al., 2000). In addition, the USSR became the largest arms supplier to African states and insurgents, supplying (as Lamb, 1990—on p. 189— points out) 11 times more weapons than the USA and four times more than France.

The Angolan civil war was a typical Cold War proxy war. Armed conflict in Angola started in 1961, when nationalist movements launched their liberation war against Portuguese colonial rule. Three important nationalist movements emerged, namely the northern and Zaire-based National Liberation Front of Angola (FNLA), the mostly urban-based People's Movement for the Independence of Angola (MPLA) and the southern-based National Union for the Total Independence of Angola (UNITA) led by Jonas Savimbi. Independence came about after the fall of the Salazarist regime in Portugal in 1974. A negotiated settlement of January 1975 failed to incorporate the three factions into a coalition government, and Angola became independent amid political chaos as the three factions turned on each other. In the civil war that ensued, foreign powers quickly intervened, with the MPLA receiving backing from the USSR and Eastern bloc allies, Cuba and Yugoslavia. The FNLA, by contrast, was supported by the USA and Zaire, while UNITA was backed by the USA, Zaire and South Africa. Official US involvement came to an end in 1977. The MPLA managed to defeat the FNLA and took control of the capital, Luanda, on 10 November 1975, the day prior to independence, making them the de facto Government of the country. This was contested by UNITA and ensured the continuation of the civil war, which resulted in the military intervention of the USSR and Cuba on the side of the MPLA and of the South African Defence Force in support of UNITA. The Cold War phase in the Angolan civil war came to an end in the late 1980s, following the signing of the 1988 New York Accords, which required the disengagement of the foreign powers. This was followed by the 1991 Bicesse Accords, which brought the conflict to an end for a short period. Savimbi's unwillingness to accept an electoral defeat in 1992 led to the resumption of hostilities, which continued, despite various attempts to negotiate peace, until the death of Savimbi in January 2002. His death led to a cease-fire and the formal declaration of peace on 2 August 2002 (O'Neill and Munslow, 1995; Kambwa et al., 1995).

Secessionist Wars

The division of Africa by the European colonial powers at the end of the 19th century led to the creation of colonies with artificial borders that seldom reflected the political, economic, ethnic, social and geographical realities of the regions.

The arbitrary nature of the African states, which often grouped competing ethnic groups together, along with a colonial legacy in which groups were often played off against each other, ensured that identification with the nation became an illusive ideal in many post-colonial African states. The exclusive nature of politics in independent Africa, the domination of ethnic groups and competition over scarce resources further exacerbated the competition and tensions between ethnic groups, and resulted in a number of secessionist wars in which the ultimate goal was the creation of independent states. Examples of wars of secession include those in Katanga and South Kasai in Zaire (1960–64), Biafra in Nigeria (1967–70), Casamance in Senegal (1982–2005), southern Sudan (1963–72, 1983–2005), the Caprivi Strip in Namibia (1999), several regions in Ethiopia (e.g. Ogaden since the 1980s) and Somaliland in Somalia, which seceded in 1991, but has yet to be recognized by other states (pp. 78–79, in Francis et al., 2005; p. 401, in Englebert and Hummel, 2005).

The Nigerian civil war was considered the bloodiest war in Africa until the Rwandan genocide of 1994. The origin of this secessionist conflict dates back to the colonial era, during which the British combined three distinct regions (East, West and North), each dominated by a single ethnic group (the Igbo, the Yoruba and the Hausa-Fulani, respectively), into a single colony. These differences were further entrenched by religious differences, with the Igbo being predominantly Christian, the Yoruba, at that stage, being predominantly animist and the Hausa-Fulani being mainly Muslims. British colonial rule ensured the regionalization of Nigerian politics and loyalties, which continued after the colony obtained independence in 1960. The immediate causes of the civil war were: the political instability preceding and following the two coups of 1966, the first one led by Igbos in January 1966, with a counter-coup by northerners in July 1966, which brought Lieut.-Col Yakaby Gowon to power; the intensification of ethnic conflict in the North, which saw the killing of thousands of Igbo labourers; the increasing importance to the national economy of petroleum, which was found in the East; the personal ambitions of the Igbo military leader, Col Chukweumeka Ojukwu; and the breakdown of national conciliation efforts. The final catalyst was Gowon's announcement on 27 May 1967 that the country would be redivided into 12 regions, instead of the then four, which would break up the Igbos' domination in the East. Ojukwu reacted to this announcement on 30 May by announcing the secession of the East from the Nigerian federation and the establishment of a 'Republic of Biafra'. A civil war ensued, in which Biafra received support from France, while the federal Government was supported by the United Kingdom and the USSR. Biafra surrendered unconditionally to the federal Government on 15 January 1970. During the civil war an estimated 1m. people died, many from hunger and disease (Isichei, 1976).

Inter-state or Conventional Wars

Inter-state, conventional conflict has been relatively limited in independent Africa, where the vast majority of conflicts have been fought within states. Conventional conflict refers to conflicts between states and normally involves the regular military forces, though these are sometimes supplemented with paramilitary forces. In independent Africa, inter-state conflicts have resulted mostly from border disputes, especially when these borders contain strategic resources, from territorial claims and corresponding intentions to annex a disputed territory and from interference in the internal affairs of neighbouring states. Examples of inter-state, conventional conflicts include: the Ethiopia–Somalia war of 1977–78 over the Ogaden region; Uganda–Tanzania in 1978–79; Mali–Burkina Faso over the Agacher strip in 1974 and 1985; the ongoing dispute between Nigeria and Cameroon over the Bakasi peninsular; and that of Eritrea and Ethiopia over three regions, Bad'me, Alitena and Zalembassa, and Burie, which led to conflict in 1998–2000 and again in 2005 (p. 79, in Francis et al., 2005; pp. 66–67, in Zartman, 2001).

The origin of the Uganda–Tanzania war of 1978–79 lies in the territorial claims made by the Ugandan dictator Gen. Idi Amin shortly after he came to power in a *coup d'etat* in February 1971. Amin claimed territories on Uganda's borders with Rwanda, Kenya and Tanzania, while the last was also accused of harbouring guerrilla supporters of the previous Ugandan Government. Sporadic violence along the Uganda-Tanzania border started in September 1971 with a Ugandan cross-border raid into Tanzania. War followed in 1978 when political unrest in Uganda led Amin to allege a Tanzanian invasion of his country. Reconnaissance raids and bombings were followed, on 30 October, by the invasion of Tanzania by the Ugandan military. Encountering little opposition, the Ugandan forces quickly advanced to the Kagera river, but were forced to withdraw by a Tanzanian counter-attack. Other Ugandan attacks followed in December and in January 1979, both repelled by Tanzania. In response, the Tanzanian President, Julius Nyerere, decided to launch an attack on Uganda with the ultimate goal of removing Amin from power. This attack was launched at the end of January, with the invading force made up of the Tanzanian military forces, a group of Ugandan dissidents organized into the Ugandan National Liberation Army and a Mozambican field artillery unit. By April the Tanzanian forces had overrun Ugandan opposition, Amin had fled to Libya and an interim President, Yusufu L. Lule, had been sworn in. Political instability and civil war followed, until the National Resistance Army, headed by Yoweri Museveni, took control of the capital, Kampala, in January 1986 and subsequently succeeded in re-establishing an effective central Government in Uganda (pp. 293–303, in Ibingira, 1980; pp. 104–08, in Clayton, 1999).

Identity-based Wars

Identity-based wars (according to Francis et al., 2005—p. 80) refer to ethnic and religious conflicts, in that people perceive that core identities and values are under threat and consequently mobilize along ethnic and/or religious lines to oppose that threat. Identity-based conflicts are not confined to ethno-religious wars, but also include conflicts fought along regional and/or political lines, where political ideology and regional identity provide the basis for group identification and the exclusion of outsiders. The entrenchment of ethnic, religious, political and regional identities has led to numerous conflicts in independent Africa, including between the Hutus and Tutsis in Rwanda and Burundi, between north and south in Chad and Sudan (1963–72, 1983–2005), Algeria (1991–99) and Liberia (1989–2003) (Ihonvbere, 1994; Abubakar, 2001; Blanton et al., 2001).

During the Rwandan genocide of 1994 ethnic and regional differences were exploited by the Hutu political elites to the detriment of moderate Hutus and the Tutsi population. The origin of the genocide dates back to the colonial era during which the Belgian authorities divided Rwandan society on the basis of three clearly identifiable ethnic groups, proceeding to favour the numerically fewer Tutsis above the Hutu majority and the Twa. During the independence process the Belgian authorities shifted their support to the Hutu majority, which exacerbated existing ethnic tensions, and conflict erupted on 1 November 1959 with Hutu attacks on Tutsis and Tutsi reprisals. This conflict continued until the country became independent in July 1962 and flared up sporadically during the post-colonial era. Ethnic tensions increased in the 1980s, mainly owing to population pressure, crop diseases and dismal economic conditions that resulted from the drastic decline in world coffee prices. In reaction to the ongoing marginalization of the Tutsis, the Tutsi-dominated Rwandan Patriotic Front (RPF) launched an attack on the Hutu government forces from its base in Uganda in October 1990. This attack initiated a period of conflict that lasted until a cease-fire was negotiated in July 1992. Negotiations led to the UN-brokered Arusha Accords of August 1993, which allowed for greater Tutsi participation in Rwandan politics. Despite the presence of a UN peacekeeping force under the command of the well-known Canadian, Gen. Romeo Dallaire, ethnic tensions continued to build up. The genocide broke out on 6 April 1994 when the aircraft carrying the Rwandan President, Gen. Juvenal Habyarimana, and the Burundian President, Cyprien Ntaryamira, was shot down on approach to the airport in Kigali. Led by the Hutu militia, the Interahamwe, the mass killing of the Tutsis and of Hutu moderates started, and continued—without foreign intervention and under the watchful eyes of the UN—until the RPF took control of most of Rwanda by the end of July. By that time an estimated 800,000 people had already been killed. Order was eventually restored with the help of the international community, and the Tutsi-dominated RPF, headed by Paul Kagame, took control of the Rwandan Government (pp. 439–40, in Gregory, 2000; Hintjens, 1999).

Resource-based Wars

Conflict in Africa is increasingly being waged to secure access to scarce resources. A key characteristic of the post-colonial African state is the state's control over economic resources and, consequently, political power in Africa has more often than not been identified with economic wealth, especially where the resources hold the promise of making a secessionist state economically viable. In recent years resource-based conflicts have increased in number and include the conflicts in Sierra Leone (mainly diamonds, 1991–2002), Angola (petroleum, diamonds and wildlife resources, 1992–2002), Sudan (petroleum, 1983–2005) and Nigeria's Niger delta (petroleum, since 1998).

The Sierra Leone civil war of the 1990s illustrates the complex nature of resource-based wars. The origins of this civil war can be traced back to the political and economic instability prevalent in Sierra Leone by the late 1980s, which resulted from widespread corruption, governmental mismanagement and the political and economic marginalization of the rural majority. The conflict started when the Revolutionary Front (RUF) launched their armed campaign against the Government in 1990, with the backing of Liberia's Charles Taylor. As the International Institute for Strategic Studies (2006) points out, the RUF struggle was rather unique in that the organization made no specific demands, was not a separatist movement and did not enjoy much national or ethnic support. The RUF insurgency plunged Sierra Leone into a civil war and created a climate of opportunism in which many government soldiers became so-called 'sobels'— soldiers by day and rebels by night. Numerous military coups and mediation attempts failed, including the short-lived civilian Government that come power following the 1996 multi-party elections. The conflict and instability led to intervention by the Nigeria-led Economic Community for West African States (ECOWAS) Monitoring Group (ECOMOG), which aided the Sierra Leone Civil Defence Force in ousting the military junta and restoring the 1996 civilian Government in 1998. UN intervention followed in July, but failed to bring lasting peace, with rebel action resumed shortly thereafter. A new peace agreement was signed in May 2001 and, following the demobilization of nearly 72,000 comba-tants, President Ahmed Tejan Kabbah declared an end to the civil war on 18 January 2002 (Kandeh, 2003). Diamonds featured prominently in the conflict and were used to finance the war, by buying weapons and paying combatants. Foreigners, both intervening governments and mercenaries, were compensated with diamond contracts and mining concessions. The use of diamonds to fund the civil war in Sierra Leone (and in Angola and Liberia) led to diamonds originating from insurgent-controlled territories to be termed 'conflict diamonds' by the UN and a ban being placed on trade in them on international markets in July 2000 (United Nations, 2001).

CONFLICTS IN THE 21ST CENTURY

Africa entered the 21st century with at least 15 conflicts of various proportions being fought across the continent. According to the International Institute for Strategic Studies, based in London (United Kingdom), the fatalities in 21 conflicts in 19 African states between 2000 and 2005 alone amounted to over 185,000.

Conflicts that Came to an End

Probably the most significant developments in conflict management in Africa in the past few years have been the resolution of six long-running conflicts. The

Angolan civil war was finally brought to an end after 27 years on 4 April 2002, but only after the death of the UNITA leader, Jonas Savimbi. Similarly, the 10-year civil war in Sierra Leone was also brought to an end in 2002, and this country, like Angola, has started the long process towards rehabilitation. Peace was brought to the Casamance region in southern Senegal, where there had been peaceful campaigning for a separate state since 1947. An armed struggle was launched against Senegalese rule in 1990 and sporadic fighting continued until December 2004, when a peace accord was signed, under the terms of which the region remained part of Senegal.

A significant development was the peace process in southern Sudan that brought the 22-year old secessionist war to an end in January 2005. The war in southern Sudan revolved around religious, ethnic and cultural differences, access to resources, the political ambitions of some southern leaders and the northern reaction to southern demands. The origin of the southern Sudan secessionist war dates back to the colonial era, during which the United Kingdom governed the south as a separate unit until 1946, while the north was controlled by Egypt. Despite southern objections, the predominately Christian and animist, black ethnic groups of the south were united into one country with the predominantly Muslim and Arabic north at independence in 1956. The Government was seated in Khartoum in the north, and this region remained in firm control of the country and its resources. Armed resistance to northern rule was launched in 1963, in opposition to northern attempts to spread Islam and Arabic to the south and to the appointment of northerners to key positions in the south. The ultimate aim of the insurgents was the establishment of an independent state in southern Sudan. The secessionists were plagued with discord from the outset, which led to widespread splintering of the movement and violent conflicts between the various southern factions. The secessionist war with the north continued until a cease-fire was negotiated in 1972. Peace lasted until September 1983, when the Government introduced *Shari'a* law, implemented other restrictive measures and removed southern self-rule. These measures, along with the discovery of petroleum resources in the south, led to the resumption of southern resistance. Important southern factions to emerge included the Dinka-dominated Sudan People's Liberation Army (SPLA—headed by Col John Garang), the Nuer-dominated Anya Nya II and the United Democratic Salvation Front (headed by Riek Mashar). The southern resistance was again characterized by ethnic tension between the various groups, and much of 1992, for example, was spent fighting each other instead of the Sudanese Government. The conflict between the southern factions and the Government continued despite various international attempts at mediation, such as the 1995 cease-fire brokered by the former US President Jimmy Carter. Protracted peace negotiations started in Kenya after the turn of the century, mediated by Ugandan President Museveni (a key supporter of the southern factions). These negotiations eventually led to the signing of a Comprehensive Peace Agreement on 9 January 2005, which brought the conflict to an end and which allowed for a referendum on southern secession after an interim period of six years (Johnson, 2003).

A few identity-based conflicts, influenced greatly by access to resources, were also brought to an end, including the 15-year old Burundi conflict (1988–2003), the 14-year civil war in Liberia (1989–2003) and the comparatively short war in Chad (1999–2000), the last launched by the north against southern domination. The conflict in Burundi revolved around a power struggle between the dominant Tutsi minority and the Hutu majority. As is the case in Rwanda, the origin of the ethnic tensions dates back to the colonial era, and specifically to the way in which the Belgian colonial authorities politicized ethnicity and promoted Tutsi interests to the detriment of the Hutu majority. Independence in 1962 exacerbated ethnic and regional tensions and resulted in frequent ethnic and regional violence. Hutu uprisings in the north in 1988 sparked a new wave of violence when the Tutsi-dominated army reacted by killing an estimated 20,000 Hutus and forcing about 100,000 to flee to Zaire and Rwanda. International peace initiatives were countered by internal developments in 1993, while the Rwanda genocide further complicated ethnic relations and directly led to the systematic killing of Hutus by the Tutsi army of Burundi between 1995 and 1996. The Arusha peace process was launched in 1998 and negotiations were mediated by former Tanzanian President Nyerere and then by former President Nelson Mandela of South Africa. Six Hutu factions, including the two major factions, refused to sign the August 2000 Arusha Peace and Reconciliation Agreement for Burundi. Renewed efforts in 2003 by the President, Maj. Pierre Buyoya, who came to power in a military coup in 1996, eventually led to the signing of the Pretoria Protocol on Political, Defence and Security Power Sharing in Burundi between the Government and the largest Hutu faction, the National Council for the Defence of Democracy. Although not all factions have agreed to end hostilities, relative stability exists in Burundi, monitored by a UN peacekeeping force, which took over from the African Union (AU) peacekeeping force in June 2004 (Ndikumana, 2000; Reyntjens, 2006).

Fragile political stability also exists in Liberia following the cessation of 14 years of civil war in 2003. The Liberian civil war had origins that dated back many years, to the settlement of freed black slaves from the USA in the territory in the 19th century. The country became independent in 1847 and its politics, economics and social structures were dominated by the Americo-Liberians (mainly descendents of people taken from the Congo region), who marginalized the country's 13 indigenous ethnic groups. The immediate causes of hostilities were two-fold, namely ethnic tensions and control over natural resources, mostly diamonds and timber. The established political order came to an end with the April 1980 *coup d'état* that brought Sgt Samuel K. Doe, a Krahn, to power. Political instability, repression, violence and economic mismanagement followed, along with the increased politicization of ethnicity. Armed resistance to the Doe regime broke out in December 1989 when the National Patriotic Front of Liberia (NPFL), headed by the Americo-Liberian Charles Taylor, attacked from Côte d'Ivoire. Civil war ensued, characterized by factionalism, massacres and destruction. An ECOMOG force, staffed mainly by Nigerian and Ghanaian soldiers, intervened without success and also failed at numerous attempts to broker a cease-fire and to initiate peace talks. The initial civil war was brought to an end with the Abuja II Accords in August 1996. By that stage about 150,000 people had been killed and 80% of the population had been uprooted and forced to flee their homes. Taylor came to power in the July 1997 elections that were conducted under ECOWAS supervision. His abuse of power, corruption, economic mismanagement and the marginalization of other ethnic groups, in particular the Krahn, led to the resumption of hostilities in 2000. Opposition forces united into Liberians United for Reconciliation and Democracy (LURD) in Freetown, Sierra Leone, in February 2000, intent on removing Taylor, and received military and financial support for their struggle from Guinea, Sierra Leone, the United Kingdom and the USA. The conflict continued until the signing of a UN-brokered Comprehensive Peace Agreement by the Government, LURD and other factions and parties on 18 August 2003. Following this agreement, a National Transitional Government of Liberia, composed of all factions and headed by Gyude Bryant, took control of the country in October 2003, under the supervision of the UN Mission in Liberia. Taylor had by that time fled to Nigeria, where he was granted asylum. He was extradited to Sierra Leone in 2006 to stand trial for his role since November 1996 in the atrocities in Sierra Leone (Harris, 1999; International Institute for Strategic Studies).

Old Wars and New Conflicts

While fragile political stability returned to a number of conflict-ridden African states, in many others the 21st century has meant the continuation of the same violence, repression, death and destruction, with no real end yet in sight. In Nigeria, for example, ethno-religious conflict in the north and resource-and ethnic-based conflicts in the Delta region in the east continues to destabilize these regions. The Niger Delta region, in particular, has been plunged into a general state of lawlessness, with violence, kidnappings, oil siphoning and sabotage being the order of the day. The causes of these widespread conflicts in the region are directly related to two important issues, namely the political, economic and social marginalization of ethnic minority groups, which make up the bulk of the Delta population, and the vast petroleum and gas resources that are found in this region. While the rest of the country in general, and the majority ethnic groups in particular, have benefited from the oil wealth, the Niger Delta is characterized by widespread poverty, lack of development, lack of basic infrastructure, mass unemployment and widespread environmental degradation and pollution due to oil-related activities (Human Rights Watch, 1999 and 2002).

Political instability also continues in previously stable African states such as Zimbabwe, Côte d'Ivoire, and São Tomé and Príncipe, while the Moroccan Government is yet to allow the referendum on the future of Western Sahara provided for in the 1991 UN-brokered cease-fire agreement with the Polisario Front. Consequently, the latter is still engaged in a secessionist struggle against Moroccan domination. The same is valid for the Oromo people and the Somalis living in the Ogaden region in Ethiopia. Both groups have continued their struggle against the Ethiopian Government, albeit on a low-intensity level. Somalis, meanwhile, have not succeeded in re-establishing law and order following the disintegration of the Somali state in the 1980s. Fuelled in particular by clan rivalry and access to scarce resource due to prolonged droughts, the Somali conflict has continued despite numerous mediation attempts by continental and international actors. A recent breakthrough in the peace talks and the signing of the Somali National Charter in January 2004 have not led to the much-needed political co-operation and compromise, with disagreement and clan rivalry still dominating the political landscape. The implosion of the Somali state has led to the establishment of two breakaway states, namely Somaliland in northern Somalia in 1991 and Puntland in July 1998. Both states have succeeded in establishing working state structures and emerging civil societies, although none has been recognized internationally (Doornbos, 2002; International Institute for Strategic Studies). In Uganda the armed conflict by the Lord's Resistance Army (LRA) against the Government and its own people in the north, the Acholi, also continues with no real end in sight. Like Somalia, the LRA resistance was born out of the political instability that prevailed in Uganda in the early 1980s, to which the LRA have added millenarian religious motivations (Van Acker, 2004).

Conflict also continues to engulf the Great Lakes region in Central Africa, where the so-called 'Great War of Africa' has been waged in the DRC (formerly Zaire) with the involvement of more than eight neighbouring and other African states. This war is very complex and is often described as three wars being fought at the same time, namely: the ethnic conflict between the Tutsis and the Hutus; the armed insurgency by Congolese factions aimed at overthrowing the Government; and a series of proxy wars involving the military forces of Uganda, Burundi and Rwanda, which fight in the DRC alongside the rebel factions, and the military forces of Chad, Namibia and Zimbabwe, which fight on the side of the Government. The origins of this war can be traced back to two main elements: the repressive dictatorship of Mobutu Sese Seko, who controlled Zaire from 1966 until 1997; and the ethnic conflict between the Hutus and the Tutsis. Of particular importance to the latter were the Rwandan genocide and the influx of more than 1m. refugees from Rwanda into neighbouring Zaire, Tanzania and Uganda, many of whom were Hutu militia members fleeing Rwanda in fear of reprisals. The conflict started in 1996 when the Tutsi-dominated Rwanda and Burundi Governments, and Uganda, supported the insurrection launched by an Alliance of Democratic Forces for the Liberation of Congo-Zaire (ADFL-CZ), headed by Laurent Kabila, against Mobutu's rule. This insurrection gained momentum very quickly and eventually led to the removal of Mobutu from power in 1997, with Kabila taking control of the Government and renaming the country the DRC. Kabila soon lost the backing of his former allies, who transferred their support to a Tutsi-dominated rebel faction, the Congolese Rally for Democracy (CRD). The CRD, aided by Rwandan and Ugandan military forces, launched a struggle against the Kabila regime, taking control over a third of the country. With the help of Zimbabwe, Angola, Namibia, Chad and Sudan, Kabila managed to retain control over the west of the DRC. Mediation efforts were intensified at the end of the 1990s, culminating in the signing of the Lusaka Agreement in July 1999 between the Kabila Government, three rebel factions and five intervening states. The peace process, along with the conflict, continued after Kabila was assassinated by a bodyguard in 2001, to be succeeded by his son, Joseph Kabila. While the transitional Government that has emerged from the protracted peace process has proven to be a relative success, conflict and instability have continued in the Ituri and the North and South Kivu districts, despite the presence of a large UN peacekeeping force. Nine Bengali UN peacekeepers, for example, were killed in the Ituri district in February 2005 (Reyntjens, 2001; International Institute for Strategic Studies).

International efforts have also not been successful in bringing an end to one of Africa's most deadly new conflicts, in the Darfur region in Sudan. Conflict in this region started back in the 1980s, when inter-communal violence and banditry resulted from increased competition over scarce resources and from political changes. The current violence was caused by local frustration with national politics and the inability of the Khartoum Government to address the region's problems and aspirations. Darfur frustration with the Government resulted from the 1999 split in the ruling Congress Party, in which Omar al-Bashir replaced his former mentor, Dr Hassan al-Turabi, as president. Turabi was very popular in Darfur and the Bashir regime took steps to replace local administrators and the leaders of the Popular Defence Forces (PDF) in the region with people loyal to the new factional set-up. In this process the PDF became politicized and started to intervene in ethnic conflicts, in particular those between Arab and other ethnic groups in the region. Armed resistance to the Government broke out in Darfur in February 2003. Initially the rebel forces, organized into the Darfur Liberation Front (later renamed the Sudan Liberation Movement/Army, SLM/A), enjoyed some early successes, leading to their demand for a united, secular Sudan in which all ethnic groups would be equal. The SLM/A was also joined in its struggle by the Zaghawa-dominated Justice and Equality Movement (JEM), which has strong links with the Islamist movement. The Government reacted to the crisis in Darfur by making use of the local PDF, popularly known as the Janjaweed, against the insurgents in a campaign that has become notorious for the brutality against the civilian population and the insurgents. The Khartoum Government miscalculated the international repercussions of its actions in Darfur, which were condemned internationally, and Sudan was consequently reported to the UN Security Council in July 2004. The international attention, along with the AU-mediated peace talks, however, have not been able to bring this conflict to an end, and the Janjaweed attacks on innocent civilians consequently continue (De Waal, 2005).

MAKING AND KEEPING THE PEACE IN AFRICA

William Thom noted back in 1984 that African armies were better at mobilization than demobilization. The experiences in an increasing number of African states, such as the DRC, Liberia, Sierra Leone and Somalia, or in the Nigerian Niger Delta, have confirmed this to be the case in whole societies as well. It has proved very difficult to reverse entrenched patterns of conflict, repression, suspicion and intolerance. Indeed, demobilizing Africa's militarized and conflict-ridden societies remains a challenge, and is an extremely slow process, as shown in the so-called success cases of Burkina Faso, Mozambique and South Africa. Consequently, political stability remains fragile at best in many of Africa's former war-torn states, such as Angola, Burundi, Liberia and Sierra Leone.

Making and keeping the peace in contemporary Africa is no easy task, in no small part due to the internal nature of most African conflicts. The long duration of many African conflicts underlines the depth of divisions that led to the conflicts in the first instance, and these divisions have become more entrenched over time. In addition, the general unwillingness of many governments and opposition forces to compromise and bring the violence to an end have unnecessarily prolonged many conflicts. Owing to Savimbi's unwillingness to compromise and co-operate, for example, the UNITA leader managed to prolong the Angolan civil war for almost a decade. Only after his death in January 2002 was it possible for UNITA and the Angolan Government to negotiate a lasting settlement. Peacemaking has also been complicated in recent years by the regionalization of internal conflicts, in particular those of the DRC, Somalia, Liberia and Sierra Leone. These conflicts spilled over to neighbouring countries, thereby aggravating the problems involved in keeping the peace, and complicating the mediation process that now has to take account not only of the demands and grievances of internal factions, but also of neighbouring governments and movements.

Marrack Goulding (p. 160 of his 1999 publication) points out that the internal nature of African conflicts make them much more difficult to mediate than inter-state conflicts because of six factors. First, the sovereignty principle in international law makes it difficult to intervene in sovereign states without the invitation of the government. Second, the law and methodology of conflict mediation are based mainly on resolving inter-state conflicts and not intra-state conflicts. Third, the causes of intra-state conflicts tend to be fundamental social cleavages within societies, which strengthen sovereignty-related arguments to exclude outside mediators. Fourth, at least one party is likely to be an insurgent group. Such groups are in general difficult to work with owing to their general lack of experience in negotiations and international law. Fifth, the government will most likely resent and resist being regarded as being equal in status as the insurgent groups and as having contributed equally to the outbreak of the conflict. Sixth, civilians suffer the most in intra-state conflicts, which makes it impossible for humanitarian and relief agencies to respond to the crisis without getting drawn into the politics that underlie the conflict.

Making and keeping the peace in Africa involve individual states, leaders and/ or groups of states (e.g. France in the Central African Republic), regional multinational force intervention (e.g. ECOWAS in West Africa) or continental and/or international multinational force intervention (e.g. the UN and AU peace-keeping forces). The proliferation of conflict in Africa in the post-Cold War era has increased the involvement of the UN in African conflicts. Since the late 1980s the UN has been officially involved in 15 African states, in which 22 peace-keeping operations were launched. The effectiveness of these operations varied greatly, from the general successes in Namibia (UN Transition Assistance Group—UNTAG) and Mozambique (UN Operation in Mozambique—ONU-MOZ) to the dismal failures in Somalia (UN first and second Operations in Somalia—UNOSOM I and II), which led to the humiliation of the US Rangers in Mogadishu in October 1993 and the hasty withdrawal of American troops involved in the peacekeeping operation. UNOSOM was not only a failure, but, more importantly, made the USA very reluctant to become involved in African conflicts in general; it is further credited with being one of the main reasons why the Western powers and the UN did not intervene in the Rwandan genocide of 1994. At mid-2006 the UN had 15 peacekeeping operations around the world, of which seven were in Africa, namely Western Sahara, the DRC, Eritrea-Ethiopia, Liberia, Côte d'Ivoire, Burundi and Sudan.

The reluctance of the global powers to intervene in African conflicts is a growing trend in conflict resolution and peacekeeping on the continent. Conse-quently, the role of regional organizations and the AU in peacekeeping has greatly expanded, despite problems such as a lack of resources and long-term logistics capabilities and a heavy reliance on outside expertise and funding hampering all-African peacekeeping operations. Both ECOWAS and the AU are currently focusing on building up their capacity to carry out peacekeeping operations, with the AU developing a permanent African security force known as the AU Standby Force. The Standby Force will consist of five or six brigades, which will be stationed around Africa with the aim of being able to intervene quickly in any conflict situation on the continent. Despite the challenges to all-African peace-keeping operations, the African Mission in Burundi (April 2003–April 2004, comprising South African, Ethiopian and Mozambican troops) did succeed in stabilizing 95% of the country. The AU is now involved in its AU Support Operation in Darfur, attempting to bring peace to Africa's newest deadly conflict.

Managing and preventing conflict in contemporary Africa is no easy task, and no quick solution exists for the continent's multiple conflicts. Of crucial impor-tance in limiting current and future conflicts is the reduction of small arms (deadly leftovers from the Cold War era, in the aftermath of which the international weapons market was flooded with cheap, surplus arms) and the implementation of arms control mechanisms, since wars start and continue because of the widespread availability of small arms across the whole continent. Foreign intervention in disputes and conflicts should also be timely and not after the fact, as was the case in Rwanda in 1994. To reduce the possibility of the renewal of conflict, it is further important to establish security in the country concerned and to work towards social reintegration of combatants, reconciliation between the opposing groups (e.g. truth and reconciliation commissions, as in South Africa, Rwanda and Sierra Leone) and the economic recovery of the country. Education for peace is also of utmost importance, since the promotion of the peaceful resolution of political, ethnic, religious and other differences remains a key aspect of preventing deadly conflicts. Until these fundamental principles take root in African societies, civilians will continue to suffer the consequences of the multiple conflicts that are fought because of the unwillingness of African political elites to compromise and co-operate.

Ethnic Conflicts in the Caucasus and Central Asia

EMMANUEL KARAGIANNIS

INTRODUCTION

In the aftermath of the break-up of the USSR, the Caucasus and the Central Asian regions were hit by a wave of ethnic conflicts. The Caucasus region is bounded by the Black Sea and Azov Seas to the west and the Caspian Sea to the east; it shares international borders with Turkey and Iran to the south and is roughly delimited by a horizontal line drawn between the Don and Volga rivers to the north. The Caucasus has asymmetrical political structures, which include three independent states—Georgia, Armenia and Azerbaijan—inside which there exist three autonomous entities claiming de facto independence: Nagornyi Karabakh, Abkhazia and South Ossetia. In addition, there are seven autonomous republics that are all parts of the Russian Federation, one of which has also claimed independence: Chechnya. Central Asia is bounded by the Caspian Sea to the east, Iran to the south, Russia to the north and the People's Republic of China to the east. The disintegration of the USSR in December 1991 led to the establishment of five independent states in Central Asia: Uzbekistan, Kazakhstan, Turkmenistan, Kyrgyzstan and Tajikistan.

The aim of this chapter is to present a comprehensive account of the major ethnic conflicts in the Caucasus and Central Asia. It will cover ethnic conflicts in Nagornyi Karabakh, South Ossetia, Abkhazia, North Ossetia (Osetiya) and Chechnya, as well as the Fergana Valley and Tajikistan. More specifically, I will be focusing on: the origins of ethnic conflicts; the involvement of great powers and international organizations; the present state of affairs; and the prospects for conflict resolution for the unresolved disputes.

THE NAGORNO-KARABAKH CONFLICT

The predominantly Armenian-populated Nagorno-Karabakh Autonomous Oblast (NKAO) within the Soviet Republic of Azerbaijan was established in July 1923. The enclave covers 4,400 sq km and is surrounded entirely by the rest of Azerbaijan; its nearest point to Armenia is across the so-called Lachin (Laçin) corridor, a distance of roughly 4 km. The essence of Armenian discontent lay in the fact that the Azerbaijani authorities in Baku deliberately severed the ties between the enclave and Armenia and pursued a policy of planned Azerbaijani settlement, squeezing the Armenian population of the NKAO and neglecting its economic and social needs. Although ethnic Armenians constituted the largest group in the NKAO, they received no Armenian television broadcasts and had no Armenian-speaking institution of higher learning. As long as Communist rule held in the USSR, however, so did the uneasy but peaceful relationship between the enclave and Baku.

New possibilities for the Armenians to protest were opened up in the late 1980s. In the enclave itself, a petition campaign in favour of reunification with Armenia was in progress from the second half of 1987. The Azerbaijani authorities, indignant over what they viewed as an Armenian-orchestrated drive to unite Nagornyi Karabakh with Armenia, responded with repressive measures. Secession was illegal in the context of the 1978 Soviet Constitution, which stated that the borders of a republic could be changed only if the republic itself permitted the change. The Armenians, inspired by Mikhail Gorbachev's politics of *glasnost* (openness) and *perestroika* (restructuring), claimed that Karabakh had been Armenian land for time immemorial and that it had been forcefully annexed to Azerbaijan by the Bolsheviks. In 1989, according to the last Soviet census, Nagornyi Karabakh was home to 192,000 people; ethnic Armenians represented 76% of the population and Azeris 23%. There were also small communities of Russians, Kurds and Greeks.

Violence was soon unleashed, with each side claiming that the other initiated the hostilities. Hundreds of thousands of Armenian and Azeri refugees fled to avoid the fighting or were forcefully expelled. In January 1989 the authorities in the Kremlin—in Moscow, the Soviet capital—attempted to regain control over the area by imposing direct rule on Nagornyi Karabakh, dispatching interior ministry troops there. In December 1989, however, Armenia declared Nagornyi Karabakh part of a 'unified Armenian republic'. The Soviet Government responded in January 1990 by declaring the move unconstitutional. In September 1991, though, the Karabakh leaders declared their territory an independent Soviet republic. The disintegration of the USSR in December 1991 allowed Karabakh Armenians to go one step further, proclaiming in January 1992 the independence of the Republic of Nagornyi Karabakh (Artsakh in Armenian). The war ended with a cease-fire in 1994; the conflict had claimed some 15,000 lives and produced up to 1m. refugees, of which three-quarters were Azeris (p. 38, in Baev, 1997). In addition to Nagornyi Karabakh, the Armenian forces succeeded in taking control of Kelbajar (Kelbacar) and Lachin provinces, which provide the enclave with common borders with Armenia.

Early mediation initiatives between the two warring parties were attempted by a number of countries. In September 1991, for example, President Boris Yeltsin of Russia, in conjunction with Kazakhstan's President Nursultan Nazarbayev, brokered an agreement between Armenia and Azerbaijan, which involved, notably, a pledge by the former to revoke its territorial claim to Nagornyi Karabakh. However, the agreement failed to halt the violence. Finally, a Russian-mediated cease-fire was agreed on 12 May 1994, formalized by an armistice signed by the ministers of defence of Armenia and of Azerbaijan and the commander of the Karabakh army on 27 July 1994.

In the initial stage of the conflict, the authorities in Moscow backed the Azerbaijani position, because their policy was based on the principle of the sanctity of borders. Mikhail Gorbachev equated acceptance of the right to redraw internal borders to opening a 'Pandora's box' of ethnic strife throughout the Soviet federation. The collapse of the USSR transformed the Karabakh crisis from a domestic dispute into an international conflict. In 1992, however, the Yeltsin administration began to support—morally and militarily—the Armenian separatists. The main reason for Moscow's change of policy was the coming to power of Azerbaijan's Popular Front Party, led by Abulfaz Elchibey, and Baku's subsequent shift from a pro-Russia policy towards a pro-Turkey one.

The Organisation for Security and Co-operation in Europe (OSCE) has played a leading role in negotiations since 1994. A subset of OSCE members, dubbed the 'Minsk Group' of countries, so called after the location of its first convening in Belarus, has been formed to supervise the negotiations. The group is chaired jointly by Russia, France and the USA. Representatives of Armenia, Azerbaijan, France, Russia and the USA met in Paris (France) and in Key West, Florida (USA), in the spring of 2001 to discuss the future status of Nagornyi Karabakh, but no agreement was reached. Further talks between the Azerbaijani and Armenian presidents, Ilham Aliyev and Robert Kocharian, were held in September 2004 in Astana, Kazakhstan, and in February 2005 in Rambouillet, France, but attained no results.

The conflict has entered a state of populist and nationalistic fever from which it is difficult for any government to retreat. The opposition parties, in both Armenia and Azerbaijan, demand an even harsher line. The Armenian Government insists that Baku must recognize Karabakh's independence and deal with the Karabakh leadership directly as a full-fledged party to the conflict. Moreover, the Armenians refuse to promise that the territorial integrity of Azerbaijan will be restored, although they are willing to return to Azerbaijan some of the territory seized during the war. From the Armenian point of view, Nagornyi Karabakh is the last line of defence: if the enclave is lost, the Armenian nation itself may be lost. The unconditional support of the Armenian diaspora for the Karabakh Armenians is another obstacle to the settlement of the conflict in the near future.

On the one hand, it is unlikely that Karabakh Armenians will ever agree to hand over the town of Shusha, which was populated before the war mainly by Azeris, since until its capture it was from where Azerbaijani forces shelled Stepanakert, the capital of the NKAO. The Lachin corridor is also too strategic a position for Karabakh Armenians to let Azerbaijan place military forces in, as that would drive a wedge between the enclave and Armenia. On the other hand, Baku's position has been that Armenian forces must withdraw from all Azerbaijani territory outside the enclave and that all refugees must be allowed to return to their homes before the status of Nagornyi Karabakh can be discussed. The Azerbaijani Government has often stated that it will never accept the inclusion of Nagornyi Karabakh in Armenia or recognize it as an independent state. Azerbaijan views the self-proclaimed 'Republic of Nagornyi Karabakh' as an illegal entity, artificially created by Armenia and governed by a puppet regime.

There is clearly considerable pressure on the Azerbaijani Government to reclaim territory—with 16% of its area currently occupied and several hundred thousand internal refugees hampering economic and social development, this is hardly a surprise. Nevertheless, the Aliyev Government has offered to grant the enclave of Nagornyi Karabakh the highest degree of autonomy within Azerbaijan.

THE GEORGIAN–SOUTH OSSETIAN CONFLICT

South Ossetia covers an area of about 3,900 sq km on the southern side of the Caucasus, separated by mountains from Russia and extending southwards almost to the Mtkvari river in Georgia proper. According to the 1989 Soviet census, 98,000 people lived in South Ossetia. Ossetians accounted for approximately two-thirds (66.61%) of the population and Georgians most of the other third (29.44%); there were also small communities of Russians, Armenians and Jews. Ossetians are believed to be descendants of Iranian-speaking tribes. Most Ossetians are Orthodox Christians, but there is also a sizeable Muslim minority. The modern-day South Ossetia was annexed by tsarist Russia in 1801, along with Georgia itself. Following the 1917 October Revolution, South Ossetia became a part of the Menshevik Georgian Democratic Republic. In April 1922 the South Ossetian Autonomous Oblast (region) was established within the Soviet Socialist Republic (SSR) of Georgia.

The tensions between Georgians and Ossetians began to rise in 1989. Prior to this the two communities had been living in peace with each other. In August 1989 the authorities in Tbilisi finally responded positively to public nationalist demands to introduce a Georgian-language state programme, which promoted the language in education and administration and made Georgian the 'working language' of the SSR parliament. Ossetians and other minority groups viewed such measures as discriminatory and abusive. Earlier in the year the South Ossetian Popular Front, a nationalist organization, had started campaigning for the unification with the North Caucasus autonomous republic (ASSR) of North Ossetia (Osetiya), which is part of the Russian Federation. In November the South Ossetian Supreme Soviet (legislature) approved a decision to unite South Ossetia with the North Ossetian ASSR. A day later the Georgian parliament revoked the decision and abolished South Ossetian autonomy.

In late November 1989 Zviad Gamsakhurdia, a former dissident and an opposition leader, organized a march of thousands of ethnic Georgians to Tskhinvali, the capital of South Ossetia, in order to 'defend the Georgian population'. However, Ossetian nationalists and Soviet forces blocked the road to Tskhinvali and clashes took place in which several people were wounded. The victory of Gamsakhurdia's Round Table-Free Georgian Bloc in the October 1990 elections led to a more militant phase of state-building process. The legacy of a weak and ethnically divided state and a worsening domestic situation led Gamsakhurdia to stress national unity, strong leadership and a unitary state. The Gamsakhurdia Government based much of its nationalities policy on the distinction between 'indigenous' people and 'settlers'. Such policies in multi-ethnic Georgia reinforced the Ossetians' sense of alienation from the new Georgian state, despite the religious affiliation of most of them.

Fighting broke out in early January 1991 and lasted for about a month. Sporadic violence involving Georgian and South Ossetian forces continued until July 1992, when agreement on the deployment of Georgian, South Ossetian and Russian peacekeepers was reached. As a result of the war approximately 1,000 people were killed and 60,000 Ossetians forced to flee Georgia proper and find refuge in South and North Ossetia, as well as 10,000 Georgians leaving South Ossetia (UNHCR, 2004). From then until mid-2004 South Ossetia was relatively peaceful. In June 2004, however, small-scale fighting re-erupted when the new Georgian Government under Mikheil Saakashvili pledged to bring the breakaway region back under central control.

Georgian officials have often criticized Russia's role in South Ossetia. Moscow provides political, economic and military support to the region; indeed, many South Ossetians have acquired Russian citizenship. The Georgian authorities in Tbilisi claim, with some justification, that the 500-strong Russian peacekeeping force offers protection to Ossetian criminal gangs engaged in smuggling, while ignoring Ossetian reprisals against the remaining Georgian population in South Ossetia.

In late January 2005 the Saakashvili Government presented a peace initiative for the resolution of the South Ossetian conflict to the Parliamentary Assembly session of the Council of Europe in Strasbourg (France). In October the US administration of George W. Bush and the OSCE expressed their support for the Georgian action plan, which had been presented by Prime Minister Zurab Noghaideli at the OSCE Permanent Council in Vienna (Austria), but was subsequently rejected by the South Ossetian authorities. Although the two sides have signed agreements on economic issues and the return of refugees, the prospects for conflict resolution in South Ossetia look rather grim. South Ossetia has enjoyed de facto independence for 15 years and has cultivated strong ties with neighbouring North Ossetia. By contrast, the Government in Tbilisi advocates a unified Georgian state, albeit an asymmetrical one. Therefore, the Georgian Government has expressed willingness to grant widespread autonomy to South Ossetia. Nevertheless, the Georgian-South Ossetian remains unresolved.

THE OSSETIAN–INGUSH CONFLICT

Following the 1917 October Revolution Ingushetia (Ingushetiya) became part of a short-lived Soviet Mountain (Gorskaya) People's Autonomous Republic. By 1924 a separate Ingush autonomous district had been established, but in 1934 it was integrated into a joint Chechen-Ingush ASSR. The latter was abolished during the 1944 deportation and reinstated in 1957. When Chechenia or Chechnya unilaterally declared its independence in 1991, Ingushetia was left to become an autonomous republic in the Russian Federation.

The Ingush-populated Prigorodnyi District (raion) around the city of Vladikavkaz was given to North Ossetia in 1944, and Ingush-owned property was distributed among the Ossetian (Osetiyan) population. When the Ingush came back to the North Caucasus, however, the Soviet authorities prevented the repatriation of the Ingush population in the Prigorodnyi District. Nevertheless, Ingush continued to protest and seek full repatriation and compensation. Prior to 1992, according to official statistics, some 33,000 Ingush lived in North Ossetia (p. 253, in Cornell, 2001).

Violence erupted in Prigorodnyi District in late October 1992 (less than a year since the dissolution of the USSR) and lasted until 6 November. Russian troops were sent almost immediately to North Ossetia, ostensibly as peacekeepers, but apparently they actively participated in the fighting on the Ossetian side. President Yeltsin also issued a decree that the Prigorodnyi District was to remain part of North Ossetia. As a result of the short war, there were about 500–600 deaths and almost all Ingush were forced to flee North Ossetia and find shelter in neighbouring republics (p. 18, in Human Rights Watch, 1996).

The Russian-brokered Ossetian-Ingush agreement of 1995 finally induced the North Ossetian authorities to allow Ingush refugees from four settlements in the Prigorodnyi District to return to their homes, but their return has since been blocked by the Ossetian population. The presence of Ossetian refugees from Georgia in Prigorodnyi is another obstacle to the repatriation of Ingush refugees. Although talks have been held periodically between the two sides, little progress has been achieved. On 11 October 2002 the presidents of Ingushetia and North Ossetia signed an Agreement for Promoting Co-operation and Neighbourly Relations between the republics. However, the 2004 Beslan hostage crisis in North Ossetia, with the rumoured participation of Ingush terrorists, hampered the return process and worsened Ossetian-Ingush relations. North Ossetia is Moscow's chief regional ally and the Kremlin is unlikely to impose a peace settlement in Prigorodnyi given the ongoing insurgency in Chechnya. At the same time, the Ingush are not yet willing to give up their territorial claims against North Ossetia, so the possibility of renewed hostilities cannot be excluded.

THE ABKHAZIAN–GEORGIAN WAR

Abkhazia, an autonomous republic in Georgia, is situated on the Black Sea coast and had in 1989, according to the Soviet census, a population of 537,000, of whom 45% were ethnic Georgians, 17% Abkhazians, 14% Russians and 15% Armenians. There were also large Greek and Jewish communities. Ethnic Abkhazians are not related to Georgians; linguistically and culturally they are akin to the North Caucasus peoples.

Abkhazia was integrated into the newly established Soviet state in 1921, following the Red Army's takeover of Georgia. Under Stalin's rule Abkhazia endured a period of a 'Georgianization' policy in the late 1940s and early 1950s, when the Georgian language was imposed on Abkhazian students in schools and, for the Abkhazian language, they were forced to use a Georgian-based alphabet, instead of a Cyrillic one,. These policies aroused in the Abkhazians the fear of extinction as an ethnic group through forced assimilation. This anxiety was compounded by an unfavourable demographic trend in the republic, because the Georgian population was growing at a faster rate than the Abkhazian. The death of Stalin led to the relative liberalization of Soviet society, including cautious redress of minority grievances. In 1978, however, the Abkhazian leadership launched a campaign for secession from the Georgian SSR and for subsequent incorporation into the Russian Federation. The Abkhazian demands were rejected by Moscow, but the federal Government did agree large-scale political and cultural concessions to the Abkhazian authorities in Sukhumi.

In July 1989 the Georgian Government tried to establish a branch of the Georgian State University in Sukhumi, to replace the Georgian department of Abkhazia's university and thus upgrade the status of Georgian-language education in the republic. Georgian and Abkhazian students clashed in the first round of what became ongoing hostilities between the different nationalist groups. A large-scale conflict was avoided at that time thanks only to the introduction of a state of emergency in the republic. The ousting of Georgian President Gamsakhurdia in early 1992 directly fuelled Abkhazian separatism. Numerous Georgian laws were nullified in Abkhazia and a special regiment of internal troops was established and placed under the command of the Presidium of the Abkhazian Supreme Soviet. In July 1992 the 1978 Constitution, which specified that the Abkhazian Autonomous Republic was a constituent part of the Georgian SSR, was repealed and replaced by the long-dormant 1925 Constitution, which declared Abkhazia a sovereign republic with only alliance commitments to Georgia.

Military confrontation began in August 1992, when Gen. Tengiz Kitovani's National Guard, a paramilitary force allied with the Edward Shevardnadze-controlled ruling Military Council, marched on Abkhazia. The Georgian forces occupied most of the republic, including Sukhumi, forcing the Abkhazian leadership to retreat to the regional centre of Gudauta. In late July 1993 an agreement was signed in a Russian town, Sochi, by the Georgian, Abkhazian and Russian sides. It provided for a cease-fire, the withdrawal of the Georgian army from Abkhazia and mutual demilitarization by the belligerents, to be followed by the 'return of a legal government to Sukhumi'. In mid-September 1993, following the eruption of a miniature civil war between pro-Shevardnadze and pro-Gamsakhurdia forces in western Georgia, the Abkhazians launched an all-out attack on the Georgian forces. With the help of freelance Russian soldiers and North Caucasus volunteers, they drove the Georgian army from Abkhazia, capturing Sukhumi on 27 September. As a result, up to 300,000 people, the majority ethnic Georgians, fled Abkhazia, creating a humanitarian crisis (p. 1, in UNDP, 2005). Shevardnadze appealed to the Russian Government, as a guarantor of the Sochi agreement, to restore the status quo, but Moscow did not intervene. However, the Kremlin condemned the Abkhazian actions and imposed economic sanctions on the republic. Under Russian pressure, finally, the two sides agreed to accept the deployment of a Russian-dominated peacekeeping force along both sides of the Inguri river, the dividing line between Abkhazia and rest of Georgia.

Russia's role in the Abkhazian conflict was both crucial and controversial. A number of factors compelled the Russian leadership to play a prominent role in the conflict. First, Moscow had to contend with the active participation of its citizens in the conflict. The North Caucasus-based Confederation of Mountain Peoples of the Caucasus had sent volunteers to fight alongside the Abkhazian forces, while Russian ultra-nationalists and Cossacks came to the aid of the Russian population in Abkhazia. Also, the presence of a sizeable Russian minority in Abkhazia, as well as the large number of Russian citizens vacationing there when the conflict erupted and the death of some of them, forced the Kremlin to adopt a more proactive policy towards the conflict. Finally, the Russian troops that remained in Abkhazia, and the airborne division that arrived in the republic after the violence erupted to protect these units and to assist in the evacuation of Russian citizens, soon became targets for armed raids, eventually drawing Moscow into the conflict. Georgian officials have claimed that the Abkhazian military campaign was planned by Russian officers and that many Russian servicemen joined Abkhazian units.

The Abkhazians also relied for support on Turkey, where there is a large Abkhazian community. In August 1992 the Caucasian-Abkhazian Solidarity Committee (Kafkas-Abkhaz Dayanisma Komitesi) was founded by Turks of Abkhazian origin to co-ordinate the assistance given to Abkhazia and to help in the development of relations between Turkey and the breakaway republic. In late September 1992 demonstrations were held in Turkey against the Georgian invasion of Abkhazia and the passive attitude of the Turkish Government. Tens of young Turks also fought in the breakaway republic and many more planned to emigrate there to regain their ancestral lands. Nevertheless, the authorities in the Turkish capital of Ankara advocated sustained dialogue between Georgia and Abkhazia, within the framework of the Geneva process. In this context the Turkish Government organized a conference in Istanbul (Turkey) on 7–9 June 1999, and brought the parties together with a view to contributing to the peace process.

International efforts to bring about a fair settlement in Abkhazia have included over a dozen UN Security Council resolutions, activities by the special envoy of the UN Secretary-General and the constant endeavours of Russia. A group calling itself Friends of Georgia, composed of representatives of the USA, the United Kingdom, Germany, France and Russia, has also done much to encourage a peaceful settlement. Despite all this, no real breakthroughs have occurred so far.

While Georgia may have tasted the bitterness of defeat in this war, however, Abkhazia's part was to suffer massive and widespread destruction. Even before Russia began to enforce the blockade, Abkhazia's economy had been devastated by the war. Its well-developed tourist industry had been destroyed, while the interruption of rail services from Russia had isolated the republic and interrupted trade. In any case, the situation between the two sides remains volatile. Small-scale fighting continues along the border between Georgia and Abkhazia. In mid May 1998, for example, after hostilities involving Georgian guerrillas, Abkhazia poured heavy artillery and tanks into the district of Gali and exiled thousands of Georgians from their villages.

The current state of affairs in the relations between Georgia and Abkhazia inspires little optimism. Tbilisi is offering the Abkhazians a special political status, with provisions for extensive self-rule within a unitary federal republic; former President Shevardnadze even used the word 'statehood' to describe his vision of Abkhazia's status. Yet, there is a de facto independent Abkhazian state and the Abkhazian public rejects any close reintegration with Georgia. Indeed, Abkhazians now see the preservation of their statehood as essential to securing not only their self-determination, but also their very survival. The demographic issue is the single biggest irritant to a rapprochement between Tbilisi and Sukhumi, which otherwise have deep historic roots of co-existence. It is very unlikely that the Abkhazians will accept a repatriation programme that restores the demographic balance of 1989. Moreover, any peace settlement must include the right for the Abkhazians to have free trade and traffic with their North Caucasus kinsmen. Nevertheless, Georgia receives a considerable amount of moral support and sympathy from international organizations and Western powers vis-à-vis its dispute with Abkhazia. Yet, the state of the Georgian economy and of its armed forces make it unlikely in the foreseeable future for the country to forcefully, or in any other way, return Abkhazia to its control.

THE RUSSO-CHECHEN WARS

The North Caucasus republic of Chechnya covers an area of 15,300 sq km and has a population of approximately 1m. Chechnya declared independence from the Russian Federation in late 1991; its independence bid stemmed from the personal ambition of the Chechen leader, Gen. Dzhokar Dudayev, but had its roots in Chechen history. Conquered by tsarist Russia in the mid-19th century, after decades of fierce resistance, the Chechens were long considered to be disloyal. In 1921 Chechnya became part of the Soviet Mountain Republic, but that was later divided. In 1934 Chechnya and Ingushetia were combined into the Chechen-Ingush Autonomous Region, which in 1936 was transformed into a republic. During the Second World War some Chechens joined the Nazi anti-Communist campaign. For this treachery the Chechen people were deported en masse to Central Asia on Stalin's orders in 1944; their republic was redistributed between Georgia and the Russian territories of Dagestan, North Ossetia and Stavropol province (krai). Thousands of Chechens died in the deportation. In 1957, after Stalin's death, the Chechen-Ingush ASSR was restored, with a partial return of the population and less territory than it had previously.

In late October 1991 a Chechen presidential election was held. Dudayev was elected President; on 5 November he declared the Chechen Republic's independence from Russia. Initially, Moscow refused to recognize Chechnya's independence, but attempted periodically to enter into negotiations with Dudayev. In addition, the Kremlin tried to support the Chechen pro-Russian opposition. However, by 1994 Moscow, with its political and economic house in better order, began to worry about Chechen separatism. For three years covert operations designed to topple Dudayev failed; the federal Government sponsored one more anti-Dudayev coup in November 1994, but the Chechen President was able to remain in power.

In December 1994, finally, President Yeltsin sent 40,000 Russian troops to suppress the separatist uprising in Chechnya. Armed with light equipment and weapons, the Chechen forces clashed with the Russian army. When Dudayev, a former Soviet air force general, declared independence from Russia, he had immediately begun building up paramilitary forces. Moscow considered Dudayev and his army to be a criminal gang that would be intimidated at the first sight of a Russian tank. The Russian Government failed to understand that Dudayev and many of his key lieutenants were Soviet military veterans, who were well aware of Russian capabilities and weaknesses. Also, traditionally, the Chechens are a warrior people, for whom resistance and fighting are national virtues. Another factor aiding the Chechen rebels was the sorry state of the Russian armed forces. By April 1995 the Russian army's inability to contain a rebellion led by a small group of guerrilla forces, whose continued success was making international news headlines, was clearly becoming an embarrassment for President Yeltsin. More than 30,000 Chechens, mostly civilians, and some 3,000 Russian soldiers died in the fighting, which lasted for more than 16 months.

Turkey played an active role in the Russian-Chechen conflict. Ankara offered moral support to the Chechen rebels and, through private channels, possibly even logistical, military and financial help. The link between Chechnya and Turkey was revealed first in late September 1992 when, during his visit to Turkey, Dudayev stated that Turkey was a regional power and ought to help the Chechens. More-over, the Chechen leader declared that the Chechen capital of Groznyi was reviewing the issue of recognizing the 'Turkish Republic of Northern Cyprus'; indeed, he later visited Northern Cyprus and discussed co-operation between the self-declared 'states' of Chechnya and Turkish-occupied Cyprus. In addition, Dudayev chose for the flag of independent Chechnya a wolf and crescent, which are, respectively, pan-Turkish and Islamic symbols. The seizure of the ferry *Avrasya* by Chechen sympathizers, but Turkish nationals, in the Turkish Black Sea port of Trabzon in January 1996 drew international attention to Turkish-Chechen ties. There are an estimated 25,000 Turkish citizens of Chechen descent (p. 45, in Bezanis, 1995). In addition, there are several million inhabitants of Turkey whose families originate in the Caucasus. In response to the Russian army's attack on Chechnya, on 18 December 1994 the Kafkas-Çeçen Dayanisma Komitesi (Caucasian-Chechen Solidarity Committee) was established in Ankara by North Caucasus associations. There is no reliable information on the number of Turkish volunteers that joined the war in Chechnya, but their number was probably insignificant. In January 1996 the Russian Government officially complained to Ankara that it allowed Chechens a free hand and failed to prevent members of the North Caucasus diaspora from training and sending volunteers to fight in Chechnya.

Finally, the Russian security chief Aleksandr Lebed negotiated a peace agreement with Chechen rebel commanders in late August 1996. The agreement stated that Russian troops would withdraw immediately from Chechnya, under the joint supervision of the two adversaries. A cease-fire was agreed upon and the rebels took control of Groznyi. However, the question of Chechnya's independence was deferred for five years. In May 1997 the two sides signed a Treaty of Peace and Principles of Relations between the Russian Federation and the Republic of Ichkeria (i.e. Chechnya), according to which the two sides agreed 'to renounce forever the use of force and the threat of its use in resolving all disputed questions'.

Despite the Russian withdrawal, however, the state-building process in the breakaway republic was not particularly successful. After the end of the fighting Chechnya was plagued by a crime wave, which brought the republic to the brink of anarchy. In the absence of strong authority beyond the capital, veteran commanders were able to establish personal fiefdoms and undermine the elected Government in Groznyi. Moreover, the idea of unification between Chechnya and parts (or all) of neighbouring Dagestan was gaining momentum in the breakaway republic. The Islamic Nation movement, founded in Groznyi in August 1997 at a congress of Chechen and other North Caucasus delegates, declared as its proclaimed goal the creation of a political entity that should incorporate all the lands unified by the Chechen warlord Imam Shamil in the 19th century.

The second Russian-Chechen war began in early August 1999, when Islamic militants under the command of Shamil Basayev crossed the border between Chechnya and Dagestan and occupied several villages in the south-west of that republic. Three days later the self-styled Islamic Council of Dagestan issued a statement in Groznyi declaring an independent Islamic state in Dagestan. The rebels took advantage of Dagestan's high mountains and porous borders to pursue their aim of establishing an independent Islamic state in the North Caucasus with access to the Caspian Sea, thus increasing their stakes in the geopolitics of oil transportation from the Caspian Sea to Western markets. The developments were seen by the Kremlin as a serious threat both to political stability in Dagestan and to the territorial integrity of the Russian Federation. Following the Russian military's success in expelling Chechen-based rebels from Dagestan in mid-September, it turned its attention toward Chechnya. A series of terrorist bombings in Moscow and other Russian cities, for which the Russian Government blamed Chechen terrorists, provided added incentive for a new offensive against the secessionist republic and generated widespread popular support for Russia's military campaign in the North Caucasus. In late September Russian forces crossed Chechnya's northern border and, over the next several days, occupied all the territory north of the Terek river. Russian forces then proceeded to move southward across the Terek and began encircling Groznyi. In late January 2000 the federal army seized the Chechen capital.

South of the Terek, however, Chechnya consists of mountainous countryside, where guerrilla forces are most effective. Most importantly, by broadening the military operation against Islamic militants based in Chechnya to include a large-scale ground and air campaign against the breakaway republic, Moscow unified Chechnya's disparate guerrilla factions, regardless of whether they sought the establishment of an Islamic state. The current hostilities in the republic have only deepened Chechen enmity towards Moscow, making it all but inconceivable that Chechnya will ever become a normal subject of the Russian Federation. One of the strengths of the Chechen guerrilla campaign is that it is low cost and, therefore, easy to sustain. Moreover, the security corridor that Russia established around Chechnya might be effective against guerrilla forces conducting large-scale cross-border assaults, but has questionable effectiveness in identifying individual terrorists or small groups of militants, especially as Chechen refugees continue to flee across the border. Furthermore, the question of Chechnya's independence has only been postponed, and the Russian Government will face the unenviable choice of either letting the Chechens secede or offering them economic and political inducements to remain within the Federation—which would encourage other republics and regions to press their cases for greater sovereignty.

ETHNIC CONFLICTS IN THE FERGANA VALLEY

The Fergana Valley is located at the heart of the Central Asian region; it is 300 km long and 170 km wide, occupying 22,000 sq km. With a population of about 10m., it is divided between Uzbekistan, Tajikistan and Kyrgyzstan; the valley is the most densely settled area in Central Asia.

In June 1989 clashes broke out between Uzbeks and Meskhetian Turks in the Uzbekistan part of the Fergana Valley, after a disagreement in an open market between an Uzbek vendor and a Meskhetian buyer. Meskhetian Turks have mixed origins, some being descended from Turks, others from Turkicized and Islami-cized Georgians. They lived in the region now known as Samstkhe-Javakheti, in south-west Georgia, until November 1944, when they were deported en masse to Central Asia, mostly to Uzbekistan, on the pretext that the military security of the Turkish-Soviet border needed to be strengthened. The group numbered at that time approximately 100,000 people. The 1989 incident triggered widespread violence, which spread to several cities, including Namangan, Kokand and Margilan. More than 100 people were killed and many more wounded. Meskhetian Turks were forced to flee and were scattered across Central Asia, Russia, Ukraine, Azerbaijan and Turkey.

In June 1990 discord between Kyrgyz and Uzbeks erupted into disastrous turmoil in the Kyrgyzstan part of the Fergana Valley, in and near the city of Osh. The historic and cultural differences between the Kyrgyz and Uzbek peoples— descendants of nomadic and agricultural cultures, respectively—run deep. The so-called trigger factor was the news that the local administration was going to distribute plots of land to landless Kyrgyz at the expense of the Uzbek commu-nity. Violence resulted in the death of hundreds of people and ceased only after the arrival of Soviet troops. Officially, the Soviet authorities listed the casualties at 200 killed and some 300 injured, but local sources put the death toll at more than 1,000 (p. 68, in Rashid, 2002).

THE TAJIK SUB-ETHNIC CONFLICT

Tajikistan has been the only country in the former USSR to experience a sub-ethnic conflict. The geography of Tajikistan has led to the development of localism, specifically known in Tajik as *Mahalgaroi*, which is defined as a fierce competition among clans for scare resources (e.g. land or clean drinking water) or influence. Tajik clans are communities or groups of extended families originating from the same region and united by a common identity and, often, a common dialect. Despite Soviet attempts to impose a new national identity on the Tajiks, clan identity has remained a significant factor in Tajik politics. During the Soviet period clan membership determined career prospects, especially in the public sector, influenced social status and functioned as a defence mechanism against outside competitors. Clan politics in Tajikistan encouraged the establishment of patron-client relations, which produced 'winners' and 'losers', eventually generating armed conflict. The main clan groupings can be identified with the main cities of western Tajikistan (the mountainous east consists of Gornyi Badakshan), the capital Dushanbe in the centre, with Khojand (Leninabad) to the north, Garm to the east and Kulyab and Kurgan-Tyube to the south.

The sub-ethnic conflict started with the collapse of the USSR. The political elites from Kulyab region in the south-east and Soghd (then known as Leninabad) region in the north, which had enjoyed privileged economic status during the Soviet era, supported the Communist Party of Tajikistan (CPT). The newly established opposition parties received support from regions that were generally under-represented in government and politics during the Soviet era. Supporters of the Islamic Revival Party (IRP) were mainly from the Garm region in east-central Tajikistan. The separatist Lali-Badakhshan party had supporters from the Gorno-Badakhshan Autonomous Oblast (GBAO), which is populated by small Eastern Iranian peoples, the so-called Pamiris after the mountain junction, who differ from the rest of the Tajik population because they speak distinct Iranian languages and have a different culture. The Western-orientated Democratic Party of Tajikistan and the nationalist Rastokhez movement were composed mainly of Dushanbe-based Pamiri intellectuals.

At the end of August 1991 the leader of Tajikistan, Kakhar Makkhamov, was forced to resign after supporting the failed anti-Gorbachev Soviet coup. Parliamentary chairman Kadriddin Aslonov replaced Makkhamov. Aslonov immediately banned the CPT and froze its assets in the republic (independence was proclaimed on 9 September). In parliament the CPT retaliated by forcing Aslonov's resignation, replacing him with Rakhmon Nabiyev as acting President and parliamentary chairman. Nabiyev annulled the ban, but the demonstrations organized by the opposition eventually forced him to organize a free presidential election. The opposition parties supported the candidacy of Davlat Khudonazarov. The election of Nabiyev on 24 November provoked a storm of protests from opposition parties, which denounced the elections as rigged. In March and April 1992, pro-government groups and opposition parties staged demonstrations in Dushanbe. Fierce armed clashes between the two blocs erupted in early May, when opposition supporters gained control of the Tajikistan state television in the city. In mid May the severity of the clashes compelled Nabiyev to form the so-called Government of National Reconciliation with the admission of opposition parties. In the summer pro-government forces unleashed violence against Tajiks of Garmi origin and Pamiris who supported the opposition.

In late November 1992 the Communist-dominated parliament selected Imamali Rahmonov, former chief executive of Kulyab region, as parliamentary chairman and head of state. From the winter of 1992/93 onwards, the conflict between the Rahmonov Government and opposition forces spread from Dushanbe to the countryside, especially in the Karategin Valley and areas surrounding Dushanbe. By early 1993 tens of thousands of Tajiks had fled to neighbouring Afghanistan. In response to government repression, the IRP, together with the Democratic Party, the Rastokhez movement and Lali-Badakhshan formed the United Tajik Opposition (UTO). The new coalition set up bases in Afghanistan and begun launching hit-and-run attacks against government forces.

Although officially neutral, the Russian Government offered the Rahmonov regime aid in the form of moral, logistical and covert military support. More specifically, the 201st Division, headquartered in Dushanbe, was involved in some battles against opposition forces. In 1993 a Russian-led Commonwealth of Independent States (CIS) peacekeeping force was sent to Tajikistan to stabilize the political situation in the country and to restore the integrity of the Tajikistan-Afghanistan border. The peacekeeping force, which included the 201st Division and units of Russian border troops and some from Kazakhstan, Kyrgyzstan and Uzbekistan, also aimed to protect key installations and to accompany relief convoys. A small international force, the UN Mission of Observers in Tajikistan (UNMOT), was also deployed in December 1994. By mid-1996 Moscow began to view the rise of the Taliban in Afghanistan as a greater threat to its interests in Central Asia than the UTO. Therefore, the Kremlin put pressure on the Tajikistan Government to negotiate a peace agreement with the UTO.

The Uzbekistan Government initially also supported the Rahmonov regime; the launching of an armed struggle against the Russia-aligned secular elite in Tajikistan by a coalition of pro-democracy and Islamic groups was perceived in Tashkent as a security threat, because it served as an example for the Uzbek opposition. Over time, however, Uzbekistan's support for Rahmonov diminished. The Uzbekistan Government eventually supported a negotiated solution to the civil war.

In June 1997 the UTO and the Government agreed a cessation of hostilities, culminating in the General Agreement on the Establishment of Peace and National Accord. As a result of the civil war, approximately 60,000 people lost their lives and about 700,000 people were displaced (p. 35, in UNDP, 1998). The UN-brokered peace deal entitled the UTO to 30% of senior government posts, with the IRP taking the lion's share. Moreover, refugees from Afghanistan and other countries were to return, UTO fighters were to be demobilized or integrated into the Tajik armed forces and the political system had to open up, leading to fair and open elections and the formation of a new coalition government. Despite the establishment of a fragile post-war political system and the endurance of sub-ethnic identities, the Tajikistan peace process has been largely successful.

CONCLUSION

Since the late 1980s the Caucasus and parts of Central Asia have been the scenes of ethnic conflicts, which had deep historical, political, economic and social roots. Nagornyi Karabakh has the sad privilege of being the first region plagued by ethnic warfare and, given the national interests at stake, conflict resolution seems for the time being improbable. The Georgian–Abkhazian war devastated the breakaway republic, but resulted in the creation of a de facto independent Abkhazian state that Georgians are not prepared to recognize as a distinct political entity. North Ossetians and Ingush battled fiercely for the control of Prigorodnyi District, with the latter facing ethnic cleansing. Russia has attempted twice to crush Chechen separatism, but so far the hostilities continue in the secessionist republic. In fact, the Russian authorities are actively involved in all the Caucasian ethnic conflicts that remain unresolved. Where no great power involvement took place, matters were settled in a far more peaceful way. For example, the Tajikistan sub-ethnic war ended in the late 1990s and the country's successful peace process has in fact set a regional precedent. Despite the fighting between Uzbeks and Meskhetian Turks and between Kyrgyz and Uzbeks in 1989 and 1990, respectively, the Fergana Valley has not since witnessed another ethnic conflict and remains relatively peaceful.

Conflicts in South Asia: Kashmir and Sri Lanka

RAJAT GANGULY

INTRODUCTION

At the beginning of the new millennium South Asia seems to be standing at a crossroads. Barring a few exceptions, South Asian states have made significant progress over the last decade in fostering economic and industrial development, lowering poverty, improving literacy and public health, and promoting the general well-being of their populations. Over the same period, however, South Asia has regressed politically and in terms of human, national and regional security. Democracy, human rights and rule of law have been undermined or significantly eroded in several states. Sectarian, communal and ethnic violence has flared up in almost the entire region, undermining state and human security and subjecting even the established democratic polities to enormous amounts of strain. The tentacles of transnational terrorism have spread rapidly, no doubt aided and abetted by short-sighted regimes in power and by the existence of various types of disgruntled non-state groups professing various forms of extremist ideology. Even regional economic progress seems to have unleashed brutal class warfare in some areas, highlighting perhaps the injustice and inherent danger associated with rapid but unequal development brought about by the forces of globalization and liberalization. Intractable regional conflicts, too, such as between India and Pakistan, have become more dangerous and unpredictable as a result of the introduction of nuclear weapons into the equation; new lines of conflict, such as between India and Bangladesh and Pakistan and Afghanistan, have added to the further destabilization of the regional security environment. Conflicts—in various shapes, sizes and forms—thus seem to have become an enduring feature of the landscape in South Asia.

In this essay, I focus on two major 'internal' conflicts in South Asia: the secessionist insurgency in Indian Kashmir, which has extracted a huge cost in terms of human lives and development and has periodically threatened to precipitate a major war between India and Pakistan, with potentially catastrophic consequences for the entire region; and the Tamil–Sinhalese conflict in Sri Lanka, where a ruthless insurgency run by the Liberation Tigers of Tamil Eelam (LTTE) is met head on by an equally uncompromising counter-insurgency operation mounted by the Sinhalese-dominated Sri Lankan Government, leading to the creation of a highly internationalized 'dirty war'.

74

THE KASHMIRI INSURGENCY AND THE
INDIA–PAKISTAN CONFLICT

Origins

The genesis of the Kashmiri insurgency lies deep in history. The State of Jammu and Kashmir was the largest and the fourth most populous of the 565 princely states in British India.[1] It consisted of five distinct regions: the Vale of Kashmir; Jammu; Punch (Poonch); Ladakh and Baltistan; and Gilgit. Out of a population of 4m. on the eve of India's independence, approximately 77% were Muslim, 20% Hindu, 1.5% Sikh and 1% Buddhist. The State was ruled by a Hindu dynasty, the Dogras, with help and advice from the British Indian Government.

With British colonial disengagement and the partition of the subcontinent in 1947, the rulers of the princely states were given a choice of joining either of the newly created dominions of India or Pakistan.[2] The two principal criteria guiding this choice were to be the communal allegiance of the people of the state and its geographical contiguity with India or Pakistan. All the princely states, except for Hyderabad, Junagadh and Kashmir, joined either India or Pakistan before 15 August 1947. Hyderabad and Junagadh were subsequently forced to join India. However, Kashmir, being geographically contiguous to both India and Pakistan, was claimed by both sides for ideological and geostrategic reasons. The Dogra ruler of Kashmir, Maharaja Hari Singh, calculated that by not joining either India or Pakistan during the transfer of power, he would emerge as the ruler of an independent Kashmir state. The Maharaja's plans were thwarted by pro-Pakistan groups in Kashmir; they established contact with Pathan (Pashtun) tribes in Pakistan and laid the foundation for an armed invasion and forcible seizure of power in the state. In October 1947, as the Pathan tribal invasion pushed rapidly into the Kashmir Valley, the Maharaja appealed to the Indian Government for help. Prime Minister Jawaharlal Nehru agreed to provide military assistance in return for Hari Singh's acceptance of Kashmir's legal accession to India, a move that was supported by Sheikh Muhammad Abdullah, the leader of a popular, secular and democratic political movement in Kashmir. Once the Instrument of Accession was signed, Indian troops were airlifted into the Vale of Kashmir. By early 1948 the battle had been joined by the regular Pakistan army. A UN-sponsored cease-fire agreement, which came into effect on 1 January 1949, finally brought the war to an end. At that time India occupied roughly two-thirds of the erstwhile princely state, with Pakistan controlling the other third. Over the next 20 years, both India and Pakistan sought to absorb their respective portions of Kashmir and the 1949 Cease-fire Line (CFL) gradually became the de facto border between the two states, bifurcating Kashmir.[3] The Indian portion of Kashmir consisted of three main regions: the Vale, Jammu and Ladakh. In 1956 the Jammu and Kashmir Constituent Assembly approved the merger of the state with India.

Outbreak of Secessionist Insurgency

Politics in Indian Kashmir (particularly in the Valley) has always been marked by an undercurrent of turbulence, but it was not until the late 1980s that secessionist sentiments became widespread and a well-organized insurgency sprang up. The outbreak of secessionist insurgency in Indian Kashmir in the late 1980s is attributable mainly to fundamental demographic, economic and political developments in the state. By the 1980s a relatively younger, educated, ambitious and politically conscious generation had emerged in Kashmir. Economic and employment opportunities did not expand commensurably, however, leading to a rise in the numbers of the educated unemployed. The simmering discontent that existed among the educated unemployed received further impetus when, after the death of Sheikh Abdullah in 1982, the Congress Government at the centre started meddling in local Kashmiri politics in order to further the interests of the Congress party in the state. This first led to the dismissal of the legitimately elected National Conference (NC) Government in Jammu and Kashmir, led by Farooq Abdullah (the son of Sheikh Abdullah), in 1984. Subsequently, the Congress and the NC entered into an electoral alliance and blatantly rigged the 1987 assembly elections in the state. This flagrant electoral abuse and Farooq Abdullah's 'betrayal' sparked widespread resentment among Kashmiri Muslim youth against the Congress and the NC, which soon escalated into acts of violence against and calls for secession from the Indian federation.

From its inception, the Valley-based secessionist insurgency split into two factions based upon ideology and objective. One faction, represented by the Jammu and Kashmir Liberation Front (JKLF), advocated the formation of an independent and secular Kashmir state comprising the five main regions of the erstwhile princely state; this was to be achieved by the secession of Indian and Pakistani parts of Kashmir, followed by a merger of the two areas. A second and more dominant faction within the secessionist movement, represented by Islamic fundamentalist groups such as the Hizbul Mujahideen, the Lashkar-i-Taiba and the Jaish-i-Mohammad, advocated Indian Kashmir's secession from India followed by either a merger with Pakistan or, at the very least, the creation of an independent Islamic state with close ties to Pakistan. Those who espoused Islamic fundamentalist ideology also endorsed the 'ethnic cleansing' of the minority Hindu Pandit community from the Valley and the Tibetan Buddhist community from Ladakh. Massacres of Hindu and Sikh families were also carried out in the Jammu region. Islamic militants from Kashmir even carried out terrorist attacks in other parts of India, often with help from international terrorist organizations, such as al-Qaida, disgruntled domestic groups, such as the Students' Islamic Movement in India (SIMI), and the criminal underworld.

Indian Counter-Insurgency Strategy

While keeping the door open for political negotiations, the Indian Government mainly resorted to coercion and force while responding to the secessionist insurgency in Kashmir. In the early 1990s forces from the Central Police Organizations (CPOs)[4] and the Army were deployed in Kashmir to begin counter-insurgency operations, along with the Jammu and Kashmir Police (JKP). The counter-insurgency operations had two objectives: to destroy local insurgent organizations and their support networks within Kashmir; and to prevent the infiltration of armed insurgents from across the Line of Control (LoC—as the CFL had become known). In order to accomplish the first objective, the security forces created and maintained secure zones, launched combing (cordon and search) operations and administered both judicial and extra-judicial punishments. Border sealing and counter-infiltration operations were launched to fulfil the second objective. The security forces also created a network of informers and an anti-insurgency force comprised of former insurgents. The federal authorities in the Indian capital of New Delhi further imposed President's Rule (direct rule by the centre) in Kashmir.[5]

Understandably, the Indian counter-insurgency offensives led to widespread alienation among Kashmiri Muslims from the Indian state and drew heavy criticism from human rights groups and activists in India and abroad. To answer its critics and win back the confidence of the local civilian population, from around the mid-1990s onwards the Indian Government began to exercise tighter control over the behaviour of security personnel. New Delhi also started to encourage foreign dignitaries to visit Kashmir, to see first-hand the destruction and massacres caused by the insurgents, and Indian diplomats began to present evidence of human rights abuses committed by the insurgents in various inter-national forums and foreign capitals. Additionally, the Indian Government opened discussions with several Kashmiri political organizations, such as the NC, the All-Party Hurriyat Conference (APHC) and the JKLF, with an aim to re-start the state's political machinery.

In May 1996 national elections were held for the Indian Parliament. In spite of a call for a boycott by the insurgent groups, polling took place in Jammu and Kashmir state, with around 35%–45% of eligible voters voting for the first time since 1989. The general election was followed by state elections in Indian Kashmir in September 1996. Voter turnout was a respectable 53% and, with many of the pro-independence and pro-Pakistan groups boycotting the poll, the NC led by Farooq Abdullah stormed back to power.[6]

Pakistani Intervention

Pakistan having failed in previous attempts to seize Indian Kashmir by force and operating under conditions of 'existential deterrence',[7] the diffusion and encouragement of the Kashmiri insurgency offered Pakistan a relatively inexpensive and effective way to tie India down in costly and unpopular counter-insurgency operations, to discredit its secular and liberal ideological moorings and slowly to undermine New Delhi's hold over Kashmir. The sponsorship of insurgency, terrorism and subversion in Indian Kashmir was tightly controlled by the Pakistani Army's Inter Services Intelligence (ISI) Directorate and formed a major part of the Pakistani military's policy of acquiring 'forward strategic depth'.[8] In implementing this strategy, the ISI benefited immensely from the experience it had gained during the Afghanistan war. During the 10-year-long war, the USA trained and equipped the Afghan *mujahideen* (freedom fighters) and volunteers from Muslim countries for guerrilla operations against the occupying Soviet forces and Afghanistan government troops. These operations were run by ISI agents, under the supervision of US Central Intelligence Agency (CIA) officials, from bases located in the North-West Frontier Province (NWFP) and the autonomous tribal areas of Pakistan near the border with Afghanistan. Through these covert operations, the ISI developed an expertise in unconventional warfare and established close ties with the Afghan *mujahideen*. Once the Afghan war was over in 1989, the ISI turned its attention towards Kashmir. Most of the ISI-run training centres for Kashmiri insurgents were located either in the Pakistani part of Kashmir or along the Pakistan-Afghanistan border. Apart from training in guerrilla warfare, large quantities of sophisticated weapons, including Stinger anti-aircraft missiles and automatic rifles, which the USA had brought into Pakistan to be used by the Afghan *mujahideen*, were given by the ISI to the Kashmiri insurgents.[9] The ISI also encouraged veteran guerrillas of the Afghan war, who were left aimless after the Soviets withdrew from Afghanistan, to infiltrate into Kashmir and carry out a *jihad* (holy war) against India.[10] To facilitate the infiltration of insurgents across the LoC, the Pakistani military periodically fired upon and shelled Indian forward positions and border villages.

While the ISI was organizing and supporting the Kashmiri insurgents and foreign *mujahideen*, the Pakistani Government lost no opportunity to internationalize the Kashmiri dispute by highlighting in international forums New Delhi's corrupt rule in Jammu and Kashmir and the human rights abuses carried out by the Indian military and counter-insurgency forces against the Kashmiri people. The authorities in the Pakistani capital of Islamabad also consistently demanded international mediation in the Kashmir dispute and called for the holding of a UN-sponsored plebiscite to ascertain the wishes of the Kashmiri people regarding the state's future political status.

The Indo-Pakistani Nuclear Tests, Bus Diplomacy and US Crisis Management

The simmering tensions between India and Pakistan over Kashmir suddenly escalated in May 1998 when India, breaking its self-imposed moratorium of 24 years, tested several nuclear bombs; Pakistan immediately matched India by conducting its own nuclear weapons tests.[11] In the aftermath of the Indian and Pakistani nuclear weapons tests, a legitimate concern of the international community was the prospect of a real nuclear exchange (no matter how limited) between India and Pakistan, given the long history of animosity between them, their zero-sum mentality regarding Kashmir and the hardening of emotions on both sides of the LoC in the immediate aftermath of the nuclear weapons tests.

Acting upon these fears, the Western states, led by the USA, imposed economic and military sanctions on India and Pakistan in order to put pressure on them to sign the Comprehensive Test Ban Treaty (CTBT) and the Non-Proliferation Treaty (NPT). The US Government also put pressure on New Delhi and Islamabad to put in place credible command-and-control systems to handle nuclear warheads, to prevent the meshing of warheads with delivery vehicles, to initiate confidence- and security-building measures (CSBMs) and to resume bilateral dialogue. In a major policy statement, the US Ambassador to India, Richard Celeste, made it clear that the USA viewed the entire pre-1947 State of Jammu and Kashmir as a 'disputed territory' and believed that an ultimate resolution of the Kashmir dispute must be achieved through negotiations between India and Pakistan, taking into account the interests and desires of the Kashmiri people; the Clinton Administration, however, ruled out any kind of US mediation.[12]

Under American pressure, foreign-secretary level talks between India and Pakistan resumed on 15 October 1998, after a stand-off of almost a year. Nevertheless, tensions escalated again with the news that *jihadis* (Islamic holy warriors) funded by a noted terrorist, Osama bin Laden, had begun to infiltrate into Indian Kashmir, with the help of the ISI, to boost the strength of the secessionist forces.[13] The smooth passage of the Fifteenth Constitutional Amendment Bill (the so-called Islamicization of the Constitution Bill, which made *Shari'a* the highest law in Pakistan—and gave the Prime Minister extraordinary powers) through the Pakistan National Assembly also began to ring alarm bells in New Delhi.[14] These developments, together with the continued shelling of the LoC by the Pakistani military and the massacres of large number of Hindus in Jammu by Muslim insurgents, provoked India into holding a massive military exercise along the Indo-Pakistani border.[15] This sparked off yet another round of instability and tension.

Under intense American pressure to de-escalate the tensions generated by the Indian decision to hold military exercises, the Government in New Delhi allowed the Pakistan cricket team to tour India in January–February 1999. Thereafter, in February, Prime Minister Atal Bihari Vajpayee took the bold initiative to visit the Pakistani city of Lahore by bus from India, with an entourage of politicians, bureaucrats and prominent personalities from different professions and walks of life. At the conclusion of Vajpayee's visit, India and Pakistan signed the Lahore Declaration and a Memorandum of Understanding (MOU). The most important aspect of the Lahore Declaration was a series of nuclear weapons-related confidence-building measures (CBMs) between India and Pakistan.[16]

The Kargil War and Military Coup in Pakistan

In the aftermath of the Indian Prime Minister's historic bus trip to Lahore, a short, intense, but undeclared border conflict broke out between India and Pakistan across several sectors of the LoC in Kashmir. The border conflict started in May 1999, when Kashmiri insurgents and foreign *mujahideen*, backed by regular Pakistani soldiers in civilian garb, crossed the LoC in the Kargil sector and occupied large tracts of land and several unmanned peaks and ridges on the Indian side. Initially stunned by the suddenness and scope of the border incursion, New Delhi responded militarily with vigour and determination. The undeclared war that followed, from May to July, eventually resulted in the restoration of the status quo ante, after Pakistan was forced, by a massive Indian counter-offensive and intense American pressure, to withdraw its soldiers and the *mujahideen* forces under its control from the Indian side of the LoC.[17]

The Nawaz Sharif Government in Islamabad blamed the Pakistani military for the Kargil fiasco. The growing rift between Sharif and the Chief of Army Staff (COAS), Gen. Pervez Musharraf, rang alarm bells in the US capital of Washington, DC, and President Clinton, fearing for Pakistan's political future, pointedly warned the Pakistani military not to undertake any action that would jeopardize democracy in Pakistan. The American apprehension about a possible military *coup d'état* in Pakistan came true on 12 October 1999. In a televised address, Gen. Musharraf offered several reasons for seizing power: systematic destruction of political institutions by the Sharif regime; the perilous state of the national economy caused by the self-serving policies of the Government and the high levels of corruption among civilian politicians; and the politicization of the armed forces.[18] He promised that his military regime would give top priority to economic revival, national integration and accountable and transparent governance. Musharraf subsequently assumed the title of Chief Executive and imposed a state of emergency in the country, curtailing the power of the judiciary and the scope of fundamental rights, suspending the Constitution and the parliament and freezing the bank accounts of top politicians and their family members to prevent capital flight. He also appointed new provincial governors and constituted a new National Security Council.

Post-Kargil Stalemate in Kashmir

The Musharraf regime tried to overcome the frustrations over the Kargil fiasco by stepping up its support of insurgent and terrorist groups operating in Indian Kashmir and by constantly harping on the possibility of a catastrophic nuclear showdown with India as a ploy to attract foreign attention and involvement in the dispute. Due mostly to Pakistan's help, by the turn of the century the secessionist insurgency in the Kashmir Valley came to be dominated by foreign *jihadi* outfits with strong links to transnational terrorist groups such as al-Qaida. These groups were more interested in promoting a pan-Islamic cause and were as guilty as the Indian security forces in committing human rights abuses on the local populace. The massacre of 35 Sikhs in Jammu by Lashkar-i-Taiba during President Clinton's visit to India in March 2000 was a case in point; it had little to do with Kashmiri grievances against India, but was clearly intended to create communal tensions across the region.

Such blatant communal attacks by foreign *jihadi* groups seemed to put off the local people and some of the indigenous insurgents in Indian Kashmir.[19] After a decade of fighting, local people also seemed to be tiring of the conflict and yearned for peace.[20] The indigenous insurgents were therefore willing to enter into peace negotiations with New Delhi. The Indian Government, too, favoured a dialogue with the local insurgents and, to facilitate the process, released a number of prominent Kashmiri leaders from prison. Several rounds of talks were held between representatives of the Indian Government and various Kashmiri insurgent groups, but these failed to reach any breakthrough in understanding.

9/11 and After

No single event in modern history has had as much impact on global affairs as that of the 11 September 2001 terrorist attacks on the USA, on the World Trade Center in New York and the Pentagon in Washington, DC. In the USA and across the globe the catastrophic strikes evoked widespread shock, sorrow and anger at the same time. Once the initial shock wore off, American intelligence and counter-terrorism experts quickly sifted through the evidence and pinned the blame for the attacks on Osama bin Laden, a Saudi millionaire and well-known sympathizer and financier of Islamic *jihad* and fundamentalist regimes, his al-Qaida terrorist network fanning across many countries and continents. American intelligence agencies further found Osama bin Laden to be hiding in Afghanistan, where he was being sheltered and protected by the Taliban regime, his most ardent ally. When US threats and its ultimatum to the Taliban Government failed to produce bin Laden and his key advisors, US President George W. Bush decided to use military force in order to topple the Taliban regime and to ferret out Osama bin Laden.

The planned US military action in Afghanistan (with assistance from the British), as part of what President Bush called the global 'war on terror', resurrected Pakistan once again to the status of a 'frontline state' in American strategic thinking and planning and presented President Musharraf with a 'Devil's choice': siding with the Taliban would be a popular move domestically, but would invite the wrath of the USA, which would exacerbate the country's myriad social, economic, political and security problems; contrarily, siding with the USA would bring substantial benefits to Pakistan, but would be domestically unpopular and strengthen the religious hardliners. President Musharraf eventually chose the second option, after the Bush Administration made it explicitly clear that 'fence sitting' would not be allowed.

As part of the deal, Pakistan provided three distinct services to the US military during its military offensive in Afghanistan: first, the Pakistani military provided military airports and bases in Balochistan to American special forces, from where they launched raids into southern and eastern Afghanistan; second, the ISI provided intelligence on the Taliban and bin Laden to the Americans; and, third, Pakistani soldiers and border guards went after suspected al-Qaida personnel who had taken up shelter in the tribal belt in north-western Pakistan. In return, President Bush further acknowledged and appreciated the enormous personal risk President Musharraf had taken when he decided to join the global war on terrorism and the difficult job he faced in curbing religious fanatics and terrorists at home. The Bush Administration also offered economic and financial assistance to Pakistan and promised to reassess the issue of US arms sales to that country.

With credibility restored, the Musharraf regime stepped up its support for the *jihadi* insurgent organizations operating in Indian Kashmir, much to the chagrin of India. In late 2001 and early 2002 a series of spectacular terrorist attacks in India were carried out by groups such as Lashkar-i-Taiba, Hizbul Mujahideen and Jaish-i-Mohammad, including an attack on the Indian Parliament. Public opinion in India was outraged and opinion polls showed that an overwhelming majority favoured a 'decisive war' with Pakistan. The Vajpayee Government reacted by mobilizing and deploying the Indian military on the Indo-Pakistani border and putting the forces at the highest state of alert (Pakistan responded in similar fashion). New Delhi also recalled its ambassador from Islamabad and revoked Pakistan's over-flight permission.

Sensing trouble, the Bush Administration's crisis managers, such as Secretary of State Colin Powell, Assistant Secretary of State Richard Armitage and Secretary of Defense Donald Rumsfeld, made several trips to New Delhi and Islamabad in 2002 and 2003. The US officials essentially followed a dual approach to building a peace process in the subcontinent. On one hand, they impressed on Pakistan that in the post-Kargil and post-9/11 milieu Islamabad was required to take specific steps (such as stopping infiltration of and support to insurgents in the Vale of Kashmir) in order to create political space for New Delhi to agree to bilateral peace talks. On the other hand, they firmly indicated to India that the USA did not consider New Delhi's decision to suspend bilateral talks with Pakistan until Islamabad stopped all cross-border terrorism as realistic.

Although India remained unconvinced by President Musharraf's pledge that his regime stood against terrorism and was doing its best to crack down on insurgent outfits operating out of Pakistan, coming under intense American pressure, New Delhi grudgingly agreed to demobilize its forces and initiate a composite dialogue with Islamabad with the aim of finding a lasting solution to the Kashmir problem. The public mood in both countries also seemed to favour peace. Several rounds of official talks took place between India and Pakistan and several CBMs were initiated, including the start of a Srinagar–Muzaffarabad bus service linking the two parts of Kashmir. The two countries' cricket teams and large contingents of supporters also visited each other and, for the first time in history, the cricket matches were played in very cordial environments. While these gains were noteworthy, not much forward movement was seen on the vexed issue of Kashmir. Terrorist attacks in Indian Kashmir and in other parts of India (most recently in Varanasi and Mumbai) also continued to be carried out by Pakistan-based fundamentalist organizations such as Lashkar-i-Taiba. The infiltration of militants across the LoC has continued as well, putting a further dampener on the bilateral negotiations.

Pakistan's inability to curb the activities of the *jihadi* organizations may mean one of two things. First, it may mean that, in spite of joining the global war on terrorism, the Musharraf regime has little intention of clamping down on terrorist groups operating out of Pakistan. The Government may even have come to an understanding with Islamic fundamentalist groups in Pakistan that, as long as these groups do not create problems for the regime over the issue of Afghanistan, their jihadi aspirations in Indian Kashmir would continue to be supported. If this scenario is true, as many in Indian government and policy circles tend to believe, then not much gain should be expected from the resumption of bilateral talks between New Delhi and Islamabad. Citing the various terrorist attacks in recent months, India has once again reiterated that Pakistan needs to demonstrate emphatically its commitment to fighting terrorism before progress can be made in bilateral discussions. An alternative scenario could be that President Musharraf has actually given firm instructions to the Pakistani military and the ISI to stop the infiltration of terrorists into Indian Kashmir and to dismantle training camps in Pakistan. However, since infiltration has not come down significantly and since insurgent training camps are still in operation in Pakistan, it could mean that President Musharraf may not have total control over his own military and that factions within it are pursuing their own agenda; the Government, therefore, may not have complete control over the *jihadi* groups based in Pakistan. If the second scenario is closer to reality, as many Western governments and academics seem to believe, then giving President Musharraf more time to reform the military and the ISI and to effectively neutralize the *jihadi* organizations in Pakistan may seem to be the most prudent course of action; indeed, this is what the Bush Administration is trying to convince India to do. Only time will tell whether the USA's 'unofficial mediation' will be ultimately able to break the Indo-Pak deadlock over Kashmir.

TAMIL–SINHALESE CONFLICT IN SRI LANKA

Origins and Evolution of Sri Lankan Ethnic Conflict

Sri Lanka (formerly Ceylon), an island located off the southern coast of India, has a total population of around 20m., of which roughly 74% are Sinhalese, 18% Tamils, 7% Moors and the rest mainly Burghers, Malays and Veddhas.[21] The Sinhalese are mostly Buddhists and inhabit the southern, western and central parts of Sri Lanka. The roots of their civilization are largely Indian, although over the years they have been influenced by other cultures, including the Portuguese, the British and, to a lesser extent, the Dutch, the Burmese and the Thais. The bulk of the Tamil population is Hindu and remains concentrated in the drier northern and eastern parts of Sri Lanka. The Tamils are split into two distinct groups: the Jaffna Tamils, who are mainly descendants of tribes that first arrived on the island well over 1,500 years ago, and the Indian Tamils, who originate from indentured plantation workers, brought to the island by British tea planters during the 19th and early 20th centuries.

Historically, Tamil-Sinhalese relations in Sri Lanka have been marked by traditional rivalry as well as peaceful co-existence. However, in the past three decades conflict between these groups has severely challenged the sovereignty and territorial integrity of Sri Lanka, choked off economic growth and caused unprecedented human sufferings. Several contentious issues, such as territorial and linguistic rights of ethnic minorities, the status of a minority religion and economic and political opportunities for minorities, lie at the root of the present-day ethnic conflict. During British colonial rule these issues, though present in society, remained in check. After independence successive Sinhalese-dominated governments, pandering to Sinhalese-Buddhist nationalism and giving hardly a thought to minority well-being, used political power to resolve these contentious issues in a way that favoured the Sinhalese at the expense of the minorities, especially the Tamils.

The first sign of trouble came when, contrary to assurances made by Prime Minister D. S. Senanayake that no harm would come to the minorities, the United National Party (UNP) Government passed the Ceylon Citizenship Act of 1948 and the Indian and Pakistani Residents (Citizenship) Act of 1949. These two pieces of legislation, along with the Parliamentary Elections (Amendment) Act of 1949, laid down strict requirements and documentation for eligibility for Sri Lankan citizenship, which very few Indian Tamils could meet. Consequently, the vast majority of Indian Tamils became stateless.[22] Thereafter, successive Sinhalese-dominated governments tried to win and retain power by adopting an anti-Tamil stance. For instance, the Government enacted discriminatory legislation, such as the Official Language Act of 1956,[23] and adopted discriminatory policies, such as the policy of 'standardization';[24] the Government also encouraged state-aided programmes of colonization of Tamil areas by Sinhalese peasants.[25] Even at the societal level, persecution of minorities continued, often with tacit governmental approval.

Faced with grim prospects after independence, the Sri Lankan Tamils resorted to agitation, strikes and civil disobedience. Initially, the Tamils' demands were autonomist in nature, but in the mid-1970s demand for an independent Tamil state was made. A key reason for the rise of secessionist militancy among the Sri Lankan Tamils was the failure of moderate Tamil leaders to secure concessions from the Sri Lankan Government through political negotiations. Tamil youths were also encouraged by the successful secession of East Pakistan and the creation of the new state of Bangladesh in 1971. Finally, the immediate precipitating factors behind the rise of militancy were three-fold: a new Constitution was adopted by Sri Lanka in 1972, which did not contain any provisions for a federal organization of political power and reiterated the pre-eminent status of Sinhalese as the sole official language; the Constitution bestowed a special status on Buddhism, which is the religion of the majority Sinhalese; and Sri Lankan Tamil youths were impatient with conventional methods of political agitations.

By the early 1980s a number of guerrilla organizations had cropped up. The largest and most ferocious insurgent group was the LTTE, led by Velupillai Prabhakaran. Founded in 1972 as the Tamil New Tigers, the group changed its name to Liberation Tigers of Tamil Eelam in 1976, which coincided with the demand for a separate Tamil state to be called Eelam. In 1981 a faction of the LTTE led by Uma Maheswaran broke away to form the People's Liberation Organization of Tamil Eelam (PLOTE). Some other groups were the Tamil Eelam Liberation Organization (TELO), the Eelam People's Revolutionary Liberation Front (EPRLF), the Tamil Eelam Liberation Army (TELA) and the Eelam

Revolutionary Organization of Students (EROS). At frequent intervals, these groups clashed with each other.

In the initial years of the Tamil militancy the acts of violence and terrorism were mainly in the nature of assassinations of government personnel and robberies. However, after the anti-Tamil riots that swept Colombo, the capital, and other towns in July 1983, the LTTE and the other insurgent groups intensified their attacks on government forces, which brought harsh retaliation against Tamils in Jaffna. The intensification of the Tamil insurgency after the 1983 anti-Tamil riots also signalled the growing marginalization of the moderate Tamil United Liberation Front (TULF) from mainstream Tamil politics in Sri Lanka.

International Involvement

As the ethnic conflict in Sri Lanka intensified after the 1983 anti-Tamil riots, neighbouring India, which contained around 80m. Tamils in the southern state of Tamil Nadu became directly affected. The Tamils residing in Tamil Nadu were naturally concerned by the plight of their ethnic kin in Sri Lanka during the anti-Tamil riots and urged the Indian Government to get involved. New Delhi took the view that the protection and promotion of India's national interest required an immediate de-escalation of the ethnic conflict and the commencement of a peace process. For India, the resolution of the conflict required the satisfaction of two objectives: Sri Lanka's sovereignty and territorial integrity had to be preserved, but, simultaneously, the Tamils' earlier demand for devolution of power and regional autonomy had to be honoured.

Through India's diplomatic support, the Sri Lankan Tamil political parties were able to reach a wide global audience with accounts of systematic Sinhalese discrimination against their community. Western countries were sympathetic towards the plight of the Sri Lankan Tamils. The United Kingdom, for instance, offered prominent Tamil politicians asylum and allowed the LTTE to open public relations offices in the country. Canada also took a sympathetic stand and allowed many Sri Lankan Tamils who fled the island to escape the war to settle in Canada. The USA and the USSR also professed full faith in India's ability to affect a successful resolution of the conflict. Hence, when President J. R. Jayewardene visited the USA in June 1984 to seek US support for the Sri Lankan Government's position on the ethnic issue, and to obtain military assistance, the Americans declined to provide such help. Similarly, the USSR also refused to involve itself in Sri Lanka, leaving the field open to India.[26]

To tackle the growing Tamil insurgency, the Sri Lankan Government actively sought military help from foreign states. Within South Asia, it received some arms and military training from Pakistan. The People's Republic of China, South Africa, Singapore and Malaysia also supplied arms to Sri Lanka. British, Rhodesian and South African mercenaries were reportedly hired to impart training in counter-insurgency warfare to the Sri Lankan forces. Assistance was even sought from Israel, a country with which Sri Lanka had severed diplomatic relations in 1970; responding to Sri Lanka's call, Israel set up an interests section in the US Embassy in Colombo and Mossad and Shin Beth, the Israeli agencies that deal with espionage and counter-insurgency, started training the Sri Lankan security forces.[27]

The Sri Lankan Tamil insurgent groups received covert military assistance and training mainly from the Research and Analysis Wing (RAW), India's leading spy agency. Training camps were established by RAW in the Ramanathapuram district in southern Tamil Nadu. The first Tamil group to be trained by RAW was TELO. However, later on, RAW provided military training to the LTTE, PLOTE and EROS.[28] Apart from RAW training, political parties in Tamil Nadu provided the Sri Lankan Tamil insurgent groups with substantial financial support, as well as lots of free publicity and media exposure.

Attempts at Conflict Resolution

In August 1983 the Indian Prime Minister, Indira Gandhi, announced that President Jayewardene of Sri Lanka had accepted India's offer of good offices and agreed to have a broad-based conference with the Sri Lankan Tamil leaders to work out a political settlement to the ethnic problem. Indira Gandhi's personal envoy, G. Parthasarathy, was given the task of mediating between the Tamil groups and the Sri Lankan Government. What emerged from Parthasarathy's efforts came to be known as the Parthasarathy Formula. The key provision of this formula was 'Annexure C', which envisaged the creation of elected and auton-omous regional councils in the northern and eastern provinces of Sri Lanka. An all-party conference was called to discuss these proposals, but it failed to reach agreement.

In July–August 1985 another attempt was made by India to bring the Tamil insurgents and political groups and the Sri Lankan Government to the negotiating table. Bhutan's King Jigme Wangchuk's offer of his capital, Thimphu, was accepted as the neutral site for a comprehensive peace conference. Under intense Indian pressure, five Tamil militant groups (LTTE, TELO, EROS, TELA and EPRLF) agreed to co-operate with one another and came to the negotiating table, united as the Eelam National Liberation Front (ENLF). In addition, the PLOTE, the TULF and the Governments of India and of Sri Lanka were represented at the talks. During the discussions, the Tamil delegation insisted that the following basic principles were cardinal in any settlement of the Tamil problem:

the Sri Lankan Government's recognition of the Sri Lankan Tamils as a distinct nationality;

the Sri Lankan Government's recognition that the northern and eastern provinces together constituted the Sri Lankan Tamils' traditional homeland;

the Sri Lankan Government's recognition of the Sri Lankan Tamils' right of self-determination; and

the Sri Lankan Government's granting of Sri Lankan citizenship to all Tamils on the island.

The Sri Lankan delegation argued that recognizing the principles was tantamount to conceding Eelam. Consequently, the talks fell through.

Following the failure of the Thimphu talks, the Tamil insurgents and the Sri Lankan Government sought a decisive military victory. Heavy fighting was reported in the northern and eastern provinces. Internecine fighting also broke out among the various Tamil insurgent groups. Sensing that the situation was rapidly slipping out of control, India made a last-ditch effort in December 1986 to effect a settlement between the Tamil groups and the Sri Lankan Government. Under Indian pressure, President Jayewardene met Prime Minister Rajiv Gandhi of India, Tamil Nadu Chief Minister M. G. Ramachandran and the LTTE supremo, Prabhakaran, in Bangalore (India). At this meeting President Jayewardene suggested breaking up the eastern province into three separate units, representing Tamils, Sinhalese and Muslims. In so doing, he rejected the 'traditional homeland' theory of the Sri Lankan Tamils (comprising the northern and eastern provinces), because the Sri Lankan Government did not consider the eastern province to be a predominantly Tamil area. The proposal, therefore, was not acceptable to the Tamils.

In early 1987 intense fighting broke out in Sri Lanka after President Jayewardene, facing mounting pressure from Sinhalese hardliners, authorized the military to launch a major operation in the Jaffna peninsula, a LTTE stronghold. Bombing of Jaffna was started in earnest and a food and fuel embargo was imposed in the region. The attack on Jaffna by the Sri Lankan military created a tremendous backlash in Tamil Nadu. Faced with intense criticism from the Tamil Nadu Government that it had betrayed the Tamils, the Indian Government announced its intention to send relief supplies to the people of the beleaguered and embattled Jaffna peninsula. Despite warnings from President Jayewardene that such an act by India would be considered an infringement of Sri Lankan sovereignty, India initially attempted to send the supplies by sea. When the Indian flotilla was intercepted and turned back by the Sri Lankan Navy, 25 tons of food and relief supplies were para-dropped in Jaffna by Indian Air Force jets. Amid rumours of a possible Indian military intervention, a visibly shaken Jayewardene started sending feelers to India to work out a political solution to the conflict and, as a gesture of sincerity, the Government terminated the military operations in Jaffna and released a large number of Tamil detainees from prison. This set the stage for renewed Indian diplomatic efforts, leading to the signing of the Indo-Sri Lankan Accord on 29 July 1987.

The key provisions of the Indo-Sri Lankan Accord were as follows. First, the Accord recognized the unity, sovereignty and territorial integrity of Sri Lanka, thereby 'eliminating Tamil claims for a sovereign state (Eelam) and averting the threat of an Indian invasion.'[29] Second, the Accord also recognized Sri Lanka as a 'multi-ethnic and multi-lingual plural society' comprised of Sinhalese, Tamils, Muslims (Moors), Malays and Burghers. Third, although the Accord recognized that the northern and eastern provinces of Sri Lanka constituted 'areas of historical habitation of Sri Lankan Tamil-speaking peoples', it also recognized the territorial rights of other groups who have at all times lived in this territory.

Fourth, the Accord provided for the temporary merger of the northern and eastern provinces as a single administrative unit, after the holding of elections to the provincial councils by December 1987; the permanency of this merger was to be determined by a referendum to be held no later than December 1988. Fifth, the Accord provided for the cessation of hostilities, the surrender of arms by the Tamil militant groups and the return of the Sri Lankan Army to barracks. It also provided for a general amnesty to all political detainees and the repeal of the Prevention of Terrorism Act and other emergency laws. Finally, under the Accord, India agreed to provide military assistance as and when requested by Colombo in order to implement the provisions of the agreement.[30]

On 30 July 1987 (one day after the Accord was signed) orders were given for an Indian Peace Keeping Force (IPKF) to move into Sri Lanka to help the Sri Lankan Government to implement the Accord. Because no fighting was anticipated, the maxim of concentration of force was ignored. For the same reason, heavy weaponry was left behind in India. Within a few days of its induction, however, the IPKF suffered reverses. On 4 August, addressing a huge rally in Jaffna, LTTE chief Prabhakaran categorically rejected the Indo-Sri Lankan Accord, giving the following reasons: the Accord did not redress the main grievances of the Sri Lankan Tamils, but was concerned primarily with Indo-Sri Lankan relations; the Accord called for the Sri Lankan Tamils to disarm without first guaranteeing their safety and protection from the Sri Lankan military; and the Accord did not guarantee that the Sri Lankan Government would fulfil the promises made. The LTTE, therefore, refused to surrender weapons and ammunition to the IPKF. Under scathing criticism from the Sri Lankan Government for failing to restrain the Tamil militants and to protect civilian life and property, Prime Minister Gandhi ordered the IPKF to apprehend anyone carrying arms or who was involved in the massacre of civilians. For the next two years the IPKF was engaged in a fierce war with the LTTE that it had little chance of winning.

As the IPKF became bogged down, opposition to the Accord gathered momentum in Sri Lanka and India. In Sri Lanka the main opposition party, the Sri Lanka Freedom Party (SLFP), openly criticized the Accord as violating Sri Lanka's sovereignty and demanded the IPKF's withdrawal. Similar sentiments were expressed by the right-wing, pan-Sinhalese Janatha Vimukthi Peramuna (JVP) or the People's Revolutionary Front. The Sri Lankan Tamil groups were also critical of the Accord and wanted an early withdrawal of the IPKF. In India, too, most political parties and key military leaders favoured the immediate return of the IPKF, which was suffering heavy losses. After high-level talks in September 1989, a cease-fire between the IPKF and the LTTE was arranged and the IPKF finally left Sri Lanka in March 1990.

Back to War

With the withdrawal of the IPKF and the annulment of the merger of the northern and eastern provinces (which was to be affected under the Indo-Sri Lankan

Accord) by the Premadasa Government (Ranasinghe Premadasa became President of Sri Lanka in December 1988), in deference to Sinhalese sensitivities, the civil war resumed in the north with renewed vigour. In the early 1990s another angle was added to this complex conflict—that is, violence between Tamils and Muslims in the eastern province. In the south of the island, too, violence broke out, in the form of the JVP insurrection. The Premadasa Government responded to the JVP threat by organizing pro-government death squads, consisting of off-duty security personnel and UNP supporters. These death squads killed thousands of youths and students belonging to or supporting the JVP and even captured and killed the leader of the JVP, Rohana Wijeweera, and his immediate followers.

President Premadasa was eventually assassinated by a LTTE suicide bomber in 1993. A new presidential election took place in 1994, which was won by Chandrika Bandaranaike Kumaratunga of the People's Alliance (PA). In January 1995 the Kumaratunga Government entered into a cease-fire agreement with the LTTE and promised to come up with a new set of proposals for the devolution of power. However, after waiting patiently for three months to see these new peace proposals, the LTTE finally became tired of waiting and repudiated the cease-fire agreement in April. Armed clashes between the LTTE and the Sri Lankan military once again intensified. In frustration, President Kumaratunga endorsed the Sri Lankan military's plan to launch a massive operation, codenamed Riviresa (Sunrays), to re-establish government control over the northern city of Jaffna, the main LTTE stronghold. By June 1996 the Sri Lankan military was able to recapture most of the Jaffna peninsula. However, after lying low for a while and regrouping, the LTTE retaliated through a series of spectacular terrorist attacks on civilian and military targets.

Colombo responded to these LTTE attacks through another aggressive and forceful counter-insurgency campaign. In 1997 the Sri Lankan military launched Operation Jayasikuru, with the aim of establishing a secure land corridor between Jaffna and the rest of Sri Lanka, clearing the northern jungles of the Wanni district and gaining full control of the upper sectors of the eastern province. By mid-1999 the military was also engaged in a two-pronged offensive in the north-east. The LTTE regrouped quickly, to inflict heavy casualties on the armed forces, leading to large-scale desertions from the ranks. The Tigers also did not show any sign of giving up the armed struggle for a separate Tamil state. The group continued to benefit from a seemingly endless supply of basic and advanced combat weapons and from funds raised primarily by Sri Lankan Tamil expatriates in North America, Western Europe and the Australasia region. Additionally, defying expectations as the conflict dragged on, the LTTE appeared to have little problem in recruiting new cadres.[31]

To make things hard for the LTTE and to placate hardline elements within the Sinhalese community in the wake of an LTTE bomb attack on a Buddhist shrine in Kandy in January 1998, President Chandrika Kumaratunga outlawed the LTTE. The Sri Lankan Government also stated its intention to grant regional autonomy to Tamil areas and to create a civilian administration in Jaffna; for this reason, it tried to work out a deal with several moderate Tamil groups. The LTTE scuttled these moves by assassinating pro-government Tamil leaders, such as Dr. Neelan Thiruchelvam, a Member of Parliament and leader of the TULF, in July 1999 and N. Manickathasan, vice-president of PLOTE, in September 1999.

International Apathy

During the decade-long 'dirty war' in Sri Lanka in the 1990s, prominent international actors showed little intention of getting involved to stop the violence and to figure out a way to resolve the conflict. In part, the international apathy towards Sri Lanka's ethnic conflict was due to the horrible experience of the IPKF. Additionally, by the 1990s most international actors, including India, had come to regard the LTTE as the main obstacle to peace in Sri Lanka and considered its military defeat as the only way out of the quagmire.

The Indian Government, having burnt its fingers in trying to enforce peace and being fed up with the LTTE's terrorist methods and its refusal to accept anything less than Eelam, stopped all aid to the LTTE in the early 1990s. It also dismissed the Dravida Munnetra Kazhagam (DMK) Government in Tamil Nadu and placed the state under President's Rule in order to prevent it from being used as a sanctuary by the Tamil Tigers. The assassination of former Prime Minister Rajiv Gandhi during an election rally in Tamil Nadu in 1991 at the hands of LTTE suicide bombers further turned up the heat on the Tigers and pro-LTTE political parties in Tamil Nadu. In the aftermath of Gandhi's assassination, the Indian Government classified the LTTE as a terrorist organization and blamed it for prolonging the ethnic conflict in Sri Lanka. The United Front (first under Prime Minister Deve Gowda and then under Prime Minister Kumar Gujral), which came to power in the mid-1990s, further advocated strengthening the Sri Lankan Government's hands in its fight against the Tamil Tigers. This policy was continued by the National Democratic Alliance (NDA) Government of Prime Minister Vajpayee from 1998 and the United Progressive Alliance (UPA) Government of Prime Minister Manmohan Singh from 2004.

India's changed attitude towards the LTTE influenced wider international opinion and adversely affected the group's international reputation. The LTTE came to be generally regarded in international circles as a terrorist organization and there were rumours that the Tigers were involved in drugs trafficking to raise money to fund their military campaigns.[32] The LTTE was also accused of being involved in the smuggling of weapons and ammunition obtained from the international underground arms market. The Tigers' attempts to forge links with insurgent groups in India, such as the People's War Group, also did not endear them to India and the international community. Consequently, when the Sri Lankan military launched Operation Riviresa (Sunrays), the Sri Lankan Government received widespread international sympathy and support. The LTTE's military reverses during this offensive also found few mourners in the wider world, even though the group's public relations office in London (United Kingdom) tried to project the Sri Lankan military offensive as a 'genocide' of the Tamil nation.

The Onset of Peace Negotiations

Early in the new millennium Norway took the initiative to facilitate peace negotiations between the LTTE and the Sri Lankan Government. The key player in this facilitation process was Erik Solheim, special adviser to Norway's foreign minister and previously the leader of the Norwegian Socialist Left Party. Several developments made it likely that both the Sri Lankan Government and the LTTE could be persuaded to come to negotiating table.

On the Sri Lankan Government side, the national elections of December 2001 resulted in a change of regime and a realignment of political forces in the country. The opposition United National Front (UNF), led by Ranil Wickremasinghe, replaced the PA as the largest group in Parliament and formed the new Government. For the UNF Government, negotiation and not confrontation with the LTTE was advantageous for a number of reasons. First, in the post-9/11 world, the LTTE leadership was clearly under pressure to move away from its hitherto steadfast demand of a separate Tamil state to be achieved through armed struggle. Secondly, in the aftermath of 9/11, world opinion had clearly turned against groups that employed terrorism, irrespective of their just cause. The Sri Lankan Government therefore received lots of pledges of support in its war against the LTTE from different quarters. Since almost no one of significance within the international community (especially neighbouring India, which contained so many millions of fellow Tamils) supported the LTTE's demand for a separate state, the Sri Lankan Government's hands were further strengthened for negotiations with the Tamil Tigers. Thirdly, creation of a stable and lasting peace was crucial for the economic regeneration and recovery of Sri Lanka. As an island economy, Sri Lanka is heavily dependent on external trade and tourism. Throughout the 1990s, as the civil war continued to cause havoc, GDP growth had been badly affected. In the new millennium, however, Sri Lanka's economy had started to revive, mainly as a result of the economic liberalization policies of the Government and experts forecasted a faster growth rate if peace could be achieved on the island. Finally, Prime Minister Wickremasinghe represented a new generation of political leadership in Sri Lanka, which was less concerned with ethno-religious nationalism and zero sum military confrontation, but focused more on achieving a substantial peace dividend in the context of globalization and market liberalization. Wickremasinghe was also unencumbered by past failures and hence was in a position to take bold decisions to achieve peace.

The LTTE also found it difficult to say no to Norway-facilitated peace talks with the Sri Lankan Government. First, unlike the previous regimes, the newly formed Wickremasinghe Government showed a willingness to negotiate directly with the LTTE and was not averse to discussing the creation of an 'interim self-governing authority' (ISGA) for the Tamil-majority north and east, which had been a key demand of the Tigers. Secondly, after the 2001 general election, through the Tamil National Alliance (TNA), a conglomeration of four pro-LTTE Tamil parties, the LTTE had a political presence in the Parliament, which was bound to strengthen the Tigers' hands at the negotiating table. Thirdly, having been branded as a terrorist organization in a post-9/11 world, the Tigers were facing difficulties in raising funds in Western countries, which may have adversely affected their military preparedness and fighting capability.[33] Fourthly, there were clear indications that the Sri Lankan military was actively seeking weapons and counter-insurgency training from a number of sources. The LTTE therefore faced the future prospect of being challenged militarily by a more confident and better trained and equipped Sri Lankan military backed politically by powerful allies. Finally, it was reported that the Tamil Tigers were suffering from war fatigue and facing problems in recruiting new personnel.

After months of separate talks with representatives of the Sri Lankan Government and the LTTE, Norwegian facilitators were able to procure an indefinite cease-fire agreement (CFA) between the two sides on 23 February 2002. The signing of the CFA was followed by a visit to Jaffna by Prime Minister Wickremasinghe. Providing a further impetus to peace, following the Prime Minister's visit to Jaffna, the Sri Lankan Muslim Congress (SLMC) declared that it was willing to enter into discussions with the LTTE regarding problems of the Muslims in the north-east region. In a reciprocal gesture, the LTTE acknowledged that Muslims had suffered severely at its hands and apologized for past misdeeds. The Tigers also recognized the Muslim people's 'unique cultural identity' and pledged to address Muslim concerns and apprehensions.

In April 2002 LTTE chief Prabhakaran came out of his jungle hideout to hold a press conference in Kilinochchi in northern Sri Lanka with the national and international media. Flanked by the LTTE's chief negotiator and political strategist, Anton Balasingham, Prabhakaran indicated that he was extremely pleased with the peace process and thanked Prime Minister Wickremasinghe for his bold actions. He pledged that the LTTE was 'sincerely and seriously committed to peace', but also cautioned that 'the right conditions have not arisen for the LTTE to abandon the policy of an independent statehood.' He stressed that for any solution to Sri Lanka's ethnic conflict to be acceptable to the LTTE it must incorporate three fundamentals—Tamil homeland, Tamil nationality and Tamil right to self-determination—and 'once these fundamentals are accepted, or a political solution is put forward by Sri Lanka recognizing these three fundamentals and if our people are satisfied with the framework of a solution that recognizes these core issues, then we will consider giving up the demand for Eelam.'[34] Balasingham further expanded the LTTE's understanding of self-determination: 'We mean the right of people to decide their own political destiny—it can also apply to autonomy and self-governance. If autonomy and self-governance is given to our people, we can say that internal self-determination is to some extent met. But if the Sri Lankan Government rejects our demand for autonomy and self-governance and continues with repression, then as a last resort we will opt for secession—that also comes under self-determination.'[35]

The much anticipated peace talks between representatives of the Sri Lankan Government and the LTTE, which were to begin in Thailand, were delayed as several snags developed. It seemed that the Wickremasinghe Government, like its predecessor, had suddenly developed apprehension that the formation of an

LTTE-controlled ISGA in the north and east would, over time, lead to the formation of a de facto sovereign Tamil state. In a speech to the European Parliament in May 2002, Prime Minister Wickremasinghe stressed that the unity of Sri Lanka was non-negotiable and categorically denied that his Government had given any blanket assurance to the LTTE that an ISGA under the Tigers' sole control would be established in the north-east. He also indicated that his Government had no plans to repeal the Prevention of Terrorism Act (POTA), which gave sweeping detention powers to the police and armed forces against the Tamil rebels, and expected the LTTE to respect human rights and democratic norms.[36]

After a lot of persuasion by the Norwegian facilitators, a first round of peace talks between the LTTE and the Sri Lankan Government was held in Thailand in September 2002. At the end of the three-day talks, the chief negotiator and political strategist of the LTTE, Balasingham, clarified that the Tigers were ready to accept 'autonomy and self-governance' in north-eastern Sri Lanka, the details of which could be worked out if both parties first agreed to a particular political system for the whole country. The head of the government delegation, Gamini Lakshman Peiris, also stressed that the LTTE's political aspirations could be fulfilled 'within one country'. The two sides agreed to meet for further talks and decided to set up a joint task force for humanitarian reconstructive activities.

Another round of talks was held in Oslo, Norway, in December 2002. The most crucial outcome of this round of negotiations was the agreement by both sides to develop a federal political system that would give the Tamils 'internal self-determination' in the Tamil-dominated areas of the north-east. Norway's Special Envoy termed this agreement as a 'major step', but warned that a 'long and bumpy' road was ahead before a final solution could be agreed upon.[37] G. L. Peiris, head of the government delegation, also cautioned that the Oslo decision to explore a 'federal model' was just the outer perimeter of a complex conflict resolution process and that more contentious issues such as 'division of power' and 'human rights' would be taken up for discussion later.[38]

Suspension of Peace Talks

By mid-2003 the peace process was under severe strain because of a number of developments. First, both sides continued to build up their military strength and war preparedness by recruiting heavily, which indicated that they did not place much faith in negotiations. Secondly, President Kumaratunga developed deep apprehensions regarding the nature of the concessions being made to the LTTE by the Government and felt that the Tigers had already set up a de facto independent Tamil state in north-eastern Sri Lanka. Her concern was shared by her party, the SLFP, and allies such as the JVP. The Sinhalese-Buddhist clergy was also vehemently opposed to the concessions being granted to the Tamils. Finally, key international actors and major donors expressed serious reservations about the behaviour of the LTTE and stressed that any solution to Sri Lanka's ethnic conflict must ensure principles of democracy, pluralism and human rights.

In April 2003 the LTTE abruptly suspended the peace talks. Frustrated and angry at the breakdown of the peace talks, President Kumaratunga evoked the executive presidency's enormous powers on 5 November to declare a state of emergency in the country, under which she suspended Parliament and took over control of the ministries of defence, the interior and the media from the Government.[39] She also asked her party, the SLFP, to form a political alliance with the JVP, which came to fruition in January 2004 with the formation of the United People's Freedom Alliance (UPFA). In early February President Kumaratunga dissolved Parliament and declared 2 April to be the date for fresh elections.

In March 2004 reports of a split between the LTTE's northern and main unit, led by Prabhakaran and based in Kilinochchi, and its eastern unit, led by V. Muralitharan (alias 'Col Karuna') and based in the eastern Batticaloa-Amparai district, began to circulate. The split greatly undermined the LTTE's political standing and bargaining power at the negotiating table. For instance, the LTTE's claim to be the 'sole representative' of Sri Lankan Tamils was badly dented by Karuna's claim that the LTTE represented 'North Eelam' while he and his forces represented 'South Eelam'. In an exercise in damage control, Prabhakaran predictably expelled Karuna from the organization and ordered his troops to crush the budding revolt by force.

The 2 April 2004 parliamentary elections drastically altered the political landscape in Sri Lanka again. The UPFA emerged as the single largest grouping (105 seats) in a Parliament with a total strength of 225 and formed the new Government under Mahinda Rajapakse. The election results indicated a strong ethnic polarization in Sri Lanka, which did not bode well for the peace process. The UPFA Government was critical of Norway's facilitation, refused to recognize the LTTE as the sole representative of the Tamil people and rejected the 'federal model' that had been agreed to in principle earlier. Not surprisingly, the LTTE categorically refused to participate in any peace talks with the UPFA.

Tsunami Disaster and the Return of War

In December 2004 Sri Lanka suffered a major tragedy when a giant tsunami, that also devastated northern Indonesia, southern Thailand and parts of south-eastern India, hit the northern and eastern parts of the island, causing massive destruction and loss of life. As international humanitarian and relief aid poured in, a tussle developed between the Sri Lankan Government and the LTTE over aid allocation and distribution. The LTTE accused the Government of meting out step-motherly treatment to the Tamil-speaking areas of the north-east, which made reconstruction work difficult. On its part, the Sri Lankan Government refused to form a joint LTTE-Government mechanism (as suggested by the LTTE and Norway) for reconstruction work as long as LTTE paramilitaries continued to operate in the north-east. Both sides refused to budge from their respective positions and preferred to take their case to the international community.[40]

The bad blood and air of mutual suspicion that developed between the LTTE and the Sri Lankan Government over the post-tsunami aid distribution and reconstruction work eventually took its toll on the peace process. The first sign of major trouble came in August 2005, when the Sri Lankan foreign minister, Lakshman Kadirgamar, was assassinated by an unidentified sniper. Although the LTTE denied any role in the Kadirgamar assassination, Sinhalese-Buddhist opinion was vehemently critical of the organization and put enormous pressure on the Government formally to terminate the peace process. In this tense climate, Sri Lanka held a fresh presidential election, which was won by the UPFA's candidate, the hardline Rajapakse. In his election manifesto, Rajapakse had made it clear that he supported a 'unitary' rather than a 'federal' polity in Sri Lanka. Rajapakse had also been a strong critic of the Norway-facilitated peace process and had in the past advocated a 'military solution' to Sri Lanka's decades old ethnic conflict. The prospects for peace thus looked extremely grim.

By December 2005 Sri Lanka was back to civil war. In a spectacular landmine attack in the northern Jaffna peninsula, the LTTE executed 11 government soldiers and a policeman—this was the biggest Tiger attack since the signing of the CFA in 2002. The Government's military response was swift and harsh, and over the next few months massacres were committed by both sides with impunity. As the death toll climbed sharply in Sri Lanka and thousands of civilians started fleeing the combat zones in the north and east, international condemnation of the LTTE came thick and fast. The US Government, for example, called the LTTE a 'reprehensible terrorist group' and mainly blamed it for the resumption of civil war in Sri Lanka; Canada also labelled the LTTE as a 'terrorist group'.[41]

From April–May 2006 major confrontations between the LTTE and the Sri Lankan military became a daily occurrence in the north and east. A series of major sea battles took place between the Sea Tigers (the LTTE's naval wing) and the Sri Lankan Navy; in support of its naval forces, the Sri Lankan Air Force also resorted to aerial bombardment of Tamil areas. In retaliation, the LTTE carried out suicide terrorist attacks against the Sri Lankan army headquarters in Colombo, killing several people and seriously wounding the head of the army, Lt-Gen. Sarath Fonseka. Violence also broke out between the LTTE and the Karuna faction, which was probably being used by the Sri Lankan military against the Tigers. Communal violence between Tamils and Sinhalese or Muslims was reported from the east. Violence was also directed at the international truce monitors belonging to the Sri Lanka Monitoring Mission (SLMM). In this climate of spiralling violence, human rights abuses were committed by all sides. For example, while the LTTE was accused of intimidating and targeting foreign truce monitors, especially those who were European Union (EU) nationals, the Sri Lankan armed forces were criticized by human rights groups such as Amnesty International for killing unarmed Tamil civilians, including children, in the Jaffna peninsula and 17 aid workers in the eastern town of Muttur.[42]

In August 2006 serious clashes flared up on the Jaffna peninsula, in Batticaloa in the east and around Trincomalee port in the north-east. Heavy shelling and aerial bombardment of these areas by the Sri Lankan Army and Air Force was reported. Fierce artillery exchanges and hand-to-hand combat between LTTE fighters and government troops were also reported. A major confrontation between the Sri Lankan Navy and the Sea Tigers took place near Trincomalee harbour, in which around 70 Tamil Tigers were reportedly killed. While it seems that in these recent battles the Tamil Tigers have taken a major hit, the Sri Lankan military, too, has suffered heavy casualties. Aid agencies reported that over 100,000 people had become displaced in the north and east as a result of fighting.[43]

Sri Lanka's return to all-out war has all but destroyed the CFA and is a huge reverse for the peace process facilitated by Norway. Although both the LTTE and the Sri Lankan Government continue to pay lip service to the importance of holding peace talks to resolve the ethnic conflict, in reality neither side has shown any inclination towards making the kind of concessions needed to carry the peace process forward. On the contrary, both sides seem to believe in a 'decisive war' in order to swing the outcome conclusively in their favour. Having joined the American-led global 'war on terror' and having received international sympathy and support, Colombo probably feels emboldened and confident that it can win a decisive military victory over the LTTE and smash the power and influence of the organization, which would then allow it to dictate the terms of peace. For the LTTE, however, a decisive military victory would help solidify the de facto Tamil state, which many experts believe has already come into existence in the north and parts of the east. The stakes are, therefore, high for both sides. Only time will tell how this conflict will ultimately be resolved.

NOTES

1. During the British rule of India, two categories of states existed. In the first category were the areas of British India that were ruled directly from London, via the viceregal Government. The second category of states, known as the princely states, was ruled indirectly by the British under the Doctrine of Paramountcy. Under this scheme, the princely states were nominally independent, but the rulers recognized the British Crown as the paramount power in India, received imperial titles and agreed to be guided by the British Government.

2. Since the Doctrine of Paramountcy, which had guided relations between the princely states and the British Crown, was to lapse with the colonial disengagement from India, in a technical sense this meant that the rulers of the princely states had the right to decide if they wished to accede to either India or Pakistan, or preferred to remain independent.

3. India and Pakistan fought two more wars (1965 and 1971), the former directly over Kashmir. Except for some minor alterations after the 1971 war, the CFL line remained intact. After 1971 it came to be known as the Line of Control (LoC).

4. The CPO forces came mainly from the Border Security Force (BSF), the Central Reserve Police Force (CRPF), the Indo-Tibetan Border Police (ITBP) and the Rashtriya (National) Rifles (RR).

5. See pp. 147–54 of R. G. Wirsing's 1994 publication, as listed in the Bibliography.

6. See p. 39 of *The Economist* 1996 (14 September) article, as listed in the Bibliography.

7. For a detailed discussion of existential deterrence and its applicability in South Asia, see Devin Hagerty (*International Security*, Winter 1995/96).

8. Pakistan adopted the policy of aquiring 'forward strategic depth' first under Zulfiqar Ali Bhutto in the 1970s, primarily to offset its lack of territorial depth and early warning capabilities. The strategy envisioned that, in the event of an impending Indian military invasion of Pakistan, Pakistani intelligence agents and Pakistan-sponsored insurgents and terrorists carrying out subversive activities in India would be able to provide early warning of the attack and launch guerrilla warfare against the Indian Army before it could reach the Indo-Pakistani border. See Bodansky, 1995 (on Freeman Center for Strategic Studies website, at http://freeman.io.com/m_online/bodansky/axis.htm).

9. Sanjoy Hazarika, 'India Says Pakistan is Stirring Up Kashmir Unrest', in *The New York Times*, of 1 February 1990 (p. 5), and John Ward Anderson, 'Pakistan Aiding Rebels in Kashmir: Muslims Reportedly Armed and Trained', in *The Washington Post* of 16 May 1994 (p. 1).

10. Hazarika, 'Afghans Joining Rebels in Kashmir', in *The New York Times* of 24 August 1993 (p. 4), and P. S. Suryanarayana, 'Afghan Support to Pakistan in the Event of War', in *The Hindu* (International Edition) of 15 October 1994 (p. 3).

11. Ashok Sharma, 'India Conducts 3 Nuclear Tests', in *The Washington Post* of 1 May 1998, and John F. Burns, 'Pakistan, Answering India, Carries Out Nuclear Tests', in *The New York Times* of 29 May 1998.

12. US Department of State, Daily Press Briefing of Friday, 9 October 1998 (DPB No. 113, 2.30 pm).

13. Vijay Dutt, 'Pak Mercenaries Establish Bases in Kashmir', in *The Hindustan Times* of 5 October 1998.

14. Christopher Thomas, 'Sharif: Invoking Islam to Keep Nation Together', in *The Times* of 17 September 1998, and Zahid Hussain and Manoj Joshi, 'In a Holy Mess', in *India Today* of 14 September 1998.

15. Julian West, 'Indian Exercises Spark Fears of War', in the *electronic telegraph* of 11 October 1998.

16. Swapan Dasgupta and Harinder Baweja, 'Breaking Barriers', and Harinder Baweja and Raj Chengappa, 'From Breakdown to Detente and Entente Cordiale', in *India Today* of 1 March 1999.

17. John Lancaster, 'Kashmir Crisis Defused on Brink of War', in *The Washington Post* of 26 July 1999.

18. See the transcript of Gen. Musharraf's address to the nation, 'Dawn', of 13 October 1999.

19. 'Rift among J&K Militant Groups Comes to the Fore', in *The Times of India* of 17 August 2000.

20. Prem Shankar Jha, 'Yearning for Peace', in *Outlook* of 28 August 2000.

21. The Moors are descendants of the ancient Arab traders that used to visit Sri Lanka before the advent of the Europeans. They practice Islam, speak mostly Tamil and are concentrated in major trading centres like Colombo and in the east of the island. The Moors living in the trading centres are usually wealthy and literate, while those living in the east are economically backward with a low literacy level. The Burghers are of mixed European and Sri Lankan descent. They are mostly Christians and speak English. They are mainly concentrated in Colombo and are economically prosperous. The Malays are descended from the Malay traders and guards brought to the island during the colonial period. Finally, the Veddhas are the descendants of the aboriginal tribes of ancient Sri Lanka, whose numbers have been greatly reduced over the years, as many of them have been absorbed in the Sinhalese race. The remaining Veddhas continue to rely on hunting for their food and live in extremely primitive conditions in the forests of eastern Sri Lanka. This information is attributed to the Ministry of Finance and Planning's *Statistical Pocketbook of the Democratic Socialist Republic of Sri Lanka, 1998* (Colombo, Dept of Census and Statistics, 1998); see pp. 9–26.

22. Under the Citizenship Act of 1948, Indian Tamils could no longer become citizens of Sri Lanka by virtue of their birth on the island and had to prove three or more generations of paternal ancestry to become citizens by descent. It was virtually impossible for most Indian Tamils to provide such proof. As a result, they were made stateless. Similarly, the Indian and Pakistani Residents (Citizenship) Act of 1949 and the Ceylon (Parliamentary Elections) Amendment Act of 1949 also disenfranchised most of the Indian Tamils, who had participated in the country's general elections since 1931. The total outcome of all three Acts was that about 975,000 Indian Tamils were rendered stateless.

23. In the initial years after independence, the Sri Lankan Government's position was to recognize both the Sinhalese and Tamil languages as official languages of Sri Lanka. When the Sri Lanka Freedom Party (SLFP) under S. W. R. D. Bandaranaike won the 1956 elections on a 'Sinhala Only' platform, things changed for the worse. One of the first major acts of Bandaranaike's Government was to pass the Official Language Act of 1956, by which the two-language policy was abandoned and Sinhalese was made the sole official language of Sri Lanka. The Act granted no concessions to the Sri Lankan Tamils, the national minority, with regard to

the use of the Tamil language for education, employment or administrative purposes. The Sri Lankan Tamils resorted to protest. Faced with such mounting ethnic tension, the Government passed the Tamil Language Act of 1958, to provide for the 'reasonable use' of Tamil in education, administration and public service examinations in the northern and eastern provinces. The implementation of the Act was, however, minimal.

24. This plan was devised in order to squeeze the Tamils out of higher education. Under this plan, for admission purposes in higher educational institutions, the marks obtained by Tamil students were 'weighted' downward against marks obtained by Sinhalese students.

25. Because the Tamils have always claimed the northern and eastern provinces to be their traditional homeland, based on their constituting a numerical majority in these areas, the Sinhalese-dominated governments of independent Sri Lanka deliberately started the policy of settling large numbers of Sinhalese families in the northern and eastern provinces. The purpose behind this policy was two-fold: first, by changing the population ratio between Tamils and Sinhalese in these areas, the Sri Lankan Government sought to eliminate any legitimate claims the Tamils might have over these areas; and, second, a changed population ratio would have been beneficial to the Sinhalese politicians during elections. With election results reflecting a clear polarization of politics (Sinhalese parties and Tamil parties won clear victories in their respective areas), a changed population ratio would give the Sinhalese greater control of traditional Tamil areas.

26. See p. 425 of P. Venkateshwar Rao, 1988.

27. See p. 67 of Kadian, 1990, and pp. 67–69 and 127–31 of Ostrovsky and Hoy, 1990.

28. For details of Indian covert involvement and the role played by RAW in the training of Tamil guerrillas, see pp. 98–109 of Kadian, 1990.

29. See p. 678 of Premdas and Samarasinghe, 1988.

30. See p. 346 of Rupesinghe, 1988.

31. Peter Chalk, 'The Liberation Tigers of Tamil Eelam Insurgency in Sri Lanka', in Ganguly and Macduff, 2003 (pp. 128–65).

32. Walter Jayawardhana, 'Guns for Drugs', from *Sunday* of Calcutta, 4 November 1990 (p. 82).

33. See *The Economist* in 2001 (p. 38, 10 March) and in 2002 (p. 39, 12 January).

34. 'Pirapaharan Commits to Peace, Self-determination', in *Tamil Guardian* (Online) of 10 April 2002.

35. Ibid.

36. K. Venkataramanan, 'No Assurances on Interim Administration to LTTE: Ranil', in *The Hindustan Times* (Online) of 13 May 2002, and 'Lankan

Government Says It Has No Plans to Repeal POTA', in *The Times of India* (Online) of 9 May 2002.

37. V. S. Sambandan, 'Colombo, LTTE Agree on Federal Structure', in *The Hindu* (Online) of 6 December 2002.

38. Sambandan, 'Peace Negotiators Face Uphill Task', in *The Hindu* (Online) of 10 December 2002.

39. David Rohde, 'Sri Lankan President Declares a State of Emergency', in *The New York Times* (Online) of 6 November 2003.

40. P. K. Balachandran, 'Lankan Government, LTTE Take their Fight to Global Arena', in *The Hindustan Times* (Online) of 18 April 2005.

41. Balachandran, 'LTTE is "Reprehensible", Says US', in *The Hindustan Times* (Online) of 23 January 2006, and 'Canada Labels LTTE a Terrorist Organization', *The Hindu* (Online) of 11 April 2006.

42. 'LTTE Wants EU Monitors to Go, Says Sri Lanka', in *The Hindustan Times* (Online) of 9 August 2006, and 'Sri Lanka "Must Probe" Killings', from BBC News (Online) of 17 May 2005, and 'Sri Lanka Blamed for Aid Deaths', from CNN.com of 30 August 2006.

43. 'Deadly Clashes Flare in Sri Lanka', from BBC News (Online) of 12 August 2006.

Conflicts in South-East Asia: Decolonization, Modernization, Nationalism and State-Building

YOKE-LIAN LEE AND ROGER BUCKLEY

INTRODUCTION

South-East Asia covers an area of approximately 1.6m. sq miles (4.1m. sq km) and is divided into two regions: Indochina and the Malay Archipelago. Indochina consists of Cambodia, Laos, Myanmar (Burma), Thailand and Viet Nam, while Brunei, Indonesia, Malaysia, the Philippines, Singapore and Timor-Leste (East Timor), fall in the region of the Malay Archipelago. The entire region has a population of more than 593m. Few similar-sized regions in the world are as historically complex and as culturally, ethnically, religiously and linguistically diverse as South-East Asia. Although, historically, it has played an important role in world politics and there is every reason to believe that it may continue to do so in the future, since the end of the Indochina Wars (1947–79) it has not, from a global perspective, been particularly visible. It was not until the terrorist attacks of 11 September 2001 (known as 9/11) and the aftermath of the 2002 Bali bombing in Indonesia, when the US authorities in Washington, DC, began to describe South-East Asia as the 'second front' of its 'global war on terror' that the region became once again the focus of world attention. Most of the major recent conflicts in South-East Asia have involved indigenous ethnic and religious regional armed insurgencies rather than inter-state confrontations. The insurgencies are generally the result of a desire for political inclusion on the part of distinct ethnic and religious groups—inclusion in terms of a greater share in socio-economic and political power, regional autonomy or outright independence.

In this chapter we will first outline some general features of South-East Asia. Then we will focus on the profile of individual countries, examining their conflicts and their roots. Our concluding remarks are rather pessimistic: since each South-East Asian state handles religious and ethnic claims differently, a holistic conflict resolution framework cannot be applied to the region.

GENERIC FEATURES OF SOUTH-EAST ASIA

Although the countries of South-East Asia vary significantly from one another, there is one characteristic, with the exception of Thailand, they all share: a post-colonial history since the end of the Second World War and a resultant reconfiguration as nation-states with initial broadly liberal constitutional arrangements. Indonesia proclaimed its independence from the Dutch in 1945; the transfer of sovereignty to the Philippines from US colonial rule occurred in 1946; Burma (now Myanmar) became a sovereign state when British rule ended in 1948; Cambodia and Laos gained independence from France in 1954; Malaysia left British rule in 1957, and Singapore left Malaysia in 1965, to become a republic; Viet Nam proclaimed independence from the French in 1954 and, through the unification of North and South Viet Nam, became the Socialist Republic of Viet Nam in 1976; Brunei regained full sovereignty from the United Kingdom in 1984; finally, East Timor ended its annexation by Indonesia and achieved full independence in 2002.

The entrenching of democratic constitutions as part of the process of state-building in these now independent states has been problematic, not least because there is no history or shared commitment to liberal democracy in the region. More importantly, post-colonial state-building processes require the centralization of national political authority based on ideologies of 'national identity' by the injection of particular norms, values and systems of belief that are often forged through the medium of the state. Such a state-building strategy is often incompatible with the cultural and religious beliefs of minority groups. Among the 'justifications of modernity', Homi Bhabha lists those of 'progress, homogeneity, cultural organicism, the deep nation, the long past'. All these, he suggests, 'rationalize the authoritarian, "normalizing" tendencies within cultures in the name of the national interest or the ethnic prerogative' (Bhabha, 1990—see Bibliography). The wholesale introduction of modernization by the political elites in South-East Asia, in the attempt to achieve rapid socio-economic growth, has been the dominant model for the post-colonial nation-building process in the region. In this way, the articulation of differences, in terms of language, culture, religion and political traditions, has been suppressed by centralized political forces, which have attempted to assimilate the population within a modernizing project to establish a coherent national identity.

The democratization of politics in the region found support mostly among Western-educated nationalist elites, who believed that a programme of modernization, urbanization and the spread of some form of capitalism was the best way of curing social ills and bringing prosperity to all. The expectations underpinning the process of modernization, however, often went unrealized, notwithstanding spectacular economic growth in some countries of the region. The centralization of political and economic power has tended to lead to one particular ethnic political group gaining advantage over other groups in society. The result has usually been the isolation and effective disenfranchisement of sections of the population and, correspondingly, the development of insurgencies and separatist wars. Democratization, in particular, was often short-lived as minorities began to challenge exclusionary state practices and the imported political and economic models. For example, in the late 1950s President Sukarno of Indonesia dissolved the legally elected legislature, in Malaysia the 1969 racial riots led to the suspension of Parliament for 22 months, while President Ferdinand Marcos of the Philippines imposed martial law in 1972. From the mid- to late 1960s, it became increasingly evident that decolonized countries in South-East Asia had to a large extent turned their back on liberal democracy: constitutional democracy gradually gave way to authoritarianism or dictatorship, in which political opposition was restricted. Social and political movements were frequently brutally crushed by military force, opposition leaders detained without trial and human rights abuses, sometimes on an extensive scale, became the norm. In South-East Asia legal and political institutional structures and enforcement have been, and remain, weak, inefficient and corrupt.

Authoritarianism and oppressive or exclusionary state policies that are politically, ethnically and religiously discriminatory against opposition political parties and minorities have created resentment and violent resistance among dissident groups. The relationships between the governing elites and/or military regimes and the minority groups have tended to break down. Ethnic and religious conflicts, secessionism and the demand for self-determination from insurgency forces have resulted, such as: the activism of minority groups in East Timor (now independent and officially known as the Democratic Republic of Timor-Leste), Aceh and Irian Jaya (West Papua) in Indonesia; the upsurge of Islamic separatist violence from the Muslim minority, mainly on Mindanao, lead by the Moro Islamic Liberation Front (MILF) in the southern Philippines; the conflicts between the centralized military Government of Myanmar (Burma) and ethnic minority groups seeking autonomy and/or independence; the Malay-Thai Muslim secessionist movement in southern Thailand; and the threats and acts of violence from extremist Islamists with links to Jemaah Islamiah in Malaysia and Singapore. These are some of the revolutionary or separatist movements that reflect the regional pattern of resistance to dominant political regimes. The rise of these and other movements can be attributed in large measure both to the failure of modernity and to the failure of the nation-states to assimilate diverse minority groups into mainstream political discourse. This violence undoubtedly poses serious threats both to the unity and integrity of the nation-states of South-East Asia and to the region's stability and security as a whole.

The phenomenon of intra-state violence in South-East Asia can therefore be explained partly as the legacy of imperialism and also of existing inter-community conflicts in the form of ethnic insurgencies and secessionism. The centralization of state power based on the idea of the nation-state has almost always involved the totalization of a particular ethnic culture as the dominant national culture, privileging one group over another and displacing any possibility of cultural pluralism.

Since independence the economic performance of the South-East Asian countries has, in general, been particularly impressive. References to the Asian 'tiger' economies during the 1980s and early 1990s indicate how the performance of certain South-East Asian countries caught the imagination of outside observers, at least until the 1997–98 Asian economic collapse, when inflation and pressure upon domestic currencies saw growth rates tumble across the region. From the 1970s the move by foreign investors to take advantage of lower labour costs and other incentives in the region generally acted as a boost to growth rates. This, combined with government policies to promote openness of the economy, trade and investment, led to the industrial structures of many of the countries in the region changing very rapidly as manufacturing rose as a percentage of output.

However, it has not been all positive news. Countries such as Malaysia, Indonesia and the Philippines have been affected by internal conflicts and political instability. This has contributed to a far more erratic economic performance in both Indonesia and the Philippines. A dependency upon the export of primary commodities, particularly in the early post-independence years, saw countries such as Malaysia affected by changes in the international markets in the mid-1980s. Economic mismanagement in the Philippines during the 1970s and 1980s, plus the hyperinflation in Indonesia in the 1960s, were further factors contributing to poorer performances, while Myanmar experienced lower economic growth rates as a result of US-led sanctions and the cessation of most international development assistance.

Strong performances across South-East Asia have led to improvements in average living standards. A relevant measure here is the UN Development Programme's human development index (HDI). The HDI is a composite indicator measuring longevity, knowledge and a decent standard of living and has seen steady increases since independence in all South-East Asian countries for which figures are available. However, the benefits of economic growth and human development improvements have been unevenly distributed and have not been felt by all the poorest people in many of these countries. Where the benefits have not been shared, for instance between ethnic or religious groups or between rural and urban populations, this has fuelled discontent and promoted political instability.

INDIVIDUAL PORTRAITS

Myanmar (Burma)

Myanmar is one of the most ethnically diverse countries in South-East Asia. Since decolonization its politics have been marked by widespread internal conflicts between the Government and opposition political groups and ethnic minority groups such as the Karen and the Shan. The war between the military regime and armed ethnic groups has continued for almost 60 years.

The war on the Karen ethnic minority in Toungoo District has been especially brutal. Rather than a case of counter-insurgency, as claimed by the military junta, Karen minorities have been faced with the Government's widespread systematic policy of 'ethnic cleansing' by forcible relocation (an estimated 650,000 internally displaced persons in eastern Myanmar, most from the large Karen minority, are now living over the Thai border in camps), burning and looting of Karen villages, torture, rape and extra-judicial killings, and conscription of labour. Myanmar is ruled by a strong military dictatorship and dominated by corrupt military personnel with little sense of how to run a country. The most basic grievance of ethnic minority and opposition groups, with the exception of the Karen National Union (KNU), which wants a separate Karen State, is not about outright independence. Rather it is primarily about their lack of political participation and influence on governmental policy formulation and decision-making. Despite the fact that ethnic minorities constitute 35% of the country's approximately 52m. people, their position has been seen as a relatively minor issue, rather than as an integrated part of Burma's history and politics. The 'Burmanization' policies of the Government not only serve to marginalize the cultural identity of minorities, but also to diminish their social, economic and cultural autonomy. What these groups seek to secure is a greater sense of local autonomy and administrative authority providing them, in turn, with the freedom to practice their own language, culture and religion and to a greater share of economic benefits.

The minorities seek to replace the Union of Myanmar with a new and more equal institutional, and federal, framework, which fosters pluralistic accommodation and negotiation among diverse communities. Since 1988 and the subsequent cease-fire agreements between the Government and most of the armed ethnic minority groups, they have embarked on a long process of political negotiations about ' weapons for peace', with particular focus on development and social welfare reforms. In 1988 the ruling leader, Gen. Ne Win, was brought down by widespread pro-democracy demonstrations. Aung San Suu Kyi had returned to Myanmar in 1988, becoming caught up in the pro-democracy protests and forming the League for Democracy party. She was placed under house arrest in the following year. Her National League for Democracy Party won a landslide victory (83% of the votes) in the May 1990 general election. However, the military junta refused to recognize Aung San Suu Kyi's mandate and she remains under house arrest, despite international objections. The May election prompted the military regime to launch military operations against the Pao, Shan and Kachin minorities, living in the north-east region of the country, in which hundreds of villages were destroyed and thousands fled. Fighting also started in the north-west region of Rakhine, where approximately 250,000 Muslims were forced to leave the region to seek refuge. Cease-fires in Myanmar have meant a reduction in the violence against ethnic minorities by the Government, but it has not meant that basic human rights are essentially being observed by the military regime. Freedom of speech and information are severely restricted. In fact, Myanmar operates the most restrictive form of control over access to the internet in the world. Political dissidents and their families are routinely and violently targeted and intimidated.

Cambodia

The modern post-colonial history of Cambodia has been marked by years of armed opposition, factionalism and civil war. The horrific bombing raids by the US military forces during the Viet Nam War in the 1960s and a *coup d'état* launched by Gen. Lon Nol on 18 March 1970, which succeeded in deposing

Prince Norodom Sihanouk, have been followed by years of manoeuvring by various political factions seeking to take control of the country. For four years from 1975 the country was ruled by the notorious Khmers Rouges regime headed by Pol Pot, during which time 1.5m. Cambodians were brutally murdered. In 1978 the Vietnamese army invaded Cambodia (then known as Kampuchea), defeating the Khmers Rouges, and continued to occupy the country for the next 10 years, until its withdrawal in 1989. Cambodia, thus, experienced well over 30 years of political trauma leading to the destruction of its social, economic and political structures. Relative peace began to return in 1991 under the Paris Peace Accords, in which the notion of human rights and a pluralistic liberal-democratic system of rule were introduced to facilitate the rebuilding of the country. Following the introduction of democracy, a relatively successful post-war election was held in 1993 under the auspices of the UN Transitional Authority in Cambodia. A short-lived post-war democratic coalition Government was formed in October 1993. Politically, Cambodia has enjoyed relative peace and stability, with democracy, elections, constitutional forms of rule and law and respect for human rights having been introduced as parts of the post-war political system.

However, there remain very considerable challenges to be tackled: democracy is fragile; there appears to be a lack of commitment to undertake democratic reform in the governance system; and the rule of law remains open to political interference as well as corruption. The current Prime Minister, Hun Sen, from the Cambodian People's Party, has increasingly taken Cambodia back to the era of authoritarianism, with greater centralization of political power, governmental suppression and the jailing of members of opposition groups. Human rights violations are increasing and ethnic minorities continue to endure repression and harassment from the authorities. For example, the Vietnamese minority's citizen status is being stripped from them and they face forceful eviction from their 'floating village' along the Bassac river. Those who dare to oppose the authorities often 'disappear', being arrested, deported or sent to prison, where torture is routine. The police, the military, local authorities and powerful business elites are evicting the indigenous peoples in north-east Cambodia from their land through forcible confiscation. There is widespread disregard of Cambodia's Land Law and the deployment of violence, intimidation and harassment are some of the illegal land-grabbing strategies deployed by often-corrupt government officials who have allowed the land conflicts to continue. In addition, the judicial system is open to political interference, with the law frequently deployed to criminalize or intimidate dissidents. Centralization of political power, the lack of pluralistic political voices and the failure to seek public consultation, as well as the lack of transparency in legal and governmental institutions and procedures, has contributed to the isolation and disenfranchisement of individuals and groups. The Government's failure to forge positive reforms in addressing the pressing political and social problems in Cambodia has inevitably contributed to high levels of dissatisfaction. What we see today in Cambodia is a society increasingly plagued with political intolerance, corruption and lawlessness.

Timor-Leste (East Timor)

Following the decolonization of East Timor from Portugal in 1975, it was invaded by Indonesia in the following year and forcibly annexed, to become a province of Indonesia until 1999. During this time Indonesia ruled Timor brutally, with the Indonesian army committing gross human rights violations to the extent that it can be described as 'ethnic cleansing'. According to recent reports, about 200,000 people were killed during Indonesia's occupation. Mark Rolls (2003—pp. 168 and 173) suggests that, 'the origins of the ethno-nationalism that fuelled the conflict in East Timor from 1975–99 lay in the experience of European coloniza- tion', adding that the imposition of colonial rule by Indonesia failed to integrate East Timor not only because the 'people of East Timor ... [do] not share the historical experiences that underpin the ideology of modern Indonesia national- ism', but also because of cultural, linguistic and religious differences. The Armed Forces of the Liberation of East Timor (FALINTIL) strongly opposed the Indonesian military rule through armed resistance. In August 1999 East Timor overwhelmingly voted for independence from Indonesia. Violence broke out, with pro-Indonesia militia groups attacking pro-independence groups. Thousands of East Timorese became refugees and fled to West Timor (part of Indonesia). Despite protest from the UN, Indonesia continued to assert its authority over East Timor and claimed that the conflict was essentially a domestic affair. Following the declaration of martial law, approximately 4,000 military personnel were sent into East Timor. Faced with political pressure and the threat of economic sanctions from the USA, Indonesia eventually agreed to let UN forces, mostly drawn from regional states such as Australia, New Zealand, Thailand and the Philippines, restore peace and order in East Timor. The Indonesian Government in Jakarta announced that it would accept the outcome of the East Timor referendum. The UN Transitional Administration in East Timor was established on 25 October 1999 to help with the task of government during the transition period.

After 25 years of military rule by the Indonesian Government over its territory, the Democratic Republic of Timor-Leste eventually became the world's newest sovereign state on 20 May 2002, with Xanana Gusmão as President and Mari Bim Amude Alkatiri as the first Prime Minister. Violent conflict in this newly independent country remains a distinct possibility, as it still faces many problems. One of the major challenges is to gain reconciliation among the many rival factions. Since late April 2006 East Timor has again been in political crisis. Conflicts erupted within the local security forces when Alkatiri sacked 600 soldiers, one-third of the military forces, on what was thought to be an ethnically motivated basis. Clashes broke out between rebel soldiers and troops that were loyal to Alkatiri. Conflicts between political opponents and rivalries between civilian gangs further ignited the crisis. As a result, more than 150,000 people have been made refugees, and between April and June 30 people were reported killed. The violence severely crippled the fragile Timorese Government; Prime Minister Alkatiri resigned on 26 June, following weeks of political unrest in the country, and José Ramos Horta was appointed as the interim Prime Minister by

President Gusmão on 8 July. On 25 August the UN Security Council established the UN Integrated Mission in Timor-Leste, a new non-military peacekeeping support mission to assist the country in restoring and maintaining peace and order. Its mandate has been to support the post-conflict Government in consolidating stability, enhancing a culture of democratic governance and facilitating political dialogue among Timorese stakeholders in their efforts to bring about a process of national reconciliation. Troops from Australia, Malaysia, New Zealand and Portugal have been deployed as peacekeepers and a general election was due to be held in 2007. Meanwhile, the Timorese interim Government is working with UN personnel to address the social, economic and political problems of the country.

Malaysia

In Malaysia racial tension between the Chinese and the Malays led to the race riots of 13 May 1969 and a 22-month suspension of parliament. The main focus for Malaysia, especially under Prime Minister Mahathir Mohamad, was to forge and strengthen 'Muslim' social, political and economic modernization schemes through the New Economic Policy (NEP). The NEP is an affirmative action policy to help the ethnic Malays (Bumiputra). The goal has been to construct a Malay-Muslim cultural identity and maintain Malay political domination. State economic and education systems were restructured on racial lines to give pre-ferential treatment to the ethnic Malays, specific government-funded economic projects were created to bolster the income level of Malays and higher education placements and scholarships were also largely allocated to Malays. The declared aim of the NEP was to enable the Malays to 'catch up' with the non-Malays, especially the Chinese business and Indian professional classes. The NEP undoubtedly helped to heighten racial tensions further in Malaysia—non-Malays were acutely aware that the NEP programme was essentially a state-sanctioned policy designed to produce inequality. There is a sense that the Muslim Malays are the 'proper' citizens, privileged by the state, and non-Muslims largely see themselves as second-class citizens.

Although there has not been any recurrence of racial riots since 1969, there have been intra-Muslim conflicts. The NEP initiatives have undoubtedly improved the life of some sectors of society, and this has led to the emergence of an urban, middle-to-upper-middle class 'modern' Malay. Meanwhile the rural Malays remain poor, in some cases even worse off than they were before. The Government and national elites' commitment to modernity and high levels of state intervention in social, economic and development matters has also created opposition and resistance among Malaysia's radical Islamists. Economic devel-opment based on rapid political and economic modernization has created the situation in which Malaysia's Islamic resurgence has become 'embroiled in struggles with different groups of national elites concerning the rule, scope, and force of Islam in Malaysia's modernity project' (p. 5, in Peletz, 2002). Islamic political groups, such as the opposition Islamic Party of Malaysia (PAS), assert that the Government's 'Islamicization' of society has not gone far enough in that it has failed to create an Islamic state governed by *Shari'a* law. Islamic military insurgency, with alleged links to organizations such as Jemaah Islamiah and Kampulan Mujihedduin Malaysia, could be viewed as a violent political struggle aimed at overthrowing the Government in order to undo the state's political, cultural and economic modernization programmes.

Although there are diverse Islamist groups in Malaysia, these movements all share a broadly similar ideology seeking to create an Islamic state. The intensification of religio-political conflicts between the moderate Muslim Government and radical Islamist movements has led the state to rely excessively on the Internal Security Act (ISA) as a counter-terror measure. The ISA is used to deny suspects' civil liberties, including the constitutional right to due process. Some would argue that the ISA has served as the tool of political oppression, as it gives the police the power of arrest and indefinitely detain political opponents and terrorist suspects without evidence or trial. Since 9/11 Islamic conflicts have been simplistically labelled as 'terrorist conflicts' and, in the name of the 'war on terror', it has been suggested that suspects have been subjected to torture and inhumane treatment during interrogation.

Philippines

The Philippines' experience has been one of intermittent conflict. This can be traced from its struggle against Spanish colonization in the 19th century to resistance against Japanese occupation in the 1940s during the Pacific War, before becoming an independent state free from the USA in 1946, with the later 'people's power' struggle that defeated President Ferdinand Marcos in the 1980s. However, the longest internal conflict in the Philippines has been the armed rebellion against the Government by the separatist Islamic factions. The Moro National Liberation Front (MNLF) began the struggle, but more militant groups, such as the MILF and the Abu Sayyaf Islamic group (which split from the MNLF in 1977 and 1991, respectively), have intensified their opposition to the state. The Sayyaf group is the most radical, with alleged links to Osama bin Laden's al-Qaida network, and is said to be responsible for a series of the most recent bombings, killings and kidnappings of Western foreigners (and Philippines nationals) in exchange for substantial ransoms. The aim of these groups is primarily to establish an independent Islamic state in Mindanao and the Sulu islands in the southern Philippines, a region that was colonized by the Spanish and later by the American and the Philippines administrations.

The emergence of the Moro separatist movement can be attributed, to some extent, to 'American colonialism', whereby the US authorities created Moro province in 1906 as part of the modern state system, although it is also a product of the wider resurgence of political Islam. The centralization of power in the Manila-based administration became the mode for governing the Moro Muslims. In April 1940 the US Government abolished the sultanate. The emergence of the MNLF can be traced back to the late 1960s: the struggle for a separate Moro state for Muslims; an alleged massacre of Muslims in Manila Bay; and a demographic change in the Moro population, which contributed to increasing alienation among the Muslims. After negotiations began in 1974, the MNLF signed the cease-fire Tripolis Agreement with the Marcos Government in 1976. The agreement broke down later and fighting continued. In 1996 the MNLF made another peace agreement with the Government, which created the Autonomous Region in Muslim Mindanao (ARMM). That, in turn, eventually ended the MNLF's 25 years of armed struggle for autonomy. However, the breakaway MILF refused to accept the Government's semi-autonomy offer, mainly because its principal objective was to create an independent Islamic state. In 2001 the MILF signed a peace agreement with President Gloria Arroya, but the violence was resumed soon afterwards and the situation continued to worsen as the MILF launched more bomb attacks and kidnapping of foreigners. In March 2003 Davao City airport was bombed, killing 21 people. Again, in January 2005 the MILF attacked the Philippines army in Maguindanao, and 23 people were killed. Clashes erupted between 28 June and 6 July between the MILF and armed civilian volunteers (CVOs) under Maguindanao Governor Andal Ampatuan, the latter backed by the military forces. The conflict started after Governor Ampatuan accused the MILF of perpetrating a car bomb attack in June in which five of his entourage were killed. The MILF denied the allegation, but Ampatuan sent police and CVOs to arrest those MILF Islamists who had allegedly taken part in the attack. Four thousand families were reported displaced by the fighting. Since 2002, as part of the 'war against terror', US troops have joined with the Philippines military forces against the Abu Sayyaf rebels. Although a cease-fire agreement between the MILF and the Government in Manila was signed on 10–11 July 2006, which ended the fighting, without a comprehensive implementation strategy and the mobilization of ethno-religious popular support, the conflict is by no means resolved.

Indonesia

After bitter fighting to gain independence from the Netherlands, Indonesia became a sovereign state in 1949. As in most decolonized states in South-East Asia, a liberal democratic system was introduced. However, internal conflicts and political unrest became the norm, though disputes concerned the reconfiguration of the Indonesian nation-state rather than the promotion of direct separatism. The management of these internal conflicts was mainly exercised through emergency powers. In 1965 Suharto's New Order was an effort to build an ethno-nationalist Javanese identity based on the idea of a single 'organic' Indonesian nation and economic modernity. The expectation was that varying traditions, 'ethnic loyalties and so-called primordial sentiments would fade, and new loyalties to the modern nation of Indonesia would become the central aspect of every citizen's identity' (p. 323, in Berger, 1997). The New Order involved the construction of a centralized and authoritarian military regime as a stabilizing force to control social and political conflicts. It enabled Indonesia to industrialize rapidly, thereby leading to higher levels of economic growth. Yet the New Order was not without its drawbacks, politically, socially, culturally and economically. It gave rise to considerable discontent, resentment and unrest among intra-political elites, to contention among the rural poor over land disputes and to the soured relationship between the centralized governmental trade union organizations. These political difficulties triggered the student unrest that paved the way for Suharto's downfall in 1998 and later led to secessionist politics in East Timor, Aceh and Irian Jaya. Suharto's centralized, authoritarian (military) regime was organized along socio-ethnic lines (Javanese) and the Government was deeply immersed in institutio-nalized corruption and nepotism. Repressive state agencies used indiscriminate violence to suppress rebellions, and Javanese-led political elites heavily influ-enced the legal system.

Indonesia continues to face a challenging series of insurgency issues. The use of military force to combat threats from provinces such as Aceh and Papua leads inevitably to the risk of uncontrolled violence and allegations of major human rights abuses. Successive Indonesian governments have feared that the loss of East Timor might prompt yet more attempts to dismember the nation and that influential powers overseas are encouraging separatist movements. Despite post-Suharto moves towards greater democratization, there are limits to the extent to which any government in Jakarta can be expected to agree to separatist demands. The difficulty of gaining effective domestic compromises suggests that measures to contain ethnic and religious violence would be difficult. Indonesia's national slogan may be 'Unity in Diversity', but achieving any such political reality with-out bloodshed will be a major test.

Thailand

Separatist conflict has plagued Thailand's Muslim-dominated, Malay-speaking southern provinces of Narathiwat, Yala and Pattani. These southern Thai pro-vinces were originally know as the Pattani sultanate, an independent Muslim kingdom that was annexed by Thailand in 1902 and later divided into the current three Muslim provinces. The causes of Islamic resurgence could be attributed to the Thai Government's official cultural and social assimilation policies to create an ethnically homogeneous national identity. The southern Malay-Muslims feel that their own sense of history, culture and language has not been recognized and acknowledged by the state. For the past two generations Thailand has experi-enced high economic growth, and this has undoubtedly raised the living standard of the Thai population. However, despite the growth in manufacturing, agricul-tural exports, tourism and the financial market, southern Muslims have enjoyed limited benefit. They are by far the most poor and economically marginalized sector of the population. The southern Muslim separatist movement is not new and can be traced back to the 1960s, when the National Liberation Front of Pattani and Barisan Revolusi National were formed to fight against the Thai Government. In the 1970s and 1980s the Pattani United Liberation Organization (PULO) was established in order to carry out war against the Thai administration.

The principal aim of these Islamic groups has been to establish their own sense of Malay Islamic identity and to reclaim the Pattani Muslim kingdom as a sovereign entity.

However, by the 1980s Islamist movements had lost some of their momentum and it was not until recent years that there was a resurgence of ethnic Islamism in southern Thailand. This revival of activism derived largely from the forging of links with the regional radical Islamic group Jemaah Islamiah, thus becoming more active and dangerous. From the beginning of 2004 until the middle of 2006 the Government's excessive use of force against the armed Islamist insurgents and demonstrators caused the loss of nearly 1,300 lives. On 25 October 2004 nearly 2,000 Muslim demonstrators at Takbai in Narathiwat were detained. Most were then crammed into overcrowded army trucks by Thai security forces and taken to detention centres. Upon arrival, 80 Muslim protesters were found to have died of suffocation. The excessive use of police force fuelled further violence. Unrest erupted again in July 2005, forcing the Prime Minister, Thaksin Shinawatra, to declare a three-month state of emergency in the southern provinces, subject to renewal.

Thaksin Shinawatra, however, was ousted in a bloodless coup following months of popular protests and military disquiet over the allegation that Thaksin was trying to interfere with the internal affairs of the armed forces. The coup, which took place while Thaksin was in New York (USA) on 19 September 2006, was led by army commander Gen. Sonthi Boonyaratglin, who seized power and revoked the 1997 Constitution. He asserted that a temporary constitution would be speedy enacted and a general election held in October 2007. It was reported that the Thai military had declared martial law, banned political assemblies of more than five people and arrested political activists who protested the coup. The reasons for the deposition of Thaksin concern allegations of corruption, abuse of power and the failure to respond effectively to the Islamist separatist insurgency in southern Thailand. The 19 September coup marked the 18th successful military coup in Thailand's 74 years of constitutional monarchical rule. According to correspondents in Bangkok, the Thai capital, on 5 October 2006 leaders of the Muslim rebel groups PULO and Bersatu made contact through Malaysian high officials, proposing peace negotiations. Gen. Sonthi, himself a Muslim, had proposed before the coup to enter into negotiations with the Muslim separatist groups. The interim premier, Gen. Surayud Chulanont, indicated that resolving the Islamist armed conflict would be his Government's top priority.

Singapore

The politics of the Republic of Singapore since the island state's independence from the Federation of Malaysia in 1965 have been dominated by the People's Action Party, initially under the leadership of Prime Minister Lee Kuan Yew. Lee stood down as Prime Minister in 1990, to become Senior Minister, and was succeeded by Goh Chok Tong, who served until Lee Hsien Loong, the eldest son of Lee Kuan Yew, became Prime Minister in 2004. Of all the countries of

South-East Asia, it is Singapore that has achieved the fastest rate of economic growth, despite its small size and lack of natural resources. This has led to significant increases in the standard of living of Singaporeans. However, it could be argued that this level of economic success would not have been possible without the creation of an authoritarian democracy in Singapore. Owing to Singapore's size and location, the ruling party has justified such authoritarianism, as the party sees the island state in a position of perpetual vulnerability in the Muslim world of South-East Asia, with Malaysia to the north, Indonesia to the south and Muslim groups in the Philippines. Such fears mean that Singapore has committed as much as 30% of state expenditure to its defence establishment. However, it is the drive for economic improvement that is regularly used by the ruling elite to justify the lack of liberal democratic principles in the governance of Singapore. As a result, political opposition exists in the form of 20 registered political parties, but they play only a limited role in the political process, to the extent that in the general election of 2006 the People's Action Party won 82 of the 84 parliamentary seats. In addition, neither political opposition nor dissent is allowed free expression through the state-controlled media and all trade unions and civil organizations are regulated by the state. Where there have been instances of such dissent being seen as a threat to national security, the state has not been slow to use organs such as the Internal Security Act to create a climate of intimidation to silence its actual and potential critics.

Singapore's fears of the activities of its Muslim neighbours have increased in recent years. Regional terrorist attacks, such as the Bali bombing of 2002, the bombing outside the Australian embassy in Jakarta in 2004 and the second Bali bombing in 2005, all with links to Jemaah Islamiah, contributed to a series of counter-terrorist measures being introduced in Singapore. In addition, specific incidents have occurred within Singapore, such as the discovery in December 2001 of a plot to bomb foreign embassies and other installations on the island. As a result, more than 30 members of Jemaah Islamiah were arrested under the Internal Security Act. Then, in August 2002, more than 20 members of the same organization were arrested in Singapore while similar arrests were being made throughout South-East Asia. Ultimately, it is the imperative of continued economic progress that is central to Singapore's future and, in order to achieve this, the ruling party argues for the means to defend national security and ensure political stability. As a result, Singapore's authoritarian system will be maintained and its position, in the words of Lee Kuan Yew, as a state but not a nation, will continue.

Laos

Laos is one of the few countries in the world that is still ruled by a Communist Government, the Lao People's Revolutionary Party. The Communist regime came to power when it overthrew the monarchy in 1975. During the last general election, that of 10 May 2006, the ruling party won 113 of 115 seats. Laos endured years of isolation, but increasingly opened up to the world community during the 1990s and became a member of the Association of South-East Asia Nations (ASEAN) in 1992. In spite of economic reforms, such as reintroducing free markets and private enterprise from the late 1980s, and an impressive average annual growth of 7%, Laos is still one of the poorest countries in the world, relying heavily on international aid. The Secret War that was fought in Laos during the second Indochina War from 1962 to 1975 (when North Viet Nam established the Ho Chi Minh trail to infiltrate South Viet Nam) severely destabilized the country and, ultimately, this led to civil war and a number of *coups d'état*. Like in most South-East Asian countries, the post-1975 Laos Communist regime adopted the modernization project of building a legitimate national identity based on the cultural preferences of the political elites, and it reclassified its ethnic groups in accordance with official criteria. Although Laos has the most ethnic minorities in South-East Asia, there are only 49 officially recognized groups. Today, Laos is a relatively peaceful and unified country, and the human rights situation has improved. However, the decades-old conflict with the Hmong radical rebels has intensified and, in 2004, there were several attacks against the Government. On 6 April 2006 it was reported that Lao government forces had carried out an armed military massacre of at least 26 ethnic Hmong, mostly women and children, who were hiding in the jungle from the military. Ill treatment of Hmong political prisoners and religious activists by the gerontocratic Lao Government continues. Political protest and media freedom are generally suppressed.

Viet Nam

From 1945 to 1979 Viet Nam was subject to three successive Indochinese wars. Generations of French colonization, combined with imperial Japan's military occupation during the Pacific War, and the subsequent Viet Nam War inevitably led the country into factional strife. The USA's intervention, part of the Cold War global contest between Western liberalism and Soviet Communism, was especially tragic. Although French rule had come to an end with the 1954 Geneva Agreement on Indochina, Viet Nam remained temporarily divided into North and South Viet Nam at the 17th parallel (latitude 17°N), with the hope of unification pending on free elections supervised by international bodies. The failure to implement the Geneva Agreements in Viet Nam over unification fuelled further hostility, which led to years of conflict until the end of the Viet Nam War in 1975. During this period the country's political, social and economic structures collapsed. Approximately 4m. Vietnamese lost their lives and vast devastation occurred throughout the countryside as the USA launched massive bombing campaigns in an attempt to 'smoke out' the Communist guerrillas embedded in the forests. Approximately 8m. metric tons of bombs were dropped on Indochinese soil, to defoliate Viet Nam's jungles, and an estimated 70m. litres of Agent Orange poured over 1.7m. hectares of Vietnamese jungle; an estimated 20% of South Viet Nam's forests were chemically damaged.

The Socialist Republic of Viet Nam was formally established on 2 July 1976 with the reunification of North and South Viet Nam. Viet Nam is a single-party state resting on the ideological framework of a socialist republic. The Communist Party of Viet Nam (CPV) has authority over all major state policies, including their determination and enforcement. In April 1992 a new Constitution further reaffirmed the centralization of power in the hands of the CPV in political and socio-economic affairs. Economically, the country has adopted market reform models, but politically, there are, however, no free elections, as the CPV chooses the candidates to be elected to the National Assembly and local people's councils. The next elections are to be held in 2007. Legal and political opposition to the regime has been crushed; freedom of the media is severely restricted and laws punish internet users suspected of harming national security or causing social disorder. High levels of corruption are widespread in Viet Nam. Civil and political rights are limited. The Vietnamese Government is opposed to freedom of expression, although freedom of religion is generally permitted, provided it is an officially recognized religion in accordance with the legal framework of the 2004 Ordinance on Belief and Religion. Believers of non-recognized religious groups are subjected to governmental crackdowns, particularly those Protestant and Roman Catholic Montagnards who live in the Central Highlands. The Montagnards are distinct tribal peoples who do not share Viet Nam's dominant culture, nor are they given the political opportunity to participate in state institutions. The CPV has long had a history of suspicion of the Montagnards, who seek independence from Vietnamese rule. The 1958 uprising of the Montagnards against the Vietnamese forces, and the recruitment of 40,000 highlanders by the US military to fight against the Communists during the Viet Nam War, have contributed to the reprisals against them by the Communist regime. The Montagnards are persecuted peoples and those who take part in peaceful protests concerning issues such as political representation, land owner-ship and access to education face possible imprisonment. Arbitrary arrest and torture is routinely deployed against dissidents. Notwithstanding, there is a general sense among the majority of the Vietnamese people that they are now enjoying a greater degree of social, religious and economic freedom than ever before.

PROSPECTS FOR CONFLICT RESOLUTION?

To adopt a universally preconceived conflict resolution framework for South-East Asia is likely to fail, since each state handles religious and ethnic claims differently. Much depends on each country's legal and political framework. The emergence of rebel sub-groups opposed to particular states often stems from localized historical grievances compounded by coercion. Any prospect of conflict resolution may well depend on whether governments have understood and responded to the root political, economic, social and religious causes of the conflicts in question. Any peacemaking would require state recognition and accommodation of the rights of minority groups and a willingness to adopt steps to build pluralistic societies where cultural, religious and ethnic differences were both accepted and nurtured. In this context, the involvement of outside powers, such as the USA, Japan, China and Australia, must be less imperial and more accommodating to the expressed needs of the regional parties in conflict. If outside intervention appears imperialistic, then the prospect of external mediation for the local problems will be greatly reduced. True, South-East Asia is enjoying an unprecedented era of peace and prosperity. Memories of colonization, military occupations and the first heady days of decolonization and independence still persist, although they are not as strong as they used to be. As a result of generally favourable economic development, aided by American, Chinese and Japanese capitalism, the region has seen the emergence of a larger and more politically conscious middle class, which identifies closely with many of the goals of the ruling factions. The continuation of such economic growth, often through state-directed and authoritarian policies, seems to bode well for the region.

The enhancement of a growing regional identity is the continuation of practices that began in the Cold War era, when the birth of ASEAN in Bangkok on 8 August 1967 prompted the process of cautious integration among previously antagonistic or aloof states. ASEAN today has evolved to incorporate all states in the region by working through quiet diplomacy to establish closer relationships that may defuse issues that threaten the region's general stability. Links have also been created through wider, albeit looser, institutions in the ASEAN (or Asian) Regional Forum, to reckon with a post-Cold War international order. Attempts to promote confidence-building measures and to encourage states to think more broadly of wider responsibilities will continue.

While national sensitivities may preclude closer co-operation in some areas, it ought to be possible to promote a regional human rights order in the next decades, as well as paying greater attention to such issues as terrorism, drugs smuggling, piracy and human trafficking. In all instances there is a common interest in tackling non-traditional security questions through enhanced exchanges of infor-mation, border liaison and regular meetings of military and civilian elites. Successes in these fields will demonstrate the degree to which South-East Asia is able gradually to create a shared identity and is prepared to think regionally.

The greatest hurdles facing the states of South-East Asia today are internal. By contrast, the challenges that the first generation of leaders faced concerned the creation of a shared zone of stability and security. By 1987 the ASEAN 'experiment' had succeeded to the extent that it was increasingly being forgotten that 'ours was once an area of turmoil, of mutual suspicion, of mutual hostility, of mutual dislike, even of mutual disinterest' (according to a 1987 ASEAN report, *ASEAN: The Way Forward*). A decade later and the ASEAN Standing Commit-tee's annual report for 1997–98 was able to boast of a concert of South-East Asian states acting through regular summit meetings and eager to extend its contacts to China and Japan.

What has yet to be achieved, however, is the goal of a 'community of caring societies'. The domestic difficulties facing the nation-states remain substantial. A coercive state policy that bans or criminalizes ethnic and religious discourse can only make matters worse. To employ violence against violence will fail to create stability or to resolve deep-rooted ethnic and religious conflicts. It is far too easy for the national governments to ascribe the root of the conflicts to ethnic and religious separatism. In many cases, conflict resolution means arbitrary arrests, military/police brutality and persistent violence, yet ethnic and religious conflicts are usually the results of the failure of the state to provide for fundamental human freedoms and material wants. The need to recognize the distinctive rights and identities of minorities, and to offer political representation and economic equality to such groups, would be a first step towards conflict resolution and thereby contribute to greater stability in South-East Asia. Anything less deserves to fail.

The Arab-Israeli Conflict

RORY MILLER

BIRTH OF A CONFLICT AND THE BIRTH OF ISRAEL

The origins of Arab–Israeli conflict can be traced back to the 1890s and the formal establishment of the Zionist Organization, the Jewish national movement seeking the return of the Jews to their ancient homeland in Palestine, a geographic area that includes both present-day Israel and Jordan. Both of these territories had been part of the vast possessions of the Ottoman Empire since 1516. From this time until the end of the First World War Palestine did not exist as a unified geopolitical entity. It was divided between the Ottoman province of Beirut in the north and the district of Jerusalem in the south. The Muslim inhabitants of Palestine, the vast majority of the population, were subjects of the Ottoman sultan-caliph, the religious and temporal head of the Islamic world, and local governors were appointed by the Ottoman court in Constantinople (now Istanbul in Turkey).

There had been a dwindling Jewish presence in Palestine since biblical times, when part of this area comprised a Jewish state. By 1914, primarily due to immigration from Eastern Europe, Palestine's Jewish community (commonly known as the Yishuv) numbered 70,000–85,000, about 12% of the total population. Following the Ottoman decision to enter the First World War on the side of Germany in November 1914, the Zionists looked to the United Kingdom, the leading anti-Ottoman power in the Middle East, for political support (pp. 11–13, in Friedman, 1992—see Bibliography).

In November 1917 the British Government issued the Balfour Declaration. Named after Arthur Balfour (later Earl Balfour), the British foreign minister, it was issued in the form of a letter to Lord Rothschild, the leading figure in British Jewry. The Balfour Declaration called for the 'establishment in Palestine of a national home for the Jewish people' and pledged that the United Kingdom would 'use its best endeavours to facilitate the achievement of this object, it being clearly understood that nothing shall be done which may prejudice the civil and religious rights of existing non-Jewish communities in Palestine' (pp. 291–92, in Vital, 1987).

The following month the British army under the command of Gen. Sir Edmund Allenby captured the holy city of Jerusalem. The end of 1917 marked the beginning of almost three decades of British rule in Palestine, which was formalized in July 1922, when the League of Nations approved a British Mandate for this former Ottoman possession. The key clauses of the Balfour Declaration were incorporated into the Mandate. This allowed the Yishuv to develop extensive educational and welfare services and to acquire large parcels of land from Arab landowners, absentee landlords and peasants and to develop rapidly the construction, industrial and agricultural sectors in a period of rising Jewish immigration. A 1922 census estimated the total population of Palestine at 752,048, of which Muslims numbered 589,177 (78% of the population) and Jews 83,790 (11%). By 1947 the Jews comprised 31% of a total population of over 1.7 million. This rise in the Jewish population was due largely to an influx of Jews escaping Nazi persecution in Europe. However, Palestine's Arabs viewed Jewish immigration into the country as a political rather than a humanitarian issue. In 1921, 1923, 1930 and 1936 Palestinian Arab delegations visited the British capital of London to express opposition to Zionism and to continued immigration (p. 241, in Tannous, 1988).

International diplomacy aside, the primary instrument available to the Arabs of Palestine in opposing Zionist aspirations was civil unrest, violence and guerrilla warfare. In April 1920 Arab nationalists in Palestine sought to thwart Zionist activity (and to rally support for incorporating the country into the short-lived Syrian kingdom headed by King Faisal ibn Hussein) by carrying out attacks on Jews in Jerusalem. Similar attacks occurred in 1921 and 1929, and Arab opposition intensified in 1936–39, when a general Palestinian uprising against the British, known as the Arab Revolt, claimed hundreds of lives (pp. 111–14, in Sherman, 1997).

The Arab world vehemently opposed the July 1937 recommendation of a British Royal Commission on Palestine (the Peel Commission) that the Mandate be abrogated and that Palestine be partitioned into Jewish and Arab states, with a permanent mandate for Jerusalem. In November 1938 partition was rejected as unworkable and, instead, in May 1939 the British Government introduced the Palestine White Paper. This document severely restricted Jewish immigration into Palestine, to a maximum of 75,000 between April 1939 and 1944, after which time 'no further Jewish immigration will be permitted unless the Arabs of Palestine are prepared to acquiesce in it'. The White Paper led to a severe breakdown in relations between the British and the Zionists, who viewed this policy as a subversion of the Jewish national revival in Palestine and the abandonment of European Jewry to their Nazi persecutor. In May 1942 the mainstream Zionist leadership for the first time officially endorsed the call for the creation of a Jewish state in Palestine, as opposed to a Jewish National Home. At the same time extremist Jewish groups like the Irgun Zvai Le'umi and the Stern Gang increased their attacks against British targets in Palestine, the most notorious of which was the 1946 bombing of the British military headquarters at the King David Hotel in Jerusalem, which killed 91 people (p. 103, in Jones, 1986).

In 1947, in the face of Jewish insurgency and Arab hostility, the United Kingdom turned the Palestine problem over to the UN. On 29 November 1947 the UN General Assembly passed Resolution 181(II) calling for the partition of Palestine into two independent states—one Jewish, the other Arab—linked in an economic union. The City of Jerusalem was to be placed under an international regime, with its residents given the right to citizenship in either the Jewish or the

Arab state. Thirty-three UN members supported the resolution, 13 voted against and 10, including the United Kingdom, abstained. The Arab world rejected UNGA Resolution 181 and, on 15 May 1948, less than 24 hours after the proclamation of the establishment of the State of Israel by the country's first Prime Minister, David Ben-Gurion, the combined armies of Egypt, Iraq, Lebanon, Jordan and Syria invaded the nascent Jewish state.

Israel was victorious in this war, known as the War of Independence by Israel and al-Nakba (the Catastrophe) by the Arabs, and by the summer of 1949 the new country found itself in possession of far more territory than had been originally envisaged under the UN partition plan (for example, the capture of Eilat, on the northern tip of the Gulf of Aqaba, enabled Israel to assert its sovereignty over the southern Negev, an area originally excluded from the Jewish state). During the war Jordan captured east Jerusalem, along with the entire area of the west bank of the Jordan River. This meant that King Abdullah ibn Hussein, the founder of the Hashemite Kingdom of Jordan, now ruled both banks of the River Jordan as, during the 1920s, the British had placed the area of Palestine to the east of the river under Hashemite control. In April 1950 King Abdullah annexed East Jerusalem and the West Bank into his kingdom. Egypt also took control of the Gaza Strip during the war. Both prior to and during the war, large numbers of Palestinian Arabs from the main urban centres of Jerusalem, Jaffa and Haifa, and from villages along the coastal plain of Palestine fled their homes to Jordan, Lebanon, Syria and the Gaza Strip. The actual number of Palestinians who became refugees at this time is unknown. Israel estimates the figure at 538,000, the UN at 720,000, while Palestinian sources believe it to be 850,000 (pp. 1–2, in Lapidoth, 2002).

SUEZ TO YOM KIPPUR

This mass Palestinian exodus and the accompanying birth of the refugee problem is the most formative event in Palestinian history, if not the most important and controversial issue relating to the Arab–Israeli conflict and Middle Eastern politics. It led to the crystallization of Palestinian national identity and the development of the conflict. Moreover, it is a subject that bears directly on contemporary peace negotiations between Israel and the Palestinians and one that will have tremendous centrality in any final settlement, or in any failure to find a lasting settlement.

The early 1950s was a period of waning British influence in the region and heralded a new reality in which the USA, preoccupied with the evolving Cold War, emerged as the key Western player in the Middle East. The regional pro-Western nations—Turkey, Iran, Iraq and Pakistan—saw their ties to both the USA and the United Kingdom not primarily in terms of containing the Soviet threat, but as a way of furthering their own national interests and advancing their position vis-à-vis local rivals—India in the case of Pakistan, Greece in the case of Turkey, and Israel and Egypt in the case of Iraq (p. 130, in Cohen, 2005).

The tumultuous upheaval in the Middle East during the 1950s came to a climax with the Suez War, the Anglo-French-Israeli invasion of Egypt, in late 1956. The previous July the Egyptian President, Gamal Abd an-Nasir (Nasser), the leading pan-Arab nationalist of the era, had nationalized the Suez Canal. Both the French and British Governments were infuriated by this move and viewed it as a challenge to their economic security and prestige (the United Kingdom was responsible for the military defence of the canal and felt humiliated by the Egyptian action; France viewed Nasser as the major patron of the anti-French rebels in Algeria, and both saw the act as a blow to their international standing as great powers).

France, a close ally of Israel at this time, approached the Jewish state regarding the possibility that Israel might participate in a military action to retake the canal. Israel faced continuous guerrilla attacks from Egyptian-controlled Gaza and in April 1956 Egyptian artillery had initiated a sustained assault, also from Gaza, on Israeli settlements in the Negev. Nasser' blockade of the Straits of Tiran prevented merchant ships from reaching the Israeli port of Eilat, while the nationalization of the canal had enabled Egypt to enforce the Arab economic boycott of Israel by preventing ships destined for Tel Aviv or Haifa from using the canal. Moreover, co-operation with France provided Israel with the opportunity to avail itself of generous amounts of French military equipment that would allow it to counter the growing military strength of Egypt (which received massive arms transfers from the Soviet bloc) at a time when Nasser was becoming increasingly outspoken about his determination to destroy the Jewish state. In the last days of October 1956 Israeli troops crossed the Egyptian border and within a week had overwhelmed Sinai. On 5 November French and British forces landed in Egypt, ostensibly to separate the warring parties, but in reality as part of a prearranged plan, for which the Israeli action provided a pretext to force Nasser to denationalize the canal. The scheme was brought to a halt by Soviet and US pressure on France, the United Kingdom and Israel, and the whole affair had major implications: for relations between the USA and its foremost Western allies, the United Kingdom and France; for Soviet involvement in the region; for Israel's strategic relationship with France; and for the standing of France and the United Kingdom in the Middle East (p. 532, in Kyle, 1991).

Nasser's international status grew immensely following the Suez crisis and, in February 1958, Syria and Egypt joined together under his leadership to form the United Arab Republic (UAR).[1] Nasser's claim to be the champion of Arab unity greatly worried his pro-Western neighbours, Lebanon's President, Camille Chamoun, and King Hussein of Jordan, who had succeeded his father, King Talal in 1953. Both faced significant challenges from pro-Nasserite domestic opponents. Of particular concern to King Hussein was Nasser's decision (between 1959 and 1964) to establish gradually a Palestinian entity that would ultimately evolve into the Palestine Liberation Organization (PLO). This group directly challenged Hashemite sovereignty over the West Bank by appealing to Jordan's large Palestinian population (pp. 67–68, in Shemesh, 1988).

The key question regarding the PLO at this time was whether it would work to become a broad popular base in the struggle to liberate Palestine or, alternatively, whether it would simply develop into a propaganda/political organization supporting whatever its Arab government-sponsors might do. This question was answered in the wake of the 1967 Arab–Israeli War (the Six Day War). The immediate events that led to the outbreak of the war can be traced back to 18 May 1967, when the UAR terminated its consent to the presence of the UN Expeditionary Force (UNEF) on Egyptian territory and requested its immediate withdrawal. UN Secretary-General U Thant acceded to Nasser's demand and recalled the UN force, which had been created in November 1956 to patrol the Egyptian-Israeli armistice and demarcation lines, delineated in the 1949 armistice accords between the two countries. Four days later, on 22 May 1967, President Nasser declared his intention to reconstitute the blockade of Israel in the Straits of Tiran. This constituted a direct threat to regional peace as Israel, in the face of economic and diplomatic isolation in the Arab world, viewed interference with its ships as they exercised free and innocent passage in the Gulf of Aqaba and through the Straits of Tiran, as an act of war under article 51 of the UN Charter.

In the early morning of 5 June 1967 Israel initiated a major air campaign against Egypt that marked the beginning of the war. Apart from reuniting Jerusalem under Israeli sovereignty, and seeing the West Bank captured from Jordan, the Golan Heights from Syria and Gaza and the prized Sinai from Egypt, the stunning Israeli victory in the ensuing war fundamentally altered the strategic balance in the Middle East. On 22 November the UN Security Council (UNSC) unanimously adopted the hugely significant Resolution 242, the basic premise of which—'land for peace'—though subject to widely differing interpretations, has provided the basic framework for a negotiated settlement up to the present day. UNSC Resolution 242 called for an Israeli withdrawal 'from territories occupied in the recent conflict', and called for 'a just settlement of the refugee problem' (p. 102, in Lall, 1968). Israel, together with the vast majority of UN member states, endorsed Resolution 242, but the Arab world, which two months previously, at the Khartoum Summit, had passed the infamous 'Three No's' resolution—no peace, no recognition and no negotiation with Israel—rejected it (pp. 78–79, in Lukacs, 1992). Such a response was hardly surprising given that since 1949 the Arab world had demanded the absolute right of refugees to return to their former homes, or the right to choose between repatriation or compensation, on the basis of UNGA Resolution 194 of 11 December 1948.

The war between Israel and the Arab states in June 1967 saw the displacement of a further 200,000 Palestinians, which exacerbated the existing refugee problem and deeply influenced international political attitudes to the conflict. Indeed, from this time on it became increasingly difficult to separate the humanitarian issue relating to the fate of the Palestinian Arab refugees from the political issues concerning the Israeli occupation of the West Bank and Gaza and, more generally, the relationship between a solution of the Palestinian refugee problem and a settlement of the Arab–Israeli dispute. This evolving attitude was also influenced by the fact that Israel's military victory in June 1967 and its subsequent occupation of the West Bank and Gaza came at a time of growing international sympathy for developing world causes and for an anti-colonial ideology that enhanced the belief that Zionism was an anachronistic, even illegitimate, cause, while the Palestinian struggle was one of liberation (Wistrich, 1979).

Israel's victory in the 1967 war left the Arab world—especially Egypt—both militarily and psychologically wounded. It resulted in rising Soviet influence over the Arab states, as they looked for a sponsor to help them rebuild their military capability. It also established Israel as a true military force in the Middle East and cemented the US-Israeli strategic relationship. Following the war, the Arab–Israeli conflict entered a new phase, characterized by intensive cross-border shelling between Israel and Egypt (known as the War of Attrition) and an upsurge in the PLO's guerrilla warfare and terrorist operations. The summer of 1968 saw the first Palestinian hijacking of an international airliner and the formulation of the PLO's National Covenant, which declared the existence of the State of Israel to be null and void (article 19) and rejected any form of compromise (article 21). The following year Yasser Arafat became head of the PLO, following the success of Fatah (Arafat's power base) in winning control of the Palestine National Council (PNC), the governing body of the PLO (p. 6, in Shirabi, 1970).

The USA now began to use its rising influence with Israel to increase its political leverage over the Arab states. The US Administration in Washington, DC, brokered a cease-fire in the War of Attrition in 1970, and the death of Egypt's President Nasser, later in the same year, provided the USA with an opportunity to capitalize on both the recent cease-fire and the growing tensions between Egypt's new President, Anwar Sadat, and his Soviet patron, following the USSR's refusal to supply Egypt with the massive arms shipments requested (p. 79, in Golan, 1990). In turn, Sadat was motivated to move closer to Washington by his belief that only the USA was capable of persuading Israel to return the Sinai. In July 1972 Sadat opened a secret channel of communication with the USA and, the following year, he expelled 4,000 Soviet advisors. This ultimately resulted in Sadat's repudiation of the 15-year Treaty of Friendship with the USSR in 1976 (pp. 269–70, in Heikal, 1978).

Despite the fact that Egyptian-US relations were improving in the early 1970s, President Sadat realized that he needed to restore Arab pride, which had been shattered in the 1967 war, before his people, and the wider Arab world, would be psychologically ready to consider supporting a compromise peace agreement with Israel. As such, October 1973 saw the invasion of Israel on its holiest day by the combined forces of Syria and Egypt. This war (known in Israel as the Yom Kippur War and in the Arab world as the Ramadan War) caught Israel by surprise and, in the early stages, the Jewish state suffered heavy losses as Egyptian forces crossed the Suez Canal and overran Israeli strongholds, while the Syrians infiltrated deep into the Golan Heights. Israel's counter-offensive pushed the Syrians east of the 1967 cease-fire line and the Egyptian army back across the canal. On 24 October, with Israeli soldiers about one kilometre from the main Cairo–Ismailia highway and the USSR threatening direct military intervention, the UN imposed a cease-fire. The 1973 war raised the real possibility that the

Arab–Israeli conflict could escalate into a confrontation between the super-powers. After several months of negotiations, during which sporadic fighting continued, Israel reached disengagement agreements with Egypt in January 1974 and Syria the following May. In September 1975, after further negotiations, a second Sinai Disengagement Agreement (Sinai II) was signed between Egypt and Israel.

President Anwar Sadat felt vindicated by Egypt's victories early in the conflict and, in 1977, in a truly heroic and historic move, he visited Jerusalem. This culminated in the signing of an Israeli-Egyptian peace treaty in March 1979, known as the Camp David Accords. Camp David provided for a partial Israeli withdrawal from Sinai within nine months and a total withdrawal from the area within three years (this occurred on 25 April 1982). In return, Egypt offered Israel full diplomatic ties, freedom of Israeli passage through the Straits of Tiran, an international police force on shared borders and bilateral talks on economic and cultural normalization. However, Camp David endorsed the preferred Israeli option of Palestinian autonomy (rather than statehood) in the Occupied Territories and was thus rejected by the PLO and most Arab states. Egypt was expelled from the Arab League, on the grounds that the idea of self-rule envisaged in the proposals was a denial of the existence of the Palestinian people and an attempt to legalize the Israeli occupation of Palestinian land (p. 259, in Stein, 1999).

THE CASE OF LEBANON AND THE FIRST INTIFADA

Since the late 1960s, particularly after the PLO had been expelled from Jordan by King Hussein in the early 1970s, an area of southern Lebanon known as 'Fatahland' (after Fatah, the major constituent group in the PLO) developed into the principle PLO base for attacks into Israel. In March 1978 Operation Litani, the first Israeli invasion of Lebanon, was initiated in order to neutralize this threat. In June Israeli forces officially withdrew from Lebanon, but the raging civil war and instability on Lebanon's southern border with Israel continued. In early June 1982 Shlomo Argov, Israel's ambassador to the United Kingdom and Ireland was shot in the head as he left an official reception at London's Dorchester Hotel. Abu Nidal's Black June group claimed responsi-bility for the assassination attempt and, in response, the Israeli Cabinet author-ized retaliatory strikes against Palestinian bases in Lebanon. This, in turn, saw the PLO open fire on the Galilee in northern Israel. On 5 June 1982 Israel's Cabinet approved a major military action inside Lebanon, codenamed Operation Peace for Galilee. Variously termed the 'war of desperation' or the 'war of choice', Israel's invasion and subsequent entanglement in Lebanon (which lasted until the last of its troops were withdrawn in the summer of 2000), would have a profound impact on an Israeli society divided over the war; on a Lebanese society that was radicalized by the war and on the PLO, the leadership of which was forced to take refuge in Tunisia, its military infrastructure in Lebanon destroyed (p. 306, in Schiff and Ya'ari, 1984).

On a tactical level the Israeli invasion of Lebanon in 1982 succeeded in destroying the PLO as military force in the country. However, for Israel the cost of the invasion was to prove extremely high, not only in terms of the lives of its own soldiers and growing opposition within Israel to the war, but also in terms of its relations with the international community. Indeed, the invasion greatly increased anti-Israeli sentiment, as well as international support for the PLO. It also spawned Hezbollah (Party of God), an umbrella organization of various radical Shi'ite Muslim groups, which quickly evolved into the major anti-Israel force and an instrument of both Syrian and Iranian influence in Lebanon. Moreover, the death of several hundred Palestinian civilians at the Sabra and Chatila refugee camps at the hands of Christian Phalangists, who were allied to Israel, was presented as evidence of Israel's brutal approach to dealing with the Palestinians.

In December 1987 the *intifada* (uprising) began. This mass Palestinian uprising was an expression of resentment against the Israeli occupation and the rapid growth of Jewish settlements in the territories. The *intifada*, like the invasion of Lebanon, greatly damaged Israel's international standing, but it also highlighted the existence of a local Palestinian leadership capable of challenging the dominance of the Tunis-based PLO. The PLO's influence was further weakened by the growing appeal of Islamist groups like Hamas, the Palestinian branch of the Muslim Brothers, in Gaza. These factors, as well as the PLO's desire to improve ties with the USA, which in 1975 had signed an agreement with Israel promising not to meet with, or recognize, the PLO until it accepted UNSC Resolutions 242 and 338,[2] led to a declaration by the PLO leadership, in Algiers (Algeria) on 15 November 1988. The Algiers Declaration called for the convening of an international peace conference, under the auspices of the UN and on the basis of Resolutions 242 and 338. It also renounced terrorism, but with a significant caveat that exempted those fighting foreign occupation, and proclaimed a Palestinian state, without defined borders, but with Jerusalem as its capital (pp. 415–19, in Lukacs, 1992).

Although the Algiers Declaration was the first time that the PNC had verbally endorsed a settlement of the conflict along the lines set out in UNSC Resolutions 242 and 338, Israel rejected it as a deceptive propaganda exercise intended to create the false impression of PLO moderation. The international community welcomed the declaration and, in its immediate wake, 27 Muslim, developing-world and non-aligned nations explicitly recognized an independent Palestinian state. It also led to growing international consensus over the need to convene an international conference and comprehensive multilateral negotiations between Israel and the Arab parties, including the PLO. This completely contradicted the Israeli position at the time. Distrustful of both the USSR and the European Community (EC, now the European Union—EU), Israel opposed an international conference, preferring to build on the Camp David formula of bilateral negotiations. Israel opposed a multilateral process in which it had to deal with all the Arab states and the PLO as one, instead favouring negotiations with Arab states (in particular Jordan and Egypt) and elected local Palestinian leaders in the territories it ruled, without dealing with the PLO.

THE FIRST GULF WAR AND THE OSLO PEACE PROCESS

On 2 August 1990 Iraq invaded Kuwait, its smaller but far wealthier neighbour on the Persian (Arabian) Gulf. This action and the subsequent war between Iraq and a US-led international coalition would have profound implications for the Israeli–Palestinian conflict, as well as the future of Iraq.

In the months of pre-war diplomacy the administration of US President George H. Bush (1989–93) had increasingly warmed to the idea put forward by coalition allies, including France and Egypt, as well as Russia, of convening an international conference on the Middle East once Iraqi leader Saddam Hussain had been defeated. By March 1991, following the expulsion of Saddam's devastated army from Kuwait, the USA began to capitalize on its predominant international position in the post-Cold War era and its post-Gulf War prestige in the Middle East to bring the major regional parties to the conference table (p. 440, in Freedman and Karsh, 1993).

The American success in convening the conference was not only because of its new global predominance, but also because vital domestic considerations made it unwise for any of the parties to say no to the USA at this time. For example, Israel agreed to attend the meeting in Madrid (Spain), despite long-time opposition to an international conference, because it felt increasingly secure in the region following the collapse of the USSR and the defeat of Iraq in Kuwait. More importantly, Israel agreed to attend Madrid because the cost of absorbing the hundreds of thousands of Soviet Jewish immigrants made the Jewish state increasingly financially dependent on the USA. However, the right-wing Likud Government was unbending in its refusal to negotiate with the PLO and, as such, a compromise was found, whereby 'non-PLO' Palestinian representatives from the Occupied Territories (though not from Jerusalem or the Palestinian diaspora community) would participate at Madrid as part of a joint Jordanian-Palestinian delegation.

The PLO leadership was in no position to dispute this arrangement. The *intifada* had highlighted to both Israel and the international community that there existed a viable Palestinian leadership within the territories that had the potential to represent the Palestinians of the West Bank and Gaza as well, if not far better, than the Tunis-based PLO leadership. While the collapse of the USSR not only denied the PLO an important source of diplomatic support and military equipment and training, but left the USA—a country that had refused to meet or recognize the PLO for almost its entire existence—as the only global superpower. Moreover, the PLO's decision to support the Iraqi invasion of Kuwait had been a major strategic miscalculation. In the wake of the liberation of Kuwait, the Arab Gulf states, led by Saudi Arabia and Kuwait itself, set about punishing the PLO for its stance during the war. The large Palestinian work-force in the Gulf was expelled en masse, thus reducing the amount of income that was funnelled from this constituency to the PLO, while the petroleum-rich Gulf states also cut off their financial support for the PLO.

The Madrid conference provided for bilateral talks between Israel and delegations from Jordan-Palestine, Syria and Lebanon, under US supervision, and for multilateral track talks on arms control, refugees, water, the environment and regional economic development, under EU auspices. Madrid was significant because it set a precedent for Israel entering into bilateral political discussions with representatives of the Palestinian people. However, the conference failed to produce any immediate breakthrough and the ongoing bilateral discussions between Israel and the various Arab delegations, which were taking place in Washington, DC, became bogged down.

The victory of the Labour party in the Israeli national elections of 1992 was greeted with optimism in the international community, as an opportunity for the process to regain momentum. Between 1977 and 1992 Labour's only taste of government had been in a national unity coalition with the Likud party in the period between 1984 and 1990. Now the Labour leader, Yitzhak Rabin, promised to make the promotion of peace with the Palestinians his Government's central goal. Despite Rabin's promise to try to reach an agreement with the Palestinians within nine months of taking power, by the summer of 1993 few substantive gains had been made in any of the 11 rounds of bilateral talks between Israel and the Palestinians (as well as other Arab states) in Washington, DC.

However, parallel to the official negotiations, secret discussions had been going on for some time in Oslo, the Norwegian capital, between senior Israeli and PLO figures. In August these talks resulted in the signing a draft peace agreement, which was followed shortly after, on 13 September 1993, by a White House signing ceremony in Washington, DC.

On that historic day Israeli foreign minister Shimon Peres and the PLO's Mahmoud Abbas (Abu Mazen), Arafat's second-in-command, signed an agreement setting out a framework for providing (prior to a permanent peace agreement) for Palestinian self-rule in the entire West Bank and the Gaza Strip for a transitional period not to exceed five years, during which time the territories would be administered by a Palestinian Authority (PA), which was to be freely and democratically elected after the withdrawal of Israeli military forces both from the Gaza Strip and from the populated areas of the West Bank. Prime Minister Rabin and Chairman Arafat also attended and they sealed the deal with an historic and highly symbolic handshake.

The Oslo process raised real hopes that a comprehensive, just and lasting settlement to the Arab–Israeli conflict was near. The first practical success to emerge from the 1993 Oslo Accords was the Israeli-PLO Cairo Agreement of 4 May 1994, which established PLO rule in Gaza and Jericho. This was followed by a peace agreement between Israel and Jordan in October 1994 and then, on 28 September 1995, by the Israeli-Palestinian Interim Agreement (Oslo II), which extended Palestinian autonomy in the Occupied Territories and established a framework for Israeli military redeployment that, it was hoped, would provide the basis for Palestinian presidential and general elections to take place.

On 4 November 1995, just over a month after the signing of Oslo II, Prime Minister Rabin was assassinated by an Israeli citizen opposed to the peace process. The killing of Rabin sent shock waves through an international community concerned that the death of such a key architect of the Oslo agreement might impact negatively on a permanent settlement between Israel and the Palestinians. Rabin's murder occurred at a time of increased Palestinian terror attacks against Israeli targets, which continued after Shimon Peres had replaced Rabin as head of the Labour-led coalition Government. By this time the situation had become so unstable that President Hosni Mubarak of Egypt and President Bill Clinton of the USA felt compelled to convene a meeting in March 1996, at Sharm esh-Sheikh (Egypt), to shore up the floundering peace process. Moreover, in the May 1996 general election Peres was defeated by Likud's Binyamin Netanyahu, a former Israeli UN ambassador, and (with the support of leading 'neo-conservatives' in Washington, DC, like Richard Perle) was an outspoken opponent of Oslo while in opposition. Likud's election victory was viewed in the Arab world, and much of the international community, as a significant reverse for the Oslo process. Nevertheless, under Netanyahu there was some progress in the process, with agreements in 1997 (Hebron Protocol) and 1998 (Wye River Accords) extending Palestinian autonomy and providing for a gradual Israeli military redeployment and for co-operation on security issues.

During the Oslo era the international community provided significant support for the economic, political and social development of the PA-controlled territories, with the World Bank estimating that annual donor assistance averaged US $1,000m. per annum in these years. However, this massive investment did not result in ordinary Palestinians experiencing a noticeable rise in their living standards. This was due in part to Israel's repeated closure of its borders to Palestinian goods and workers, in response to the wave of Palestinian terror attacks, but it was also due to the widespread corruption and gross inefficiency within the PA.

Like Rabin's 1992 election victory, the success of Labour's Ehud Barak in the 1999 Israeli elections was once more greeted by the international community as an opportunity to restart the stalled peace process, after three years of Likud obstructionism. This culminated in an unprecedented series of negotiations between Clinton, Barak and Arafat, at Camp David, the US presidential retreat in Maryland, between 12 and 24 July 2000. However, the Camp David meeting failed to achieve an agreement and, following Likud leader Ariel Sharon's visit to the Temple Mount (Haram ash-Sharif, the site of the al-Aqsa mosque) in Jerusalem in late September 2000, there was an eruption of wide scale Palestinian violence. This uprising came to be known as the al-Aqsa *intifada* and led to the disintegration of the Oslo process and the electoral defeat of Barak by Likud's Sharon.

AFTER OSLO: NO END OF CONFLICT IN SIGHT

In the months, and years, since the collapse of the Oslo process, the Palestinian leadership, much of the Arab world and supporters of the Palestinian cause in the West have challenged the generosity of Barak's various peace proposals between July 2000 and January 2001. They have explained the collapse of the Oslo process and the outbreak of the al-Aqsa *intifada* in terms of general Palestinian frustration with ongoing statelessness and anger over the visit of then Israeli defence minister Ariel Sharon to the Temple Mount (the holiest Muslim site in Jerusalem). Others (perhaps most notably senior US negotiator Dennis Ross and President Clinton) reject this interpretation and have argued that in the six-month period beginning with Camp David Israel did make significant concessions on the size of a prospective Palestinian state—agreeing to give the Palestinians all of Gaza and 92% of the West Bank at Camp David, and then, at the 21–27 January 2001 meeting in the Egyptian Red Sea resort of Taba, agreeing to hand over 98% of the West Bank and Gaza—as well as on the Palestinian claim to Jerusalem and on the highly contentious issue of the 'right of return' for Palestinian refugees to their former homes in Israel (though in a way consistent with the continued status of Israel as the homeland of the Jewish people). Following the Israeli army's reoccupation of most of the major Palestinian-controlled cities in the West Bank following the assassination of a government minister in October 2001, Israel faced criticism from the international community on a number of interrelated issues. This ranged from public condemnation of Israel's destruction of EU funded infrastructural projects in the Occupied Territories to the far more serious allegation over Israel's treatment of the Palestinian people.

In March 2002, for the first time, a resolution (UNSC 1397) referring explicitly to the idea of Palestinian statehood was adopted by the UN Security Council. In April 2003 the international quartet of the USA, Russia, the EU and the UN adopted a performance-based plan known as the Road Map for Middle East Peace. In its original format it did not deal directly with the size of any future Palestinian state, the status of Jerusalem or the question of Palestinian refugees, but rather envisaged a three-phase path to peace beginning with the end of terror and violence and the normalization of life in the Palestinian areas. Once this had been achieved, the second phase would focus on the transition to a Palestinian state with provisional borders and attributes of sovereignty based on a new Palestinian constitution. The final stage was to see a permanent status agreement on the boundaries of a Palestinian state between Israel and the PA. The Road Map was accompanied by the election of senior PA official Mahmoud Abbas as the PA's first ever Prime Minister. This appointment resulted from a demand by the international community that Arafat share power in order to bring transparent and democratic government to the Palestinians.

Israel used Abbas's accession to the political leadership of the PA to further its objective of isolating Arafat, whom it held primarily responsible for the collapse of Oslo and the outbreak of violence. Though the international community embraced the appointment of Abu Mazen, it refused (with the exception of the USA, which in June 2002 had called on Arafat to cede political power) to adopt a policy of excluding the long-time Palestinian leader from the political process. In September 2003, citing Arafat as the major cause of the collapse of his Government, Abbas resigned his position as Prime Minister. Egypt gave Arafat an ultimatum to implement reforms; the Mubarak Government's call for reform and holding of Arafat as personally responsible for the chaos inside the PA was joined by King Abdullah II of Jordan and a number of Palestinian officials and personalities. Moreover, the Palestinian Legislative Council—the Palestinian parliament—published a report that concluded that Arafat and the PA's failure to live up to the responsibilities of leadership was a significant contributing factor to the growing anarchy and disillusionment of the Palestinian people. As such, by the time of his death in November 2004, Yasser Arafat, who for over a quarter of a century had embodied the Palestinian struggle as 'Mr Palestine', had lost much of his domestic and international credibility.

The succession of Abbas to the Palestinian presidency was heralded as an opportunity to relaunch the peace process. Javier Solana, the EU foreign policy chief, attempted to put forward a proposal to relaunch the Road Map in a manner that was widely interpreted as a call for the immediate establishment of a Palestinian state. George W. Bush (US President since January 2001) rejected any proposals to relaunch a 'fast track' version of the Road Map following Arafat's death, on the grounds that democratization must precede, rather than follow, the establishment of a Palestinian state. During his White House meeting with Abbas in May 2005, President Bush made it clear that the USA would support the establishment of a Palestinian state only if, and when, it made a definitive commitment to democracy and fully cracked down on terrorism. Abbas's attempt to reach a peace agreement with Israel was impeded both by the continuing Israeli policy of building settlements in the West Bank and by the efforts of Hamas to challenge the Fatah-led PA for power in the Palestinian territories following Arafat's death. By 2000 Hamas, which came to prominence during the 1980s, at the time of the first Palestinian *intifada* and which increased its power further in the 1990s by establishing an extensive social services network, had developed into the dominant political and military player in Gaza (Levitt, 2006).

In the third round of the Palestinian municipal elections of May 2005, Hamas won 27 local councils, compared to Fatah's 33, gaining more than twice as many votes as Fatah. This growing influence of a group that had used terrorism throughout the 1990s to undermine the Oslo peace process, as well as Abbas's refusal to take military action against Hamas or any other militant group for fear of starting a civil war, further added to the Israeli belief that the PA was unable to deliver a negotiated settlement. As such, in August 2005 Israel carried out its unilateral disengagement from the Gaza Strip. This unprecedented decision led to the dismantling of all 21 Jewish settlements in Gaza (as well as four in the northern West Bank). It was welcomed across the international community, where it was viewed as the first stage of a complete Israeli withdrawal from territories captured during the 1967 Six Day War, as well as the first real opportunity for the Palestinians to govern themselves, free from Israeli military intervention or settlements, since the 1994 Cairo Agreement established Palestinian self-rule in Gaza and Jericho.

The international community pledged significant sums to help the Palestinians develop Gaza's infrastructure and economy following the Israeli withdrawal. It also acknowledged the huge political and personal risks that Israeli Prime Minister Ariel Sharon had taken by implementing his disengagement plan in the face of staunch domestic opposition. The international quartet also began to pressure Abbas and the governing Fatah party to try harder to re-establish control over Gaza. However, to the shock of many, not only in the Palestinian political establishment but also in Israel and across the world, Hamas was victorious in the January 2006 PNC elections, winning 76 of the 132 seats in the Palestinian parliament. Hamas's political success was due to the group's ability to capitalize on popular Palestinian disillusionment with the corrupt and faction-strewn Fatah, as well as its track record of providing extensive social services to a large number of Palestinians living in poverty. Since entering government, Hamas has refused to renounce or amend its constitution, which promises that 'Israel will exist ... until Islam will obliterate it', and Israel has refused to negotiate with representatives of a group that openly calls for its destruction. All of this makes it likely that any future Israeli withdrawal from the West Bank will be unilateral and based on an evaluation of the potential military threat from Hamas. This is unacceptable to all Palestinian parties, the Arab world and much of the international community, all of which continue to support a negotiated settlement along the lines of that set out in the Road Map. At the same time, Arabs refuse to countenance any solution to the refugee crisis outside the context of full repatriation (right of return), something that is unacceptable to Israelis across the political spectrum. All of which, when combined with the summer 2006 war between Israel and Hezbollah in Lebanon, means that the circumstances required for the establishment of a viable, sovereign Palestinian state living side by side with Israel in the West Bank and Gaza, a development that is vital to the end of the century-long Arab–Israeli conflict, is unlikely to occur in the foreseeable future.

NOTES

1. Despite the dissolution of the Union during the 1960s, Nasser demanded that Egypt be known as the UAR until his death in 1970.
2. UNSC Resolution 338 was passed unanimously by the Security Council on 21 October 1973. It called on the warring parties to cease fighting and resume diplomatic efforts, in accordance with Resolution 242.

Re-examining the
Northern Ireland Conflict

JOHN DOYLE

INTRODUCTION

The Northern Ireland conflict has its roots in the failure of the British state-building project to consolidate the territorial gains of colonization in Ireland. A decade of intense political activity in the early 20th century, a failed armed rebellion in 1916 and a guerrilla war by the Irish Republican Army (IRA) in 1918–21 led to the establishment of an independent Irish state. The British Government, after a bitter but ultimately failed attempt at counter-insurgency, withdrew its forces from most of Ireland, but the price to be paid was partition. The particular circumstances of the settler plantations from the 17th century onwards had led to well-organized opposition in the north-east to Irish independence, and these supporters of union with Britain were termed 'unionists'. They had a sufficiently strong alliance with elements of the British political establishment to persuade the British Government to adopt a policy of partition, even after they had failed to defeat the wider challenge of Irish nationalism.

Irish nationalists split on the terms of the treaty offered by the United Kingdom and fought a brief but bitter civil war. After the defeat of radical forces in the civil war the new Irish Government was preoccupied with stability, not with the completion of Irish unity. Unionists for their part accepted a devolved parliament in Northern Ireland as a means of ensuring greater control over their own political destiny. They accepted a smaller geographical area that the traditional northern province of Ulster where their majority was very small and instead drew the partition boundary around an area where they made up approximately 66% of the population.[1] Faced with a nationalist minority and a new southern Irish Government, unionist political culture was grounded in a siege mentality. In this context elites were able to control a political party that ruled in a single-party Government, with no significant internal division, for nearly 50 years. The unionists cemented this position by asserting a nakedly privileged position for their own within the system. It had a strong internal class inequality, but even those at the bottom of the unionist hierarchy still possessed advantages over their nationalist counterparts in employment, cultural rights and security. As Richard Rose (p. 465, in Rose, 1971—see Bibliography) put it, nationalist compliance with the new regime, not consent, was sought.

THE ORIGINS OF THE MODERN CONFLICT

The political divisions between Irish nationalists and unionists continued after partition, but there was little serious armed resistance to British rule until the present conflict erupted in the late 1960s. The international context at the beginnings of the modern conflict was framed by the US civil rights movement, student protests and new social movements. The utter failure of a minor IRA armed campaign in 1956–62 (Coogan, 1980), the inability of moderate conservative nationalism to offer any realistic political strategy, British unwillingness to disturb the status quo and the absence of any significant international support for Irish unity meant that by the late 1960s a traditional nationalist campaign was an unlikely vehicle for the mounting frustration of nationalists and others concerned with the nature of unionist rule.

The Northern Ireland Civil Rights Association formed in 1967 was based on the US model—adopting its terminology and its tactics of peaceful marches (McCann, 1993; Farrell, 1976). While unionists point out that the present Sinn Féin leader Gerry Adams was (as a young and unknown political figure) among its founding members, it was in reality a broad movement, focused on issues of discrimination, not partition. Its demands included: an end to the provision restricting voting rights in local elections to property owners; an end to the manipulation of electoral district boundaries;[2] an end to discrimination in the provision of public housing and jobs; the repeal of emergency laws; and the disbandment of the B Specials (a particularly ill-disciplined element of the security forces). The relationship between the civil rights protests and the subsequent armed conflict remains contested. Unionists predominantly see the civil rights protests as a deliberate effort by republicans to begin civil strife. Nationalists overwhelmingly blame the British Government for its failure to respond adequately, or in time, to what they regarded as reasonable and moderate demands for reform.

Civil rights protests gained momentum throughout 1968 and were banned and eventually violently attacked by both police and unionist protestors. Counter protests by unionists—leading to the emergence of Ian Paisley as a political figure—led to widespread street violence. Thousands of nationalists were forced to leave their homes in mixed areas or at sectarian boundaries. Rising levels of street violence led some within nationalist communities to look to their traditional defenders—the IRA. However the IRA leadership was opposed to an armed campaign at this time, leading to graffiti appearing in Belfast saying, 'IRA—I Ran Away' (p. 83, in Smith, 1995). Almost inevitably the IRA split and it was the new 'Provisional' leadership—the 'Provos' in journalistic shorthand—who were to emerge as the only effective successor to the IRA; it is from this split that the modern Sinn Féin party and IRA emerged (Feeney 2002; English, 2003).

The British Government left political control in the hands of the regional unionist administration, though they did deploy the British army on to the streets in August 1969, when protests had stretched the Royal Ulster Constabulary (RUC—the local police force) to breaking point. An initial period of calm ended quickly as the British army was deployed to quell nationalist protests and defeat the emerging IRA. As civil rights protests continued and there were signs that the IRA was reorganizing, the unionist Government in Belfast responded in August 1971 by introducing internment—detention without trial. Only nationalists were arrested, many if not most with no IRA connections, despite the fact that unionist paramilitaries[3] had also been involved in killings. The response was a huge escalation of the IRA campaign—more people were killed from August to December 1971 than had been killed between 1967 and July 1971 collectively.[4] The armed conflict had begun.

THE ARMED CONFLICT AND ITS POLITICAL ACTORS[5]

There is a very contested literature on the role of the British state in Northern Ireland. Arthur Aughey (1989), for example, reflects a typically unionist view, arguing that the British state is a less than convinced ally. Former Irish Taoiseach Garret FitzGerald (1991) saw British policy on Northern Ireland as a problem of low priority and inconsistency. Republicans such as Gerry Adams (1995; 2003) see the United Kingdom playing a colonial role. Whatever is thought of the United Kingdom's strategic motivations, over the last 30 years or so there has been a consistency to its public position. The United Kingdom seeks a restoration of stability over all else and believes this will be accomplished by remaining as the sovereign power, trying to defeat the IRA, introducing a power-sharing government between moderate nationalists and unionists, and improving its relationship with the Irish Government. After some military confusion in the early 1970s the United Kingdom ran an intense counter-insurgency campaign to defeat the IRA, leading to widespread criticisms from human rights organizations (Human Rights Watch, 1991). However, British policy showed little strategic thinking on how to deal with the fact that for over 20 years there was little sign of progress either in defeating the IRA or in reaching a political agreement. The British state never adopted a firm view as to the relative balance to be achieved between its relationship with unionism and the Irish Government, where it was often pulled in opposite directions. In the late 1960s and early 1970s it still retained the view that the Irish Government had no business 'interfering' in Northern Ireland. As street violence escalated in late 1969 the British Government refused to meet the Irish Government or even to discuss the crisis (Fanning, 2001; Kennedy, 2001). This view softened somewhat in the 1970s; however, a senior Irish civil servant involved in high-level talks through the 1980s and early 1990s said that, until the lead up to the peace process of the 1990s, there was little real acceptance on the British side that a good relationship required them to take Irish government concerns seriously[6] and so, in general, unionist concerns were generally given priority over those of the Irish Government.

The Irish Government, like the United Kingdom, was conflicted in its strategic goals. It favoured stability over high-risk strategies to achieve Irish unity but faced a public with a strongly nationalist political culture. The Irish

Government, for example, banned all Sinn Féin and IRA members from appearing on TV or radio from the early 1970s—15 years before the British did so. In a justification for the measures before parliament, the minister then responsible explicitly referred to the ability of Sinn Féin and the IRA to mobilize public opinion through 'emotive' appeals.[7] After a disastrous 'economic war' with the United Kingdom in the 1930s, an ineffective diplomatic campaign against partition in the 1950s and repeated failed attempts to persuade US governments to intervene with the British, Irish governments had reached the conclusion that for all their frustrations they had no alternative but to seek (slowly) to persuade the British Goverment to adopt a position of reform. This also fitted with the relatively conservative instincts of Irish governments over this period, which often led northern nationalists to believe that they had in effect been abandoned.

Sinn Féin and the IRA, sometimes collectively referred to as the Republican Movement, are both organized on an all-Ireland basis, though they have much greater support in the north. Re-emerging as a credible force out of the civil rights period, their political strategy in the 1970s was characterized by a focus on a military campaign. Until 1981 Sinn Féin refused to stand for election, saying it would only lend legitimacy to British rule. However, in the aftermath of a major political crisis around a hunger strike by prisoners (see below) the focus shifted to, first of all, a dual strategy of 'armed struggle' and party political organization and eventually, in the peace process, to a strategy focused exclusively through Sinn Féin (Murray and Tonge, 2005). Sinn Féin denies any organic link with the IRA (which is illegal) and the clandestine nature of the IRA and a very active campaign of attempted infiltration by the British security forces means that in practice the vast majority of Sinn Féin members could not be in the IRA. However, it is commonly assumed by journalists that there is overlap at leadership level. Sinn Féin has a strong focus on community activism and this, along with radical left-wing and militant separatist politics, saw them develop broad support (Doyle, 2006). While the IRA campaign continued, Sinn Féin was unable to overtake the more conservative nationalist Social Democratic and Labour Party (SDLP) in Northern Ireland and remained a small party in the south. After the cease-fire Sinn Féin has become the dominant nationalist party in Northern Ireland (polling 26.2% of the votes, compared to the SDLP's 15.2%, in the 2007 Assembly election) and are a growing but still smaller political force in the south, with approximately 10%–11% in 2006 opinion polls.[8]

The SDLP was founded amid the political crisis of civil rights, replacing a conservative and ineffective Nationalist Party, with an agenda focused on internal reform. In response to the collapse of a 1973 experiment in power-sharing, the SDLP shifted to a more explicitly nationalist agenda and its strategic focus has oscillated over the years between attempts to secure internal reform with moderate unionists and attempts to mobilize international opinion, especially in the USA, to persuade the United Kingdom to introduce more far-reaching political changes over the heads of unionist opinion (Murray, 1998). It has always opposed the use of political violence and this was the key point of differentiation from Sinn Féin during the conflict, leading to a broad support base. In the aftermath of the IRA ceasefire it has, however, struggled to redefine itself and has seen its support continually shrink, so that it now reflects an older, more conservative voter to an increasing extent (Murray and Tonge, 2005).

Ulster unionism remained a cohesive political force between 1920 and the late 1960s, organized in a single Ulster Unionist Party (UUP). Divisions in how they should respond to the civil rights movement saw the emergence of rivals, one of which—the Democratic Unionist Party (DUP), led by Ian Paisley—survived and became the largest unionist party in 2003. Apart from opposing Irish unity, unionism has adopted a relatively exclusionary form of politics. There is no attempt to persuade nationalists to become pro-union with the British, but rather, nationalists are seen as a threat to the state, and this has served as the basis for exclusion not only from the political domain but also in employment, cultural rights and policing (Doyle, 1994). Unionists have been divided in their strategic response to the conflict, uncertain as to whether full integration with the United Kingdom (ending any attempt to restore regional government) or restoration of devolution would best secure their position. While united in opposition to Irish unity, the British Government is often seen as a less than secure ally (pp. 3–4, in Doyle, 2003).

Armed groups also emerged in unionist areas but political parties associated with loyalist paramilitaries have tiny electoral support. This reflects to a large extent the unionist community's support for the official security forces, which are seen as reflecting their concerns. None the less, unionist paramilitaries were sizeable organizations, responsible for the deaths of nearly 1,000 people since the late 1960s. Despite their declared goals of attacking the IRA, most of their victims were nationalist civilians. Steve Bruce (1992) argues that 'pro-state terrorism' rather than 'counter-terrorism' is a more accurate reflection of their position. Indeed their attacks both preceded the re-emergence of the IRA and were as much linked to periods of political reform as they were to IRA activity.

Until the ending of the Cold War the international pressures for a resolution of the Northern Ireland conflict were very minimal (Guelke, 1988). The USA was unwilling to challenge its most important NATO ally and US government policy was firmly within the context of the 'special relationship' with the United Kingdom (O'Grady 1996). Northern Ireland was seen as an internal British affair and Irish governments were politely informed that the US administration would not intervene (Cronin, 1987). Other international interventions were equally low key. The UN Security Council was never likely to get involved as the United Kingdom held a permanent seat and a veto. The European Economic Community (EEC—later the European Community, EC, or European Union, EU) also refrained from involvement (p. 280, in Ruane and Todd, 1996). There were occasional signs of a countervailing view, such as with US President Jimmy Carter's ban on arms sales to the RUC, and there was constant non-governmental organization (NGO) criticism of British policy in Northern Ireland, but the level of international pressure was never enough to have a significant impact.

FROM WAR TO PEACE

In its essentials the conflict endured a period of stalemate between the early 1970s and the early 1990s, with little change in the internal dynamics or the international context. However, three key episodes are discussed below, as they had an enduring impact on the direction of the conflict.

Until 1998 the only agreement to be reached between the parties (and even then excluding Sinn Féin) was the 1973 Sunningdale Agreement, which included power sharing between centrist unionists and the SDLP and an advisory cross-border council. The Agreement only survived a few months. The UUP split down the middle and in an early British general election in 1974 every unionist candidate elected was publicly hostile to the Agreement. The Executive limped on, as its mandate came from Northern Ireland regional elections held before Sunningdale. In May 1974 a strike was called by a group including loyalist paramilitaries, anti-agreement unionist parties and workers in the power stations (who were almost exclusively unionist). The British Government refused to use its security forces to keep electricity plants open or to remove roadblocks, and the power-sharing Executive collapsed (Fisk, 1975). The collapse of Sunningdale led to a stronger nationalist position being articulated by the SDLP (Murray, 1998), which was highly critical of the British Government's failure to defend the Agreement. From this point on, the SDLP refused to consider any proposed agreement that did not include an institutionalized role for the Irish Government, believing that an agreement with another state would be harder for the British Government to walk away from.

The military stalemate in the late 1970s led some within Sinn Féin and the IRA to question the dominant role of the military campaign in republican strategy (Adams, 1996). The pace of change was increased dramatically in late 1980 by a decision of IRA prisoners to launch a hunger strike to win improved prison conditions (Beresford, 1987; Campbell et al., 1994). Ultimately 10 prisoners died between May and October 1981. The leader of the protests and the first victim, Bobby Sands, was elected to the British Parliament in a by-election and became an iconic figure for republicans. Two other prisoners were elected to the Irish parliament in a general election that June. Further elections of prisoners were only prevented by new British legislation banning prisoners from standing for election. Sinn Féin had previously refused to stand for election on the grounds that it would amount to recognition of British sovereignty, but changed strategy on seeing the huge political impact of Sands's election and quickly established a support base of between 33% and 40% of the nationalist vote.

The electoral rise of Sinn Féin led the Irish Government to launch new political initiatives designed to show that moderate nationalism had a strategy for political progress (p. 462, in FitzGerald, 1991). A cross-party convention was held in Dublin to try and agree a common moderate nationalist position and in November 1985, following more than a year of talks, the two Governments signed the Anglo-Irish Agreement, which granted the Irish Government a consultative role in the governance of Northern Ireland. In return, the Irish Government confirmed there would be no change in the 'status' of Northern Ireland without the agreement of a majority there and promised greater security co-operation. Unionists launched a campaign of opposition based on the rejection of any input by a 'foreign' government in the governance of Northern Ireland. In her memoirs, Margaret Thatcher (pp. 402–06, in her 1995 publication) said she regretted signing the Agreement as it alienated unionists and as, she claimed, she did not get the security co-operation she desired from the Irish Government. Nationalists were also ultimately disappointed that 'consultation' led to very limited impact on policy, but it was the first institutionalized role for the Irish state and laid some basis for later progress. The unionist campaign, involving public protests, resignations from Parliament and a major escalation of unionist paramilitary attacks failed to force a British change of policy, unlike the campaign against power-sharing in 1973 (Aughey, 1989). This point was not lost on unionist politicians and it made them very reluctant to boycott talks during the peace process of the 1990s.

The new electoral strength of Sinn Féin altered the political dynamics and pressurized moderate nationalists, but it also gave the SDLP options, other than seeking a deal with unionism. In April 1992 news broke that the leaders of Sinn Féin and the SDLP, Gerry Adams and John Hume, were engaged in a series of secret talks. The Hume-Adams process as it was labelled was hugely popular among nationalists where, despite electoral rivalry and differences on the IRA's campaign, there was a popular desire for a more united nationalist position to exert pressure on the United Kingdom.

THE PEACE PROCESS

It is beyond the scope of this chapter to provide a narrative of the peace process,[9] but the talks between Hume and Adams, involving the Irish Government behind the scenes (Mansergh, 1995), ultimately led to an IRA cease-fire in August 1994. There is no evidence of a secret deal with the British to produce the cease-fire. Rather it reflected a strategic move by the IRA to get itself out of a position of military stalemate and create a new nationalist momentum.

It is possible to see the peace process as an affirmation of William Zartman's (2005) theory of 'ripeness', in particular of the impact of a 'mutually hurting stalemate', in creating positive conditions for peace processes. Sinn Féin knew it could not on its own pressurize the United Kingdom to withdraw; it needed a broader political base and this is confirmed from a leaked document in 1994.[10] Sinn Féin was fearful that a long stalemate would ultimately weaken its movement. It was also clear that the British Government did not believe that it could militarily defeat the IRA (FitzGerald, 1999). While the IRA was relatively contained, incidents like the bombing of London's financial district[11] and of Downing Street itself[12] caused significant financial and psychological damage. The United Kingdom too was open to a new approach. For the United Kingdom and the IRA it is possible to use Zartman's model of ripeness. There was, at least potentially, a mutually hurting stalemate, recognized spokespersons on each side and a possible way forward in the short term (even if long-term objectives differed fundamentally). It is difficult, however, to fit Ulster unionists into this model. They did not accept that the IRA could not be defeated and accused successive British governments of being over concerned with their international image in their security decisions (p. 12, in Doyle, 2003). Unionists favoured the status quo over a high-risk peace process, but they feared being totally sidelined in a bilateral nationalist-British dialogue if they refused to join talks.

There were underlying socio-political factors that also influenced Sinn Féin, in particular demographic changes. From the 1920s to the 1980s nationalist emigration, driven by high levels of unemployment and discrimination was much higher than emigration by unionists. This reversed in the late 1980s, partly as a response to new anti-discrimination legislation. In addition, as the nationalist-unionist balance in the university student population neared parity, increasing numbers of young unionists chose to study in England and Scotland, rather than in the effectively bi-national local universities, and many of them did not return to Northern Ireland. While the nationalist percentage of the population had remained static at one-third for 50 years, by the early 1990s nationalists made up over 40% of the voting population and a majority of the primary-school-going cohort. A nationalist majority is unlikely in the near future, but many nationalists believe a majority will now eventually emerge and that a growing nationalist population will in the meantime give them added political strength.

A leadership change in the governing party in the Republic of Ireland saw a new Taoiseach,[13] Albert Reynolds, effectively reverse key elements of Irish government policy (p. 352, in Coogan, 1995). Previous conflict resolution strategies had been based on trying to isolate Sinn Féin and build a centrist agreement around the SDLP and the UUP, with the hope that this would erode support for the IRA and eventually bring peace. Reynolds opened a dialogue with Sinn Féin with the aim of getting a cease-fire before political negotiations and based on including Sinn Féin in government, not excluding them. He also played a large role in persuading US President Bill Clinton to join the process. US visas for Sinn Féin leader Gerry Adams and IRA leader Joe Cahill were crucial confidence-building measures in the run-up to the cease-fire. This new approach survived a change of government in early 1995, as a senior advisor in the new Irish Government argued that any agreement that excluded Sinn Féin was 'not worth a penny candle'.[14]

The Conservative British Government was clearly not convinced of this new approach of the Irish Government and sought to prioritize restarting talks, excluding Sinn Féin, with a focus on internal reform and a strategy to contain the IRA campaign. British reluctance to engage with the process led to delays in opening talks with Sinn Féin after the 1994 IRA cease-fire and this ultimately precipitated the ending of the cease-fire in February 1996. However, following the election of the Labour Party in the United Kingdom in 1997 and the return of the more nationalist Fianna Fáil to power in the Republic of Ireland later that year, a new IRA cease-fire was declared and talks, including Sinn Féin, began in September.

THE IMPACT OF A CHANGING INTERNATIONAL ENVIRONMENT

The ending of the Cold War opened up greater possibilities for international involvement in the conflict. It weakened the importance of the US relationship with the United Kingdom—a crucial factor, as the USA was the only international actor likely to be able to exert influence on the United Kingdom. While Northern Ireland was a low-risk intervention for the USA, it did involve President Clinton in a breach with an ally—to the extent that British Prime Minister John Major refused to take his phone calls—and was taken against the advice of almost the entire foreign policy, defence and intelligence establishment (p. 373, Coogan, 1995).

While the new world order permitted President Clinton's intervention, it did not prompt it. For motivations, it is necessary to look at the domestic pressure on Clinton (O'Cleary, 1996). His party needed to win back Irish Americans, who had become part of the Reagan-Democrat bloc. Clinton himself needed the Irish vote to win the Democratic primary and it was before the crucial New York primary, with its large and well organized Irish American vote, that he made his public commitments on the 'Irish' issue. He was also under pressure from a much more professional and influential Irish American lobby, itself partly a response to the changing strategy of Sinn Féin in Ireland, where better working relationships with other nationalists were being sought. The fact that President Clinton was personally involved increased the pressure on political actors to reach agreement and, as nationalists had least interest in accepting the status quo, this intervention inevitably favoured nationalists (as they wanted change), even if the process of intervention was even-handed, which it was.

Other international factors were also significant for the peace process. 'Struggles' that the Sinn Féin leadership had drawn inspiration from or sought to compare themselves with in South Africa, Palestine and Central America were moving towards peace negotiations (Cox, pp. 676–82 in 1997, and pp. 75–77 in 1998). Though the IRA did not face significant financial or military material losses they were affected by the political climate that these developments created and were part of. At an ideological level and, in the case of South Africa, at the level of extensive personal contacts[15] the emergence of international peace processes had a significant impact on republican thinking, a process of influence that Sinn Féin then played in the Basque conflict.

Prior to the end of the Cold War, unionists by virtue of their siege mentality had made limited use of international contacts. Such parallels as were drawn tended to be with what were perceived as similar communities under siege, such as Israel, Turkish Cypriots, apartheid South Africa or other 'abandoned' British settlers, such as the white community in Rhodesia/Zimbabwe (pp. 40–46, in Clayton, 1996).[16] Such comparisons were clearly damaging by the 1990s and unionists could not credibly argue that the conflict was a purely internal 'British' matter once the British Government accepted US and Irish government involvement (p. 289, in Ruane and Todd, 1996). However unionists were undoubtedly pleased with the election of George W. Bush as US President and the lower level of engagement it promised, but their general distrust of any international involvement was seen after '9/11' when they made no serious attempt in the USA to try and use the new environment to damage Sinn Féin.

THE 1998 AGREEMENT

The Agreement[17] reached by the two Governments and the main Northern Ireland parties (excluding the DUP) in April 1998 included a power-sharing consociational-style government, a new Northern Ireland regional assembly and a structured set of cross-border institutions. Sinn Féin was to be included in the power-sharing government, the cease-fire was to be reinforced, prisoner releases provided for and a programme of reform for police, criminal justice, cultural rights and economic equality set in place.

The Agreement provided for a new Assembly to be elected by proportional representation, which would have 'full legislative and executive authority' in respect of matters devolved from London. Elected members, on taking their seats, have to designate themselves as 'unionist', 'nationalist' or 'other'. Key decisions are made with either 50% support from each community or a 60% overall majority, including at least 40% support from each bloc. The First Minister and Deputy First Minister are elected by the process of parallel consent, designed to ensure that one will be a unionist and one a nationalist. They effectively operate as a single institution. Other ministerial posts are allocated to parties on the basis of the number of Assembly seats held, and ministers have a good deal of autonomy in running their departments. To ensure that the North-South Council actually operates and is not frustrated by unionist opposition to such cross-border institutions, the Assembly and the North-South Council are declared to be 'mutually interdependent ... one cannot successfully function without the other'. Participation in the Council is declared to be 'one of the essential responsibilities' attaching to a ministerial post. Also, the British and Irish Governments agreed to redraw their constitutional expressions of sovereignty on Northern Ireland, stating:

> 'it is for the people of the island of Ireland alone, by agreement between the two parts respectively and without external impediment, to exercise their right of self-determination on the basis of consent, freely and concurrently given, North and South, to bring about a united Ireland, if that is their wish, accepting that this right must be achieved and exercised with and subject to the agreement and consent of a majority of the people of Northern Ireland.'

Most of the UUP leadership, including party leader David Trimble, had been active in the unionist opposition to the more modest Sunningdale Agreement, which only involved power sharing with the SDLP and a purely consultative cross-border Council of Ireland. The 1998 Agreement did commit the two Governments to maintaining the Union with Britain, even if qualified by saying that it was only for as long as that was the wish of a majority. The Agreement also meant the return of a government and parliament to Northern Ireland, with David Trimble as the most likely First Minister. Also, the Irish Government agreed to hold a referendum seeking to amend the Irish Constitution to reframe the Republic's position on unity from a territorial claim to a 'firm will'. Unionists, however, also had to face a number of previously unthinkable propositions. They would be forced to share power not only with the SDLP but also with Sinn Féin and they had to agree to a cross-border body with a strong structural position, police reform, equality measures and prisoner releases.

Unionism was, however, faced with an Irish nationalist position that had formed an effective alliance with a US administration and a reasonable working relationship with a British Labour Government that was likely to be in power for another eight or nine years. Northern nationalists now made up over 40% of the voting population and moderate unionism, as represented by Alliance, combined with loyalist paramilitaries who supported the deal for different reasons might mobilize another 8%. Mainstream unionism, for the first time since partition did not have a secure majority. Nationalists were still a long way from securing a majority for a united Ireland, but with minimal other support they could secure a majority in a referendum for far-reaching political change. The UUP leadership was quite explicit about this threat during the negotiations. Senior UUP negotiator Anthony Alcock argued that if the UUP walked out it was likely that a section of mainstream unionists would vote in a referendum to accept a peace deal that had been negotiated in their absence.[18] The bottom line for the UUP leadership was that however unhappy they were with key elements of the deal, any likely alternative was going to be much worse from a unionist perspective, as a British Government keen to secure the IRA cease-fire was going to agree to some sort of deal with or without the unionists.

The rejection of the deal by the DUP—and almost half of all UUP supporters— was not surprising as they had been on the record over many years as opposing compromises and reform well short of what was in the Agreement. Unionist parties have traditionally insisted that there is little point having a veto on the 'final hand-over' of sovereignty if they cannot prevent political decisions which change the character of the state and/or which move them towards a united Ireland (Doyle, 2003). This strong linkage of equality issues and constitutional issues means that reform is seen as undermining the state and paving the way for further change. This position was articulated by all the major unionist parties, including those which ultimately supported the Agreement, as recently as 1997.[19]

For Sinn Féin, the Agreement fell short of achieving a united Ireland, but it saw this as an agreement in transition, not its end point. While there are specific gains in the deal such as the North-South Council and internal reform, the detail is less important than a clear commitment by the two Governments to move away from the status quo. Sinn Féin leaders recognized early on that a united Ireland was not going to be available at these talks, as they did not have the political support to achieve it. However, they could achieve—in alliance with other nationalists, the Irish Government and the USA—a much strengthened equality agenda and institutional links between north and south and they could create a dynamic for further progressive change. Given the stalemate that the IRA campaign had reached, Sinn Féin was willing to accept the Agreement on this basis.

THE PROSPECTS OF CONFLICT RESOLUTION

In some respects the Northern Ireland conflict is regarded as 'resolved' in a comparative context. There are almost no conflict-related deaths. The IRA has destroyed all of its weapons in a process witnessed by a Canadian, Gen. John de Chastelain, and an international commission.[20] British and Irish security sources agree with Gen. de Chastelain's analysis that IRA disarming was complete. The IRA also issued a public statement calling an end to its armed conflict.[21]

The underlying political conflict remains however. The power-sharing executive set up under the 1998 Agreement was suspended in 2001 and was not restored until May 2007. The UUP refused to remain in the Executive until the IRA fully disarmed. The IRA in turn would not disarm until the Agreement was fully implemented. Without a champion to argue the case for the Agreement within the unionist community, support for it fell dramatically and the consistently anti-agreement DUP emerged as the largest unionist party in 2003, consolidated in 2007 with some 30% of the total to the UUP's 15%. However, disarming by the IRA in 2005 did not see unionists rejoin the government at that time. The DUP now demanded IRA disbandment and Sinn Féin support for the police among other issues before they would agree to share power.[22] Nationalists were sceptical that they had any intention of ever doing so, as they believe unionists prefer direct rule from London to sharing power regionally with Sinn Féin. Sinn Féin for its part refused to support the police until further reforms were implemented—as proposed in a review chaired by the former British politician and (perhaps symbolically) last Governor of Hong Kong, Chris Patton. In particular it sought the transfer of political control from London to the power-sharing Executive.[23]

Opponents of the Sinn Féin leadership from the perspective of IRA dissidents (McIntyre, 2001; Moloney, 2003), pro-agreement unionists (Bew, 1998) and academic analysts (such as Murray and Tonge, 2005) have characterized the Sinn Féin leaders' acceptance of the 1998 Agreement as an abandonment of their republican objectives, as there is little evidence of an imminent united Ireland. Jennifer Todd (1999) disagrees, arguing that Sinn Féin has rather redirected its energies towards a radical egalitarianism. While Sinn Féin has embraced the language of equality as the core theme of its recent publicity, it also pursues the objective of a united Ireland (Doyle, 2006). It sees the 1998 Agreement as part of a process, not a settlement. It always uses that language.[24] Sinn Féin remains committed to the peace process as it believes it has a greater possibility of achieving its objectives than an 'armed struggle' that had been contained. In addition, its commitment to a process that does not self-evidently deliver a united Ireland is based on three assumptions. First, the Sinn Féin leadership assumes that demographic trends will continue to reduce the unionist percentage of the population in Northern Ireland. Secondly, Sinn Féin argues that increased functional co-operation through cross-border institutions will create a political dynamic towards unity—a point also feared by unionists.[25] Finally, Sinn Féin believes that unionism at its most fundamental rests on a position of privilege over nationalists—reflected in unemployment figures, policing, cultural rights, etc. Sinn Féin does not have the political power to achieve Irish unity at present, but it does believe that it has the power to create much greater equality between nationalists and unionists and that such reform will strengthen nationalism and weaken unionism, boosting the political dynamic towards unity.

Some unionists who still support the 1998 Agreement assume that if nationalists have a role in government, greater equality and some institutional links with the Republic of Ireland then this will effectively end the militant nationalist challenge to British rule. The dominant voices in unionist politics, however, do not believe that nationalists will alter their underlying perspective and see the reform process as strengthening nationalist claims by undermining the security forces and the 'British' ethos of Northern Ireland. There is therefore little internal dynamic in unionism to reach any form of agreement. However, unionists traditionally rejected power sharing with the SDLP and refused to have any talks with the Irish Government, both of which they now accept. If the unionist parties could resist power sharing or further reform by simply accepting continuing rule from London they would gladly do so. However, the real prospect of political change being agreed by the two Governments without them forced the unionists to make a decision.

The confidence in the IRA's commitment to the peace process is partly responsible for the stalemate in the political process. As the British Government has become convinced that the IRA is unlikely to resume its armed campaign, it has felt under less pressure to respond to nationalists' political demands for reform of policing, troop withdrawals and more proactive equality measures, or to pressurize unionists to rejoin the power-sharing Executive. This was a high-risk strategy. While there is no evidence of any intention by the current IRA leadership to relaunch an armed campaign, a long-term stalemate could have led to disillusionment among members and a crisis event of some sort could see street violence re-emerge in the future. Certainly throughout 2006 former IRA members opposed to the peace process were attempting to reorganize.[26] Ultimately, in the 2007 election the dissidents only received a tiny vote, consolidating Sinn Féin's leadership in the nationalist community.

The Irish Government is always under pressure to achieve progress. It faces an increased electoral challenge from Sinn Féin; the largest and currently (2006) governing party, Fianna Fáil, has sought to protect the traditionally nationalist element of its support base by projecting a more strongly nationalist position and, in this context, it needs to assert itself against the United Kingdom. The British Government could resist such pressure given its more powerful position, but it also wants good relations with the Irish Government. This led the two Governments (under Irish pressure) effectively to threaten the imposition of a 'plan B' over the heads of local parties if unionists did not rejoin the power-sharing Executive. The agreed phrase 'joint stewardship of the process' was designed to hint at the possibility of something close to de facto joint governance by the two Governments if unionists refused to share power with Sinn Féin, although without being explicit enough to cause a unionist revolt. While still leaving the United Kingdom as the sovereign state and most powerful actor, such an arrangement would have been likely to lead to further reform measures in policing, cultural rights, etc., and to the renewal of cross-border institutions, with London appointing the 'northern' representatives. This would be an acceptable fall-back position for Sinn Féin—not as advantageous as being in government but better than stalemate and probably enough to sustain the IRA cease-fire.

For unionists the possibility of an inter-governmental 'plan B' was seen as a threat that the status quo is an unlikely future scenario and that they were faced with a choice between sharing power with Sinn Féin or seeing the Irish and British Governments share (some) power over their heads. The DUP chose to share power rather than allow a greater institutional role for the Irish Government in co-operation with a British Government that it did not trust. DUP leader Paisley accepted power sharing only because the alternative was worse. The unionists extracted some concessions from Sinn Féin, but joined government with good grace in May 2007—confirming that you do not need to like or agree with those with whom you share government

NOTES

1. Space does not permit a more detailed analysis of the historic roots of the conflict. For a good overview see O'Leary and McGarry (1993).

2. In the most famous case in Derry City, a unionist population of approximately 33% of the city's voters returned a majority of councillors on the city corporation.

3. 'Paramilitaries' is the term widely used to describe illegal armed groups in Northern Ireland and not 'paramilitary police' as is common elsewhere. 'Loyalist' is usually used to describe a militant unionist; for clarity, in this article it is only used to describe those with links to illegal unionist paramilitaries.

4. See website with statistical analysis (http://cain.ulst.ac.uk/issues/violence/stats.htm).

5. Two excellent introductions to the academic literature on Northern Ireland are McGarry and O'Leary (1995) and Ruane and Todd (1996). The best international and comparative studies are McGarry (2002) and Cox, Guelke and Stephen (2006).

6. From a confidential conversation with the author.

7. Contribution by the Irish Minister responsible for Broadcasting in the Seanad Éireann, the Irish upper house of parliament, on 12 March 1975.

8. E.g. *Sunday Business Post* of 25 March 2006 gave Sinn Féin 11%.

9. There are many books that do so; the two best journalistic accounts are Mallie and McKittrick (1996) and De Bréadún (2001). Mansergh (1995) and Adams (2003) provide insider's accounts.

10. Reproduced in full in the appendices of Cox et al. (2006).

11. In particular two unusually large devices caused hundreds of millions of pounds in damage in 1992–93 in London's financial district, at the Baltic Exchange in April 1992 and a year later in the Bishopsgate area.

12. Mortars landed in the rear garden of 10 Downing Street during a cabinet meeting on 7 February 1991.

13. The Irish term for Prime Minister.

14. Fergus Finlay, adviser to then Irish Foreign Minister Dick Spring, in *The Irish Times* of 26 April 1996.

15. *The Irish Times* of 20 April and 30 April 1998.

16. See also: *Combat*, August 1974 and September 1974; Jim Kilfedder in the House of Commons on 6 March 1978; and David Trimble in the House of Commons on 30 October 1996.

17. Full text available at foreignaffairs.gov.ie/angloirish/goodfriday/. For commentary, see Doyle (1998).

18. Northern Ireland Forum of 3 October 1997 (Vol. 45, p. 10).

19. For example, the UUP response to the framework documents on the internet at www.uup.org and Alcock in the Northern Ireland Forum of 7 February 1997 (Vol. 27, p. 21).

20. On 26 September 2005.

21. On 28 July 2005.

22. See www.dup.org.uk for latest positions from the party.

23. See www.sinnfein.ie/ for up-to-date policing statements.

24. At www.sinnfein.ie/ are copies of all recent manifestos and policy documents.

25. E.g. Robert McCartney in the Assembly on 22 November. 1982.

26. E.g. *Sunday Tribune* of 27 August 2006.

Yugoslavia: Why Did it Collapse?

Stevan K. Pavlowitch

In this chapter I would like to narrate the Yugoslav story as a tragedy that is strewn with misapprehensions. Yugoslavia was not a nation in the sense given to that word since the French Revolution: it was never really a 'community of citizens', and yet its concept was not artificial. The modern nation, with a political identity, was built on the ethnic community, characterized by cultural and historical affinities. In western Europe, political unity had been established well before the emergence of modern nationalism, but in the eastern part of the continent, ethnic communities developed without turning into political communities. Each new so-called nation, as it emerged, wanted to coincide with a territory and to blend its population into a whole so as to constitute a nation-state.

Yugoslavia extended across a zone of fault lines, but also of passageways and crossroads. In the 19th century a source of unity came to be seen in the speech and way of life of the South Slav populations, but for as long as empires existed, the Yugoslav idea remained a unifying ideology, not an identity, subject to a variety of interpretations. When that dream came true at the end of the First World War, the articulation of several South Slav identities was already well advanced, yet the founders of the Yugoslav state wanted to treat them as subgroups of one nation—an ideal or an illusion? In spite of differences and problems, because Yugoslavia was generally seen to be the most reasonable framework for the coexistence of its related ethnic groups, the Yugoslavs went on searching for a viable political solution for over 70 years, from crisis to crisis.

The Second World War brought to an end what has since been called the 'First Yugoslavia'—with occupation, dismemberment and civil, ideological and ethnic strife, as the conquerors destroyed the state and set its components against each other. However, the outcome of the war led to a 'Second Yugoslavia', because the defeat of Nazism destroyed those movements that had sought to solve the problems of ethnic differences by withdrawing into tribalism under foreign protection. The Communist Party of Yugoslavia under Tito reunified the country as a federation of related ethnic communities, but wartime wounds went unhealed in the certainty that communism would cauterize them.

The social revolution was no less radical than the political revolution. Its climax was not reached until the 1960s when the challenges to central control by the wartime revolutionaries' generation had become such that a redistribution of power was called for. What happened then was that sovereignty was distributed to regional leaderships, in what amounted to a feudalization of party rule under the paramount suzerainty of the ageing dictator. From the 1970s the regime degenerated into a coalition of local oligarchies, which allowed the majority ethnic group to assert itself in every constituent unit as a way of finding a new legitimation.

The changes had brought about an institutionally decentralized but unarticulated society lacking effective means of ensuring the recomposition of society along the lines of its emerging interests. The result was regional autarky with neither central nor democratic control. Citizens as individuals had no representation. Political institutions were able to express a plurality of interests only through the mechanisms of the ruling party, but the party was unable to govern the differences created by the changes.

Tito, like Lenin, had known how to use ethnic feelings, but after his death, and with the erosion of communist legitimacy following on increasing economic misery and political paralysis, the system held on through inertia for another decade until communism collapsed elsewhere in Europe. Centrifugal tendencies intensified in the privileged regions, more and more reticent to support the cost of the underprivileged regions and of the central power structure. The federal Government, paralysed by juxtaposed vetoes, was unable to do anything for the economy. That reinforced the image of the individual republics as the only repositories of national interests—presented as challenged by recently arrived immigrants from poorer regions, by other regions and by the federation. Two tendencies pulled in opposite directions. The new Serbian leadership under Slobodan Milošević wanted to tighten up the federation again, others to loosen it even more. The conditions under which the 1990 elections were held in all the republics rendered local governments vulnerable to populism, and the running was done by the constituent territories, which emphasized their role in the definition of group identity.

Fifty years of the dictatorship of the party under the prestigious but cumbersome figure of Tito had certainly not denied the Yugoslavs their ethnic rights, whatever their leaders and spokesmen have since said, but it had done nothing for democracy. With the collapse of communism, democracy came to be regarded as nothing more than the expression of freedom of individual ethnic groups.

Surprised by the sudden outbreak of violence, observers have tended to explain it as a return to ancestral hatreds, yet there is no need to go back further than the Second World War. The immediate cause of the cycle of warfare that started in 1991 ('the wars of the Yugoslav succession' as they have been called) was the brutal and officialized revelation, the orchestration of recollections of horrors then committed against us by others. The massacres of half a century previously fed perceptions and fears. Public opinion, as it emerged from decades of brainwashing, was pounced upon by new agitators, the worst remains of Tito's power structure. The absence of a civil society and the political ideological void caused by the collapse of communism determined conditions for the instrumental use of the past.

Milošević came to power in Serbia in 1987 by using the grievances of the dwindling Serb population in Serbia's autonomous province of Kosovo which had by then become in all but name an Albanian ethnic republic in federal Yugoslavia. He was determined to break the constitutional deadlock, to restore

Serbia's control over its provinces, and personally to dominate the federal party structure. Fear of a strong Serbia under Milošević provoked a chain reaction, which accelerated after his attempt to climb to the top of the Yugoslav party caused its final break-up.

Slovenia led the way. Nationality and territory happened to coincide in that republic. Croatia too went for a nation-state within the borders of the existing federated republic, but contained a 12% Serb minority. Franjo Tudjman's newly elected nationalist administration behaved towards the minority with incompetence, reinforced by discrimination and some violence. About half lived in poor and compact rural border areas (the one-time Austrian Military Border, or Krajina, with the Ottoman Empire) where they were organized by hardliners into the secessionist Serb Krajina, which local Croats were pressed to leave. The rest of Croatia's Serbs, mainly in larger towns, felt threatened and unprotected.

The war in Croatia started when the Krajina Serbs—encouraged and backed by what remained of the federal authority and army—voted in their own referendum to stay in Yugoslavia if Croatia went. When Milošević sensed that continued action in Croatia was endangering his claims to be master of what was left of the federation, he stopped championing the cause of the Croatian Serbs. After holding out for five years, the Krajina Serbs caved in as Croatia reconquered the territory in the summer of 1995. Most of them have fled, from fear or through pressure, and the Serbs of Croatia, down to some 5% or less of the population of that country, no longer present a problem except as refugees—mostly in Serbia.

Slovenia and Croatia having gone independent, the other non-Serb components did not want to stay in a rump Yugoslavia obviously dominated by Serbs, however much a Yugoslav structure was necessary for their survival. Bosnia and Herzegovina was the mirror image of Yugoslavia. Its population was made up of three communities, distinguished only by their nominal religious affiliation—44% Muslims, 33% (Orthodox) Serbs, 18% (Roman Catholic) Croats and some 5% who were plain Yugoslavs. During the Second World War Bosnia had been made part of a greater Croatia by the fascist Ustašas, who had tried to convert, expel or kill as many Serbs as they could, and to use the Muslims as their auxiliaries.

It was in Bosnia that ideological and ethnic strife had been at its most vicious. It had been the base of Tito's Communists, who had moulded its uprooted youth into a revolutionary partisan army. After the 1948 break with Stalin, and even more so after the Soviet invasion of Czechoslovakia in 1968, Bosnia had been turned into a mountain redoubt. It was a real arsenal, with most of Yugoslavia's military–industrial complex, underground depots of military equipment and secret headquarters. More than elsewhere, local authorities were encouraged to develop territorial defence, so that arms were readily available to all.

Bosnia was also the least prepared for democracy. Indeed, multiculturalism and the absence of democracy were two sides of the same coin. The area had enjoyed the benefits of a varied tradition and of a special way of life, but at the price of remaining economically backward except in key sectors, and in a semi-colonial status. When Yugoslavia confederalized, the party elite in Bosnia was the most conservative and the most corrupt. The three ethnic groups were entangled in an almost leopard-skin pattern, but there were no institutional mechanisms for accommodating differences among them other than party authority mitigated by corrupt practices.

In that context, the electorate went for ethnic parties; Serbs looked to Serbia, Croats to Croatia. When the referendum for independence was decided by the Muslim-led collective Presidency, it was boycotted by 37.3% of the electorate, essentially by the Serbs. Only the Muslims wanted independence. Croats were their short-term allies simply in order to break away from Yugoslavia. Serbs, fearing to be cut off from Yugoslavia, and sensing another distorted echo of the Second World War, had withdrawn from republican institutions and proclaimed their own Serb Republic. Their camp had the disadvantage of being territorially undefined, but the advantage of controlling most military capacities.

It was not possible for Bosnia to survive outside Yugoslavia. Independence identified Bosnia with its Muslim component, which had nowhere else to look to, was the largest of the three communities and had political control of larger towns, especially Sarajevo. Its political leadership had come to dominate the state apparatus, which was its instrument to ensure that all Muslims would live in one state, and it opposed plans to regionalize ethnic differences under international control.

When ethnicity was in practice territorialized, it happened by force, and the stage was set for 'ethnic cleansing'. This was first and most widely practised by Serbs, dispersed throughout Bosnia in patches that were difficult to bring together into one entity, but also by Croats who had initially offered the Muslim side their military support so long as the Government of Croatia ruled in practice over areas where they formed a strong majority. With the fears and the fighting, the polarization quickly went too far to be reversed by what was left of an urban intelligentsia and of more reform-minded party elements who had formed the opposition to the initially tripartite ethnic Government and who had tried to stave off ethnic war.

In its short-lived peaceful transition to pluralism in 1990, Yugoslavia witnessed the triumph of the idea of representation based on ethnicity rather than citizenship. People found themselves becoming estranged minorities in territories that they had previously inhabited. Because of the way in which Serbo-Croat speakers in the central area were intermixed and related, those who wanted them separated irreparably had to commit irreparable crimes. Croat fascists had done so in the early 1940s, under the protection of Nazi Germany, and almost succeeded in their endeavour. Fifty years later, under the protection of a large part of Tito's anti-fascist army, Serb hardliners of the same mixed areas would justify what they were doing by the fact that their parents had been victims of a first round of 'ethnic cleansing'. The 'return match' has led to a terrible 'draw'. Each side has committed war crimes and practised mass expulsions. The most victimized have been the Muslims of Bosnia; the Serbs of Bosnia have caused most suffering; and Croatia has been effectively cleansed of its Serbs, almost as well as Turkish Asia Minor of its Greeks after the Greek invasion and defeat in the aftermath of the First World War.

Milošević wanted to hold on to as much power over as much territory as he could—originally over the whole of Yugoslavia as a new Tito, then over as much of it as could be salvaged from the secessions and, finally, over the new Federal Republic of Yugoslavia, made up of Serbia and Montenegro. Serbia had restored control over its autonomous provinces, the administrative and cultural autonomy of which remained on paper. In practice, however, Kosovo was controlled by the military in a state of emergency where ethnic Albanians had been removed from the administration, public services and utilities, and where human rights abuses were committed. And yet, the few remaining local Serbs protested against the rapacity of carpetbaggers sent from Belgrade, while ethnic Albanians ran a shadow government after a semi-clandestine referendum on independence. The Albanian leaders travelled, gave interviews, sent appeals, organized passive resistance, held elections and were tolerated by the authorities who were anxious to keep channels open. In terms of international law, it was acknowledged that Kosovo was part of Serbia. The Albanian Government in Tirana provided no more than moral support, with a blind eye to smuggling—it feared it would not be able to absorb Kosovo which, however backward by Yugoslav standards, was so much more developed than Albania. Public opinion in Albania also perceived Kosovo Albanians as arms and drugs racketeers.

This left Macedonia, in international limbo because of a Greek veto on its name, with no more than 65% of the population registered as Macedonian—a young (Slav) ethnic community, with an ancient (Greek) name, which had lost its (Yugoslav) sponsor. The former Yugoslav republic of Macedonia had avoided war, but found it difficult to establish itself in spite of US support.

Even before the rising started by the Kosovo Liberation Army at the end of 1998 and the subsequent 'Atlantico–Serbian war', the whole of Yugoslavia had suffered from the collapse of the common state. Radicalized refugees, alienated minorities and an economy disrupted by the break-up and then by the war, when not destroyed by sanctions, did not augur well for a democratic evolution. The refusal to accept differences had been the main feature of the intra-Yugoslav wars—more significant than even the collapse of communism. Those who are creating chasms want to transform the area into something it has never been—a region of separations rather than crossroads.

The West had welcomed the birth of Yugoslavia at the end of the First World War as the new state seemed to fit a new European order and to have a future at the time of the fall of empires. It had then supported Tito right from the start, as he was deemed to be the best chance for a united Yugoslavia, before it turned his regime into a bastion against Soviet advance in the Cold War and a hoped-for model for the development of the rest of Eastern Europe. However, the West's understanding of Yugoslavia was illusory. It went on supporting Yugoslavia's communist leadership to the very end, thus enabling Tito's heirs to avoid real reforms.

Things began to go visibly wrong in Yugoslavia at a time when the West was not prepared to tackle that sort of question. It was bewildered by the collapse of communism and by the break-up of the Soviet empire. Yugoslavia no longer had a special appeal. The USA lost interest and the European Community as it turned into the European Union (EU) was in the middle of a public argument about where it was going. The Yugoslav crisis threatened to destabilize the continent at a time when Europe as a whole was trying to adjust to the changes brought about by the end of the Cold War.

Both the USA and the EU had the capability to shape the outcome in Yugoslavia, but they did not have the willingness to act in unison in the crucial early phase. The USA was chopping and changing. The EU was not a security organization, and it had not been put together to deal with civil war outside its territory. The 12 EU member nations hoped to acquire a common foreign policy in handling the break-up of Yugoslavia, but in the meanwhile pretended to have one at the lowest common denominator level. All had different motivations, which reflected different domestic predicaments. United only by the wish not to appear divided by the crisis, the West gave all the wrong messages, veering from one attitude to another, and allowing various factions to believe they enjoyed its support.

As usual the powers wanted the status quo. When, however, the secessions removed the known map of Yugoslavia's international borders, there was an inflection in the interpretation of the Conference on Security and Co-operation in Europe 1975 Helsinki principles of respect of the inviolability of state borders in exchange for respect of human rights within them. The Hague principles of October 1991 assumed, or acknowledged, that Yugoslavia was falling apart, but not to the extent that the internal boundaries between federated units were also going. Resorting to internal frontiers was an attempt to impose some kind of paper order on the chaos that was emerging.

Even so, the fall-back position on the constituent units of complex states could have been made by a simultaneous recognition of all republics, conditional on strict adherence to the stipulations of Helsinki. Instead, preoccupation with domestic issues, ignorance and lack of vision and of common political will led to giving blessing initially only to Slovenia and Croatia, and then to cornering Bosnia into following—a state rejected by one of its communities, and accepted only through lip service by another. The Dayton Accord continued the process of falling back on constituent units, by acknowledging the existence of two 'entities' within a formally united and internationally recognized Bosnia and Herzegovina. The Rambouillet plan continued on that same path.

What was once Yugoslavia is special only in that it concentrates all the ailments of post-communist Europe from the Baltic to the Caucasus. Caught between a planned economy that no longer exists and a market economy yet to come, post-communist Europe is engulfed in an economic crisis that is favourable to the search for scapegoats and the rise of demagogues. In the worst cases, a siege mentality gives cohesion to remnants of old regimes, with the debris of nomenklaturas sensitive to the calls of the extreme right, whose reflexes come from the hatred of Marxism-Leninism, from xenophobia, from patriotism and from religious fundamentalism.

In societies whose ideologies in the 19th century had seen the nation-state as the only possible repository of political aspirations and where 40 years of communism had prevented both critical study of the past and political discussion of the future, there is no political culture. Living astride a geopolitical and cultural border that has moved in time and space, differed in meaning and changed frequently, people feel vulnerable. With no understanding of politics, they look for the simplest and most dangerous explanations—conspiracies, love and hate. Far from moving on to becoming nations, disillusioned ethnic communities return to tribalism, with values based on ancestry, leadership and self-mystification, cherishing the memory of injustices received while ignoring injustice committed. Each wants to be a nation-state but balks at having to share power with minorities.

Nationalism had for long been seen by the West as an antidote to communism, until it realized that, communism having collapsed, the virus of tribal conflict had appeared in Europe; it then tried to contain the old disease in Yugoslavia by remote therapy, followed by surgical bombardment. The danger is that it may view the disastrous consequences of the way in which Yugoslavia collapsed as a regional problem, which can be allowed to fester indefinitely as long as it does not spread beyond what is conveniently and disdainfully (as if reassuringly) called the 'Balkans'.

The great powers are not responsible for the Yugoslav situation, but they must confront it. The explanation that Yugoslavia was an artificial state created at the end of the First World War is a simplistic one. It was not perceived as such at the time, and it implies that there are natural as opposed to artificial states. No less simplistic is the equally unconvincing explanation that Communism was a glacial era at the end of which 'history' reappeared with all its old names and problems.

The term 'Balkanization', which referred initially to the break-up of the Habsburg and Ottoman Empires, has come to mean the fragmentation of larger political complexes into smaller and often mutually antagonistic entities. The Balkans, however, also had a uniqueness, which resided in the sense that people did belong to distinct ethnic communities, but also to a wider common background of mentality, everyday life, cultural bases, shared experiences and, at times, religion or speech.

I would argue that peace and some sort of long-term evolution towards democracy cannot be expected in the Yugoslav lands unless territorial issues are resolved and their isolation from Europe is ended. Without some alteration of internal borders—negotiated, mediated and eventually accepted—it is doubtful that an equitable solution can be found. Rather than establish some sort of balance of military power between successor states and/or factions, a disarmament programme under international control for the whole region should accompany the prosecution of war crimes.

The task is then a long-term one of changing attitudes through education, the media and international co-operation, and of overcoming the fear of living in a society not ethnically homogeneous. In other words, what is needed is to attempt an international approach that reflects the long-term needs of the area rather than the short-term needs of the outside players. If not, the rest of Europe runs the risk of being Balkanized before the Balkans are Europeanized.

In the absence of any long-term approach in depth, one must look forward to a scenario in which local authoritarian rulers continue to target their political efforts at obtaining support from rival powers for their ethno-territorial projects in exchange for services, and to some sort of a new 'scramble for the Balkans'. The view that the conflicts in the Yugoslav lands are a purely local problem resulting from the peculiarities of the Balkan mentality is, at best, dangerously simplistic and, at worst verging on the racist. The crisis should rather be viewed in terms of the broader challenge of sustaining the values that have shaped Western Europe since the end of the Second World War at a time when the struggle against communism no longer serves as a focus of unity. Ethnic nationalism is not, after all, unique to post-communist Europe.

More than any other recent event, the Yugoslav crisis has revealed the precarious political configuration not only of the EU but of its individual member states, divided as they are between the political forces favouring continued integration and those pressing for a reassertion of individual national interests. This fact alone is a destabilizing factor in the Balkans. Yugoslavia was a 20th-century attempt to 'manage differences' in an area of transition. To the extent that it came into being, not only once but twice, and survived, albeit from crisis to crisis, for over 70 years, it was a success, but it also turned out in the end to be the abysmal failure of a success. Its birth was an act of faith in ideas that had been inherited from the 19th century. Its brutal death on the eve of the 21st century is not so much a return to the middle ages, or to the barbarians at the gates, as the appearance of an all-too-modern (or should I say post-modern?) challenge—how to 'manage the differences'—a problem we are still trying to resolve with 19th-century ideas.

Placing Serbia in Context

PETER GOWAN

INTRODUCTION

There is a very strong tendency in the literature on the Yugoslav collapse to privilege the endogenous forces pushing towards disintegration and to treat the exogenous actors as both secondary and reactive. There is a parallel tendency to stress the uniqueness of the endogenous actors within Yugoslavia rather than setting these actors in a wider comparative framework, which enables us to grasp their real specificity by precisely grasping how they are distinctive species of larger genera. I will try to argue that a wider lens is indispensable to an understanding of Yugoslav dynamics in the 1990s and early 2000s.

My essay would like to raise two issues. First, I would question the adequacy of approaches to the collapse of Yugoslavia that fail to situate it in its international spatial and temporal context and that residualize the role of external actors in the dynamics of Yugoslavia's disintegration. Secondly, I would like to make some remarks about the Serbian national question and political system. I think these questions should be addressed directly.

THE NEED FOR COMPARATIVE APPROACHES

There are three obvious comparative frameworks for studying the Yugoslav collapse: state collapse after the end of the superpower confrontation; the fragmentation of multinational states in the context of transition to capitalism; and political tendencies and configurations in the context of the crisis and collapse of state socialism. We will briefly highlight each of these frameworks.

State Strain and Collapse after the End of the Superpower Confrontation

The end of the 1980s and early 1990s witnessed strains within, or even the disintegration of, a number of states the viability of which had been influenced by the rivalry between the USSR and the USA. One such case was Somalia, another Afghanistan. Yugoslavia was a third. All such countries had possessed geopolitical or geostrategic interest for the superpowers essentially because of the superpower rivalry, interests which led one or both of the superpowers to hold the state together. However, with the end of that rivalry and the consequent withdrawal of superpower support, the state concerned was plunged into crisis. Yugoslavia was one species of this genus.

Both the USA and the USSR had had an interest in preserving the integrity of Yugoslavia during the Cold War. As the superpower strategic rivalry ended, both superpowers revoked their commitment to maintaining the integrity of the Yugoslav state. As far as the USA was concerned, its commitment was formally withdrawn in the spring of 1989. However, in reality, the US Administration of Ronald Reagan had, since 1984, tended to supplement that policy objective vis-à-vis Yugoslavia with another policy objective, the overthrowing of state socialism within Yugoslavia and replacing it with capitalism. From the spring of 1989 this objective governed all others in the policy of the USA towards Yugoslavia. This was a fundamental shift in the state's geopolitical location, with enormous importance for the internal dynamics of Yugoslavia itself. It meant that secession became a viable option.

The Fragmentation of Multinational States in the Context of Transition to Capitalism

A second obvious feature of recent Yugoslav history is the fact that during the late 1980s the country was undergoing a profound social conflict, which involved an attempt by both domestic and external social groups to overthrow the socialist system and replace it with particular kinds of capitalism. This social conflict in Yugoslavia was, of course, part of a wider social conflict throughout the whole region of east-central and eastern Europe. We now know that such social conflicts place great strains on multinational states: not only Yugoslavia, but also Czechoslovakia and the USSR. We could also add that they tend to generate inter-ethnic tensions in states where one nation overwhelmingly predominates: we have seen such tensions in Russia, Romania, Slovakia, the Czech Republic, Bulgaria and, of course, the Baltic states. The existence of acute intra-Yugoslav strains between nationalities and ethnic groups does not, therefore, in itself mark Yugoslavia out as distinctive and unique—quite the contrary.

The combination of social crisis and radically divergent and conflictive political tendencies in multinational states has tended to generate powerful centrifugal tendencies pulling apart the state on national lines. It is noticeable that in all three cases mentioned, the break-up of the multinational state was the work much more of elites than of popular political will. Certainly in both Czechoslovakia and Yugoslavia there is overwhelming evidence that the majority of the populations of both countries were hostile to the break-up before it occurred. In neither case was the population of the country as a whole able to express its will on whether the state's integrity should be maintained. In all three cases, the break-up was closely linked to the ways in which elite groups identified their own political and social interests in the context of a deep crisis of state socialism and a preference among large parts of the elites for a transition to capitalism. It was these groups that organized the break-up.

The break-up was, then, orchestrated at elite level. In the Soviet case it was carried out by parts of the nomenklatura in a strongly co-operative way, with the dominant groups within both Ukrainian and Russian elites viewing the break-up as the best path towards constructing their future political and social domination and with the Belarusian elite acquiescing. Those elements within the Soviet state apparatus that had been strongly opposed to any break-up of the USSR had already been politically defeated many months before the break-up occurred. The dissolution of federation was not the product of sharp antagonisms between the groups dominating the three republics. Thus, although there was the potential for catastrophic conflicts between Ukraine and Russia, the dominant groups in both cases had not the slightest interest in exploiting those potentialities.

In the Czechoslovakian case, the break-up was closely linked to elite-level conflict over political-economy strategies, but both the Czech and the Slovakian elites shared a common interest in separation; they also shared a common interest in minimizing conflict at a popular level or over territorial issues. There was no substantial part of the Czechoslovakian elite that was strongly committed to drastic action to preserve state unity.

The Yugoslav case was different. There were powerful tendencies towards the use of conflict and force both against the break-up and within the break-up. We can briefly list these Yugoslav peculiarities:

The Yugoslav army and state security apparatus was constitutionally, politic-ally and culturally committed to the use of force, if necessary, to preserve Yugoslav unity. They had a constitutional duty to preserve the integrity of the state and—because of the special conditions in which post-war Yugoslavia was founded, through a revolution led by a partisan military resistance—the military-security apparatus had a special élan and militancy in their cause.

The social conflict between supporters of state socialism and the supporters of capitalist restoration took a clear geographical form in Yugoslavia, where the institutions of the League of Communists were far more deeply entrenched in the populations of the Yugoslav south (Serbia, Montenegro and Macedonia) than in the north-west. As in the Czechoslovakian case, the most resolutely pro-capitalist forces were those closest to the European Union (EU) and they identified their secessionist goal with a path towards Western capitalism and the EU. There was thus a potentially explosive accumulation of national cleavages and social cleavages.

As in other parts of the region, there was a tendency for elite groups most hostile to the continuation of state socialism to embrace inter-war nationalist traditions on the right. This was evident in Croatia and it also evident in Serbia, with the revival of Chetnik and royalist traditions on the anti-commu-nist Serbian right. Such trends were also seen across the whole region—in Bulgaria, Romania, Hungary, Slovakia, etc. The distinctive feature of Yugoslavia was the fact that these inter-war and wartime traditions could only be perceived as extremely threatening by the populations of one or other of the various Yugoslav national communities.

The issue of secession organized under the leadership of nationalist political leaderships raised in an acute form the question of Yugoslavia's internal republican boundaries and national rights in the context of secession. Given the context of the other distinctive Yugoslav features, which we have mentioned, this last set of issues was bound to be absolutely fundamental if war was to be avoided.

Political Tendencies and Configurations in the Context of the Crisis and Collapse of State Socialism

A cardinal weakness of Eastern European and Soviet studies in the West during the Cold War was their failure to recognize that communism in Eastern Europe depended upon the organization of popular consent. Totalitarian theory obscured this and thus obscured much of the reality of the political crisis of communism in Eastern Europe during the 1980s. This evasion was further enhanced by the false perception that 1989–90 can be thematicized as a revolt or revolution by 'civil society' against totalitarianism in the region. In reality, the political systems of east-central Europe in the late 1980s were marked by complex left–right cleavages that cannot be understood within a totalitarian-versus-civil-society perspective. Instead of viewing totalitarianism–civil society as the structural context of politics in that region, we should rather see totalitarianism–civil society as one (transient) type of political movement among other political movements, all of which should be framed within a left–right spectrum, which itself reflects a clash of political values between socialism and pro-capitalist tendencies. Both the Civic Committees in Poland and the Civic Movement in Czechoslovakia were, in reality, liberal-capitalist political formations, organized on a fairly transient basis as a variety of anti-communist liberal populisms.

The trends that emerged in the political crisis of state socialism typically included the following:[1] (a) pro-capitalist social democratic trends growing out of the communist parties; (b) anti-capitalist trends growing out of the communist parties seeking to resist capitalist restoration either through defending the state socialist order, though not the party political monopoly, or through seeking a socialist 'third way'; (c) liberal anti-communist trends directly supporting Euro-Atlantic and IMF orientations; (d) nationalist and/or religious parties harking back to inter-war political traditions on the right and marked by both anti-communism and anti-liberalism; and (e) fascist activist parties, often based upon hostility to particular ethnic groups.

This general east-central and east European pattern of emergent political trends in the crisis of state socialism was present also in Yugoslavia. The emergent Yugoslav political leaderships and movements in the late 1980s can be situated as particular species of these general Eastern European types:

The liberal, Euro-Atlantic trend was present in Ante Marković's all-Yugoslav movement. The programme of this formation on socio-economic and political orientations was not unlike those of the Free Democrats in Hungary or that of the Polish liberals.

The pro-capitalist social-democratic trend was evident, emerging from the communist parties of Slovenia, Croatia and Bosnia and Herzegovina, and it was also present in Serbian politics. These trends were similar to the social democrats emerging from the communist parties in Hungary or Poland.

The nationalist/religious trend was evident in Franjo Tudjman's party in Croatia and in Serbian Chetnik formations such as those launched by Vuk Drasković and Vojislav Šešelj. These trends were similar to movements like the Christian Nationals in Poland, and József Antall's Democratic Forum in Hungary. And as in these latter cases, they tended to overlap with more fascistic trends on the extreme right.

Trends emerging from the former communist party still committed to the traditions of state socialism were evident above all in Serbia with the Milošević-led Socialist Party, as well as in Montenegro and Macedonia, and this trend had similarities both with the Bulgarian Socialist Party, which contained strong anti-capitalist elements in the early 1990s and with the Ion Iliescu trend in Romania. In nearly all the countries of Eastern Europe, political tendencies that continued to adhere to state socialist traditions remained significant or even, at times, electorally dominant in many countries during the transition. This aspect of the transition has, on the whole, been understated in much of the Western literature. There has been a tendency to view the Serbian Socialist Party's electoral support at the start of the 1990s as deriving overwhelmingly from its leader, Milošević, championing the rights of Serbs within Kosovo and the removal of the 1974 autonomy entitlements from Kosovo and Vojvodina and so on. Yet these were by no means the only bases of the Socialist Party's support in Serbia—a point to which we will return.

When we look at the Yugoslav events within this wider comparative context, then, we can appreciate that the distinctive feature of Yugoslavia was above all the fact that dangerous tendencies that were widely generated across the whole region happened to be combined in particularly dangerous combinations in the Yugoslav context:

The collapse of the Cold War geostrategic context of the region exerted centrifugal tendencies that were especially powerful for Yugoslavia.

The combination of a deep social conflict between groups favouring capitalism and groups favouring the maintenance of state socialism with a long and particularly acute economic and social crisis within Yugoslavia.

The political strains resulting from the social conflict over the transition to capitalism were expressed in a particularly sharp series of nationalist cleavages, as well as right–left cleavages.

There was no elite-level consensus on paths forward either in maintaining state unity or in separating.

It was thus extremely difficult to handle issues of boundaries and national rights.

THE ROLE OF INTERNATIONAL ACTORS IN YUGOSLAVIA'S DISINTEGRATION

An optic which residualizes the role of international actors to one that is both secondary and reactive is inadequate for any approximate grasp of the dynamics of the Yugoslav crisis.

Western Involvement

I have written about these issues elsewhere[2] and will simply summarize some central analytical issues here. First, the Reagan and George Bush Administrations (1981–89 and 1989–93) singled out Yugoslavia for special attention as a lead state for the US drive to overthrow state socialism and to introduce a distinctive form of open-door capitalism in the region. The US Administration pursued this strategy for Yugoslavia through the US Treasury and through the IMF and World Bank in a systematic way, and their shock therapy programme, which was launched in 1990, contained a number of distinctive features. One of these was a particularly harsh bankruptcy mechanism, which had sharply asymmetrical geographical effects, hitting the southern part of Yugoslavia most severely. The linkage between these external actors and the Ante Marković Yugoslav leadership in 1990 was a powerful accelerator of the disintegrative tendencies.

This accelerator effect was multiplied by the active encouragement by other external actors of the separatist nationalist tendencies in Slovenia and Croatia: the Vatican, Hungary, Austria and Germany actively encouraged secessionist tendencies in these two republics, and the latter tendencies gained an important political lever, particularly in Croatia, through being able to campaign against the US shock therapy line of Marković. The Serbian Socialist Party was also able to strengthen its political base by opposing the US-Marković shock therapy programme.

In any crisis of the territorial integrity of a state, the role of international actors is of critical importance, since only the leading states within the international order have it in their gift to legitimate the emergence of new states. The states of the Conference on Security and Co-operation in Europe (CSCE—later the Organisation for Security and Co-operation in Europe, OSCE), including the USA, had an absolutely clear, programmatic principle for the handling of crises of state integrity in Europe: the principle that existing states should not be allowed to break up unless all the national components of the state concerned voluntarily approved the break-up. This principle had been reaffirmed as recently as the 1990 Treaty of Paris. Yet, in the case of Yugoslavia, the west European states chose not to abide by that principle, largely because of German government pressure. First, Slovenia was effectively allowed to secede from Yugoslavia by the European Community (EC—as the EU was then known) and then Croatia was allowed to follow suit. The EC simultaneously insisted upon adequate safeguards for the Serbian minority with an independent Croatia. A cardinal analytical issue is surely the need to explain this failure.

The USA acted, from the moment when Germany persuaded the EC to recognize Croatia in 1991, as a driving force for the Bosnian Government to declare itself the Government of an independent, unitary Bosnian state. The Bush Administration was well aware that its stance on behalf of Bosnian self-determination was based upon the absence of any Bosnian political nation: Bosnia was a multinational republic in which the Bosnian Muslims lacked an overall majority. The US Government was aware that this stance would lead to a civil war in Bosnia. In March 1992 the Bush Administration urged the Bosnian Government not to accept an EC-brokered settlement that would have prevented the onset of civil war. The reasons for this policy on the part of the US administration are another absolutely cardinal issue to be explored.

In 1993 the USA's new Bill Clinton Administration sought, successfully, to undermine the Vance-Owen peace plan for Bosnia and it subsequently blocked other, later moves towards a negotiated settlement during 1994.

Throughout the Bosnian war, the US Administration presented the war not as a civil war but as a war of aggression on the part of Serbia. While the Yugoslav army and the Serbian state were providing material assistance to the Serb side in the Bosnian civil war (as other states, including the USA, were providing assistance to the Bosnian Muslim Government), the characterization of the Bosnian war as aggression by the Serbian state against an independent Bosnia was both central to the US international political management of the war and not intellectually sustainable.

While the west European states and Russia sought, during 1998, to achieve a cease-fire and a negotiated settlement of the conflict between the Serbian and Yugoslav Governments and the Kosovo Liberation Army (KLA) and the political leaders of the Kosovar Albanians, the US State Department sought to exacerbate the Kosovo conflict, repeatedly signalling to the KLA that if it maintained its military offensive in Kosovo it would assist the US effort to draw the west European states into a North Atlantic Treaty Organization (NATO) war against Serbia. US tactics in the summer and autumn of 1998 were designed to assist the KLA military campaign—the US Government successfully manipulated the OSCE monitoring force to serve its military-diplomatic preparations for war. The Rambouillet conference, far from being a conference to gain a negotiated solution between the Kosovar Albanian leaderships and the Serbian state was the vehicle for an ultimatum to Serbia, an ultimatum that included the precise demand made by the Austro-Hungarian Government to Serbia in 1914, which had started the First World War: the right of the great power to move military forces anywhere in the whole of Serbia.

The US Government organized the NATO war in a way that maximized the likelihood of atrocities in Kosovo and a flood of refugees. President Clinton first withdrew the monitors, then declared that the bombing campaign would start a full five days before it started. Then the bombing campaign concentrated during the first week on targets outside Kosovo and continued for a further 11 weeks. If the Serbian Government had been what British leaders called a fascist government with a genocidal agenda, this way of organizing the war was an invitation to genocide. However, the US administration explained this way of organizing the war at the time by claiming that President Milošević wanted the bombing campaign as a way of gaining agreement from the Serbian population to the placing of Kosovo under a NATO protectorate. This entire US approach to the NATO war awaits satisfactory explanation.

The progressive fragmentation of Yugoslavia into an increasing number of tiny statelets, many of which are not viable entities if dependent upon their own resources, must surely be seen as above all the consequences of Western— especially US—efforts to shape events in the western Balkans. To present these dynamics as mainly driven by purely endogenous forces within the western Balkans, with the West confined to a reactive and secondary role is surely not adequate.

EXPLAINING WESTERN INVOLVEMENT IN THE YUGOSLAV THEATRE

There is an almost universal tendency in the Western literature on the Yugoslav crisis to view the goals of Western powers in their Yugoslav manoeuvres as being confined to objectives within the Yugoslav theatre itself. Since none of the NATO powers has significant strategic interests within the Yugoslav theatre (except Italy, Greece and Turkey), it is then assumed that the only interest of the major Western powers in Yugoslavia has been one of conflict containment or humanitarian concern. Yet most varieties of international relations theory would suggest that such notions are not credible: great powers pursue political goals based upon national-interest concepts. A glance at the wider European political arena in the 1990s demonstrates quite sharply divergent political interests on the part of the USA and some of the main west European powers as to the kinds of political structures that should be built in Europe out of the ruins of the Cold War bipolar structure. France and Germany have both shown inclinations to strengthen the autonomy and political capacity of a western Europe under Franco-German leadership, while the USA has been campaigning to restore its political hegemony in Europe, through transforming NATO into an entirely new instrument for its political leadership of Europe.

These political conflicts among leading members of the Atlantic Alliance have been played out in no small degree through competitive efforts to take command of events in Yugoslavia. The German Government's successful campaign to draw the EC into the recognition of Croatia was, as Lawrence Eagleberger of the Bush Administration said, a signal that 'Germany was getting ahead of the US' in European politics. By playing the Bosnian card, the Bush Administration ensured that Yugoslav events took a turn that the west European states could not handle. Leading US officials have made perfectly clear that the reason why the Clinton Administration prolonged the Bosnian war was to demonstrate that the EC/EU powers were incapable of leading on Bosnia and thus on European politics. The US-led NATO drive in 1995 began the process of establishing the new NATO that the US required, while Dayton was designed to demonstrate that only the USA could lead on Yugoslavia and thus on Europe. The NATO war against Serbia was within this same pattern: it was to be a demonstration of US-European political hegemony through a victory over Serbia by the new NATO, untrammelled by UN Security Council (and thus Russian) constraints. The war against Serbia was both unnecessary for those who wished to gain a Kosovo with extensive autonomy within Yugoslavia and was also dysfunctional in terms of its likely long-term consequences for building viable political and socio-economic futures for the peoples of the western Balkans. However, it seemed eminently rational for US political goals in Europe.

THE SERBIAN AND ALBANIAN NATIONAL QUESTIONS AND THE SERBIAN POLITICAL SYSTEM

One central political problem that is almost entirely ignored in the general debates on the western Balkans is the Serbian national question. This question is, in the main, simply brushed aside in the literature by being branded the threat of Greater Serbia. The Albanian question has not been ignored in the same way, although that too is now being bracketed out of much public discussion through the same device of a supposed threat of Greater Albania. These ways of posing such issues are at best failures to recognize the consequences of the policies of Western powers for fragmenting the region.

The Serbian nation, under communist leadership after the war, accepted the division of the Serb population of Yugoslavia among a number of new republics and autonomous provinces. Indeed, the internal boundaries of post-war Yugoslavia were drawn up largely in order to assure the other Yugoslav nations that the largest South Slav nation—the Serbs—would not exercise preponderant weight in the new Yugoslavia. The Serbs accepted this arrangement because of their commitment to the new Yugoslav idea under communist leadership. They also had guarantees that the division of the Serbs within Yugoslavia would be a division in form but not in fact, because Yugoslavia would remain one. This guarantee was reinforced by the Constitution of Yugoslavia, which gave constituent nations veto powers over the decisions of individual republics. The break-up of Yugoslavia has involved the Western powers' insistence that the Serb nation should be broken up and/or ethnically cleansed and has also involved an attempt to brand self-determination for the Serbs as a threat to European stability. Following the German diplomatic triumph of ending the NATO war, the US and British Governments are attempting to maintain their political campaign against the Serbian state and its elected leaders.

The Albanian national question is equally a festering sore. The Kosovar Albanian population was never content to be within Yugoslavia. The hostility to their inclusion was not simply the result of Serbian or Yugoslav oppression: for a large part of the post-war period, the Yugoslav state gave the Kosovar Albanians not only very extensive political rights but also substantial aid for economic development. However, Albanian irredentism remained strong. It remains strong today.

Some may believe that a perspective of resolving these political problems through eventual membership of the EU for the whole region offers a path towards resolving these problems. However, such a perspective would acquire meaning and credibility only if the EU itself was utterly transformed into an entirely different kind of political structure and if the external economic policies of the EU towards east-central and south-east Europe were also transformed. Neither solution seems remotely likely. In these circumstances, viable programmes for the western Balkans, which tackle the Serbian and Albanian national questions along with all the other accumulated political, security, social and economic problems, must surely involve new, inclusive structures of regional co-operation, both economic and political. Only in such a context can there be hopes of enabling both Serbs and Albanians to overcome their national divisions. Unfortunately, the recent war has made such regional solutions less rather than more likely, at least in the short term.

A specific obstacle to the development of a viable Western approach towards genuine solutions in the region lies in the gross falsification of the nature of the Serbian political system, the character of the Serbian Socialist Party, the character of the other political forces in Serbia and the consequences of Western policy towards Serbia over the last 10 years. Only when Western public opinion is re-educated on these matters can there be hopes of a European policy towards the region that is politically buttressed by domestic public opinions within western Europe. Such a re-education would involve recognition that by the standards of east-central and eastern Europe, Serbia has been a constitutional state with a democratic political system and a relatively free press. The Serbian Socialist Party had not been a party committed to genocide or ethnocidal atrocities; it is not a fascist party or an ethnic-nationalist party. Serbian society itself is a multi-ethnic society whose record of inter-ethnic relations stands comparison with any other society in the region. Of course, the Serbian polity has been poisoned by the fact that Kosovo has been attached to the Serbian republic. There has been severe repression in Kosovo and, more fundamentally, the clash of Kosovar Albanian nationalism and Serbian nationalism has been a long-term intractable problem. It is also possible to criticize the role of the Serbian state and of the Yugoslav armed forces in the Croatian war, in their support for paramilitary groups that committed terrible atrocities in the early phase of the Bosnian war. However, such criticism should also and first be applied to those Western powers, particularly the USA, which pushed Bosnia into what was bound to be an atrocious war and which deliberately sought to prolong that war for geopolitical reasons.

NOTES

1. I have attempted a survey of political forces of Eastern Europe, focusing particularly on the left, in my 'The Post-Communist Socialists in Eastern and Central Europe', in Sassoon, D. (ed.). *Looking Left: European Socialism after the Cold War* (pp. 143–76). New York, The New Press, 1997.

2. 'The NATO Powers and the Balkan Tragedy', in *New Left Review*, No. 234 (March–April 1999); and 'The Twisted Road to Kosovo: The Political Origins of the NATO Attack on Yugoslavia', in *Labour Focus on Eastern Europe*, No. 62 (Spring 1999).

Iraq and Meta-Conflict

VASSILIS K. FOUSKAS

INTRODUCTION

In this chapter I will be dealing with present-day Iraq as a meta-conflict, and not post-conflict, case. The best way to dissect and articulate the historical and political meanings of this concept is to have a bird's eye glimpse of Iraq's 20th-century history. This is what I will be doing in the first section of this chapter.

Iraq's strategic importance is paramount, among others, by virtue of its position in the heart of the greater Middle East/Persian (Arabian) Gulf region (i.e. the Middle East, as well as the Central Asia and Caspian Sea zone) and its large petroleum reserves. Almost 95% of Iraq's total revenue comes from the oil industry. Given that much of what is happening in Iraq today is about access to its oil resources and influence by regional powers in Iraq's new (geo)politics, it is important that we seek to define meta-conflict by inserting in it the realist category of 'petroleum interests'. It is clear, as we have shown elsewhere (pp. 11–37 and 179–204, in Fouskas and Gökay, 2005), that the USA and the United Kingdom went to Iraq and Afghanistan in order to reshape the strategic contours of the greater Middle East alongside the geopolitics of the petro-dollar and the principles of neo-liberalism. That Anglo-American power became entrapped in Iraq's post-invasion chaos was not a matter of a pre-war miscalculation, but a cultural strategic deficiency of enormous proportions on the part of US policy-making elites.[1] Whereas this is a discussion about which much has been said so far, we still need to shed some light as to why the three main ethnic/religious groups in Iraq are at war with each other, beyond their perceived identity differences that express themselves at societal levels. The next section, therefore, looks at the concept of 'petroleum nationalism', as it manifests itself in the specific political, social and ideological circumstances of Iraq's political/governing elites. Petroleum nationalism is a term rather consubstantial with Middle Eastern social and political orders, as well as with most social orders whose geologies are oil-rich.

Then I go on to examine three meta-conflict descriptors in Iraq, which will enable us to somewhat 'gauge' the degree of chaos and the multi-layered and complex nature of conflict there: (a) the resistance movement; (b) the Constitution (seen as an amalgamation of class, ethnic and religious struggles); and (c) the Iranian factor in Iraqi politics. This section of the contribution exemplifies further the notion of petroleum nationalism in the new geopolitical context of post-2003 Iraq.

Finally, I conclude by outlining the alternatives the USA and the United Kingdom have vis-à-vis Iraq's meta-conflict condition and Iran's strategic positioning in Iraq and the greater Middle East. My prognosis, if historians allow me to use such a word, is rather pessimistic. With the partial exception of one option, none of the alternatives the USA has at hand can address Iraq's meta-conflict condition, and if the USA is poised to attack Iran, then this may well bring about a wider conflagration, jeopardizing the cause of both regional and world peace.

IRAQI HISTORY: A NARRATIVE OF CONFLICT

Ever since the British installed in power Amir Faisal ibn Hussain—who became King Faisal I of Iraq after the Paris Peace Conference of 1919—Iraq has been in a state of perpetual conflict. One could even go as far as to argue that Iraq had experienced some significant conflict junctures and turns that could be characterized as meta-conflict. This is a type of conflict that follows great power intervention and/or 'back stage' interference[2] in the domestic affairs of a country—a conflict, however, that is unstoppable, unappeased and hampers normalization of class and political relations of the country in question.

Faisal, an instrument of British policy in Mesopotamia, broke away from the tolerance of Ottoman rule and pursued a rather inflexible and authoritarian state policy towards the ethnic and religious mosaic of Iraq. This was rightly interpreted by the deprived and the peasant as a policy of merger between Faisal's corrupt oligarchy and British imperial interests, fuelling radical nationalist movements across the country. In many respects, King Ghazi, Faisal's son, who succeeded after the first King upon his death in 1933, tried to give expression to this newly emerged anti-imperial radicalism by upsetting the very system of governance from within.

Ghazi began developing a nationalist Iraqi policy claiming, for example, that Kuwait is part of Iraq. He also invited Germany to resume its projects in Iraq in order to counter-balance British imperialism (Ghazi spoke warmly of the pre-war Berlin–Baghdad railway project) and set up a radio station criticizing British imperialism and Zionism in the Middle East and Palestine. Ghazi, who was opposed by pro-British officials in both the Government and the army, used Kurdish elements to counter this opposition. Clashes broke out between the various factions supporting pro-British elements and pro-Ghazi forces.[3] In the end, Ghazi did not survive imperial hostility and was killed in 1939, most likely by Nuri as-Said, an official famous for his corrupt dealings with the anti-Ghazi bloc and the British (pp. 341–45, in Batatu, 1978—see Bibliography).

Ghazi's death propelled further the rise of Arab nationalism both in Iraq and across the Middle East. In 1941 a coup by four pro-Ghazi colonels assumed power in Iraq and sought co-operation with both the German Government in Berlin and the Soviet Government in Moscow. The ensuing conflict, however, brought a pro-British regime back to power. A communist insurgency in 1948 was ruthlessly suppressed. Thus, the pre-Baathist era in Iraq was characterized by a constant state of class conflict and civil war after the major contours of power in the country had been shaped by imperialism. This situation of civil war, it should be noted, was at the same time hemmed in by the anti-imperial struggles of some significant social and political factions. In addition, Ghazi's case shows that the imperial power in charge of Iraq could not always be on top of things, that is controlling and manipulating government, let alone the people, at will and at all times.

Soon after the end of the Second World War, the USA and the United Kingdom increased their imperial grip on the Middle East and Iraq. This can be seen by the support they offered to the collaborating state elites of the region to suppress nationalism and communism and also by the creation of the Baghdad Pact (Iraq, Iran, Pakistan, Turkey and the United Kingdom), which aimed at consolidating the US and British military presence in the region, while guaranteeing the safe transportation of oil and gas to Western markets. A year after the Suez crisis of 1956—a triumph for Egyptian leader Nasser against Anglo-French imperialism and Zionism—a National Front including communists, nationalists and liberals was formed in order to fight against the corrupt pro-imperial Government led by Nuri as-Said. In July 1958 Brig. Abd al-Karim Kassem, leading this hetero-geneous Front, overthrew the monarchy upon assuming power. The popularity of the coup was massive, but Kassem faced huge difficulties in ruling the country from the very beginning. Iraq's oil wealth was under the control of the British-dominated Iraq Petroleum Co, whereas large landowning elites, the work of British rule in the countryside, dominated agricultural production.[4] Kassem, who attempted to model himself after Nasser, was backed by the communists and launched a programme of nationalizations and radical agrarian reforms, and this significantly defused tensions both in the countryside and in the big cities. However, Abd as-Salem Muhammad Aref, his deputy and a strong-headed Nasserite and Baathist, undermined Kassem's work. In October 1959 a military Baathist group, which included Saddam Hussain, attempted to assassinate Kassem. The attempt failed and when Kassem recovered and resumed power he began playing off the communists against the Baathists, while developing nationalist policies along the lines of Ghazi: propaganda about the retaking of Kuwait by Iraq and fierce anti-Israel rhetoric. Iraq's communists received no support from Moscow. In fact, Moscow backed Kassem's rule because any destabilization of Kassem by the communists would jeopardize Moscow's good relations with Egypt and Syria. Eventually, Kassem was overthrown by the Baathists in a coup backed by the USA's Central Intelligence Agency (CIA) in 1963—in which Saddam participated—bringing Aref to power (Morris, 2003). Kassem was tried and executed, whereas thousands of communists were tortured, hunted down and killed, including the intellectual Khalid Ahmed Zaki.[5]

From 1919 until 1968 Iraq experienced 18 uprisings or coups and anti-coups of national significance, whereas from 1919 until 1958 it saw 22 local uprisings, mostly dominated by Kurds and peasants (pp. 467–68, in Batatu, 1977). This did not mean a halt in the overall rates of growth in the long run, but it rather augmented social dissatisfaction against the regime, as both the peasants and even the middle classes suffered from inflationary trends, food shortages and an inconsiderate state policy. At the same time, and as urbanization proceeded apace (by 1975 some 63% of the total population was living in Baghdad and other big cities), the new disaffected proletarian—that is, the former peasant—could easily be radicalized, embracing the ideologies of communism, liberalism or nationalism. The history of coups, civil war and Anglo-American and Soviet secret interferences in Iraq continued unabated under the regime of Saddam Hussein from 1978 to the First Gulf War of 1991 and beyond. However, under Saddam's rule the demarcation lines of conflict began increasingly to resemble ethnic and religious cleavages in the country. This was the result of three interrelated factors.

First, Saddam's rule was extremely personal, ruthless and pro-Sunni to the extent that it pushed all other ethnic and religious groups to acquire a strongest sense of ethnic identity and mission. Second, the Iraq–Iran War of 1980–88 increased Iran's influence in Iraq through the Shi'a population in the south, many of whom refused to fight against their religious brethren. Third, the collapse of the USSR deprived the Iraqi left (Kurdish, Sunni and Shi'a) of any unifying reference point at the national level, a fact that, coupled with Saddam's persecution policy, further undermined the left's cohesion and influence in mainstream Iraqi politics. Saddam gassed the Kurds in the 1980s and persecuted both Shi'a factions and the communists. After being ousted from Kuwait in 1991 following the first post-Cold War display of power and determination by the USA, Saddam continued to rule as a monarch, although he could no longer launch major campaigns of killing against the Kurds and the Shi'as as they were somewhat protected by the no-fly zones imposed by the USA and the United Kingdom north and south of Baghdad.[6]

After the Second Gulf War and the toppling of Saddam by Anglo-American power in spring 2003, Iraq continued to be marred by violence and sectarian conflict. As with all the previous significant turns in Iraq's 20th-century history following external, overt or covert, interference, this post-2003 conflict has been—all at once—civil/class, religious, ethnic, anti-imperial, intra-governmental and anti-governmental. However, the current meta-conflict phase that Iraq is undergoing has some distinctive features. This sort of conflict is not merely a continuation or even reproduction of pre-existing structures and sites of conflict inside the country's boundaries, but rather an exacerbation and transformation of it, this time in the wake of an open and preventive war of aggression by an imperial power in order to achieve regime change. Never before in its modern history has Iraq experienced such forms of militarization and securitization imposed from outside, as more than 200,000 American and British troops, police and other agents and mercenaries are operating in the country. Moreover, in today's meta-conflict condition of Iraq, economic modernization and growth are severely hampered and obstructed by high levels of insecurity and a weak and sectarian polity. Meta-conflict is thus a conflict situation that is detrimental to economic growth and in which imperial projection of power does not produce settlement and viable governance but a continuation/exacerbation of conflict across the social and political spectrums that the imperial power itself can neither control nor manipulate at will.

Meta-conflict, it should be noted, is not post-conflict. In post-conflict situations and social regimes the conflicting parties agree to a settlement, however painful, set out the rules of reconstruction and socio-economic and political engineering under the surveillance of the imperial power(s) and somewhat obey in maintaining a form of peace, however fragile and precarious. These are, for example, the cases of Bosnia and Kosovo, but not of Iraq and Afghanistan. In post-conflict conditions, strategies of profiteering through economic reconstruction/modernization—usually viewed as conflict prevention strategies—can be employed in earnest. Meta-conflict orders do not allow any solid institutionalization of profit-making and extraction, simply because even if economic aid and donations pour into the country in question, social and political security remain elusive. We can now move on to define the concept of 'petroleum nationalism' in the meta-conflict condition of present-day Iraq.

DEFINING PETROLEUM NATIONALISM

A fundamental prerequisite for a country to be 'sovereign' and 'independent' is to have political control over its key assets.[7] In the past, for example, Scottish nationalists claimed an independent Scotland through looking to appropriate the revenues produced by the North Sea oil; petroleum revenues were seen as a means to statehood.

Nasser and classic Arab nationalism had had an agenda of nationalizing oil industries and strategic chokepoints (e.g. the Suez Canal) in order to increase their economic power and divert assets to military projects to counter Zionism and imperialism. Petroleum nationalism, in this respect, could be seen as an ideological agenda of mobilizing the people, but an agenda that it is determined by a real and decisive substratum—political control of resources and/or strategic geographical locations. One also might argue that Hugo Chavez's foreign policy agenda today borders on petroleum nationalism. Since he assumed power in Venezuela, Chavez has increased his grip on the oil industry and abolished production sharing agreements (PSAs), while using anti-imperialist rhetoric to mobilize the Venezuelans in support of his rule.[8] In Iraq's meta-conflict condition, petroleum nationalism has taken on new expressed features. Although the picture I will be presenting below is simplified and not fully accurate, it can nevertheless provide us with good judgement, as it reflects major developments and trends on Iraq's political terrain. The situation in the country today can be described as below.

A split, manifesting itself in a vicious civil war, has emerged between the Sunni Arabs (residing mostly in the middle of Iraq and representing some 23% of the total population), the Shi'as (in the centre and south of Iraq, 57% of the total population) and the Sunni Kurds (in the north of Iraq, 18%). The ruling coalition in power today under Nuri Kamal al-Maliki, although it somewhat reflects the real electoral geography of the country, is nevertheless marred by sectarian attitudes and conflict that cut across both governmental branches and the fragmented (and fragmenting) social tissue. In this respect, the coalition is not representative at all and, as the Baker-Hamilton Report of December 2006 (see in the Bibliography, under Baker and Hamilton, 2006) did not fail to mention, 'national reconciliation in Iraq is elusive'.

The Kurds have developed a nationalist discourse based on claims over the oil fields of Mosul and Kirkuk. The strategic reasoning of the Kurds is similar to that of the Scottish nationalists in the past. They view the control of oil fields as being of vital importance for them towards achieving statehood. Turkey has been opposing this all along and has taken both soft (increasing economic co-operation with Iraqi Kurds) and hard power measures (deploying its army along the Iraqi border, including incursions or forays into Iraq), but this is beside the point: politically, the Kurds remain determined to complete the institution-building of the 1990s around the oil-rich areas of Mosul and Kirkuk and to have a state in northern Iraq sooner rather than later. In this respect, the Kurds are committed to the constitutional provision—another blunder by those who oversaw the drafting of the Constitution, which is to say, the Americans—that a referendum be held by the end of 2007 to determine the fate of Kirkuk.

Similarly, the Shi'as claim control of southern oil fields, but because they constitute the majority of the population in Iraq, some of their factions have claims over the entire Iraqi state, including Kurdish lands in the north. Thus, this new form of petroleum nationalism as manifests itself in Iraq could be seen as a means to statehood, by either splitting the state in order to affirm sovereignty over a particular geographical area (the case of the Kurds) or reshaping the entire state apparatus under the aegis of a completely different religious cast (the case of the Shi'as).

The Sunnis, who reside in the middle of the country, have meanwhile developed a 'nationalistic syndrome of deprivation'. Their nationalism is a nationalism of deprivation, because they lost all the privileges and the power that they had possessed for decades, most recently through Saddam's Baathism. Moreover, as we shall see below, the new Constitution is not conducive to their social, economic and political needs. By looking at the new Constitution of Iraq and its provisions concerning oil, as well as the electoral trends and the resistance per se, we would be in a position to understand better the operational features of 'petroleum nationalism' in Iraq's meta-conflict condition.

META-CONFLICT DESCRIPTORS: RESISTANCE, THE CONSTITUTION AND THE IRANIAN FACTOR

We can 'measure' Iraq's critical meta-conflict situation by looking at three indicators: the ferociousness of the resistance against the occupation; the level and multidimensionality of the intra-societal and intra-state conflict as it has been crystallized in the new Constitution; and the relevance and role of Iran in Iraq's domestic affairs. These three indicators are basically meta-conflict descriptors, summarizing the chaotic situation in which the British and US forces are entrapped.

The swift development and endurance of the resistance, 'the speed with which it took off', Patrick Cockburn argued in *New Left Review,* has not received its due attention. The Americans started 'to suffer casualties as early as June 2003' and this resulted in the postponement of the elections for the following year (Cockburn, 2005). These remarks carry weight, for they point to the legitimate speculation that plans for resisting the occupying forces had been in store before the US-led invasion of March 2003. In addition, they suggest that the Baathists, pushed now out of power, began organizing the resistance with means and techniques acquired from the Iraqi state they ruled for decades. US and British forces are now facing departmentalized, but well-organized and considered strikes that paralyse key economic sectors and institutions and certainly obstruct reconstruction and political processes. All in all, both the USA and the United Kingdom miscalculated the tenacity, persistence and organizational skills of the insurgents, mainly, but not exclusively, recruited from among the Sunnis and the Baathists, certain Shi'a factions and also fundamentalists and anti-imperialists from other states.[9] Put unashamedly, what is happening in Iraq today is but a war of each against all; then each Iraqi faction—at times including even certain Kurdish groups—separately fires against imperial US and British forces.

Owing to the meta-conflict condition, the UN estimates that more than 1.6 million people are displaced within Iraq, whereas up to 1.8 million Iraqis have fled the country. Also, a study published in the British medical journal *Lancet* (12 October 2006), argues that the US invasion and occupation of Iraq are responsible for the deaths of an estimated 655,000 Iraqis. The number of US soldiers killed is over 3,000. The Western media are giving the wrong impression that insurgents and suicide bombers target only civilian or religious sites. Although this is happening—Iraq in going through a period of civil war—this is wrong as an overall concluding remark. What dominates the acts of the insurgents is strategic sabotage of Iraq's oil infrastructure. According to the Institute for the Analysis of Global Security (IAGS), insurgents conducted 282 major attacks on Iraq's oil and gas pipelines, oil installations, terminals and personnel from 12 June 2003 to 24 October 2005 (IAGS—Iraq Pipeline Watch, 2005). According to the Department of Energy of the USA and to former Iraqi Oil Minister Ghadban, the total of attacks on oil infrastructure during the same period was 642, at a cost of US $10,000 million (Energy Information Administration, 2005). As well as increasing overall social insecurity, this disrupted production and modernization projects, hence oil extraction, refinement and exports.

Iraq is crisscrossed by more than 4,000 miles of oil and gas pipelines, which are difficult to protect. Iraq's oil industry is in shambles. Fuel shortages, rationing and long queues at petrol stations are becoming endemic. In order to increase the level of security across the country, the USA has contracted out some security services to private companies with very low-cost personnel recruited from Africa and Latin America. One such company is Erinys, contracted by the Pentagon for US $40 million a year, an additional expense for the occupation to succeed.[10] Another, even more expensive attempt, was the establishment of a highly trained Task Force Shield, composed of US commandos, to guard the sensitive

Kirkuk–Ceyhan oil pipeline. However, current production of petroleum in Iraq remains well below pre-war levels, at 1.9 million barrels per day, although the resulting income is modest enough to allow such a luxury.

The fighting on the ground is crystallized in the new emerging institutions of the country, both by what is included in them and by what has, rather mindlessly, been brushed aside. In this context, the Iraqi Constitution is important and we shall pay attention to that document in order to clarify some of its crucial provisions, thus understanding better the resistance, the political and ideological tensions and the overall meta-conflict condition that characterize present-day Iraqi society.

Article 1 of the Constitution calls the Republic of Iraq 'an independent, sovereign nation', whereas the governing system is 'democratic, federal and representative (parliamentary).[11] Islam is considered as the official religion of the state and as its basic source for legislation, whereas Arabic and Kurdish are stipulated as being Iraq's two official languages. However, all Iraqis have the right to educate their children in whatever minority language they wish (Assyrian, Turkmen, etc.). Article 7 brings up a point of tension: 'Entities or trends that advocate, instigate or propagate racism, terrorism, "takfir" (declaring someone an infidel), sectarian cleansing, are banned, especially the Saddamist Baath Party in Iraq and its symbols under any name.'[12] The Baath Party with its Sunni components, having been in power for decades and having an established middle class inside and outside the State apparatus, is now being told that it cannot be represented in Iraq's new institutions. This in itself created a governing/institutional vacuum that had to be filled, whereas the exclusion of Baathists was bound to generate further violence, thus undermining the political process per se. As I will establish below, this institutional vacuum was filled by the Shi'as and the Kurds, also thanks to the constitutional arrangements and overseen by the occupation powers themselves.

Article 29(4) stipulates that 'the State guarantees social and health insurance', a rather nonsensical statement as the first act of the Paul Bremer-led US authorities in Baghdad—in an act of total anarchical liberalism—was to privatize the health system. Article 35 rather lacks seriousness. It says: 'No one may be detained or investigated unless by judicial decision', and: 'All forms of torture, mental or physical, and inhuman treatment are forbidden.' However, what springs to mind while reading this is the social and prison conditions under US occupation, particularly the case of Abu Ghraib prison. Acts by US occupation forces are silently exempted from Article 35 and the Iraqi Constitution as a whole, for who can bring to justice the guarantors of the new Iraqi Constitution? This is another point that irritates the Iraqis, pushing them to join the various factions of the resistance movement.

From our perspective, Chapters 3, 4 and 5 of the Constitution are the most important, for they deal with the structure of federal authorities and their competencies/powers, as well as with the management of the oil industry. The institutional architecture reflected in those chapters has ambiguous federal elements. The legislative authority is made up of two bodies, the Council of

Representatives (Parliament) and the Council of Union (dealing with the regions). The federal executive authority consists of the President and the cabinet. The President is elected by the Parliament by a two-thirds majority for a term limited to four years. The President assigns to the leader of the majority party/coalition to form a cabinet and confirm their intention to become Prime Ministers. In the judiciary branch, the key institution is the Supreme Federal Court, made up of judges who are experts in *Shari'a* (Islamic law).

According to the Constitution, the federal authority is supposed to be the sole responsible for the country's foreign and defence policy, financial and customs policy, issuing currency and organizing issues of nationality and naturalization. As for the oil question, article 109's vague formulation—'Oil and gas is the property of all the Iraqi people in all regions and provinces'—comes to be superseded by the following, article 110, which stipulates: 'The federal government will administer oil and gas extracted from current fields in cooperation with the governments of the producing regions and provinces on condition that the revenues will be distributed fairly in a manner compatible with the demographical distribution all over the country'.[13] It also says that law should privilege regions and areas that were previously treated unfairly by the former regime, a clear reference to the Kurds in the north and Shi'as in the south. Article 111, the most controversial of all, says: 'All that is not written in the exclusive powers of the federal authorities is in the authority of the regions.' Moreover, in case of conflict 'between the federal government and the regions, the priority will be given to the region's law'.[14] The governments of the regions, the Constitution goes on to stipulate, have the right to practice legislative, executive and judicial powers, 'except in what is listed as exclusive powers of the federal authorities'. Moreover, article 116(2), reconfirming the controversial provision of article 111, says that the regional government also has the right to amend the federal law in case of conflict between regional and central governments in matters that do not pertain to the exclusive powers of the federal authorities.[15] We are given a further qualification in article 128(1), which reads as a co-federal, rather than federal, stipulation: 'The revenues of the region are made up of its designated share from the state budget and from the region's local resources.'[16] It transpires, therefore, that the issue of energy management is not an exclusive matter of the central government and that it swings more to the side of the regions.

On the issue of energy resources, a matter of life and death for Iraq that represents 95% of its revenues, the Constitution, at best, is vague and, at worst, is more confederal than federal. It would not be an exaggeration to argue that, as regards the governing and institutional technicalities of the new Iraqi polity, the Constitution is federal, but as regards the governance of energy it is rather confederal. The Baker-Hamilton Report itself concedes this point, by stating explicitly that 'particularly contentious is a provision in the Constitution that shares revenues nationally from current oil reserves, while allowing revenues from reserves discovered in the future to go to the regions' (p. 19, in Baker and Hamilton, 2006). All in all, given the crucial importance of petroleum and gas and other minerals for Iraq, the Constitution is a patchwork that undermines the political cohesion of the country, encouraging pre-existing centripetal tendencies to grow. These tendencies, which are indicative of Iraq's meta-conflict situation, are found at the heart of the new Iraqi polity: the Constitution and the actual relationship of forces, which, under the aegis of the USA, have given shape to it.

Bremer's occupation authorities, in collaboration with specific Shi'a and Kurdish parties and groupings (few Sunnis were included), drafted the following political schedule: first, due chiefly to reasons that had to do with the unexpected resistance movement, Iraq had to be governed for a year by the Coalition Provisional Authority (CPA); then, on 28 June 2004, the CPA transferred authority to an interim Iraqi Government under Ayad Allawi, a secular Shi'ite and 'a long time CIA asset' (James Cogan, 2005). Elections were held on 30 January 2005, when it became clear that Shi'a and Kurdish factions were rapidly moving into the new Iraqi polity to fill the institutional and governing vacuum. The Sunnis did not participate in this election. It took the new Government more than three months to get formed (3 May 2005) under Ibrahim al-Jafari, also a secular Shi'ite. The main task of the coalition composed of Kurdish and Shi'a parties was to draft a Constitution (discussed above) by October and then organize an election, which was held on 15 December 2005.

Many analysts that adopt the main tenets of our perspective on Iraq, US foreign policy and the Middle East, think of the new Iraqi Government as a puppet in the hands of the Americans, manipulated at will. In a way, this is understandable, because the USA is the occupying power of the country. However, I would argue that the issue is far more complicated.

The USA can only set out the legal and political framework, that is the constraints, within which domestic forces can operate. Domestic forces that fall outside the perimeter of the constraints set by the USA receive dictatorial treatment. Such forces are the various groups of insurgents. However, even this sketch is very much of an 'ideal type'. In essence, the situation in both political and socio-economic terms is very chaotic and Iraqi police (some branches of which are penetrated by insurgents and anti-Western elements), security forces and US marines are unable to secure order. Factions and departments of the state itself evade American instructions and surveillance and co-operate with insurgents and Iran. Thus, US-led operations tend to be acts of indiscriminate violence and authoritarianism, particularly after President George W. Bush, decided (January 2007) to send an additional 21,000 troops to the country. Overall, the USA cannot handle meta-conflict in Iraq, hence the Baker-Hamilton proposals for initiating political, diplomatic and institutional processes, also involving Iran, Syria, Saudi Arabia and Turkey, creating the impression that domestic forces, backed by a combination of regional powers that want stability in Iraq, are democratically in charge of the post-Saddam Iraq and that the US intention is to withdraw its troops from the country, once the security problem is solved. This gambit is unlikely to succeed, not least because the acts of the administration soon after the publication of the Report point in the opposite direction: military reinforcements in Iraq are seen as the only solution to meta-conflict. Moreover, the Maliki Government, as the Baker-Hamilton Report shows, seems unable to co-operate with the USA on matters that jeopardize Shi'a security. Thus, 'Maliki has publicly rejected a US timetable to achieve certain benchmarks, ordered the removal of blockades around the Sadr City, sought more control over Iraqi security forces, and resisted US requests to move forward on reconciliation or on disbanding Shi'a militias' (p. 16, in Baker and Hamilton, 2006).

The new Iraqi polity is cut across by inexorable ethnic, religious and class tensions (the best example being the social base of Sadr's Mahdi Army), which the USA seems to be unable to manipulate and direct. The overthrow of the Baathist bureaucratic caste brought at the same time a significant destruction of Iraq's middle classes. Now there is a ferocious struggle by Kurdish and Shi'a factions, not only because they want to rise to the class status of the Baathist/ Sunni within the branches of the central state and create their own power base, but also because they want to direct developments towards complete regional autonomy/independence for their respective, oil-rich regions: the south for the Shi'as; and the north-east for the Kurds. Some Shi'a factions, in addition, being the majority ethnic group in Iraq, view themselves as representing the whole of Iraq, thus laying claims on governing the entire country from Baghdad, as well as controlling the southern regions for themselves. In this context, the Sunnis feel completely marginalized. Thus, 'The priority', *The Economist* advised after the election of 15 December 2005 and a year before the publication of the Baker-Hamilton Report, 'is to involve in government those Sunnis who have been undermining it' (p. 51, in *The Economist* of 7 January 2005). However, there is more to the affair than meets the eye.

The area in and around Baghdad, where the bulk of the Sunnis live, is very poor in mineral and energy resources. Most of the oil fields are concentrated in Shi'a (Basra) and Kurdish (Kirkuk) areas. The constitutional and political arrangements so far deprive the Sunnis of any meaningful presence in (or return to) positions of power within and outside the state. As we saw earlier, the Constitution's provisions are structured in such a way that reflect the regional and class interests of the Shi'as and the Kurds, leaving the Sunnis out in the cold. This is more than conspicuous in all of its provisions related to the governance and regional allocation of oil resources. In this respect, a new observable class reality seems to be emerging at the heart of the new Iraqi polity, which has to do with the new type of petroleum nationalism I described earlier. The Kurdish elites, wanting to build an independent Kurdistan in the north-east, need control over the oil fields of Kirkuk and Mosul in order to finance their emerging state out of petroleum revenues. This Turkey opposes ferociously, lest the Kurds one day envisage a greater Kurdistan including the 20 million Kurds of Turkey, but the Americans do not seem, as yet, to have found a comprehensive formula that can accommodate both sides. The Americans, however, and well before a similar suggestion included in the Baker-Hamilton Report, have had unofficially brought Turkey into negotiations with Sunni Iraqi factions, in their attempt to pacify those factions and convince them to join the new executive (Aras, 2006).

On their part, however, the Kurds have already started signing oil contracts with private companies, disregarding the central authorities in Baghdad.[17] The Shi'as have the numbers—they represent more than 57% of the Iraqi population—the Constitution and their strong link with Iran on their side. Their own petroleum nationalism is consubstantial with their upward social mobility in positions of central and regional power. The backbone of the Shi'a United Iraqi Alliance (UIA) is the Supreme Council for the Islamic Revolution in Iraq (SCIRI), which has close contacts with Iran. Its leaders and followers had refused to fight against Iran in the 1980–88 war between Iran and Iraq. Bayan Jabr, Interior Minister until the election of 15 December 2005, was a SCIRI member and most of the Shi'a death squads and militia are directly organized by specific branches of the Interior Ministry. On 2 August 2005 Steven Vincent, an American journalist, was kidnapped and murdered, because he exposed the Shi'a death squads. Grand Ayatollah Ali as-Sistani and various SCIRI leaders meet Iranian officials to discuss 'border security, co-operation on oil projects' and intelligence and other matters with them (Kemp, 2005).

Soon after the general election of 15 December 2005, the Sunnis accused the Shi'as of storming polling stations and terrorizing Sunni voters.[18] Thus, the Sunni petroleum nationalism is but a nationalism of deprivation—located in the centre of the country, where no major oil fields exists, and with their rights undermined by the Constitution, the Sunnis feel squeezed out of politics and power arrangements. This induces them to join the insurgents and fight on three fronts, against the Shi'as, the Kurds and the Americans.

Our analyses so far indicate that every ethnic and religious group in Iraq today has something to fight for, with the Sunnis having to fight almost for everything as they lost everything. In addition, our analyses suggest that the real winners of the US invasion and occupation of Iraq are the Kurds, but mostly the Shi'as and, through them, Iran. Electoral trends also point in this direction.

The official results of the elections of 15 December 2005, announced nearly 40 days later (20 January 2006), gave the Shi'a coalition 130 out of 275 seats in the parliament, which means that the Shi'as need partners to govern (Worth and O'Neil, 2006). The Kurdish Alliance took 53 seats, whereas the largest Sunni party, the Iraq Accord Front, won 44 seats and another Sunni party, made up of former Baathists, won 11. Allawi's grouping took 25 seats, whereas Ahmad Chalabi's Iraqi National Congress, Washington, DC's favourite to lead the new Iraq, failed to win a seat. The Shi'a and Kurdish parties now hold 40 fewer seats between them than in the old parliament. The result, albeit a truncated one, represents a victory for the Shi'as and the Kurds and a further blow for the US-backed candidates, Chalabi and Allawi. The Sunnis, although by no means all of them, now want to be part of the game, as they realize that the Shi'as need partners to govern and the Kurds are not forthcoming. Thus, Zalmay Khalilzad, the US Ambassador to Iraq, facing political chaos coupled with further attacks on both Shi'a and Sunni holy sites, in March 2006 invented a 19-member 'National Security Council' (NSC), composed of nine Shi'as, four Kurds, four Sunnis and two 'secular' politicians, with Chalabi, whose party had won no seats, being one of them. This increases rather than decreases the difficulties facing the USA in Iraq. This NSC, Iraqi-style, has been given quasi-dictatorial powers, including the right to amend the Constitution. Finally, a Government was formed in May under Maliki, which, as we saw earlier, does not entirely obey its American masters on crucial matters.

It is impossible for Maliki's coalition to affect the existing institutional crystallizations of power in Iraq without a further increase in violence. In the event, Maliki cannot effect any policy that is to the detriment of the Shi'as. However, the USA seems to be determined to challenge Shi'a social and political power. Ambassador Khalilzad mentioned that the next head of the Interior Ministry 'should be trusted by all communities and not come from elements of the population that have militias'. He also argued that the Constitution is now 'likely to be amended' in order to broaden support (Cogan, 2005). These statements were immediately denounced by Abd al-Aziz al-Hakim, the leader of SCIRI, who ruled out any constitutional changes. Thus, in the event of the USA attempting to enforce constitutional changes in order to meet Sunni demands, this would mean war for the Shi'as, while further alienating the Kurds. In fact, the Shi'as are difficult to remove peacefully from key positions of social and institutional power without skilful interference from Iran. Yet, even this is a precarious prospect, because Iran does not control the entire Shi'a spectrum in Iraq. As we shall see below, every single option, or a combination thereof, lying before the USA today is extraordinarily difficult and painful: none of them, with the partial exception of one option, can really address Iraq's meta-conflict condition.

WAYS OUT OF META-CONFLICT?[19]

The USA and the United Kingdom are confronted with several alternatives over Iraq, all of which are particularly difficult to implement and even more difficult to succeed with (where success is measured by tackling Iraq's meta-conflict, thus moving into a post-conflict situation): (a) provoking and then invading Iran and effecting 'regime change' in view of 'moving a step forward' as regards the materialization of the scheme for the 'democratization of the greater Middle East'; (b) attacking Iran by proxy (the Israel option); (c) stepping up efforts to convince NATO-European powers to do the 'peacekeeping' in Iraq, thus releasing US forces to deal with Iran (NATO already has a small training mission in Iraq); (d) deciding about when and how to start withdrawing from Iraq (the 'defeatist' option); (e) provoking Iran and then bombing suspected nuclear sites in the country; and finally, (f) negotiating with Iran in order to tackle Iraq's meta-conflict (and then maybe consider taking Iran). These options should not necessarily be seen in isolation from each other. American, Israeli and British policy-makers are working in tandem on a combination of them.

The first option is the most dangerous one for regional and global peace. Iran has a much larger military and firepower capabilities than Saddam's Iraq used to have and can still impose unilaterally a blockade in the Straits of Hormuz. It would be hard for the United Kingdom to follow the USA in such an adventure and it would be even harder for Russia and the People's Republic of China to bandwagon or stand idly by. Both China and Russia have vital energy and business-related interests in Iran and in Iran's strategic orbit, which includes the Caucasus, Central Asia and the Caspian Sea zone. Iran's co-operation, let alone its oil and gas reserves, is badly needed by both Russia and China. Similarly, France and Germany would directly oppose this US option, for a variety of geopolitical and economic reasons. If Iran is attacked and invaded, the entire Shi'a crescent in the greater Middle East, from Afghanistan to Lebanon, would rebel against Israeli and Anglo-American interests. Meta-conflict conditions would also proliferate across the region.

The second option, an Israeli attack on Iran, would be equally catastrophic. If anything, the Hezbollah–Israeli war of summer 2006 has shown that the Israeli forces are vulnerable to irregular and asymmetric warfare (guerrilla fighting, suicide attacks, rocket firing, etc.). Any attack on Iran by Israel would immediately bring the war into Israel proper, both by way of Hezbollah penetration and renewed Palestinian operations led by Hamas and other fundamentalist groups, such as the al-Aqsa Martyrs' Brigade.

The third option (involving NATO powers in Iraq) is rather unrealistic, particularly after the cleavages that emerged during the most recent NATO summit in the Latvian capital of Riga in late November 2006. The USA wants to transform NATO from a transatlantic coalition into a global military alliance, including countries such as Israel, Ukraine, Georgia, Japan, Australia and South Africa. However, both France and Germany opposed this and no decision was taken. The USA even struggled to convince Germany and France to contribute some 2,200 troops to NATO's precarious and even failing mission in Afghanistan.

The fourth option (withdrawal) appears, rather confusingly and unconvincingly, between the lines of speeches by key US and British policy-makers, officials and influential columnists: 'Once we bring about national reconciliation and security in Iraq, our forces will withdraw'. Anglo-American power can arrange for an orderly withdrawal from Iraq at any moment, yet this is highly unlikely because it is considered as defeatist and counter-productive for the USA's global imperial standing and prestige. This may also polarize further the American elites, accentuating the cleavage between pacifist and pro-war factions.

The fifth option is a very attractive one, although, if implemented, it can hardly supersede the consequential side effects of the first and second options. Testifying before the Senate Foreign Relations Committee, former US National Security Adviser, Zbigniew Brzezinski, who opposed the March 2003 invasion and occupation of Iraq, accused George W. Bush of manufacturing evidence in order to justify 'a protracted and potentially expanding war'. He also hinted at 'a plausible scenario' in the making 'for a military collision with Iran' and called the present war in Iraq 'a historic, strategic and moral calamity' (Brzezinski, 2007; Grey, 2007). The option of provoking Iran and then launching an air campaign targeting suspected nuclear sites has the advantage of diverting political and public/media attention from Iraq's meta-conflict to Iran, while trying to contain a major spill-over of Shi'a radicalism across the Middle East, an advantage that a full-scale land invasion, whether unprovoked or not, can certainly not offer. The most rational and solid option that has the potential to address the issue of meta-conflict in Iraq remains the last one: negotiating seriously and unconditionally with Tehran and Damascus.

In a testimony to the US Senate in October 2005, the Secretary of State, Condoleezza Rice, said that the administration was considering direct contacts with Tehran as part of its efforts to achieve greater co-operation on Iraq (Marshall and Daragahi, 2005). In March 2006 the USA and Iran announced that they would hold direct, face-to-face talks on halting sectarian violence and restoring calm in Iraq. White House spokesman, Scott McClellan, has indeed insisted that US negotiators would have a 'very narrow mandate' in talking to the Iranians, adding that negotiations on the nuclear issue would only take place along with the major European powers, Russia and China (Fisher, 2006). The British Government is a warm supporter of this option. Brzezinski's testimony spelled out clearly that the 'US must reaffirm explicitly and unambiguously its determination to leave Iraq in a reasonably short period of time' in order to be credible. However, as we saw earlier (see footnote 19), the Baker-Hamilton Report is ambiguous about the issue of withdrawal, which places it in a militaristic framework: a dialogue with regional powers should begin in tandem with further reinforcements being sent to Iraq.

So how serious is this diplomatic initiative, which means first and foremost beginning negotiations with Iran and Syria? How seriously will Iran take diplomacy if it is not accompanied by public guarantees that the USA will stop threatening Iran on the nuclear issue? The irony, as Brzezinski put it in his testimony to the Senate Foreign Relations Committee, is that 'both Iran and Syria have lately called for a regional dialogue, exploiting thereby the self-defeating character of the largely passive—and mainly sloganeering—US diplomacy' (Brzezinski, 2007). Officially, the USA has not elaborated further on a number of crucial issues related to this initiative, whereas the media remain suspiciously silent. The 21,000 troop reinforcements sent to Iraq in January 2007 could be seen as underpinning a project towards a possible invasion of Iran, rather than contributing to Iraq's security crisis, a rather elusive goal that US generals and military strategists are well aware of. Iranians and Americans may be negotiating behind close doors. However, if this is the case, and in view of Iran's determination to acquire nuclear weapons, then it seems that the more intransigent the Iranians become with the Americans in private, the more hawkish and provocative the USA will become in public. Whatever the case, one thing remains certain: the USA (and/or Israel) should avoid attacking Iran at all, if they still want to have any chance of tackling successfully Iraq's meta-conflict condition, a condition which could very well spread all over the greater Middle East if they opt for a military assault.

CONCLUDING REMARKS

Throughout its modern history, Iraq has been in a continuous state of conflict due to the problematic linkages between imperial/external interference and the domestic environment. Meta-conflict is a condition where previous sites, structures and subjects of or in conflict assume a destructive dynamic, preventing the transition to a post-conflict situation of economic reconstruction and development. Regime change in Iraq has brought about precisely this. In order to 'gauge' Iraq's meta-conflict condition, I have focused on three descriptors: (a) the resistance movement and its complex manifestations at both societal and governmental levels; (b) the Constitution, which is consubstantial with the issue of oil governance and, hence, the issue of 'petroleum nationalism'; and (c) the Iranian factor. All three critical descriptors and/or their aggravation and elevation are a consequence of the US invasion and occupation of Iraq—that is, a product of external interference. I would suggest that a similar analysis applies to the case of Afghanistan.

Never before in its modern history has Iraq been subject to such dire meta-conflict circumstances. However, meta-conflict is not only bad news for the Iraqis. It is also bad news for the occupying forces, that is, the Americans and the British. Both of them are entrapped in a situation of their own making, and that despite the fact that foreknowledge of what would ensue after the toppling of Saddam Hussein was available. In this context, the future for the US and the British in Iraq is rather bleak, the only serious alternative perhaps being that of launching a sincere regional diplomatic initiative, accompanied by a credible timetable for an orderly troop withdrawal. Having said this, I have also raised concerns that in the case that the Bush Administration attacks Iran before the expiration of its term (January 2009), then this would put in jeopardy the entire security arrangements of the greater Middle East, possibly leading to a more general conflagration.

The USA did not suffer from a deficient strategic culture during the First Gulf War. The USA stopped Israel from retaliating when Saddam's Scud missiles reached Israel. More to the point, the Allies were against taking Saddam in Iraq too. James Baker himself, Secretary of State during the First Gulf War, wrote in his 1995 memoirs, *The Politics of Diplomacy*: 'We believed it was essential that Iraq remains intact, with or without a more reasonable new leadership'. He continued, 'The Shi'a were quite naturally perceived as being aligned with Iran, and the Kurds, who demanded an independent state of Kurdistan for decades, were very fragmented in the leadership and were a constant source of concern to Turkey' (p. 439, in Baker, 1995).

Baker said it all back then. Now, his discourse is poor, his influence poorer and, after all, it may be too late anyway.

NOTES

1. I borrow the term 'deficient strategic culture' from Charles Kupchan. In his *The Vulnerability of Empire* (1994—see Bibliography), Kupchan defines cultural strategic deficiency as the inability of decision-making elites to reshape and adjust their strategic culture on the basis of incoming contemporary information that forms the system of their 'strategic beliefs'. 'Strategic culture'

becomes deficient at the moment when it obstructs adjustment on the basis of correct strategic beliefs. Applying this analysis to the case of Iraq, one might argue that the USA's decades-old strategic culture (e.g. the defence and security of Israel, the geopolitical primacy of the petro-dollar, the exportation/imposition of liberal values in authoritarian regimes across the globe) overrode concrete strategic beliefs of policy-makers (both American and European), which were correctly diagnosing that Iraq (and perhaps the region) will become chaotic and extremely problematic after a US invasion and occupation.

2. 'Back stage' politics shy away from the public eye (e.g. political interference and machinations by intelligence services, whether domestic or foreign). 'Front stage' politics are visible and reportable, thus subject to criticism in the public domain.

3. Nearly 100,000 people died in Iraq between 1918 and 1948. It should also be noted the great number of deaths by public hanging, such as the death of communist leaders Fahd (of Christian origin) and Yasin. This practice, with minor and rather semantic differences, continues unabated today—witness the hanging of Saddam Hussain by the Iraqi Government, tolerated by both the United Kingdom and the USA.

4. The Iraq Petroleum Company was nationalized by the Baathists in 1972.

5. Zaki, who was influenced by Latin American revolutionaries, attempted to launch an insurrection in southern Iraq. He fought heroically and was killed in action in 1968.

6. It should be noted, however, that Saddam Hussain, immediately after the ousting of his army from Kuwait, attacked Shi'a and Kurdish forces and civilians, spreading death and destruction in large areas of the country.

7. We should distinguish here between de jure sovereignty and de facto sovereignty. The former form of sovereignty is enshrined in the Constitution of every modern state, but the latter is rather far more elusive (particularly as regards 'small' states) or complicated (particularly as regards 'medium-sized' or 'big' states). The real sovereign, Carl Schmitt argued in the 1930s, is the one who can bring about a state of emergency in a given country. In this respect, one might argue that the real (global) sovereign after the Cold War is the most powerful on earth, that is, the USA. This real global sovereign, one could also argue, contributes decisively to the shaping of the pecking order of powers and sovereignties in the world.

8. Broadly speaking, oil- and gas-producing states have three legal ways to run their energy business. The first is that of a nationalized industry, where the state is in control of the entire revenue resulting from energy. The second is the so-called concession model, at times known as the tax and royalty system. In a concession framework, the private company receives a license from the state to extract, sell, refine and transport oil and in return it pays the state taxes and royalties. A production sharing agreement (PSA) is a third form of policy, with very complex legal structures and provisions. Put simply, in a PSA contract the

private company finances the entire cycle of investment (exploration, drilling, infrastructure, etc.), with the entire production of the first oil produced going to the company in order to recover the costs incurred in the investment cycle. After that, profits are divided between the state and the private company in agreed proportions. The classic work on PSAs is that by Daniel Johnston, *International Petroleum Fiscal Systems and Production Sharing Contracts* (1994). For the concession model, see Bernard Mommer, *Global Oil and the Nation State* (2002).

9. The main Shi'a factions and militia are: that led by Abd al-Aziz al-Hakim (leader of the Supreme Council for the Islamic Revolution in Iraq—SCIRI), which is the largest and best-organized Shi'a political party, also with close ties to Iran; and the Mahdi army of Hojatoleslam Muqtada as-Sadr, which draws from the impoverished areas of the Shi'as in Baghdad. Grand Ayatollah Ali as-Sistani, although he is the Shi'ite leading cleric in Iraq, nevertheless seems to have lost much of his power and it is believed that his influence is waning (see also p. 16 of the Baker-Hamilton Report, 2006). The Kurdish factions are guided by: Masoud Barzani, the President of the regional Kurdish Government and leader of the Kurdistan Democratic Party; and Jalal Talabani, the President of Iraq and leader of the Patriotic Union of Kurdistan. Sunni insurgents and squads are unidentified, but it is believed that Tareq al-Hashimi, who leads the largest Sunni party in the parliament, the Iraqi Islamic Party, has links with Sunni militias.

10. In Greek mythology, the Erinys were attendants of Hades and Persephone, three goddesses who guarded the Underworld. What a name to choose for a mercenary company operating in the modern world! Its headquarters are in Johannesburg (South Africa) and Dubai.

11. *Text of the Draft Constitution*, translated from the Arabic by the Associated Press, at www.iraqigovernment.org/constituion_en.htm (accessed on 16 December 2005), p. 1.

12. Ibid., 2.

13. Ibid., 18.

14. Ibid., 19.

15. This is further corroborated by article 136(4): 'No amendment is allowed that lessens the powers of the regions that are not among the exclusive powers of the federal authority, except with the agreement of the legislative council of the concerned region and the consent of a majority of its population in a general referendum', ibid., p. 22.

16. Ibid., 21.

17. In November 2005 an oil exploration deal was signed between the Kurdish-controlled region of Iraq and the Norwegian oil company DNO; see Borzou Daragahi, 'Kurdish Oil Deal Shocks Iraq's Political Leaders', in *Los Angeles*

Times of 1 December 2005 (at www.globalpolicy.org/security/oil/2005/ 0928heritageoil.htm). In September 2005 the Kurds had signed a Memorandum of Understanding (MOU) with Heritage Oil Corporation (HOC), which also caused uproar among the Sunnis.

18. *The Economist* concedes that 'serious offences almost certainly occurred, but probably not on a scale large enough to shift [the election outcome] more than a handful of seats', in 'The Wrong Lot Won, Dammit', on 7 January 2006.

19. I should point out that one or two of the options for the USA and the United Kingdom that I discuss here are embraced by the Baker-Hamilton Report, but, for obvious reasons, they are not spelled out clearly and, for that matter, courageously. Moreover, the Report discusses both the diplomatic options (mainly initiation of discussions with Iran and Syria) and the issue of withdrawal in a rather confusing and contradictory manner. The authors see diplomatic success in terms of reinforcing existing US deployments in Iraq, which is basically what President Bush did. Iran and Syria could hardly be engaged in serious diplomatic talks—whether overt of covert—if they can see more US troops deployed in Iraq. Their natural reaction would be to reinforce their capabilities too and, in the case of Iran, to intensify efforts toward the acquisition of a nuclear capability.

A–Z Glossary
Conflicts in the World

Vassilis K. Fouskas
with the assistance of Hazel Cameron

This glossary constitutes an attempt at presenting those (hot/actual or cold/latent) conflicts that either have been uncovered by the contributors to this volume, or the strategic importance of which is of great historical or contemporary significance in terms of security (regional or global). The list, however, cannot be exhaustive, for there are myriads of localized, low-intensity conflicts across the globe—related to immigration, drugs trafficking, small-weapons trafficking, etc.—that, being ramified with, and possibly accentuated by, other agents' interference, could potentially destabilize local and regional socio-political settings and patterns. Conflicts can crop up at any point in time once some of the ingredients producing conflict situations are there (see 'Introduction: A World in Conflict' above). These limitations aside, this glossary draws up a substantial list, in itself long enough to draw the awareness of the reader to the issues of peace, democracy and justice in a world in which great power politics seem to be reproducing, or even exacerbating, rather than resolving, ethnic, religious and other types of conflict, latent or actual.

Aegean Sea (Greece-Turkey)

Both Greece and Turkey occupy a strategic position in the eastern Mediterranean and the Near and Middle East. However, with Turkey being far more populous (c. 70 million, with the second largest army in the North Atlantic Treaty Organization—NATO, as against c. 11 million for Greece), as well as geographically stretching from the borderlands of Iran, Iraq and Syria in the east and south to Greece and Bulgaria in the west and north-west, it is arguably more important to any great power politics game than Greece. Turkey controls the straits from the Black Sea and lives at a stone's throw distance from Russia, making it constitute a major transit route for petroleum and gas to the West, the most recent addition to such real estate being the Baku (Azerbaijan)–Ceyhan (Turkey's Mediterranean port opposite Cyprus) pipeline. Yet, Greece is in a position to launch strategic initiatives by virtue of its position in the Aegean (a major international trade route from and to the Black Sea and an important trade corridor for the Suez Canal traffic); witness the fact that Germany did not bother to militarily occupy Turkey during the Second World War, inasmuch as it was in possession of the Aegean and Crete, thus controlling the sea and air traffic from the Black Sea and of most of the eastern Mediterranean. Modern Greece was one of the states emerging out of the gradual decline of the Ottoman Empire and, as a modern nation-state, took its shape in 1923 with the Treaty of Lausanne, after having lost the war to Turkey in Asia Minor (since 1923 the only territorial addition to Greece has been the acquisition of the Dodecanese islands from Italy in 1947, in the south-east Aegean). The 1930 Venizelos-Atatürk Convention of Friendship and Reconciliation aimed, among others, at strengthening bilateral relations between the two countries in the Balkan and eastern Mediterranean theatres. However, the Greek–Turkish conflict was bound to re-emerge in the first half of the 1950s over the issue of Cyprus. Turkey attributed to Greece Cyprus's wish for union with Greece in the 1950s (see entry on Cyprus below) and began adopting an overall revisionist position regarding its bilateral relations with Greece on a number of issues, such as the Greek minority in Istanbul, the Turkish minority in Greek Thrace, the position of the Orthodox Patriarchate and the Aegean Sea. In 1955 mob violence in Istanbul and Izmir severely reduced the remaining Greek communities there, while in 1973–74, in parallel with and even before invading and partitioning Cyprus, Turkey began questioning the status of the Aegean. There are several elements to the Aegean dispute. First, Turkey does not recognize that the Greek eastern Aegean islands have continental shelf, arguing that they rest on Anatolia (Asia Minor). Second, Greece has now extended its territorial waters to six nautical miles (11 km) and reserved the right to extend them to 12 miles whenever it sees fit to do so; Turkey's Grand National Assembly has threatened that this would mean war and suggested that a median line be drawn in the Aegean. Third, Turkey recognizes a limit of only six nautical miles for Greek airspace (Flight Information Region—FIR), as this should equate to territorial waters. In 1974 Turkey issued a notice to airmen (NOTAM 714) and to the International Civil Aviation Organization (ICAO) requiring aircraft flying over the eastern half of the Aegean and the Dodecanese to report to the Istanbul FIR. This NOTAM was withdrawn in 1980, but since then Turkish military aircraft fly regularly in the outer four miles of Greek-claimed airspace, the result being several dogfights between Greek and Turkish jet fighters over the Aegean. In May 2006, during a Greek-Turkish dogfight, two jets collided, resulting in the death of the Greek pilot who failed to eject. Another dangerous incident, in January 1996, concerned the islets of Imia (Kardak), half-way between the Greek island of Kalymnos and the Turkish Çavuş Adası (Kato Is.). Both Greece and Turkey amassed their warships; the crisis was defused following behind-the-scenes diplomacy and a public announcement by US President Bill Clinton. Turkey also accuses Greece of militarizing the eastern Aegean islands in defiance of the Treaty of Lausanne. Greece counters that this legal restriction no longer applies after the 1936 Montreux Convention, when Turkey militarized the Bosphorus Straits and the Metaxas regime in Athens consequently asserted Greece's rights to militarize the northern Aegean islands, as they were part and parcel of the same strategic theatre. Greece prefers international mediation and wants the issues to be resolved by the International Court of Justice, whereas Turkey prefers a bilateral resolution framework.

Afghanistan

Afghanistan is at the heart of the pivotal Eurasian region of Central Asia. With a population of over 26 million (the figure includes refugees in Pakistan, Iran and Kyrgyzstan), it constitutes a major transit route for oil and gas from and to Russia and the Caspian Sea region and is thus important for all the great powers: China, Russia, India, the United Kingdom and the USA, as well as other major Asian (e.g. Pakistan and Iran) and European (e.g. Germany and France) powers. Today Afghanistan is a major producer of opium (nearly 75% of the world's crop, another major producer being Myanmar—Burma), which is refined into heroin with the help of acetic anhydride. There are signs that the USA and NATO are no longer interested in going the extra mile to finish off the job that they started in the wake of 9/11, when they attacked the country: poppy production is way up again and the resultant earnings from drugs are again fuelling the warlords' coffers. For Alexander the Great Afghanistan represented the 'Ends of the Earth', whereas Genghis Khan, Tamburlaine, the Persians and Mughals all tried to hold sway before the advent of the modern period, when the Russian and British Empires began fighting for Afghan and other Central Asian lands in the 'great game' of the 19th century. The largest tribe in Afghanistan are the Pashtuns (known to the British as the Pathans), who make up about one-third of the population and live both in Afghanistan and Pakistan. Another group, the Hazaras (19%) are Shi'as and supported by Iran. There are also Tajiks (25%), Uzbeks (12%), Turkomen, Almaqs and Balochis. The Pashtuns are mainly Sunni Muslims and do not recognize the frontier separating Afghanistan from Pakistan. When British India was partitioned after the Second World War, the Afghan Government requested that the Pashtun areas of Pakistan become independent with a view to annexing them in the future. Pakistan refused and sought the support of the USA, which it got. In this context, the USSR strengthened its ties with the Afghan Government, becoming its major supplier of economic aid and arms. The Soviets built a road through the Hindu Kush, including the 1.6 km Salang tunnel at some 3,000 m (10,000 feet), thus connecting Kabul to the Soviet frontier. Communist ideas in Afghanistan gathered pace and a party was formed under Moscow's surveillance and sponsorship, taking power in 1978. However, tribal warfare, always mediated by external forces supporting one faction or another (e.g. Pakistan, Iran, the USSR or the USA) over disputed territories and political power, left Afghanistan a deeply divided and chaotic country. Covert action by the US Central Intelligence Agency (CIA) and US sponsorship of anti-Soviet Islamic groups (*mujahideen*, meaning 'holy warriors') was one of the key elements of the strife during 1979–89. In March 1979, in the wake of the overthrow of Shah in Iran, Shi'a and Tajik fundamentalists captured Herat and tortured and killed a number of Soviet advisers there. The Soviets, fearing Islamic domination of Afghanistan with the knock-on effects it would have over its Central Asian republics, decided to invade the country. Thus, the USSR, under Leonid Brezhnev and his geriatric ruling group, were sucked into Afghanistan, much as the USA had been sucked into Viet Nam, as predicted by Zbigniew Brzezinski, US President Jimmy Carter's adviser and the architect of America's sponsorship of the *mujahideen*. The USA spent a total of US $3,000 million in assisting the Islamic rebels, whereas another $1,000 million of aid and war materials came from the People's Republic of China, as well as Saudi Arabia and other Muslim countries. The USSR withdrew its forces completely by February 1989, admitting to having lost 15,000 military personnel, with 35,500 wounded. The retreat of the Soviets did not put an end to the conflict between the various ethnic and religious groups. Clashes occurred between Iran-sponsored militia and the Saudi-sponsored Pashtun groupings. The advent of the Taliban (who were fundamentalist Sunnis) on to the political and social scene of the country drove a pro-Pakistani wedge into the civil war, as the group pledged border control and containment of Pashtun claims to secede from Pakistan. The Taliban asserted its power over the major urban centres of Afghanistan and against the Shi'a, entered Kabul in September 1995 and assumed power (Mazar-i-Sharif in the north was taken in 1998). Pakistan, and later Saudi Arabia and the United Arab Emirates, recognized the regime, but not the USA or Iran. Iran even threatened to invade Afghanistan when the Taliban began committing atrocities against the Shi'a in Mazar-i-Sharif, while also killing Iranian diplomats (but border clashes never escalated into a full-scale war). The Taliban survived until October–November 2001, after which US forces, leading an international coalition, overthrew the regime, because they were believed to be sheltering Osama bin Laden and al-Qaida cells, the main culprits for the 9/11 terrorists attacks on the USA on 11 September 2001. President Carter had justified America's involvement in Afghanistan in terms of containing the Soviets from approaching the Persian (Arabian) Gulf and the Straits of Hormuz, a major strategic passage. The tragic events of 9/11, however, opened up an opportunity for direct US intervention in Afghanistan and the subsequent

NATO-led occupation. That intervention was linked to the strategic interests of all the great powers involved in the occupation, ranging from oil and gas pipeline projects to issues of Western and US/Israeli security vis-à-vis the perceived Chinese threat and Iran's determination to acquire a nuclear capacity.

Angola

Today Angola's population is c. 14 million and is mainly composed of four ethnic groups: Ovimbundo (39%); Mbundu (26%); Bakongo (14%); and Lunda-Chokwe (10%). The Berlin Conference of 1884–85, an event that divided Africa between the imperial European powers, had given Angola to Portugal, which had long viewed the territory as a substitute for the loss of Brazil (Angola was first colonized by the Portuguese in 1575 and, before the slave trade was stopped by the British navy, Portugal had sent about 3 million slaves from Angola to Brazil). Portuguese governors ruled Angola by decree, attracting investment from any source and trading the key export items of the territory: coffee, diamonds and petroleum. The advent to power of the Portuguese dictator António de Oliveira Salazar in 1926 altered the relationship between the metropolitan country and the colony. Salazar's regime, particularly after the Second World War, increased its grip over the colony at a time when other colonial powers were ceding control to local nationalist and anti-imperialist movements. Facing opposition, the Portuguese attempted to stir up conflict between the ethnic groups, privileging those who were somewhat integrated into the officially run economy under the authority of the Government and those of Portuguese descent. Their attempt was a total failure. The first anti-colonial movements appeared in the 1950s and were led by the Popular Movement for the Liberation of Angola (MPLA) and the National Front for the Liberation of Angola (FNLA), a splinter group of which later formed the National Union for the Total Independence of Angola (UNITA), led by Jonas Savimbi. The uprising against Portugal began in March 1961, after the independence of the Belgian Congo (Zaire—now the Democratic Republic of the Congo). The MPLA was supported by the USSR and Cuba, whereas the USA (notably the CIA), South Africa and Rhodesia (now Zimbabwe) threw their weight behind the FNLA and, later, UNITA. Although the Portuguese eventually prevailed over the three inefficient guerrilla groups, they began to experience severe strains on their resources because of the difficulties they had been facing in Portuguese Guinea (Guinea-Bissau) and Mozambique. When the regime changed in Lisbon in 1974 and democracy was restored, Angola achieved independence. Nevertheless, fighting broke out between the MPLA, on the one hand, and UNITA and the FNLA on the other. The CIA, following the USA's defeat in Viet Nam and realizing that another overseas communist victory could not be politically afforded, began sending large quantities of arms to the FNLA and to Savimbi through Zaire and Zambia. The USSR kept supporting the MPLA, quite openly, by shipping war materials directly by sea to the Angolan capital, Luanda. The communist forces, finally, emerged victorious but the victory, despite appearances, was incomplete. While the FNLA disintegrated, UNITA retreated in good order and successfully sought support from Rhodesia and South Africa. Savimbi managed to gain control of large parts of the country rich in diamonds, so UNITA could raise substantial revenue to finance his campaign against the pro-communist Government. In June 1998 the UN placed trade sanctions on UNITA and passed a protocol penalizing whoever bought Angolan diamonds without a government-approved certificate of origins. However, peace with UNITA was not to be possible until after the death of Savimbi in 2002.

B

Balochistan (Baluchistan)

This is probably the least known and rarely spoken of conflict of the greater Middle Eastern and South Asian regions, directly affecting countries such as Pakistan, Iran and even Afghanistan. Balochistan is an area that straddles the Pakistani-Iranian border and part of southern Afghanistan, the tribal inhabitants of which had in the past fought for independence, particularly in Pakistan, thus jeopardizing the territorial integrity of both Iran and Pakistan. The two main Balochi tribes in Pakistan, the Bugti and the Marri, often also fought with each other, but in the mid-2000s, thanks to Gen. Pervez Musharraf's heavy handedness, they ended their feuding and formed a combined front to advance their demands. The Balochis are numbering some 6.5 million in Pakistan and some 2 million in Iran. They are not populous but they happen to inhabit areas that are rich in gas and located around the strategic port of Gwadar, the terminal for a giant pipeline project that starts from Turkmenistan's Chardzou or Charjew (now Türkmenabat) and then crosses through Afghanistan's city of Herat. Another pipeline is projected to cross Pakistan, connecting Iran and India. Building on this venture, India's Oil Minister in 2005, Mani Sankar Aiyar, used to outline his dreams of a pan-Asian gas grid. The People's Republic of China is also very keen on participating in these projects and loaned Pakistan US $200 million, sending Chinese engineers to develop Gwadar's port, hoping to halve the distance to Xinjiang, the westernmost province of China, where the nearest oil importing port is otherwise over 2,000 miles distant. Balochi complaints include: lack of democracy and of investment in their region; deliberate efforts on the part of central government to alter the demographic balance in Balochistan; and unfair distribution of revenue coming from oil and gas projects. Just like the Kurds in Iraq, Balochi nationalists are basically coveting energy revenues out of which they could fund their own state. Pakistani Balochistan produces more than 45% of Pakistan's total gas output. The gas field is in an area called Sui, which is basically an estate of the Bugti (perhaps the most powerful of the Balochi tribes— Marri tribesmen dominated the independence movement of the 1970s, which the Government crushed with a great deal of bloodshed). Balochi guerrillas are targeting gas pipelines, power stations, railway bridges and gas fields. In 2005 Balochi insurgents targeted Chinese personnel in Gwadar, killing three engineers and injuring 11. Obviously, the Balochis resent outside involvement in oil and gas projects, as they feel they will be even more marginalized and deprived of any economic, let alone political, benefit. Pakistan receives some support from Iran in its operations, but Pakistani nationalists suspect the USA of conspiring to push Balochis to secede from Pakistan in order to control the region's oil and gas riches. Iranians, moreover, accuse the USA of inciting Balochis to secede from Pakistan in order to upset Iran's domestic balance by incentivizing ideas for a greater Balochistan, which would of course involve the break-up of their country.

Basque Country (Spain)

The Basques have been living in an area of some 20,000 sq km on both sides of the Spanish-French border for at least 2,000 years. About one-fifth of the Basque territory lies in France (the provinces of Benafarrao, Lapurdi and Zuberoa) and the rest in Spain (the provinces of Bizkaia, Araba, Nafarroa and Gipuzkoa). The Basques were brought into the Spanish state by the Carlist wars of 1833 and 1872, while modern Basque nationalism was born in the late 19th and early 20th century. Sabino Arana founded the Basque Nationalist Party (PNV) in 1895. Under Franco's dictatorship, the Spanish Basques were deprived of basic rights, such as the right to speak their language. Euskadi Ta Askatasuna (ETA—Basque Homeland and Unity) was formed in 1958 by various nationalist groupings. It was basically born out of discontent with the PNV's official policy, which ETA considered as too moderate and damaging for the cause of an independent Basque state. In the beginning ETA's actions were bank robberies and sabotage, but 10 years after its foundation, ETA got involved in killings. ETA's greatest achievement against Franco's authoritarian rule was the assassination of Adm. Luis Carrero Blanco, Franco's presumed successor. It is widely acknowledged that ETA's resistance contributed, among other factors, to the collapse of the dictatorship in the mid-1970s. However, the transition to democracy and the new Constitution of 1978 did very little to satisfy ETA's claims. Attacks on senior police officials and government agents continued and the state responded with the creation of counter-terrorist special units, such as the paramilitary Grupos Antiterroristas de Liberación (GAL). ETA's campaign continues to the present day, despite its popularity being very low. Its targets include army and police officers, journalists, members of the judiciary and parliamentary deputies. France has always played an ambivalent role with regard to this conflict. There were times when it offered shelter to ETA activists and times when it co-operated with the Spanish Government. Today there is a consensus among analysts of the Basque conflict, which indicates that the conflict is in a transition period, swinging between the end of a period of violence and confrontation and the start of a period of resolution. Be that as it may, it is worth noting that the Basque question in Spanish politics remains unresolved. It will remain so, as long as the Spanish state addresses the question in purely security terms and in the context of the global 'war on terror', following the USA's lead after 9/11.

Burma – *see* Myanmar

C

Ceuta – *see* **Gibraltar and Spanish North Africa**

Chechnya

The North Caucasus is now the new frontier of Russia, following the disintegration of the USSR in 1991. It constitutes a region of six republics and is populated by at least 18 different ethnic and religious (mostly Muslim) groups. Chechnya is one of those republics where there are claims for independence from Russia. The Chechen territory lies on the edge of the two main routes from Russia to Transcaucasia: the road from Vladikavkaz to Tbilisi in Georgia; and the Caspian coastal road. The oil pipeline from Baku in Azerbaijan to Novorossiisk, Russia's Black Sea port, also crosses Chechnya and near its capital, Groznyi. Chechnya's strategic importance was upgraded after the end of the Cold War with the discovery of additional oil and gas reserves in the Caspian Sea. In August 1991, taking advantage of the dissolution of the USSR, the Chechen leader, Gen. Dzhokhar Dudayev, demanded total independence for Chechnya (which, for a while, included the now separate Ingushetia). The Russian President, Boris Yeltsin, orchestrated a covert operation to undermine and thwart Dudayev's project, but it failed dismally. Yeltsin then decided, despite the plight of the Russian army, on a full-scale military operation to take Groznyi and restore a pro-Russian regime. The operation, which took place in December 1994, cost Russia an arm and a leg, as the Russian army failed to take the Chechen capital with an armoured dash in front of television cameras. Groznyi was finally captured in February 1995, but the Russians never really managed to restore order in the rest of Chechnya. Chechen rebels retaliated with acts of terror in Chechnya, Dagestan and in Russia proper; it has been alleged that the USA, along with Turkey, were assisting the Chechen rebels. In August 1996 the Chechen rebels signed an agreement with Moscow, stipulating the withdrawal of Russian troops. Three years later fighting broke out in Dagestan between Russian forces and pro-Chechen Dagestanis. The Russians could not allow this to continue, because violence in Dagestan could easily spill over to Chechnya and elsewhere, and decided to intervene in Chechnya proper to end the conflict. This time around, the Russian army was more successful, whereas fears of a general anti-Russian and pro-Islamic uprising in the Caucasus failed to be substantiated. Overall, and although world public opinion since 9/11 has been more sympathetic to Moscow (thanks also to Russian efforts to equate 9/11 with Muslim acts of terror on Russia's own territory), terrorist forms of resistance to Russian rule by Chechen and other Islamic groups continues to the present day.

China – *see* Taiwan *and* Tibet

Cyprus

Cyprus had effectively been a British colony since 1878, populated by an ethnic Greek majority (80%) and a significant Muslim minority (18%), the rest of the population being Armenians and Maronites. The Greek Cypriots' nationalist awakening had preceded the national-Turkic awakening of the Muslim minority, with the Greek Cypriots already seeking unification with mainland Greece after the foundation of the first Greek Kingdom (1830). The Ottoman Government, the Sublime Porte, conceded rule over Cyprus to the United Kingdom in 1878 in return for British support during the Russo-Ottoman war. Greece had its chances to acquire Cyprus from the United Kingdom between 1912 and 1922, but Greek warships, although good at keeping a grip on the Aegean islands, could not project power deeper into the eastern Mediterranean, particularly during the Balkan Wars (1912–13). Moreover, when the British offered Cyprus to Greece in return for Greece's support for Serbia in 1915, Greece, facing an internal split between Monarchists and Liberals, declined the offer. When imperial Britain (although it did not fight) and Greece lost the war in Anatolia to Turkish nationalism under Kemal Atatürk, the union of Cyprus with Greece became even more elusive. Yet, the Greek Cypriots continued to demand independence (from the British) and *enosis* (union with Greece). In 1954 they launched an anti-colonial campaign against the United Kingdom, perhaps the only anti-colonial campaign of the period led by right-wing, extreme nationalist forces. Turkey, mostly incited by the United Kingdom rather than on its own initiative, had made clear to Greece that it could not accept *enosis* or an independent Greek Cypriot state and that the only solution was *taksim* (partition) or 'double *enosis*'. In 1960 Cyprus gained an independent Government, which was bound to fail because of the equal governing rights of the two, by now deeply hostile, communities of the island. The Cyprus Constitution was chiefly dictated by the British, the masters of the policy of 'divide and rule' on the island. In 1963–64, as predicted by a secret US State Department paper drafted in 1959, the Constitution broke down due to a Greek Cypriot drive to eliminate the equal governing rights of the Turkish Cypriots. The result was an inter-communal fight, with the Turkish Cypriots withdrawing from government and settling into militarily protected enclaves. Turkey bombed Greek Cypriot positions and towns in 1964 and 1967 and threatened to invade the island to enforce partition and protect its minority from the Greeks' campaign of terror, but it refrained from doing so due to US interference. Basically, the Americans warned Turkey that if Cyprus was invaded and the USSR ran to its defence, then the USA would not defend Turkey. However, in 1974 Turkey, having received the green light from the USA, went ahead and invaded Cyprus in two military operations that took place in late July and mid-August. Greece and the United Kingdom, according to the 1960 Constitution, had the right to intervene too, but they refrained from doing so. The United Kingdom confined itself to preparing for the defence of its two military bases on the island (Dekhelia and Akrotiri/Episkopi). Greece's military junta under Brig.-Gen. Demetrios Ioannides (most of the Greek military officers who abolished the 1952 Constitution and ruled Greece from 1967 to 1974 were on the CIA payroll) obeyed its American masters and did not participate in the conflict so as to rescue Cyprus. Thus, the cohesion of NATO's southern flank was maintained (Greece and Turkey had been NATO members since 1952) and Henry Kissinger, the US Secretary of State and chief manager of the crisis, could claim diplomatic victory. Turkey established political and military control over 37% of Cypriot territory and began transferring people to the island from Anatolia. Greek Cypriot refugees number about 160,000 and any solution to the problem has to take their interests into account, particularly in view of the fact that they are the legitimate holders of many of the title deeds in the occupied areas. In 1983 a 'Turkish Republic of Northern Cyprus' (TRNC) was proclaimed, although no state has recognized it to date, except Turkey. Several efforts sponsored by the UN since 1974 to find a lasting and viable solution to the problem have so far failed (the UN also patrols a Green Line on Cyprus, separating the Turkish north from the Greek south). In 2002–04 the two sides voted in two separate referendums on the so-called Annan Plan, the latest UN blueprint for a solution to the division of the island. The Greek Cypriots, overwhelmingly, voted against the plan, whereas the Turkish Cypriots endorsed it. This did not obstruct the entry of the Republic of Cyprus into the European Union (EU), which officially took place on 1 May 2004 (together with nine other east-central European states and Malta). The de facto division of the island, however, remains, with the EU rather impotent to enforce any lasting solution to the conflict.

D

Darfur (Sudan)

Sudan is the largest African country and is located south of Egypt and has a population of c. 30 million. The cleavages cutting across the country are geographical and ethnic/religious (70% are Muslim, 10% Christian; 52% are African, 39% Arab). North of the capital, Khartoum, lies the Nubian Desert and the overall territory is rather dry; the people living there are largely of Arab descent and Muslim, but there are also Nubians and Bedouins. The southern lands in and around Sudd contain equatorial forests and are rich in petroleum reserves; the people living there are either Christian and, in terms of origin, are closer to the Africans found in neighbouring Kenya and Uganda. In the 19th century Egypt laid claim to Sudan, as did two European colonial powers, the United Kingdom and France. In 1898 Sudan finally became an Anglo-Egyptian condominium, but was effectively ruled by a British governor. The British prevailed thanks to the determination shown by Gen. Sir Horatio Kitchener, when his expedition confronted a French army led by Maj. Jean-Baptiste Marchand in Fashoda (now Kodok) on 19 September 1898 (when, in his memoirs, Gen. Charles de Gaulle listed the disasters that had afflicted France during his childhood, the first on the list was the Fashoda incident). The British did not make any effort to integrate and unite the diverse ethnic and religious landscape of the country, and in fact the north was administered in Arabic from Khartoum, whereas the south was kept separate and governed in English from Juba. More to the point, the south was subject to missionary activities, trying to convert the people to Christianity. This further aggravated the ethnic and religious tensions across the country. In the 1950s the British compelled the Egyptians to leave Sudan and then, on 1 January 1956, conceded independence to the country. However, the Christian Government that the British had set up was brought down by a coup, which installed Gen. Ibrahim Abboud in the presidency. Abboud expelled the Christian missionaries and politicians and set about unifying the country under Arab rule. A civil war ensued, in which an estimated 400,000 civilians had been killed by the mid-1960s. The Christian movement, Anya Nya, won international support from the West, as well as from Israel and Ethiopia. By 1969 Abboud had been removed from office by Gen. Gaafar Muhammad Nimeri, perhaps the most remarkable and astute leader of modern Sudan. Nimeri developed close relations with Egypt's

Anwar Sadat and vehemently supported peace between Egypt and Israel. He also opposed Muammar al-Qaddafi of Libya, as Qaddafi's main object was the acquisition of the north-western provinces of Sudan, the northern Darfur, which he wanted to use as a military base of operations against neighbouring Chad. Despite Nimeri's remarkable efforts to solve the problem of the south, mainly by promulgating constitutional reforms and integrating the Anya Nya army into the regular national army, the rebels regrouped and in 1983, assisted by Ethiopia, formed the Sudan People's Liberation Army (SPLA). In 1985 Nimeri was deposed, but six years later the SPLA suffered a major reverse, when the Ethiopian dictator, Mengistu, was overthrown and assistance cut off. The SPLA has, since its foundation, been attempting to articulate a national rather than regional (confined to the south) agenda, but this exacerbated tensions within it, between those wanting independence for the south and those aiming at over-throwing the Khartoum Government and establishing national control. Some accommodation with the southern rebels has now been achieved, but the country is still troubled by conflict. The Sudanese Government remained committed to *Shari'a* (Islamic law), refusing to separate religion from the state, thus making peace elusive. It has been alleged that the Government is now supporting groups such as al-Qaida, Hezbollah and Hamas, which are designated as terrorist by the USA. However, George W. Bush (US President since 2001), under pressure from Congress, sought co-operation with the Sudanese Government, which he obtained. In fact, like many other Middle Eastern governments and intelligence services, such as those of Syria, Sudan had been co-operating with the USA before 9/11. Among other things, this co-operation could be seen as a conse-quence of new discoveries of petroleum in the eastern Upper Nile region in 1999, provoking China's immense interest in Sudan's oil. In 2002 production stood at 200,000 barrels a day and commercial estimates put the amount of reserves at a total of several thousand million barrels. International mediation by the USA, the United Kingdom and Norway in 2002 brought about no substantial results in ending the civil war, the most disastrous incidents and mass killings occurring in the region of Darfur. In 2003 the non-Muslim Darfur Liberation Front (DLF) and the Sudan Liberation Army (SLA) mounted some spectacular operations against government interests and forces in Darfur, but in response the Government retaliated by arming the fundamentalist Muslim group of the Janjaweed, which began committing atrocities against non-Arabs. International mediation and other attempts at reaching an agreement between the warring parties have so far failed, with the scale of catastrophe having reportedly taken on genocidal dimensions.

E

East Timor (Timor-Leste) and Indonesia

East Timor was part of Indonesia's huge archipelago made up of more than 13,000 islands, with a population of now over 220 million, the majority being Muslim (87%), making Indonesia the world's largest Muslim state. There are also Christians (10%), Hindus and Buddhists. Ethnic groups comprise Javanese (45%), Sundanese (14%), Malay (8%), Chinese (8%) and others. East Timor (now the independent nation officially known as Timor-Leste) is mainly Christian, with a population of just one million. Portuguese imperialists were the first to reach Indonesia, but they were soon overwhelmed by the Dutch and British. The Dutch colonization of the archipelago began with the formation of the Dutch East India Company in 1602. During the 19th century the British established themselves in the Malay peninsula and North Borneo, although the Dutch kept colonizing Indonesia. The Dutch had though ceded the eastern part of Timor to the Portuguese in 1859. Indonesia, a major producer of petroleum in South-East Asia, had supplied nearly 30% of Japan's oil requirements during the Second World War. Japan occupied Indonesia during the war, but when it surrendered Indonesia went ahead and declared independence under the leadership of Dr Sukarno. The Dutch resisted Indonesia's independence, but by 1950 only West New Guinea (Irian Jaya) remained under Dutch control, and East Timor under the Portuguese. The Islamic regime suppressed Christian and other minorities and claimed East Timor when the dictatorship in Portugal was overthrown in 1975. The East Timorese, who preferred Portuguese to Indonesian rule, eventually opted for independence, which Portugal was keen to concede. Outside great powers stood idly by when Indonesia annexed East Timor by force in 1976. In fact, Australia assisted Jakarta in suppressing the East Timorese. East Timor's campaign for independence gained momentum when José Ramos Horta won the Nobel Peace Prize in 1996. Talks between Portugal and Indonesia, and violence between Indonesian troops and East Timorese rebels, continued, with Indonesia finally conceding the right of East Timorese to self-determination in 1999. Finally, in a referendum held in August 1999, some 78% of East Timorese voted for independence. Indonesian forces began then to withdraw under UN supervision and East Timor won its full independence in May 2002. Given broader tensions in the archipelago, Australia's neo-imperial involvement in the region, as well as China and America's business interests in the greater South Asia and Pacific region, violent conflicts in Indonesia always remain a possibility. For example, as recently as May 2006 Australia, with the backing of the UN and the USA, intervened militarily in Timor-Leste, proclaiming the 'restoration of order and the reshaping of the Constitution'. Australia's intervention has, however, more to do with obtaining control of oil and gas reserves in the Timor Sea and establishing a strong security presence in the region, acting as America's reliable strategic partner in this vital part of the world.

F

Fiji and New Caledonia

Before the advent of French and British imperialism and Christian missionaries in the South Pacific during the 19th century, Fiji and New Caledonia were basically inhabited by Melanesian tribes. Suppressing tribal resistance, France and the United Kingdom acquired New Caledonia and Fiji in 1853 and 1874, respectively. New Caledonia turned out to be one of the richest territories on earth, given its size (40 miles long and 10 miles wide, or some 64 km by 16 km; the population today is c. 150,000). Its mineral riches include cobalt, manganese, silver, gold, mercury, chrome, copper and antimony. During the Second World War, after the fall of France, the USA used the territory as a major base in the Pacific theatre of operations against Japan. This resulted in New Caledonia acquiring modern new roads, harbours and airstrips, boosting its economic development after the end of the war. Today, the conflict is between the indigenous Kanaks (43% of the population) and the settlers, mainly of European, Polynesian and Asian origin, who outnumber the Melanesians. The territory remains a French Territoire d'Outre-Mer, an overseas territory, and not a Département d'Outre-Mer, that is, an integral part of France, sending deputies to the National Assembly. The French were and are beset by a dispute of their own making, which is the conflict between the indigenous factions claiming independence (Kanaks) and the parties representing the immigrants and the descendants of the settlers, who prefer French rule and holding on to their privileges. The situation in Fiji is not very dissimilar. The British imported some 70,000 labourers from India to work in their cotton and sugar plantations. By the 1980s, after independence, the descendants of the Indian settlers were more (48.6% of the total population) than the indigenous Melanesian Fijians (46.2%). Fijians of Indian origin dominated the state machine and virtually all business. However, the army remained under the control of the Melanesian Fijians, whose political wing lost the general election in 1987, so Melanesian supremacy was restored via a coup. Another similar coup took place in 2000, holding the Labour Government led by the Fijian Indians hostage for 56 days. Over 100,000 Indians have emigrated since 1987 and, in 2002 alone, almost a quarter of the population—220,000 people—applied to emigrate to the USA through the green card lottery system. Politics and the voting pattern are racially segregated. Elections, owing to the unclear margins of majority, are always closely fought and contested. Australia and New Zealand openly supported the Labour Party and Laisenia Qarase's re-election to power in May 2006. However, another coup soon followed. The political situation remains very precarious and both Fiji and New Caledonia are just another two cases of ethnic/religious conflict initiated by imperial undertakings of the past.

Former Yugoslav republic of Macedonia – *see* Macedonia

G

Gibraltar and Spanish North Africa

Berber Algerian Muslims first reached Gibraltar in the eighth century, only to give in to the Castilian Spanish in 1309 (although it was not finally reconquered until 1462). Two centuries later British naval ascendancy led strategists to spot Gibraltar—later Malta and Cyprus—as a post through which the United Kingdom (as England and Scotland became in 1707) could maintain maritime communications and hegemony in the Mediterranean. However, the French were interested too and poised to ally with Spain against the British, but, in the run up to the Treaty of Utrecht (1713), France abandoned Spain and gave the green light to the United Kingdom to assume total control of the Rock. This Treaty ceded control of the Rock of Gibraltar and its environs to the United Kingdom in perpetuity. However, the Spanish claimed that the British were in breach of the Treaty, because they allowed other ethnicities, such as Jews, to settle in the city. Gibraltar became a Crown colony in 1830, the year in which the United Kingdom was becoming a guarantor of Greece's independence in the eastern Mediterranean. Spain never ceased to demand sovereignty over the Rock and, in 1963, under Gen. Francisco Franco, managed to obtain a favourable UN vote in the international organization's General Assembly. The United Kingdom refused to comply and in 1967 went instead ahead with organizing a referendum in which the overwhelming majority of the population voted in favour of remaining under British sovereignty (only 43 people voted to join Spain, as opposed to 12,137 who opted to remain British). Oddly enough, Spain considers Gibraltar to be Spanish, although it refuses to concede to Morocco the two Spanish enclaves on the northern African coast, Ceuta and Melilla. Morocco's claims have been ignored and episodes of tension often occur, as in 2002, when a small group of Moroccan soldiers occupied the uninhabited island of Perejil, which is claimed by Spain (there are also other islands or islets claimed by Spain as part of Spanish North Africa, with Ceuta and Melilla, and lying very close to Moroccan coast). The Moroccan soldiers were quickly outnumbered by Spain's far superior military strength, but tensions remain to the present day, both between Spain and Morocco (Algeria also asserts a claim to the Spanish exclaves) and between Spain and the United Kingdom over the territorial question and other issues, such as fishery rights. Today's inhabitants of Gibraltar barely exceed 35,000 and often cross to Spain for entertainment. The United Kingdom is discussing with Spain ways in which the Rock can either become independent or join Spain, although it refuses to discuss surrendering the exclusive use of military and intelligence facilities in Gibraltar, as well as certain privileges concerning navigation and porting rights.

Greece – *see* **Aegean Sea** *and* **Cyprus** *and* **Macedonia**

H

Haiti

Haiti has a population of c. 8.5 million and forms the western territorial area of Hispaniola, an island of which the eastern part is the Dominican Republic. Almost all the original inhabitants of the island (Arawak Indians) died of diseases brought in by Europeans in the 16th century. Haiti, ceded to France by Spain in 1697, was constantly suffering from slave uprisings against the French rulers. In 1804 it became independent, but stability was elusive, as clashes between mulattos (of mixed African and European descent) and African Haitians were a constant phenomenon. Once the USA had established control of the western hemisphere, it swiftly moved to acquire Haiti, establishing a virtual colony there. The Americans did their best to exploit Haiti's sugar and coffee trade, but very little to integrate Haitians into civil and political institutions, thus ignoring nation-building processes. The USA withdrew from Haiti in 1935, leaving behind a chaotic situation with the security forces in power, which it tried to control. After the Second World War François Duvalier and his son, Jean Claude, ruled Haiti in a dictatorial fashion from 1957 to 1986. In a county where violence of all sorts is endemic and where poverty is a mass phenomenon (Haiti is one of the poorest countries on earth), the Duvaliers organized special security forces to deal with rebels, the famous Tontons Macoutes (Creole for 'bogeymen'). Eventually, Duvalier was ousted from power by a coup in 1986 and free elections, for the first time ever, were organized in 1990, bringing into power Jean-Bertrand Aristide. Aristide tried to launch a number of reforms, particularly in the security apparatus, but he failed. In September 1991 he was overthrown by another violent coup, headed by Gen. Raul Cedras, which resulted in thousands of deaths. Under UN mediation, Cedras and Aristide met in New York and agreed that Aristide should return to Haiti to reorganize the security apparatus under UN supervision. Yet, the UN mission failed to accomplish its objectives, as it found fierce resistance by the 'bogeymen'. The UN enforced sanctions on Haiti and author-ized a 28-nation military force, led by the USA, to invade the country. More than 21,000 troops landed in Haiti in September 1994. However, assassinations had already become routine and poverty levels had increased. Once again, American forces failed to achieve any results, whereas Aristide had to organize his own security forces in order to survive politically. This increased dissatisfaction and tension among the main rivals and a policy of tit-for-tat ensued. Haiti became virtually ungovernable, with thousands of refugees pouring into Florida. When President Bill Clinton refused to take any more refugees, Aristide rebuked Clinton by saying he created a 'floating Berlin Wall'. In 2004 Aristide, under US pressure, resigned, leaving the political and economic situation in Haiti even more precarious than in the 1990s.

I

Indonesia – *see* **East Timor and Indonesia**

K

Korea (North and South)

The Korean peninsula south of China has a total population of c. 72 million, of which some 25 million live in the North, the Democratic People's Republic of Korea, a state labelled by US President George W. Bush as being part of the 'axis of evil' (the others were Iran, Syria and, until recently, Iraq and Libya). The division of Korea into two states has, in effect, been the work of the USSR and the USA, both of which occupied the respective territories north and south of the 38th parallel (38°N) after the defeat of Japan. Before the Second Word War the peninsula was mainly coveted and occupied by Japan, which also transferred settler population there. The Soviets established a communist regime in the North and then withdrew their forces, focusing on their own immediate post-war problems. However, the North Koreans advanced well into the territories south of the 38th parallel, a fact that led the Americans under General Douglas MacArthur, the US Commander-in-Chief in the Far East, to launch an offensive pushing back the communists. The American advance was stopped by Chinese intervention. The Chinese helped push back the Americans, and even occupied Seoul, but finally a separation line was established along the 38th parallel. Today, North Korea has developed into a military power, with a very large standing army. This occurred and occurs at the expense of living standards, social welfare and economic development. The South, the Republic of Korea, in essence is an American-Japanese protectorate, which lives under the constant fear of an attack, particularly a nuclear one, from the North. The situation in this strategic part of East Asia is particularly precarious, as any advance of either the USA or Japan will not be left without response and fierce retaliation from North Korea and the People's Republic of China, and vice versa. One of the reasons, in fact, that the USA did not attack pre-emptively or preventively North Korea, but preferred to topple Saddam in Iraq, was precisely the fact that North Korea had a credible deterrence as a nuclear power, and could also be assisted, as in the past, by another and far more populous nuclear power, China.

Kosovo

In 1389 the Serbs under Prince Lazar fought ferociously against Sultan Murat I in Kosovo in order to keep the Ottoman troops out of their lands. This was a battle that had more to do with land than nationalist ideologies, as modern nationalism was not part of the European and Balkan landscapes at the time. Nevertheless, modern Serbian elites have since capitalized on this epic battle in order to amalgamate consensus and advance their national demands over the region. During the First World War the Albanians, the majority ethnic majority of the province, supported the Central European Empires against the Serbs. The Serbs, in turn, suppressed Albanian rights, launching a campaign of intimidation and colonization among them. Kosovo thus became part of modern Yugoslavia (then the Kingdom of Serbs, Croats and Slovenes) in 1919, but the Serbs never managed to streamline developments in the province without violence. All Kosovar Albanian revolts in the 1920s were brutally suppressed. During the Second World War, Kosovo was incorporated into Albania under Italian suzerainty and the Albanians again fought with the Germans and Italians, this time against Soviet and Bulgarian troops, and towards the end of the war alone, when German and Italian troops were withdrawing from Greece and Albania. During Tito's communist era (1945–80) Kosovo enjoyed spells of greater autonomy, particularly after 1974, when a new Constitution was introduced. Yet, the minority Serb population (then constituting about 28% of the provincial total) enjoyed special privileges, such as high status in party membership and, in general, was more empowered. Yugoslavia suffered a severe economic crisis in the 1970s and 1980s, as a result of 'stagflation' (economic stagnation accompanied by inflation) and Yugoslav exports being blocked from Western markets. Yugoslavia thus became dependent on the International Monetary Fund for financing its debt obligations. The collapse of the USSR further accentuated Yugoslavia's problems, as the non-aligned policy envisaged by Tito and various Arab leaders became inoperative. The Kosovar Albanians, following other ethnic communities in the country, demanded independence or, possibly, annexation by Albania. Meanwhile, ethnic Albanians were already about 90% of the total population of the region (1.8 million in total). During the 1990s Serbian elites under Slobodan Milošević attempted to impose order in the rebellious province, while fighting, either diplomatically or militarily, on several other fronts at the same time (mainly in Bosnia and Croatia, but there were also issues in Macedonia, Slovenia, Montenegro and Vojvodina). In summer 1998, when Yugoslavia was already a rump composed only of Serbia and Montenegro, the North Atlantic Treaty Organization (NATO), in a show of strength, flew over Albania and Kosovo (known officially as Kosovo and Metohija) with the apparent aim of quelling the warring parties. The Dayton Accord of 1995, which stopped the war in Bosnia between the Serbs, on the one hand, and Muslims and Croats, on the other, had no provision for the Kosovo problem. Milošević continued his campaign against the Kosovo Liberation Army (KLA), which he considered to be a terrorist group. The USA, momentarily, flirted with the idea of supporting Milošević, but finally sided with the rebellious Albanians. A number of issues were at stake for the US when NATO launched its air strikes against Belgrade on 24 March 1999. First, there was a matter of European security, which is to say, a matter of the USA asserting hegemony over the Balkans and east-central Europe, driving a wedge between Russia, which wanted to have a say in Serbia's future, and an enlarging European Union. Secondly, there were a number of oil and gas pipeline projects under way, which were financed by Halliburton, the oil corporation headed by Dick Cheney (later the US-Vice President to George W. Bush). A major trans-Balkan pipeline was planned to cross Kosovo and terminate at the Albanian port of Durrës. The issue of Albanian human rights played also an important part in justifying the campaign and in amassing the coalition of NATO forces, although Greece and Italy opposed the campaign in private and raised their concerns in NATO meetings and other international forums. Milošević's forces were finally driven out of Kosovo in June 1999, but the province's status is still unspecified today, remaining nominally part of Serbia. In 2007 the international community recommended effective independence for Kosovo as a solution, with guarantees for the Serb minority, but this was strongly opposed in Serbia proper.

Kurdistan

The Kurds, the largest nation in the world without a state, live in Turkey, Iraq, Iran, Syria, Azerbaijan and Armenia. They are c. 25 million Kurds, most of them citizens of Turkey (at least 10.8 million, or 8% of the total population of Turkey), Iraq (4.1 million, or 23%), Iran (5,5 million, 10%) and Syria (1 million, 8% of the Syrian population). The Kurds, an ancient nation located at the heart of Meso-potamia, were promised a state by the 1920 Treaty of Sèvres, but this promise never materialized, as the Greeks lost the war to Turkey. The Treaty of Lausanne (1923) realigned Turkey's borders, leaving the Kurds stateless. During the nego-tiations Turkey claimed Mosul in northern Iraq, but Lord Curzon managed to keep this Kurdish region within Iraq and the United Kingdom in charge of the region's oil riches. The Kurds rose against the Turkish state several times between the wars, but with no significant success. During the Second World War the Kurds of Iran enjoyed a spell of freedom, when the Soviets allowed the foundation of a small Kurdish Republic of Mahabad (South of Lake Urmia). Soon, however, the Kurdish Republic was abolished when the Soviets, under Anglo-American pressure, withdrew from Iran and Iranian forces restored sovereignty. Both Iraq and Turkey suppressed all uprisings of their ethnic Kurdish minorities. Saddam Hussein's Iraq gassed Kurdish villages in the 1980s, whereas the Turkish military launched a ferocious campaign in the 1980s and 1990s against Kurdistan Work-ers' Party (PKK—Partiya Karkaren Kurdistan). After the First Gulf War (1991) the Kurds were encouraged to rise against Saddam, but, when they did, they received minimal help from the West and from the USA in particular. They managed, nevertheless, to build a safe area in northern Iraq around Kirkuk and Arbil, protected by the no-fly zone enforced by the Allies soon after the war. The region of Kurdistan is strategically situated in and around oil-producing areas and the Kurds claim that petroleum revenues can resource their state. Since the Second Gulf War in 2003, Iraq's Kurdistan region enjoys a wide autonomy and the local leaders have already started signing up oil exploration contracts with foreign corporations, disregarding the central Government in Baghdad. However, in order to have Kurdistan in the form of a state, a wide revision of borders is needed in the area, and this cannot take place without a major war, possibly involving all the regional powers and the West. If this ever takes place, then it is hard to speculate whether Russia and even China would stay out of the conflict. The PKK leader, Abdullah Ocalan, was captured in Kenya in 1999 and the insurgency in Turkey has since been severely handicapped. Yet, the Kurdish guerrillas are not entirely dispersed. Turkey has in the past made military incursions into Iraqi Kurdistan to fight Kurdish guerrillas. Most recently, Turkey has also threatened to do the same if a Kurdish state arises in northern Iraq. Minority rights for the Kurds in Turkey have considerably improved ever since the country began implementing European Union regulations. The whole of the greater Middle East after 9/11 is indeed in a state of war and the great powers lack a coherent strategy as to how to cope with this critical situation. The issue of Kurdistan is but a significant component of the greater Middle Eastern crisis.

L

Lebanon

Lebanon is a classic case of a Middle Eastern country the territories of which, populated by a variety of Muslim and Christian groups, have always constituted a terrain in which great powers (France or the USA) and/or regional powers (Israel, Syria or Iran) play out their conflicting interests. Of the c. 5.5 million people of Lebanon (including Palestinian refugees, as well as Syrians), some 65% are Shi'a and Sunni Muslims, whereas the rest are Christians, Orthodox and Maronites (the largest Christian sect, owing allegiance to the Roman Catholic Pope). Lebanon was part of the Ottoman Empire and, much like other Middle Eastern states, was basically created after the First World War. It became a French mandated territory, with the Maronites and other Christians receiving greater support than the Muslims. Nevertheless, in the greater Lebanon were included Muslim-majority areas often traditionally considered part of Syria, including the Akkar district and Tripoli (Tarabulus) in the north and the Beka'a Valley in the east and they often claimed union with Syria. Lebanon suffers from the fact that it has been very close to a permanent war zone since 1948—the Arab–Israeli conflict. Like Jordan (although there the numbers are greater), Lebanon also suffers from the presence of Palestinian refugees, over 500,000 of which have been accumulating there since Israel's foundation. Lebanon, which was granted independence in 1943, has abstained from attacking Israel in all the major Arab–Israeli wars since 1948, although the Palestinian Liberation Organization (PLO) under Yasser Arafat mounted some well-orchestrated attacks on Israel from Lebanese soil. Yet, Lebanon itself was already plagued by domestic problems, namely the clash between the Christian Phalangists, armed by the West, and the Muslims, reinforced by the Palestinians, who had poured into the country en masse in the 1960s and 1970s. Syria deployed an army in Lebanon in 1976 and supported the Palestinians, whereas Israel began backing the South Lebanese Army (SLA) against the Shi'a militias. In 1978 Israel occupied a zone close to the border in order to prevent Shi'a militias launching rocket attacks on Israeli towns and other targets. A full-scale invasion of Lebanon by the Israeli Defence Forces (IDF) took place in 1982, soon after an assassination attempt of the Israeli Ambassador in London. The IDF entered Beirut and, reportedly, atrocities were committed against Palestinians in their refugee camps. The IDF's presence in

Lebanon incited the creation of Hezbollah, a Shi'a militant group mainly supported by Iran and designated by the USA as a terrorist group. Hezbollah launched a guerrilla war on the Israelis and they are generally credited with the withdrawal of the IDF from Lebanon—the last troops leaving in May 2000. However, incursions by both Israelis and Hezbollah across border areas have taken place since, with the Hezbollah trying to kidnap Israeli soldiers and use them as bargaining chips in political negotiations. The last war between Hezbollah and Israel took place in the summer of 2006, which resulted, once again, in the withdrawal of the IDF from Lebanon. The tactics pursued by the Shi'a militias make them elusive, as they launch their rocket attacks on Israel and then hide among the civilian population, making it difficult for Israel to retaliate successfully without outraging world public opinion by shelling villages and towns. This type of asymmetric conflict is advantageous to the weak, being debilitating for the high-tech weaponry and other regular military techniques that Israel can master better than most armies in the developed world. The Shi'a crescent in the greater Middle East, mainly backed by Iran, is the USA's main preoccupation in its post-9/11 military adventures in a region that stretches from Central Asia and the Caspian Sea, southwards to the Persian (Arabian) Gulf and embraces the Saudi peninsula and the Suez Canal.

Liberia

Liberia lies just north of the Equator on the Atlantic coast in West Africa and borders Sierra Leone, Guinea and Côte d'Ivoire. It is Africa's oldest republic, but it became better known in the 1990s for its long-running, ruinous civil war. In 1847 Liberia was established as an independent state by freed slaves from America and, for more than 130 years, politics within the country were dominated by the small minority of the population descended from these original settlers, known as the Americo-Liberians. During this period Liberia was famed for its stability, its functioning economy and the large amount of foreign investment it attracted to the rubber plantations and the iron ore mines. The indigenous Africans of Liberia were however largely excluded from political power and dissatisfied by such political exclusion. As a result Master Sgt Samuel Doe, a member of the indigenous Krahn ethnic group, seized power in Liberia in a violent military coup in 1980. Key members of the Americo-Liberian elite, including the President and his Cabinet were summarily executed in public on the beach. Having achieved power, Doe mismanaged the economy and transformed the armed forces into an ethnic Krahn militia, which committed considerable human rights abuses against Liberia's other ethnic groups. In 1989 the National Patriotic Front of Liberia (NPFL), led by Charles Taylor, launched an uprising from Côte d'Ivoire, which quickly deteriorated into a vicious civil war. President Samuel Doe was overthrown and tortured to death the following year by Prince Johnson, at that time an ally of Taylor. Doe's fall led to the political fragmentation of the country into violent factionalism. In mid-1990 Prince Johnson's supporters split from Taylor's group and captured Monrovia for themselves, depriving Taylor of outright victory. In 1995 a peace agreement was signed leading to the election of Charles Taylor as President in 1997, but the elections brought only temporary respite as Taylor's Government set about plundering the state of its assets and stifling opposition activity. In 1999 fighting in the country recommenced as anti-Taylor rebel groups emerged or re-formed. Fighting escalated and by July 2003 Taylor had lost control of most of the country, including much of Monrovia. Peace talks in Accra, Ghana, in August led to the signing of the Comprehensive Peace Agreement (CPA). A new Economic Community of West African States (ECOWAS) peacekeeping force was deployed, which has since been replaced by the 15,000 strong UN Mission in Liberia (UNMIL) force, and Taylor was forced into exile in Nigeria. President Taylor's regime was contemptuous of democratic principles and human rights and the Liberian civil war saw appalling human rights abuses by all sides, with the warring factions recruiting child soldiers and employing sexual violence and torture as weapons. Since the end of the civil war there have been no significant prosecutions for human rights abuses, but the human rights environment has significantly improved. The Truth and Reconciliation Commission (TRC) was officially inaugurated on 20 February 2006, with the mandate to gather evidence and testimony concerning the decades of violence that the country has suffered. The TRC is mandated to recommend prosecution or amnesty for individual cases. Decades of mismanagement and conflict have made Liberia one of the world's poorest countries. The civil war left thousands of people brutalized and traumatized, with over 200,000 people killed and more than 1m. displaced from their homes. The capital remains without mains electricity and running water, corruption is rife and unemployment and illiteracy are endemic.

M

Macedonia

In a broad historical sense Macedonia is a geographical area encompassing the northern province of Greece, part of western Bulgaria and today's former Yugoslav republic of Macedonia (constitutionally, the Republic of Macedonia), which peacefully seceded from Yugoslavia in 1991–92. In essence, there was no Macedonian national identity before the Second World War. It started receiving political recognition after 1944–45, when Tito made Macedonia one of the constituent parts of Yugoslavia. Form the last quarter of the 19th century until after the First World War the area had been at the centre of three conflicting Balkan nationalisms: Bulgarian; Serbian; and Greek. The last were the beneficiaries of the First and Second Balkan wars (1912–13) and the Bulgarians the losers, as Greeks and Serbs, and eventually Ottoman Turkey, united to fight against Bulgaria. Today, Macedonia is a multi-ethnic state of c. 2 million, mainly composed of Macedonians and Albanians (the latter about one-quarter of total population). It is a poor, landlocked state with many problems. The Albanians, mainly in the west around Tetovo, want more autonomy and many covet union with Albania in a greater Albanian scheme, including Kosovo. Bulgaria has revived its interest in Macedonia, claiming historical, linguistic and other affiliations. In 1995 Greece contributed further to Macedonia's economic problems (for example, since then unemployment has been hovering around the 40% mark) by enforcing a blockade on the grounds that Macedonia had no right to using this name, as it is the name of Greece's northern province. Greece has expressed fears that the former Yugoslav republic might, one day, develop irredentist claims on Greek Macedonia. Greece's trade embargo lasted for two years and the only thing it achieved was to convince the Macedonians to change their flag. At the same time Greece's intransigent stance damaged its standing in European and world affairs. During the NATO war over Kosovo, Macedonia received some 370,000 Albanian refugees and this further compounded the country's economic crisis. In February 2001 the Albanians launched an armed insurgency, which spread in the predominately Albanian areas of western Macedonia. Seven months later a peace agreement was reached between the ethnic Albanians and the Macedonian Government, with NATO supervising the disarmament of the Albanian rebels. Macedonia lies at the crossroads of four Balkan states (Serbia, Albania, Bulgaria and Greece) and is a major route for the trans-Balkan pipeline. Turkey has also an interest in Macedonia and has since 1992 signed military and trade co-operation agreements. It seems that Macedonia has not ceased to condense the explosive contradictions of late 19th century politics, the difference being the roles of the European Union and NATO in the region, which, arguably, can contain regional conflict.

Melilla – *see* **Gibraltar and Spanish North Africa**

Myanmar (Burma)

This country of nearly 47 million people is but another case of ethnically mixed groups where foreign imperialism (British, French and Japanese, among others) in the past exacerbated, rather than moderated, open or latent societal conflict. The majority of the population are ethnic Burmese (68%), the rest being Shan (10%), Karen (8%), Rakhine, Chinese and nine other ethnic groups (10%). During the 19th century, in order to secure India's eastern flanks (water and land passages), the British went to war with the Burmese several times (notably 1824, 1852 and 1885). The British met fierce opposition from several ethnic groups and factions, but in 1937 Burma was made a Crown colony with a degree of independence and self-government. Burmese resistance to the British was, never-theless, hampered by Indians, who were brought to Burma as labour power. During the Second World War the Burmese fought against the Japanese, who invaded Burma in their effort to implement their strategy of a 'Greater East Asia Co-Prosperity Sphere'. At the same time the Burmese fought against the British in order to gain fully fledged independence, with the Burmese Communist Party playing a significant role in this struggle. However, the first act of the independent Government in 1948 under the Anti-Fascist People's Freedom League (AFPFL) was to outlaw the communists. Subsequently, the communists launched a guerrilla campaign and, in this, they were joined by the Karen ethnic group. Other ethnic groups too joined the communist resistance, not least because almost every group viewed the Burman Government as the instrument of Western imperialism, which in turn deprived them of their fundamental human and civil rights. Dictatorial rule has been common practice in Burma (the official name of which was changed to Myanmar in 1990) ever since the country's independence. In fact, the Government has one of the worst human rights records in the world and has several times drawn severe criticism from the UN, for its activities during the struggle against both the country's ethnic minorities and its political pro-democracy opposition. Until the late 1990s Myanmar was the world's leading producer of opium, a position recently conceded to Afghanistan.

N

Nepal

This is a landlocked state of 25 million between India and China. Some 90% of the population are Hindu, the rest mostly being Buddhist and Muslim. The area of people's dwelling also plays a role in defining identities and political loyalties (mountains, lowlands, etc.). Nepal began its first steps towards unity in the 18th century under the principality of the Gorkhas. Ambitious Gorkha plans brought them into conflict with the British East India Company in India. The Treaty of Sugauli of 1816 brought an end to the war, whereupon the British began recruiting Gorkha (Gurkha) fighters into their Indian army (they still serve in the British and Indian armies). India's influence in Nepal is significant, periodically supporting one ruling caste against the other. The People's Republic of China also maintains an influence through the various communist formations of Nepal, the first one being founded in 1949, and through investment projects, particularly in the railway sector. The pattern of governance in the country since the Second World War has been unstable, authoritarian and subject to violent challenges. Thus, the communists maintain a base of support and often launch insurgencies, the last large one being in 1996. The communists argued, not unreasonably, that the Government promotes an uneven type of economic development, leaving the western provinces of the country lagging far behind in terms of modernization projects, schooling, job creation and communication networks. The communist armed opposition had similarities to and, allegedly, links with other Maoist insurgent groups in India, although whether this would persist after it joined the Government of Nepal in 2007 remained to be seen.

New Caledonia – *see* Fiji and New Caledonia

Nigeria

Nigeria, the largest British colony in Africa, was established in January 1914 by the amalgamation of the Colony of Lagos, the Southern Protectorates and the Northern Protectorate. Nigeria was granted its independence on 1 October 1960 and in 1963 broke its direct links with the British Crown by becoming a republic within the Commonwealth. The independence Constitution provided for a federation of three autonomous regions, namely Northern, Western and Eastern, each with wide-ranging powers, its own constitution, public service and marketing boards. The overarching but weaker federal Government had powers limited to national issues, including control of the police and army, and economic planning. A fourth region, the Mid-Western, was created in 1964 to satisfy the demand of the minorities. In the early 1960s the inherited regional structure led to a series of crises and conflicts, both within and between the three ethno-centric regions, as competition grew for control over the federal centre. The 1964 federal elections were marred by violence and rigging. Inter-party and inter-ethnic tensions in the country continued, leading ultimately to a military takeover in January 1966. Nigeria's post-independence history was thereafter marked by a series of military interventions in politics: coups, counter-coups and a civil war (1967–70), the last when the Eastern Region attempted to secede as the Republic of Biafra. Over 1m. people died in the conflict. Indeed, post-independence Nigeria has only enjoyed three short periods of civilian rule, in 1960–65, 1979–83 and from 1999 to the present. The intervening periods, totalling 29 years, saw military governments in place. Political liberalization ushered in by the return to civilian rule in 1999 has allowed militants from religious and ethnic groups to express their frustrations more freely, and with increasing violence. Thousands of people have died over the past few years in communal rivalry, with separatist aspirations growing, prompting reminders of the bitter civil war over the breakaway Biafran republic in the late 1960s. The imposition of Islamic law in several states has embedded divisions and caused thousands of Christians to flee; inter-faith violence is said to be rooted in poverty, unemployment and the competition for land. Nigeria's current elected leadership faces the growing challenge of preventing Africa's most populous country from breaking apart along these ethnic and religious lines. The current elected Government of Nigeria is striving to boost the economy, which experienced an oil boom in the 1970s and is once again benefiting from high prices on the world market. The former British colony is one of the world's largest petroleum producers, but the industry has produced unwanted side effects, with government progress being undermined by corruption and mismanagement, and the trade in stolen oil fuelling violence and corruption in the Niger delta, the home of the industry. Few Nigerians, including those in oil-producing areas, have benefited from the petroleum wealth.

North Korea – *see* **Korea**

P

Pakistan – *see* **Balochistan**

R

Rwanda

Rwanda is a small, landlocked, mountainous country lying south of the Equator in central Africa, bordered by the Democratic Republic of the Congo (DRC), Uganda, Tanzania and Burundi. Rwanda existed as an independent, highly centralized state for several centuries, ruled by a king and noble elite drawn largely from the minority Tutsi group. Rwanda became part of German East Africa in 1899, but following the First World War it became part of the Belgian-administered territory of Ruanda-Urundi, with neighbouring Burundi, under a League of Nations mandate. The colonial authorities consolidated the power of the existing Tutsi elite but, in an attempt to head off claims for independence from them, the Hutu majority were encouraged to participate in the political life of the country. Independence from Belgium followed in 1962, after a Hutu uprising (1959–61) and large-scale massacres of Tutsis. This brought to power a Hutu-dominated Government led by President Grégoire Kayibanda, who oversaw continued inter-communal violence between the Hutus and Tutsis. In 1973 Kayibanda was toppled in a military coup and Juvenal Habyarimana, a more moderate Hutu, took up the presidency. During his regime however, Tutsis were still excluded from power and faced widespread discrimination and state-sponsored violence. Many left the country, joining those who had fled the killings of 1959. Power was concentrated in the hands of a single party, the Mouvement Révolutionnaire National pour le Développement (MRND). Habyarimana and the MRND won several uncontested 'elections' through the 1980s. Having failed to negotiate their return to the country, in 1985 Tutsi exiles in Uganda formed the Rwandan Patriotic Front (RPF), a small but highly effective rebel force. In October 1990 the RPF invaded Rwanda from Uganda, demanding representation and equality for all Rwandans. A civil war in the border area ensued, with the Habyarimana regime being ably assisted by the French Government with whom it had struck up a mutually conducive post-independence relationship. Each incursion by the RPF was followed by reprisal massacres, largely of Tutsis, by government forces. A peace agreement was brokered in 1993, which *inter alia* provided for a power-sharing arrangement involving all political forces and the RPF. Unwilling to share power, however, a group of extremist Hutu politicians planned to consolidate their hold on the country by exterminating all the Tutsis of the country, along with moderate Hutu leaders. The Hutu Government formed and trained the extremist youth militia known as the Interahamwe and disseminated hate propaganda to the largely illiterate population through state radio. Lists were compiled of Tutsis and moderate Hutu leaders who were to be massacred once the planned genocide commenced. On 6 April 1994 President Habyarimana was returning to Rwanda from attending a meeting in Tanzania to discuss the implementation of the peace agreement. As his private jet approached the airport in Kigali it was struck by two surface-to-air missiles killing all on board. There is powerful circumstantial evidence in favour of the theory that the plane was brought down by the presidential guard as part of a coup attempt to bring hardline politicians to power and to destroy the peace process and the transition to democracy. The mass killing of political opponents was the next stage in a carefully planned sequence of events. Massacres of Tutsis and moderate Hutu politicians began within hours of the death of the President and quickly spread throughout the country, propelled by the death lists and propaganda being aired over the radio. Thousands were slaughtered daily in a genocide that lasted until July and cost the lives of around 1m. Rwandans. It was halted only by the RPF taking control of the country. The extremist politicians and over 2m. Hutus fled the country, together with many members of the Rwandan armed forces and the Interahamwe, mainly into Zaire (now the DRC). The RPF has remained the dominant party in Rwanda since July 1994, when it set up a Transitional Government of National Unity, sharing power with other parties under the formula agreed at Arusha in 1993.

S

Serbia – *see* **Kosovo**

Sierra Leone

A country of western Africa, on the Atlantic coast, Sierra Leone was inhabited by the Temne when the Portuguese first visited the coast in 1460. The region was later settled by Mande-speaking peoples from present-day Liberia. In 1792 freed slaves were brought from Nova Scotia to found the colony of Freetown, which was transferred to British administration in 1808. In 1896 the interior was proclaimed a British protectorate, mainly in order to forestall French ambitions in the region, and the colony and protectorate of Sierra Leone was established. Under the British little economic development was undertaken in the protectorate, although a railroad was built and the production for export of palm products and peanuts was encouraged. After the Second World War, however, mining (especially of diamonds and iron ore) increased greatly. Sierra Leone achieved independence in 1961, with Milton Margai as Prime Minister. Several changes of government occurred over the next few years, some as a result of successful military coups. After an attempted coup in 1971 parliament declared Sierra Leone to be a republic, with Siaka Stevens of the All-People's Congress (APC) party as President. A further series of military coups in the 1990s ended with Sierra Leone returning to civilian rule when power was handed over to Ahmed Tejan Kabbah of the Sierra Leone People's Party after the conclusion of elections in early 1996. Since 1991 the Revolutionary United Front (RUF), a loosely organized guerrilla force led by Foday Sankoh, had sought to retain control of the lucrative diamond-producing regions of Sierra Leone with the aid of finance from Liberia. Most of Kabbah's time in office was marked by a bloody civil war with the RUF, until the President succeeded in negotiating a cease-fire in the war. However, more instability in the country ensued when, only 14 months into his presidency, Kabbah was overthrown in May 1997 by a military junta, the Armed Forces Revolutionary Council (AFRC), which invited the RUF to participate in a new Government. In October the UN imposed sanctions against the military Government and the Economic Community of West African States (ECOWAS) sent in forces led by Nigeria. The rebels were subdued and President Kabbah was returned to office in March 1998, although fighting continued in many parts of the country, with reports of widespread atrocities. In January 1999 over 6,000 people were killed in fighting in the Freetown area alone. A peace accord was signed in July between President Kabbah and Foday Sankoh of the RUF. The agreement granted the rebels seats in a new Government and all forces a general amnesty from prosecution. The Government had largely ceased functioning effectively, however, and at least half of its territory remained under rebel control. In October 1999 the UN agreed to send peacekeepers to help restore order and disarm the rebels. By May 2000 there was a UN force of 13,000 in the country attempting to disarm the RUF when Sankoh's forces clashed with UN troops. Some 500 peacekeepers were taken hostage as the peace accord effectively collapsed. An 800-member British force thereafter entered the country to secure western Free-town, evacuate Europeans and support the forces fighting the RUF. After Sankoh was captured in Freetown, the hostages were gradually released by the RUF, but clashes between the UN forces and the RUF continued. In July another rebel group, known as the West Side Boys, clashed with the peacekeepers. In the same month the UN Security Council placed a ban on the sale of rough diamonds from Sierra Leone in an attempt to undermine the funding of the RUF. In late August 2000 Issa Sesay became head of the RUF. British troops training the Sierra Leone army were taken hostage by the West Side Boys, but were freed by a British raid in September. Although disarmament of rebel and pro-government militias proceeded slowly and fighting continued to occur, by January 2002 most of the estimated 45,000 fighters had surrendered their weapons. In a ceremony that month, government and rebel leaders declared the civil war to have ended; an estimated 50,000 persons died in the conflict. Elections were finally held in May 2002 and President Kabbah was re-elected; and his Sierra Leone People's Party won a majority of the parliamentary seats.

Somalia

A country in the easternmost part of Africa, where imperialism played an active role in the 19th century, with the protectorate of British Somaliland established in the north in 1887. The southern territory eventually came under Italian control and in 1936 was combined with newly conquered Ethiopian territory to form Italian East Africa; after the Second World War and a brief period of British military administration, it became a UN Trust Territory (again the responsibility of Italy). At independence in 1960 the British protectorate and Italian-adminis-tered Somalia merged to form the Somali Republic, but civilian rule ended in 1969 when Gen. Mohamed Siad Barre seized power in a military coup and established a one-party system around the concept of 'scientific socialism'. In the 1980s state authority in Somalia began to crumble as assorted clan-based groups opposed to Barre's rule began to form. In the north-west (former British Somali-land), the Somali National Movement (SNM) attempted to seize control, but Barre countered with great violence, resulting in thousands of deaths and the flight of 400,000 refugees into Ethiopia. Barre was, however, forced to flee the country in January 1991, when another rebel group, the United Somali Congress (USC), gained control of Mogadishu. A full-blown civil war developed in the capital when the USC fragmented into rival, clan-based factions. As a result of the ongoing civil war the UN established a small cease-fire observer force operation in Somalia (UNOSOM) in January 1992, but it failed to make any impact and, as civil war escalated, a massive humanitarian crisis developed. In December 1992 a US-led UN task force (UNITAF) intervened to create a secure environment for relief operations. It succeeded in establishing the main relief centres in the starvation area but did not attempt to disarm the Somali clan militias or the warlords. UNITAF handed over to UNOSOM II in May 1993. In response to militia attacks, the Security Council authorized UNOSOM to take all necessary measures against those responsible and to arrest Gen. Mohamed Farah Aidid. In the confrontation that ensued, 18 US Rangers were killed, which prompted the departure of US troops in March 1994. The last UNOSOM troops withdrew in March 1995 after the loss of 70 UN peacekeepers. Somalia has been without an effective central government since President Siad Barre was overthrown in 1991. Years of fighting between rival warlords and an inability to deal with famine and disease have led to the deaths of up to 1m. people. This contest remains unresolved and control of Mogadishu is divided among a variety of warlords, principally Hawiye. In May 1991 the north-western region of Somalia (the former British protectorate of Somaliland) unilaterally declared its independence as the 'Republic of Somaliland'. A Government composed of members nominated by their clans was established and a Constitution approved. Somaliland's stability has been widely acknowledged, but it has not received formal recognition from the international community. It has stood aside from wider reconciliation processes but indicated its readiness to discuss relations with Somalia on a basis of equality once a new Government is established in Mogadishu. A distinct 'Puntland' regime was also established in north-eastern Somalia, in 1998.

South Korea – *see* Korea

Spain – *see* Basque Country *and* Gibraltar and Spanish North Africa

Spanish North Africa – *see* Gibraltar and Spanish North Africa

Sri Lanka

This island state (known as Ceylon during British colonial rule) is situated in the north-east of the Indian Ocean and has been plagued by a vicious civil war since the early 1980s. Ethnically, it is composed of the Sinhalese (73%) and the Tamils (18%), the rest mainly being Moors (8%). The total population is about 20 million. The Tamils are mostly Hindu and the Sinhalese Buddhist, yet both communities have Christian minorities (the work of European and western missionaries). Most of the Hindus were brought to the island by the British in the 19th century to work in the tea plantations. The British maintained Sri Lanka as a colony until after the Second World War (independence was granted in 1948), but their legacy of 'divide and rule' left chaos and anarchy on the island. In order to rule the island, the British created an administrative elite drawn from both main communities, as well as the Christian missionaries. The institutional arrangements, nevertheless, privileged the majority Sinhalese, a fact that set them on a collision course with the Tamil minority. Neighbouring India got involved several times in the conflict, most notably in the 1980s, when it moved in to monitor an agreement between Tamil rebels and governmental forces. In the end, Indian forces were caught in the fighting and suffered many casualties. In 1990 India finally withdrew, but the fighting between Tamils and government forces not only did not stop, but became even more ferocious. The Tamils have, since the withdrawal of the British, been demanding independence and the civil war that began in 1983 seems to be an unfinished affair.

Sudan – *see* **Darfur**

T

Taiwan

This is an island 'state' of 23 million people, with an uncertain international status: most countries have not recognized Taiwan (which claims to be the legitimate Government of China—the 'Republic of China'—rather than an independent state) and while the People's Republic of China still claims the island province, the USA would consider any move on the part of the People's Republic to conquer Taiwan as *casus belli*. Taiwan was Chinese in ancient times. The Dutch (in 1624) were the first to occupy Taiwan, and then the Spanish and Japanese also tried to lay their grip on the island. Finally, the Japanese abandoned the island in the wake of the Second World War, after facing growing resistance from its inhabitants. China was then still ruled by the regime of Chiang Kai-Shek (Jiang Jieshi). When Mao Tse-tung (Mao Zedong) and the communists defeated Chiang Kai-Shek and his Kuomintang (Guomindang) party, Taiwan was the place the defeated could find refuge. The Kuomintang managed not only to maintain the island, but also kept control of some of the small islands of just off the mainland Chinese coast, such as Quemoy and Matsu. The Kuomintang also kept China's permanent seat on the UN Security Council until 1971, when the USA conceded publicly that a communist nation of some one billion people could not be held hostage by a right-wing 'Chinese' Government on an island of 15 million people. The *modus vivendi* found between China and the USA since has been a policy of non-recognition of Taiwan on the part of the USA and most of the international community, while at the same time the People's Republic must respect the autonomy of the island and the principle of non-interference in its domestic affairs. The Chinese, however, have on more than one occasion declared that they cannot commit themselves not to resort to force, particularly if the island proclaimed its independence (hence formal separation from China) and in view of Taiwan's armament policy and the increasing militarization of the straits of Taiwan by the USA. China has responded with missile tests in the area and with mock military exercises about taking the island. A most interesting development over the last few years is the joint Chinese-Russian military exercises around Taiwan, but also in Central Asia and the Caucasus. It seems that a Russo-Chinese understanding has begun to develop, an understanding that has an anti-American military dimension, with the Russians assisting the Chinese in Taiwan and the

Chinese reciprocating and trying to help the Russians where they have difficulties: in the Caucasus and the Caspian Sea zone.

Tibet (Xizang)

This is an area of south-western China, which was finally absorbed by Mao Zedong's communist army in 1950 and is now an integral part of China as the province of Xizang. The population is both of Tibetan (c. 6 million, an ethnicity whose origins are unclear) and Chinese (7.5 million) origin. In the Middle Ages Tibet was dominated by the Mongols, although it was never absorbed into their empire. A significant moment in the evolution of the Tibetan tradition of priestly rule began in 12th century, when Gyatso paid a visit to the Mongol court in China, becoming the educator of the Mongol Emperor. The Dalai Lama was firmly established as the supreme theocratic authority in the 17th century. In the modern era, it was the British who first became interested in Tibet, basically in order to check Russian advances in the region, an extension of their policy in Central Asia at the time (the 'great game'). In the early 1900s the British managed to sign a treaty with the Tibetans, which stipulated that Tibet could make no major foreign policy decision without clearing it first with the United Kingdom. Thus, when the Chinese entered Tibet in 1912, the British had to interfere and strike an agreement with the Chinese, confining them to the eastern part of the country (inner Tibet). The Chinese were then distracted from their own claims by civil war. When Tibet was invaded by Mao's army in 1950, the Dalai Lama began working closely with India in order to counter-balance Chinese influence and presence. In March 1959 Tibetan rebels fought against Mao's troops and the Dalai Lama escaped to India. The death toll was high: some 90,000 Tibetan rebels were killed. China has militarized Tibet and this is seen by India as a direct threat to its security. There are also environmental concerns: there are waste products from nuclear stations and research centres and also from the Amdo uranium mine. Such products contaminate most of the rivers that flow from Tibet to India.

Timor-Leste – *see* East Timor and Indonesia

Turkey – *see* Aegean Sea *and* Cyprus *and* Kurdistan

U

Ukraine

Ukraine holds a pivotal geostrategic position in Europe-western Asia. It sits on the crossroads between central and eastern Europe and central Eurasia, with a land area larger than Germany and the United Kingdom combined (and a population of 55 million). It is a major transit route for hydrocarbons, holding the key to co-operation (and conflict) between the North Atlantic Treaty Organization (NATO)/European powers and Russia. For example, the European Union (EU) is dependent on the Odessa–Brodi oil pipeline, which handles petroleum supplies from the Caucasus and the Middle East to Europe. Also, gas pipelines passing through Ukraine provide Europe with Russian gas. With the accession of Poland and Hungary to both NATO and the EU, Ukraine currently shares with the West a common border of over 650 km. Western Ukraine (Ternopil, Ivano-Frankivsk, Rivne, Volyn and Lviv) is predominately Roman Catholic and ethnically-linguistically Ukrainian. Eastern Ukraine is predominately Eastern Orthodox and the spoken language is Russian. Owing to its historical legacy (over the last 300 years Ukraine has been part of various empires) and the involvement of the great powers in its domestic environment, Ukraine's population and political elites do not have a common pattern of orientation, political behaviour and economic profiles. Instability and conflict have been visible and endemic, particularly after the collapse of Soviet communism, thus impacting upon Europe's own peace and stability. Two blocs seem to be competing over influence in Ukraine today: NATO and the Euro-Atlantic area, on the one hand, and Russia on the other. This, however, needs qualification. The EU and NATO do not pursue identical diplomacy towards Ukraine. For reasons that have to do with the EU's weakness in the fields of common foreign, security and defence policies, NATO and the USA dominate policies towards Ukraine in the overall Euro-Atlantic strategic orbit, while Russia at least as much is trying to dominate Ukraine's political landscape. This conflict between the West and Russia over Ukraine is projected directly into the polity structures of Ukraine. For example, in 2000–01, President Leonid Kuchma dismissed the pro-NATO Ukrainian Foreign Minister, Borys Tarasiuk, and also forced out of office the liberal pro-Western Prime Minister, Viktor Yushchenko. Kuchma's moves were accompanied by a number of other pro-Russian initiatives, such as conclusion of bilateral trade agreements on energy and military collaboration, as well as in the aviation and shipbuilding sectors. There is, therefore, a pronounced conflict between the US-led West and Russia over Ukraine's political orientation, a conflict that unfolded in earnest during the so-called Orange Revolution of 2004. Yushchenko, supported by the West, drew support from western areas of Ukraine, whereas Viktor Yanukovich had his constituency in eastern Ukraine and was backed by Russia. The presidential election of October 2004 became the source of conflict between Yushchenko and Yanukovich, when the former accused the latter of massive fraud. Hundreds of thousands of Ukrainians demonstrated against the result in what came to be known as the Orange Revolution, after Yushchenko's chosen campaign colour. There is clear evidence that both Moscow and Washington, DC, have been interfering in Ukrainian politics since the end of the USSR. Both Russia and the West interfered in the 2004 election and, as most recent events have demonstrated, Russian influence remains very solid in Ukraine, to the degree that any attempt by the USA (or its agencies) or NATO to remove that influence could potentially destabilize the entire Black Sea and east-central European region.

United Kingdom – *see* Gibraltar

X

Xizang – *see* **Tibet**

Y

Yugoslavia

Twice there has been a country called Yugoslavia. Twice in modern times Yugoslavia, a country of c. 22 million (population data from 1985), experimented with a form of unity, the first time from 1918 to the Second World War and the second during the Cold War under communist party rule. The so-called First Yugoslavia was a form of unity underpinned by the United Kingdom and France, which wanted a large country in the underbelly of Germany and Austria in order to contain Germanic influence and possible advances towards the east and into the southern Balkans or eastern Mediterranean. The Second Yugoslavia was the result of Tito's successful manoeuvring between the two superpowers, the USA and the USSR, in the aftermath of the Second World War. Thus, Tito's communist and non-aligned Yugoslavia (Tito died in 1980) survived the Cold War through receiving assistance and partial support from both the USSR and the West, but mostly from the West through the International Monetary Fund (IMF), the World Bank, the US Export-Import Bank and from the restoration of trade relations with the West after 1949. In essence, Cold War Yugoslavia had been an important link in NATO's chain of policies in the eastern Mediterranean, acting as a barrier to the Soviets, who always wanted to gain a toehold in the region and thus reach the Suez Canal. Yugoslavia's fateful dependency on the West manifested itself most dramatically in the 1970s, when the country borrowed large amounts of money in order to finance domestic growth via exports. However, the Western economies entered a recession (the stagflation of the 1970s) and blocked Yugoslav exports. This exacerbated Yugoslavia's international debt and forced the IMF to ask the Yugoslav authorities to implement a number of neo-conservative fiscal and institutional reforms in order to regain economic credibility and repay the debt. The required set of reforms included constitutional revision of the 1974 loose federal settlement, which had conceded large powers to Yugoslavia's five constituent republics (Bosnia and Herzegovina, Croatia, Macedonia, Serbia and Slovenia—the two Serbian provinces of Kosovo and Metohija and of Vojvodina also enjoyed considerable autonomy). However, the ethnic elites of the constituent republics opposed the neo-conservative reforms, arguing that they would damage their constitutional rights, so forcing the richest of the republics, that is, Croatia and Slovenia, to foot the bill for this neo-conservative/neo-liberal reform package. Thus, in the event, violence and ethnic conflict in the Yugoslavia of the 1990s could be seen as an unintended consequence of IMF and World Bank interventions, both of which demanded fiscal discipline and a more centralized government, measures that effectively undermined the established autonomy of the republics enshrined in the 1974 Constitution. The conflict first unfolded in Croatia and then in Bosnia-Herzegovina, the latter with the most ethnically diverse population. The USA and the North Atlantic Treaty Organization (NATO) intervened in 1993–94, following the failure of the European Union (EU) to end the conflict. In 1995 the Dayton Accord was signed between the various parties, notably the USA and President Slobodan Milošević's rump of Yugoslavia. Four years later Milošević again faced NATO power, this time over Kosovo, as the West accused Serbia/Yugoslavia of pursuing genocidal policies towards the Kosovar Albanians. After 72 days of bombing, and following Russian mediation, Milošević ordered his troops to leave Kosovo, only to find himself with a legal battle in The Hague, at an international tribunal, accused of crimes against humanity. He died of a heart attack five years later, but Serbia's drama continues, as it is the only country in the Balkans still struggling to get some attention from both the EU and the USA.

Maps

Map 1: Aegean

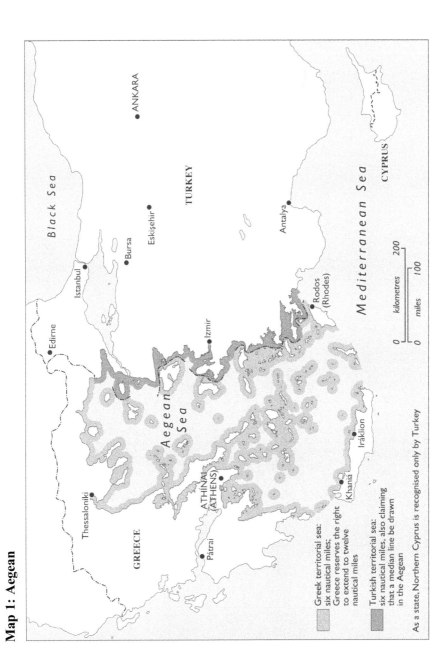

Black Sea

• ANKARA

TURKEY

• Eskişehir

• Bursa

Istanbul

• Edirne

Antalya

Izmir

Mediterranean Sea

CYPRUS

Rodos
(Rhodes)

Aegean
Sea

Thessaloníki

ATHÍNA
(ATHENS)

GREECE

Khaniá

Iráklion

Pátrai

kilometres

0   100   200

miles

0   100

Greek territorial sea:
six nautical miles;
Greece reserves the right
to extend to twelve
nautical miles

Turkish territorial sea:
six nautical miles, also claiming
that a median line be drawn
in the Aegean

As a state, Northern Cyprus is recognised only by Turkey

Map 2: The Caucasus and Central Asia

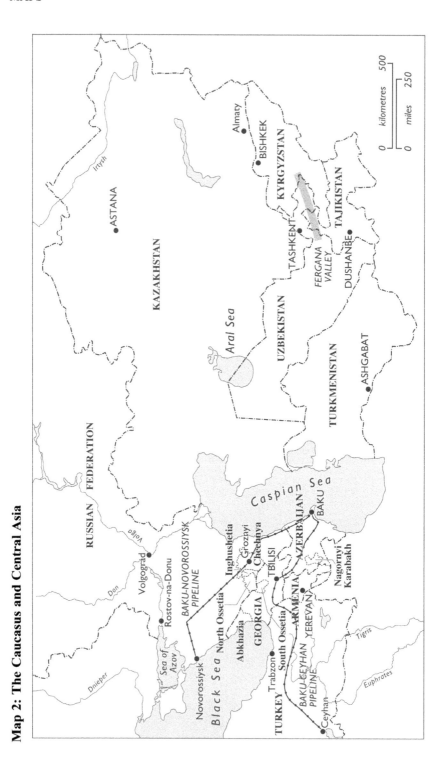

Map 3: Latin America

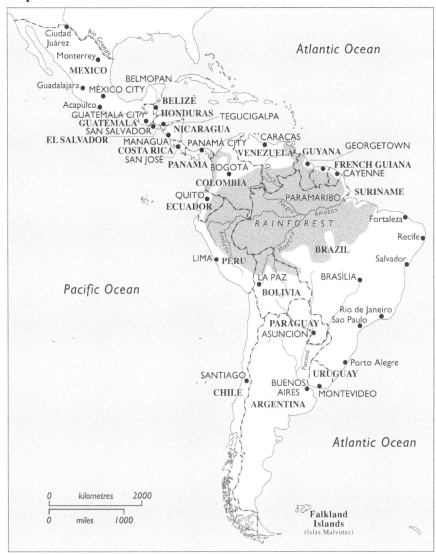

Map 4: East and South-East Asia

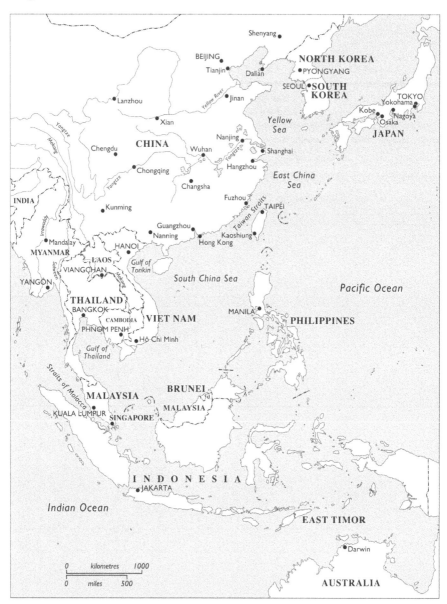

Map 5: Africa

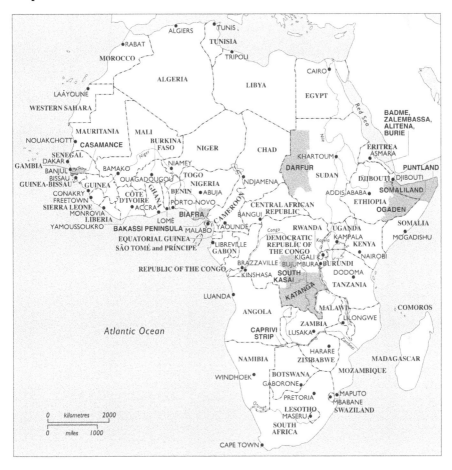

Map 6: South Asia

Map 7: Ireland

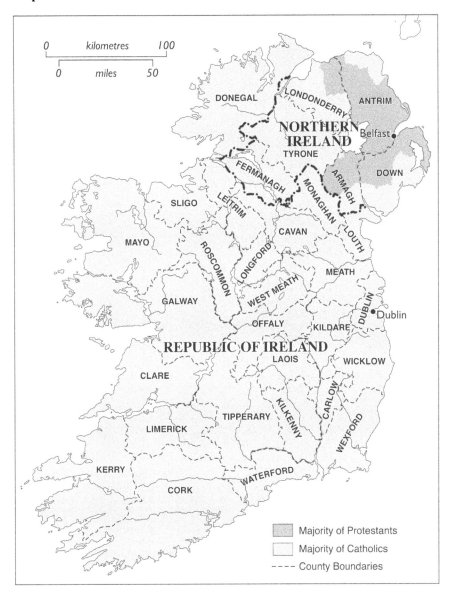

Map 8: Israel-Palestine

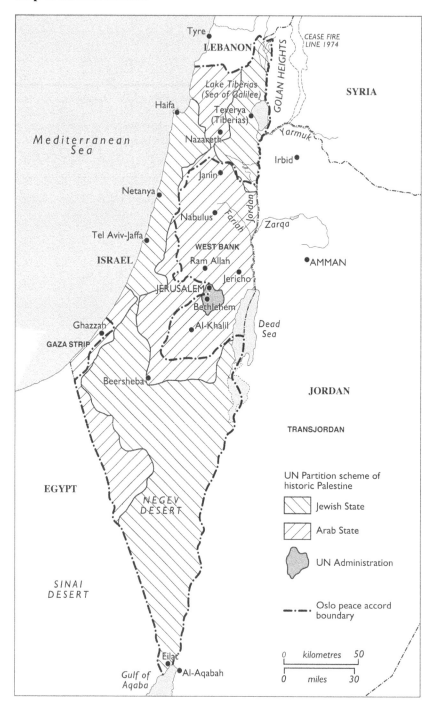

Tyre

LEBANON

CEASE FIRE
LINE 1974

GOLAN HEIGHTS

SYRIA

Lake Tiberias
(Sea of Galilee)

Haifa

Teverya
(Tiberias)

*Mediterranean
Sea*

Nazareth

Yarmuk

Irbid

Janin

Netanya

Jordan

Farah

Nabulus

Zarqa

Tel Aviv-Jaffa

WEST BANK

ISRAEL

Ram Allah

•AMMAN

Jericho

JERUSALEM

Bethlehem

Ghazzah

Al-Khalil

Dead
Sea

GAZA STRIP

Beersheba

JORDAN

TRANSJORDAN

UN Partition scheme of
historic Palestine

EGYPT

Jewish State

*NEGEV
DESERT*

Arab State

UN Administration

*SINAI
DESERT*

Oslo peace accord
boundary

0   kilometres   50

0   miles   30

Eilat

*Gulf of
Aqaba*

•Al-Aqabah

Map 9: Iraq

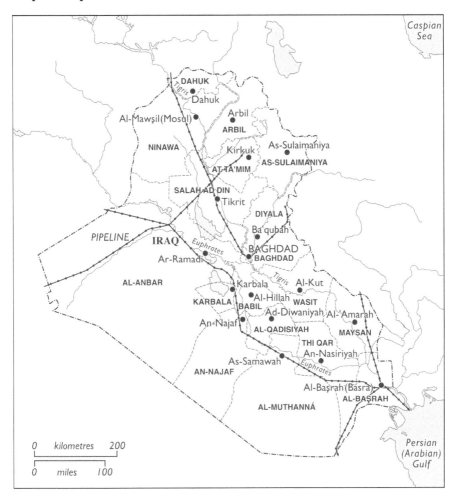

Map 10: Yugoslavia

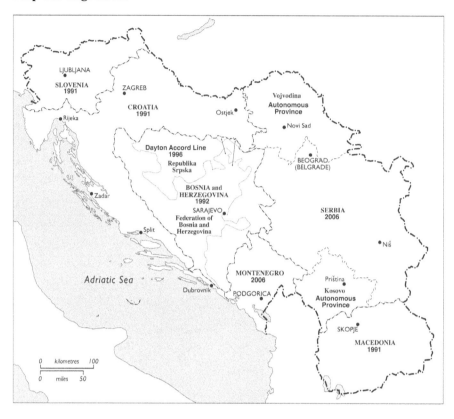

Bibliography

Bibliography

Abdullah, T., and Siddique, S. (eds). *Islam and Society in Southeast Asia.* Singapore, Institute of Southeast Asian Studies, 1986.

Abubakar, D. 'Ethnic Identity, Democratisation, and the Future of the African State: Lessons from Nigeria', in *African Issues*, 29 (1/2—pp. 33–34). 2001.

Aburish, S. K. *The House of Saud.* London, Bloomsbury, 2005.

Abuza, Z. *Militant Islam in Southeast Asia: Crucible of Terror.* Boulder, CO, and London, Lynne Rienner, 2002.

Abuza, Z. 'Funding Terrorism in Southeast Asia: The Financial Network of Al Qaeda and Jemaah Islamiya', in *Contemporary Southeast Asia*, Vol. 25. 2003.

Acharya, A. 'Culture, Security, Multilateralism: The 'ASEAN Way' and Regional Order', in *Contemporary Security Policy*, 19/1 (pp. 55–84). April 1998.

Acharya, A. *Constructing a Security Community. ASEAN and the Problem of Regional Order.* London, Routledge, 2000.

Acharya, A., and Stubbs, R. 'Theorizing Southeast Asian Relations: An Introduction' in *The Pacific Review*, Vol. 19, No. 1 (pp. 125–34). June 2006.

Adams, G. *Free Ireland: Towards a Lasting Peace.* Dingle, Brandon Publrs, 1995.

Adams, G. *Before the Dawn.* Dingle, Brandon Publrs, 1996.

Adams, G. *Hope and History: Making Peace in Ireland.* Dingle, Brandon Publrs, 2003.

Adedeji, A. (ed.). *Comprehending and Mastering African Conflicts: The Search for Sustainable Peace and Good Governance.* London, Zed Books, 1999.

Aditjondro, G. 'Ninjas, Nanggalas, Monuments, and Mossad Manuals: An Anthropology of Indonesian State Terror in East Timor', in Sluka, J. A. (ed.). *Death Squad: The Anthropology of State Terror* (pp. 1–32). Philadelphia, PA, University of Pennsylvania Press, 2000.

Adler, E., and Barnett, M. N. (eds). *Security Communities.* Cambridge, Cambridge University, 1998.

Ahmad, Z. H., and Kadir, S. 'Ethnic Conflict, Prevention and Management: The Malaysian Case', in Snitwongse and Thompson, 2005 (see below).

Akbar, M. J. *Kashmir: Behind the Vale.* New Delhi, Viking Penguin India, 1991.

Alagappa, M. 'Introduction', 'The Anatomy of Legitimacy' and 'Seeking a More Durable Basis of Authority', in Alagappa, M. (ed.). *Political Legitimacy in Southeast Asia: The Quest for Moral Authority.* Stanford, CA, Stanford University Press, 1995.

Alagappa, M. (ed.). *Political Legitimacy in Southeast Asia.* Stanford, CA, Stanford University Press, 1985.

Alagappa, M. (ed.). *Asian Security Practice: Material and Ideational Influences.* Stanford, CA, Stanford University Press, 1998.

Allen, W. E. D. *A History of the Georgian People.* New York, Routledge & Kegan Paul, 1971.

Allen, W. E. D., and Muratoff, P. *Caucasian Battlefields: A History of the Wars on the Turko-Caucasian Frontier 1828–1921.* New York, Cambridge University Press, 1953.

Almog, O. *Britain, Israel and the United States: Beyond Suez, 1955–1958.* London and Portland, OR, Frank Cass, 2003.

Amer, R. *The General Assembly and the Kampuchean Issues: Intervention, Regime Recognition and the World Community, 1979 to 1988*, Report No. 31. Uppsala, Uppsala University (Dept of Peace and Conflict Research), 1989.

Amer, R. *The Ethnic Chinese in Vietnam and Sino-Vietnamese Relations.* Kuala Lumpur, Forum, 1991.

Amer, R. 'The United Nations' Peace Plan for Cambodia: From Confrontation to Consensus', in *Interdisciplinary Peace Research*, Vol. 3, No. 2 (pp. 32–27). Oct./Nov. 1991.

Amer, R. 'The Chinese Minority in Vietnam since 1975: Impact of Economic and Political Changes', in *Ilmu Masyarakat* (Malaysian Social Science Asscn publication), No. 22 (pp. 1–39). July–Dec. 1992.

Amer, R. 'Indochina', 'Vietnam', 'Cambodia' and 'Laos', in Minority Rights Group. *The Chinese of South-East Asia*, Report 92/6. London, MRG International, Nov. 1992.

Amer, R. 'Sino-Vietnamese Relations and Southeast Asian Security', in *Contemporary Southeast Asia*, Vol. 14, No. 4 (pp. 314–31). March 1993.

Amer, R. 'The United Nations' Peacekeeping Operation in Cambodia: Overview and Assessment', in *Contemporary Southeast Asia*, Vol. 15, No. 2 (pp. 211–31). Sept. 1993.

Amer, R. *The United Nations and Foreign Military Interventions: A Comparative Study of the Application of the Charter*, Report No. 33 (2nd edn). Uppsala, Uppsala University (Dept of Peace and Conflict Research), 1994.

Amer, R. 'The Ethnic Vietnamese in Cambodia—A Minority at Risk?', in *Contemporary Southeast Asia*, Vol. 16, No. 2 (pp. 210–38). Sept. 1994.

Amer, R. 'The United Nations' Reactions to Foreign Military Interventions', in *Journal of Peace Research*, Vol. 31, No. 4 (pp. 425–44). Nov. 1994.

Amer, R. *Peace-keeping in a Peace Process: The Case of Cambodia*, Report No. 40. Uppsala, Uppsala University (Dept of Peace and Conflict Research), 1995.

Amer, R. 'Vietnam and Its Neighbours: The Border Dispute Dimension', in *Contemporary Southeast Asia*, Vol. 17, No. 3 (pp. 298–318). Dec. 1995.

Amer, R. 'Conflicts Management and Constructive Engagement in ASEAN's Expansion', in *Third World Quarterly*, Vol. 20, No. 5 (pp. 1031–48). 1999.

Amnesty International. 'Cambodia', in *Report 2003* (web.amnesty.org/report2003/khm-summary-eng).

Amnesty International. 'Laos: Massacre of Unarmed Hmong Women and Children', News Service No. 113, of 4 May 2006.

Andaya, B. W. 'Religious Developments in Southeast Asia, c. 1500–1800', in Tarling, N. (ed.). *The Cambridge History of Southeast Asia, Vol. One: From Early Times to c. 1800.* Cambridge, Cambridge University Press, 1992.

Andaya, L. Y. 'Ethnonation, Nation-State and Regionalism in Southeast Asia', in *Proceedings of the International Symposium Southeast Asia: Global Area Studies for the 21st Century* (pp. 131–49). Kyoto, Kyoto University (Center for Southeast Asian Studies), 1997.

Anderson, B. R. O'G. 'Introduction', in Anderson, B. R. O'G., et al., 1987 (see below).

Anderson, B. R. O'G. *Language and Power: Exploring Political Cultures in Indonesia.* Ithaca, NY, Cornell University Press, 1990.

Anderson, B. R. O'G. 'The Changing Ecology of Southeast Asia Studies in the United States, 1950–1990', in Hirschman, C., Keyes, C. F., and Hutterer, K. (eds). *Southeast Asia in the Balance: Reflections from America* (pp. 25–40). Ann Arbor, MI, Association of Asian Studies, 1992

Anderson, B. R. O'G. *The Spectre of Comparisons: Nationalism, Southeast Asia and the World.* London, Verso, 1998.

Anderson, B. R. O'G. (ed.). *Violence and the State in Suharto's Indonesia*, Studies on Southeast Asia 30. Ithaca, NY, Cornell University (Southeast Asia Program), 2001.

Anderson, B. R. O'G., et al. *Southeast Asian Tribal Groups and Ethnic Minorities: Prospects for the Eighties and Beyond*, Cultural Survival Report 22. Cambridge, MA, Cultural Survival Inc, 1987.

Anderson, M. (ed.). *Cultural Shaping of Violence.* West Lafayette, IN, Purdue University Press, 2004.

Andrianoff, D. 'The Effect of the Laotian Conflict on Meo Ethnic Identity', in Kang, T. S. (ed.). *Nationalism and the Crises of Ethnic Minorities in Asia.* Westport, CT, Greenwood Press, 1979 (originally 1976).

Antl'v, H., and Trnnesson, S. (eds). *Imperial Policy and Southeast Asian Nationalism, 1930–1957.* Richmond, Curzon Press, 1995.

Anwar, D. F. *Indonesia in ASEAN: Foreign Policy and Regionalism.* Singapore, Institute of Southeast Asian Studies, 1994.

Anwar, D. F., Bouvier, H., Smith, G., and Tol, R. (eds). *Violent Internal Conflicts in Asia Pacific: Histories, Political Economies and Policies.* Jakarta, Yayasan Obor, 2005.

Aragon, L. V. 'Waiting for Peace in Poso: Why has this Muslim–Christian Conflict Continued for Three Years?', in *Inside Indonesia*, No. 70. April–June 2002.

Aras, B. 'Turkey's Options', at www.bitterlemons-international.org, Vol. 4(10). bitterlemons-international (Middle East Roundtable), 16 March 2006.

Arendt, H. *Eichmann in Jerusalem: A Report on the Banality of Evil.* London, Faber & Faber, 1963.

Arendt, H. *The Jew as Pariah: Jewish Identity and Politics in the Modern Age.* New York, Grove Press, 1978.

Aspinall, E., and Berger, M. T. 'The Break-up of Indonesia? Nationalisms after Decolonisation and the Limits of the Nation-State in post-Cold War Southeast Asia', in *Third World Quarterly*, Vol. 22, No. 6 (pp. 1003–24). 1 Dec. 2001.

Assensoh, A. B., and Alex-Assensoh, Y. M. African Military History and Politics: Coups and Ideological Incursions, 1900–Present. New York, Palgrave, 2001.

Associated News. 'Despite US's Best Efforts, Cocaine Production Increases', on Fox News website (www.foxnews.com/story/0,2933,200308,00.html) on 20 June 2006.

Aughey, A. *Under Siege: Ulster Unionism and the Anglo-Irish Agreement.* Basingstoke, Palgrave Macmillan, 1989.

Aung-Thwin, M. *Pagan: The Origins of Modern Burma.* Honolulu, HI, University of Hawaii Press, 1985.

Bahadur, K. (ed.). *South Asia in Transition: Conflicts and Tensions.* New Delhi, Patriot Publishers, 1986.

Baev, P. K. *Russia's Policies in the Caucasus.* Washington, DC, Brookings Institution, 1997.

Bailey, S. D. *Four Arab–Israeli Wars and the Peace Process.* London, Palgrave, 1990.

Baker, J. *The Politics of Diplomacy.* New York, G. P. Putnam's Sons, 1995.

Baker, J., and Hamilton, L., et al. *The Iraq Study Group Report* (Baker-Hamilton Report). New York, Vintage Books, 2006.

Ball, G. W., and Ball, D. B. *The Passionate Attachment: America's Involvement with Israel, 1947 to the Present.* New York, W. W. Norton & Co, 1972.

Banlaoi, R. C. 'Southeast Asian Perspectives on the Rise of China: Regional Security after 9/11', in *Parameters*, Vol. XXXIII, No. 2. Summer 2003.

Barnes, R. H., Gray, A., and Kingsbury, B. (eds). *Indigenous Peoples of Asia*, Monograph and Occasional Paper Series, No. 48. Ann Arbor, MI, Association for Asian Studies, 1995.

Barnett, C. 'Bring Our Troops Home in 2006', in *The Spectator* of 31 Dec. 2005.

Barnett, M. *Dialogues in Arab Politics: Negotiations in Regional Order.* New York, Columbia University Press, 1998.

Bastin, J. (ed.). *The Emergence of Modern Southeast Asia, 1511–1957.* Englewood Cliffs, NJ, Prentice-Hall, 1967.

Bastin, J., and Benda, H. J. (eds). *A History of Modern Southeast Asia: Colonialism, Nationalism, and Decolonization.* London, Prentice-Hall International, 1968.

Batatu, H. *The Old Social Classes and the Revolutionary Movements in Iraq.* Princeton, NJ, Princeton University Press, 1978.

Baudrillard, J. *The Gulf War Did Not Take Place* (trans. Patton, P.). Bloomington, IN, Indiana University Press, 1995.

Baumeister, R. F. *Evil: Inside Human Violence and Cruelty.* New York, W. H. Freeman, 1997.

Bayard, D. 'Comment on "An Evolutionary Approach to the Southeast Asian Cultural Sequence"', in *Current Anthropology* (p. 229), Vol. 17, No. 2. 1976.

Bayat, A. 'Islamism and Social Movement Theory', in *Third World Quarterly*, Vol. 26, No. 6 (pp. 891–08). 2005.

Beccaria, C. *On Crimes and Punishments.* Basingstoke, Macmillan, 1963.

Becker, J. *The PLO: The Rise and Fall of the Palestine Liberation Organization.* New York, St Martin's Press, 1984.

Beeson, M. 'Southeast Asia and the Politics of Vulnerability', in *Third World Quarterly*, Vol. 23, No. 3 (pp. 549–64). 1 June 2002.

Beeson, M. 'Sovereignty under Siege: Globalisation and the State in Southeast Asia', in *Third World Quarterly*, Vol. 24, No. 2 (pp. 357–74). 2003.

Belshaw, D., and Livingstone, I. (eds). *Renewing Development in Sub-Saharan Africa: Policy, Performance and Prospects.* London, Routledge, 2002.

Benda, H. J. 'The Structure of Southeast Asian History: Some Preliminary Observations', in *Journal of Southeast Asian History*, 3 (pp. 103–38). 1962

Benda, H. J. 'Peasant Movements in Colonial Southeast Asia', in *Asian Studies*, 3 (pp. 420–34). 1965.

Benda, H. J. 'Political Elites in Colonial Southeast Asia: An Historical Analysis', in *Comparative Studies in Society and History*, 7 (pp. 233–51). 1965.

Benjamin, W. *Illuminations* (originally essays in German, trans. by Zohn, H., in 1955). London, Fontana Press, 1992.

Bentley, G. C. 'Indigenous States of Southeast Asia,' in *Annual Review of Anthropology*, 15 (pp. 275–305). 1986.

Ben-Zvi, A. *The American Approach to Superpower Collaboration in the Middle East, 1973–1986.* Boulder, CO, Westview Press, 1986.

Ben-Zvi, A. *Decade of Transition: Eisenhower, Kennedy and the Origins of the American-Israeli Alliance.* New York, Columbia University Press, 1998.

Beresford, D. *Ten Men Dead: The Story of the 1981 Irish Hunger Strike.* London, Harper Collins, and New York, Atlantic Monthly Press, 1987.

Berger, M. T. *The Rise of East Asia: Critical Visions of the Pacific Century.* New York, Routledge, 1997.

Bertrand, J. *Nationalism and Ethnic Conflict in Indonesia*, Cambridge Asia-Pacific Studies Series. Cambridge, Cambridge University Press, 2004.

Betts, R K. 'The Delusion of Impartial Intervention', in *Foreign Affairs*, 73 (pp. 20–33). Nov./Dec. 1994.

Betts, R K. 'Vietnam's Strategic Predicament,' in *Survival*, Vol. 37, No. 3. Autumn 1995.

Bew, P., in *The Irish Times* of 15 May 1998.

Bezanis, L. 'On New Footing with Turkey', in *Transition*. 23 June 1995.

Bhabha, H. K. *Nation and Narration.* London and New York, Routledge, 1990.

Bialer, U. *Between East and West: Israel's Foreign Policy Orientation, 1948–1956.* Cambridge, Cambridge University Press, 1990.

Blanton, R. T., Mason, D., and Athow, B. 'Colonial Style and Post-Colonial Ethnic Conflict in Africa', in *Journal of Peace Research*, Vol. 38, No. 4 (pp. 473–91). 2001.

Bloodworth, D. *The Eye of the Dragon: Southeast Asia Observed, 1954–1986.* Singapore, Times Books, 1987.

Bodansky, Y. 'Pakistan's Kashmir Strategy', a paper. Houston, TX, Freeman Center for Strategic Studies, 1995.

Boland, B. J. *The Struggle of Islam in Modern Indonesia.* The Hague, Martinus Nijhoff, 1971.

Boot, M. *The Savage Wars of Peace: Small Wars and the Rise of American Power.* New York, Basic Books, 2002.

Bosworth, J., and Toller, T. N. *An Anglo-Saxon Dictionary.* Oxford, Clarendon Press, 1898.

Boutros-Ghali, B. *Agenda for Peace: Preventive Diplomacy, Peacemaking, and Peacekeeping.* New York, United Nations Press, 1992.

Brands, H. W. *Bound to Empire: The United States and the Philippines.* Oxford, Oxford University Press, 1992.

Brecher, M. *The Struggle for Kashmir.* New York, Oxford University Press, 1953.

Breckon, M. L. *The Security Environment in Southeast Asia and Australia, 1995–2010.* Alexandria, VA, Center for Naval Analyses, 1996.

Bresnan, J. (ed.). *Crisis in the Philippines: The Marcos Era and Beyond.* Princeton, NJ, Princeton University Press, 1986.

British Government (Palestine Royal Commission). *Report of the Palestine Royal Commission*, Cmd. 5479. London, HMSO, July 1937.

British Government. *Palestine: A Statement of Policy*, Cmd. 6019. London, HMSO, May 1939.

Brogan, P. *World Conflicts.* London, Bloomsbury, 1992.

Brown, D. 'From Peripheral Communities to Ethnic Nations: Separatism in Southeast Asia', in *Pacific Affairs*, Vol. 61(1) (pp. 51–77). 1988.

Brown, D. 'The State of Ethnicity and the Ethnicity of the State: Ethnic Politics in Southeast Asia', in *Ethnic and Racial Studies*, Vol. 12, No. 1 (pp. 47–62). 1989.

Brown, D. *The State and Ethnic Politics in Southeast Asia.* London, Routledge, 1994.

Brown, D. 'Democracy and Nationalism: Civic, Ethnocultural and Multicultural Politics under Patrimonial Rule', in Henders, S. J. (ed.). *Democratization and Identity: Regimes and Ethnicity in East and Southeast Asia.* Lanham, MD, Lexington Books, 2004.

Brown, M. E., and Ganguly, S. (eds). *Government Policies and Ethnic Relations in Asia and the Pacific.* Cambridge, MA, MIT Press, 1997.

Brown, M. E., et al. (eds). *Nationalism and Ethnic Conflict.* Cambridge, MA, MIT Press, 2001.

Broxup, M. B. (ed.). *The North Caucasus Barrier: The Russian Advance toward the Muslim World.* New York, St Martin's Press, 1992.

Bruce, S. *The Red Hand: Protestant Paramilitaries in Northern Ireland.* Oxford and New York, Oxford University Press, 1992.

van Bruinessen, M. 'Genealogies of Islamic Radicalism in post-Suharto Indonesia' (revised), paper originally for the international colloquium *L'islam politique à l'aube du XXIème siècle*, organized in Tehran by the Institute of Political and International Studies and the French Institute of Iranian Studies on 28–29 October 2001 (www.let.uu.nl/~martin.vanbruinessen/personal/publications/genealogies_islamic_radicalism.htm). 2002.

Brzezinski, Z. Testimony before the US Senate's Foreign Relations Committee on 1 Feb. 2007.

Buss, A. 'Max Weber's Heritage and Modern Southeast Asian Thinking on Development', in *Southeast Asian Journal of Social Science*, 12(1) (pp. 1–15). 1984.

Buszynski, L. 'ASEAN's New Challenges', in *Pacific Affairs*, 70. 1997.

Buzan, B., and Segal, G. 'Rethinking East Asian Security', in *Survival*, Vol. 36, No. 2. Summer 1994.

Caballero-Anthony, M. 'Partnership for Peace in Asia: ASEAN, the ARF, and the United Nations', in *Contemporary Southeast Asia*, Vol. 24, No. 3. 2002.

Caballero-Anthony, M. *Regional Security in Southeast Asia: Beyond the ASEAN Way.* Singapore, Institute of Southeast Asian Studies, 2005.

Cahill, K. M. (ed.). *Preventive Diplomacy: Stopping Wars Before They Start.* New York, Basic Books, 1996.

CAIN Web Service (Conflict Archive on the Internet), based in the University of Ulster (cain.ulst.ac.uk/index.html).

Campbell, B., McKeown, L., and O'Hagan, F. (eds). *Nor Meekly Serve my Time: The H-Block Struggle, 1976–1981.* Belfast, Beyond the Pale Publs, 1994.

Caplan, N. *Futile Diplomacy, Vol. 3: The United Nations, the Great Powers and Middle East Peacemaking, 1948–1954.* London and Portland, OR, Frank Cass, 1997.

Carment, D. 'Secessionist Ethnic Conflict in South and Southeast Asia: A Comparative Perspective', in Ganguly and Macduff, 2003 (see below).

Carneiro, R. L. 'The Chiefdom: Precursor of the State', in Jones, G. D., and Kautz, R. R. (eds). *The Transition to Statehood in the New World.* Cambridge and New York, Cambridge University Press, 1981.

Carpenter, W. M., and Wiencek, D. G. 'Openness and Security Policy in Southeast Asia', in *Survival*, Vol. 38, No. 3 (pp. 82–98). Autumn 1996.

Carpenter, W. M., and Wiencek, D. G. (eds). *Asian Security Handbook: An Assessment of Political-Security Issues in the Asia-Pacific Region.* Armonk, NY, M. E. Sharpe, 1996.

Casino, E. S. 'Interethnic Conflict in the Philippine Archipelago', in Boucher, J., Landis, D., and Clark, K. A. (eds). *Ethnic Conflict: International Perspectives* (pp. 231–54). Newbury Park, CA, Sage Publications, 1987

Cassidy, J. 'Beneath the Sand', in *The New Yorker* of 14–21 July 2003.

Chadda, M. *Ethnicity, Security and Separatism in India.* New York, Columbia University Press, 1997.

al-Chalabi, I. 'What is Happening to Iraqi Oil?', in *Middle East Economic Survey* (Global Policy Forum) of 10 October 2005.

Chalk, P. 'Separatism and Southeast Asia: The Islamic Factor in Southern Thailand, Mindanao, and Aceh', in *Studies in Conflict and Terrorism*, Vol. 24, No. 2. 1 July 2001.

Chalk, P. 'The Liberation Tigers of Tamil Eelam Insurgency in Sri Lanka', in Ganguly and Macduff, 2003 (see below).

Chan, H. C., and Evers, H. D. 'Nation-building and National Identity in Southeast Asia', in Eisenstadt, S. N., and Rokkan, S. (eds). *Building States and Nations: Analysis by Region*, Vol. 2 (pp. 301–19). Beverly Hills, CA, Sage Publications, 1973.

Chan, S. *Hmong Means Free: Life in Laos and America* (at www.hmongnet.org). Philadelphia, PA, Temple University Press, 1994.

Chandler, D. *Empire in Denial: The Politics of State-building.* London, Pluto Press, 2006.

Chang, G. C. *Nuclear Showdown: North Korea Takes on the World.* New York, Random House, 2006.

Cheldelin, S., et al. (eds). *Conflict.* London, Continuum, 2003.

Chin, C. B. N. 'The State of the "State" in Globalization: Social Order and Economic Restructuring in Malaysia', in *Third World Quarterly*, Vol. 21, No. 6 (pp. 1035–57). 2000.

Christie, C. J. *A Modern History of Southeast Asia: Decolonization, Nationalism and Separatism.* London, I. B. Tauris, 1996.

Clad, J. *Behind the Myth: Business Money and Power in Southeast Asia.* London, Hyman, 1989.

Clammer, J. 'Secularization and Religious Change in Contemporary Asia', in *Southeast Asian Journal of Social Science*, 12(1) (pp. 49–58). 1984.

Clarke, G. 'From Ethnocide to Ethno Development? Ethnic Minorities and Indigenous Peoples in Southeast Asia', in *Third World Quarterly*, Vol. 22, No. 3 (pp. 413–36). 2001.

Clayton, A. *Frontiersmen: Warfare in Africa since 1950.* London, UCL Press, 1999.

Clayton, P. *Enemies and Passing Friends: Settler Ideologies in Twentieth Century Ulster.* London, Pluto Press, 1996.

Clinton, B. *My Life.* New York, Alfred A. Knopf, and London, Hutchinson, 2004.

Clodfelter, M. *Vietnam in Military Statistics: A History of the Indochina Wars, 1772–1991.* Jefferson, NC, McFarland & Co, 1995.

Cockburn, P. Interview with *New Left Review*, 36. Nov.–Dec. 2005.

Coedes, G. *The Indianized States of Southeast Asia* (trans. Brown Cowing, S., and ed. Vella, W. F.). Honolulu, HI, East-West Center Press, 1968 (originally in French, *Les états hindouises d'Indochine et d'Indonesie.* Paris, Boccard, 1964).

Cogan, J. 'After the Iraq Election: Washington Steps in to Shape the Next Government', from World Socialist Website (www.wsws.org) of 21 Dec. 2005.

Cohen, M. J. *Strategy and Politics in the Middle East, 1954–1960: Defending the Northern Tier.* London and New York, Routledge, 2005.

Cohen, M. J., and Kolinsky, M. (eds). *Demise of the British Empire in the Middle East: Britain's Responses to Nationalist Movements, 1943–1955.* London and Portland, OR, Frank Cass, 1998.

Cohen, S.-P. *India: Emerging Power.* Washington, DC, Brookings Institution, 2001.

Cole, P. *The Myth of Evil: Demonizing the Enemy.* New York, Praeger, 2006.

Collier, P. 'Natural Resources and Conflict in Africa', at www.crimesofwar.org/africa-mag/afr_04_collier.html. Crimes of War Project (War in Africa—the magazine), Oct. 2004.

Colombijn, F., and Lindblad, J. T. (eds). *Roots of Violence in Indonesia: Contemporary Violence in Historical Perspective.* Leiden, KITLV Press (Royal Netherlands Institute of Southeast Asian and Caribbean Studies), 2002.

Command Papers (see British Govt above).

Conley, B. 'Iraq: So Much Oil, and So Little', in IPS News (www.ipsnews.net) of 14 Dec. 2004.

Connor, W. 'Ethnology and the Peace of South Asia', in *World Politics*, Vol. 22, No. 1 (pp. 52–86). Oct. 1969.

Conquest, R. *The Nation Killers: The Soviet Deportation of Nationalities.* London, Macmillan, 1970.

Coogan, T. P. *The IRA.* London, Fontana, 1980.

Coogan, T. P. *The Troubles: Ireland's Ordeal 1966–1995 and the Search for Peace.* London, Hutchinson, 1995.

Cooper, T. 'Peru vs. Ecuador: Alto Cenepa War, 1995', in *ACIG Journal*, at www.acig.org/artman/publish/article_164.shtml. Air Combat Information Group (ACIG—Central and Latin American Database), 1 Sept. 2003.

Coppel, C. (ed.). *Violent Conflicts in Indonesia: Analysis, Representation and Resolution*, Routledge Contemporary Southeast Asia Series. Richmond, RoutledgeCurzon, 2006.

Corbin, J. *The Norway Channel: The Secret Talks that Led to the Middle East Peace Accord.* New York, Atlantic, 1994.

Cordesman, A. H. *The Israeli–Palestinian War: Escalating to Nowhere.* Westport, CT, and London, Praeger, 2005.

Cornell, S. *Small Nations and Great Powers: A Study of Ethnopolitical Conflict in the Caucasus.* Richmond, Curzon Press, 2001.

Corpuz, O. *The Roots of the Filipino.* Quezon City, Aklahi Foundation, 1989.

Cossa, R. A. 'Security Implications of Conflicts in the South China Sea: Exploring Potential Triggers of Conflict', in Pacific Forum CSIS *PacNet Newsletter*, No. 16 (1998), at www.csis.org (Publications—Newsletters). 17 April 1998.

Cotton, J. *East Timor, Australia and Regional Order.* London, Routledge, 2004.

Coufoudakis, V., et al. (eds). *Greece and the New Balkans.* New York, Pella, 1999.

Council on Foreign Relations. 'Abu Sayyaf Group (Philippines, Islamist separatists)' at www.cfr.org/publications/9235. CFR (Publication Type—Backgrounder), updated regularly.

Cox, M. 'Bringing in the International: The IRA Cease-Fire and the End of the Cold War', in *International Affairs*, Vol. 73, No. 4. 1997.

Cox, M. 'Northern Ireland: The War that Came in from the Cold', in *Irish Studies in International Affairs* 9 (pp. 73–84). 1998.

Cox, M., Guelke, A., and Stephen, F. (eds). *A Farewell to Arms? Beyond the Good Friday Agreement.* Manchester, Manchester University Press, 2006.

Cramer, C. *Civil War Is Not a Stupid Thing: Accounting for Violence in Developing Countries.* London, Hurst & Co, 2006.

Cribb, R. *Gangsters and Revolutionaries: The Jakarta People's Militia and the Indonesian Revolution, 1945–1949.* Sydney, NSW, Allen & Unwin, 1991.

Cribb, R. 'The Indonesian Massacres', in Totten, S., Parsons, W. S., and Charny, I. W. (eds). *Genocide in the Twentieth Century: Critical Essays and Eyewitness Accounts* (pp. 299–333). New York, Garland Press, 1995.

Cribb, R. 'From Petrus to Ninja: Death Squads in Indonesia', in Campbell, B. B., and Brenner, A. D. (eds). *Death Squads in Global Perspective* (pp. 181–202). Basingstoke, Macmillan, 2000.

Cribb, R. 'Genocide in Indonesia, 1965–1966', in *Journal of Genocide Research*, Vol. 3, No. 2 (pp. 219–39). 2 June 2001.

Cribb, R. 'How Many Deaths? Problems in the Statistics of Massacre in Indonesia (1965–1966) and East Timor (1975-1980)', in Wessel, and Wimhöfer, 2001 (see below).

Cribb, R. 'Unresolved Problems in the Indonesian Killings of 1965–1966', in *Asian Survey*, Vol. 42, No. 4 (pp. 550–63). July–Aug. 2002.

Cribb, R. 'From Total People's Defence to Massacre: Explaining Indonesian Military Violence in East Timor', in Colombijn and Lindblad, 2002 (see above).

Cribb, R. (ed.). *The Indonesian Killings 1965–1966: Studies from Java and Bali*, Monash Papers on Southeast Asia 21. Clayton, Vic., Monash University (Centre of Southeast Asian Studies), 1990.

Cronin, P., and Ott, M. *The Indonesian Armed Forces: Roles, Prospects, and Implications*, Strategic Forum Paper No. 126. Washington, DC, National Defense University, Aug. 1997.

Cronin, S. *Washington's Irish Policy 1916–1986: Independence, Partition, Neutrality.* Dublin, Anvil Books, 1987.

Crouch, H. *The Army and Politics in Indonesia.* Ithaca, NY, Cornell University Press, 1978.

Crouch, H., and Zakaria, A. (eds). *Military-Civil Relations in South-East Asia.* Kuala Lumpur, Oxford University Press, 1985.

Cuadra, J. 'The Lessons of Nicaragua that can be Applied to Iraq and Afghanistan', at hnn.us/roundup/entries/10663.html. History News Network, 9 March 2005.

da Cunha, D. (ed.). *The Evolving Pacific Power Structure.* Singapore, Institute of Southeast Asian Studies, 1996.

da Cunha, D. 'Southeast Asian Perceptions of China's Future Security Role in Its "Backyard"',' in Pollack, J. D., and Yang, R. H. (eds). *In China's Shadow* (CF-137-CAPP, pp. 115–26). Santa Monica, CA, RAND, 1998.

Cushman, J., and Gungwu, W. (eds). *Changing Identities of the Southeast Asian Chinese since World War II.* Hong Kong, Hong Kong University Press, 1988.

Dalby, A. *South East Asia: A Guide to Reference Material*, Regional Reference Guides No. 2. London and New York, Hans Zell, 1993.

Dale, S. F. ' Religious Suicide in Islamic Asia: Anticolonial Terrorism in India, Indonesia, and the Philippines', in *Journal of Conflict Resolution*, Vol. 32, No. 1 (pp. 37–59). 1 March 1988.

Dalpino, C. E., and Timberman, D. G. 'Cambodia's Political Future: Issues for US Policy', at www.asiasociety.org/publications/cambodia_policy.html. New York, Asia Society, 26 March 1998.

Damrosch, L. F. *Enforcing Restraint: Collective Intervention in Internal Conflicts.* New York, Council on Foreign Relations, 1993.

Danchev, A., et al. *International Perspectives on the Yugoslav Conflict.* Oxford, Macmillan, 1996.

Dann, U. (ed.). *The Great Powers in the Middle East, 1919–1939.* New York and London, Holmes & Meier, 1988.

Daragahi, B. 'Kurdish Oil Deal Shocks Iraq's Political Leaders', in *Los Angeles Times* of 1 December 2005.

Davidson, J. S. 'The Politics of Violence on an Indonesian Periphery', in *South East Asia Research*, Vol. 11, No. 1 (pp. 59–89). 1 March 2003.

Davidson, J. H. C. S. 'The Modern Short Story in South East Asia: An Introduction', in Davidson, J. H. C. S., and Cordell, H. (eds). *The Short Story in South East Asia: Aspects of a Genre.* London, School of Oriental and African Studies (University of London), 1982.

Davis, M. 'Laskar Jihad and the Political Position of Conservative Islam in Indonesia', in *Contemporary Southeast Asia*, Vol. 24, No. 1. April 2002.

Dawisha, K. *Soviet Foreign Policy towards Egypt.* London, Macmillan, 1979.

Dawisha, K., and Parrott, B. *Conflict, Cleavage, and Change in Central Asia and the Caucasus.* Cambridge, Cambridge University Press, 1997.

De Breadún, D. *The Far Side of Revenge: Making Peace in Northern Ireland.* Cork, Collins Press, 2001.

De Waal, A. 'Briefing—Darfur, Sudan: Prospects for Peace', in *African Affairs*, Vol. 104 (No. 414). 2005.

Deng, F. M., and Zartman, I. W. (eds). *Conflict Resolution in Africa.* Washington, DC, Brookings Institution, 1991.

Dentan, R. K. *The Semai: A Nonviolent People of Malaysia.* New York, Holt, Rinehart & Winston, 1968.

DeWitt, D., and Bow, B. 'Proliferation Management in Southeast Asia', in *Survival*, Vol. 38, No. 3 (pp. 67–81). Autumn 1995.

Dibb, P. 'Indonesia: The Key to South-East Asia's Security', in *International Affairs*, Vol. 77, No. 4 (pp. 829–42). Oct. 2001.

van Dijk, C. *A Country in Despair: Indonesia between 1997 and 2000.* Jakarta, KITLV Press, 2001.

Dillon, D. R. 'Contemporary Security Challenges in Southeast Asia', in *Parameters*, Vol. XXVII, No. 1 (pp. 119–33). Spring 1997.

Dinnen, S., and Ley, A. (eds). *Reflections on Violence in Melanesia.* Annandale, NSW, Hawkins Press, and Canberra, ACT, Asia Pacific Press, 2000.

Doner, R. F. 'Approaches to the Politics of Economic Growth in Southeast Asia', in *Journal of Asian Studies*, Vol. 50, No. 4 (pp. 818–49). 1991.

Doornbos, M. 'Somalia: Alternative Scenarios for Political Reconstruction', in *African Affairs*, Vol. 101 (No. 402). 2002.

Dossani, R., and Rowen, H. S. (eds). *Prospects for Peace in South Asia.* Stanford, CA, Stanford University Press, 2005.

Downie, S., and Kingsbury, D. 'Political Development and the Re-emergence of Civil Society in Cambodia', in *Contemporary Southeast Asia*, Vol. 23, No. 1. April 2001.

Downing, B. T., and Olney, D. P. (eds). *The Hmong in the West: Observations and Reports*, Southeast Asian Refugee Studies Project. Minneapolis, MN, University of Minnesota (Center for Urban and Regional Affairs), 1982.

Doyle, J. 'Workers and Outlaws: Unionism and Fair Employment in Northern Ireland', in *Irish Political Studies*, 9 (pp. 41–60). 1994.

Doyle, J. 'Towards a Lasting Peace'? The Northern Ireland Multi-Party Agreement, Referendum and Assembly Elections of 1998', in *Scottish Affairs*, 25 (pp. 1–20). 1998.

Doyle, J. 'Governance and Citizenship in Contested States: The Northern Ireland Peace Agreement as Internationalised Governance', in *Irish Studies in International Affairs*, 10 (pp. 201–19). 1999.

Doyle, J. 'Ulster Like Israel Can Only Lose Once: Ulster Unionism, Security and Citizenship from the Fall of Stormont to the Eve of the 1998 Agreement', a working paper for the Centre for International Studies DCU (available www.dcu.ie/~cis/publications.htm). Dublin, CIS/DCU, 2003.

Doyle, J. 'Republican Policies in Practical Politics: Placing Sinn Fein in a European Context', in Honohan, I. (ed.). *The Future of Republicanism in Ireland: Confronting Theory and Practice.* Manchester, Manchester University Press, 2006.

Drysdale, A., and Hinnebusch, R. A. *Syria and the Middle East Peace Process.* New York, Council on Foreign Relations, 1991.

Dublin City University (Centre for International Studies). Documents on Northern Ireland (www.dcu.ie/~cis/northernirl.html).

Dunlop, J. B. *Russia Confronts Chechnya: Roots of a Separatist Conflict.* Cambridge, Cambridge University Press, 1998.

Dunlop, J. B. 'How Many Soldiers and Civilians Died during the Russo-Chechen War of 1994–96?', in *Central Asian Survey*, Vol. 19, No. 3. Sept. 2000.

Echevarria, A. J. *Fourth-Generation War and Other Myths* (at www.strategic-studiesinstitute.army.mil/pdffiles/pub632.pdf). Carlisle, PA, Strategic Studies Institute (US Army War College), 2005.

The Economist. 'Vote, Damn You.' London, 14 Sept. 1996.

The Economist. 'Hitting the Tigers in their Pockets.' London, 10 March 2001.

The Economist. 'The Wounded Tigers.' London, 12 Jan. 2002.

The Economist. 'The Wrong Lot Won, Dammit.' London, 7 Jan. 2005.

The Economist. 'Misreading Iran.' London, 14 Jan. 2006.

The Economist. 'Colombia's Drug Wars.' London, 24 Feb. 2006.

Eklöf, S. *Indonesian Politics in Crisis: The Long Fall of Suharto 1996–98.* Copenhagen, Nordic Institute of Asian Studies, 1999.

Eldridge, P. J. *Non-Government Organizations and Democratic Participation in Indonesia.* Kuala Lumpur and New York, Oxford University Press, 1995.

Ellings, R. J., and Simon, S. W. (eds). *Southeast Asian Security in the New Millennium*, Study by National Bureau of Asian Research. Armonk, NY, M. E. Sharpe, 1996.

Emmers, R. *Cooperative Security and the Balance of Power in ASEAN and the ARF.* London, Routledge, 2003.

Energy Information Administration. 'Iraq', Country Analysis Briefs (www.eia.-doe.gov/emeu/cabs/Iraq/Full.html). Washington, DC, EIA (Dept of Energy), June 2006.

Englebert, P., and Hummel, R. 'Let's Stick Together: Understanding Africa's Secessionist Deficit', in *African Affairs*, Vol. 104 (No. 416). 2005.

English, R. *Armed Struggle: The History of the IRA*. London, Macmillan, 2003.

Evans, G. *Cooperating for Peace: The Global Agenda for the 1990s and Beyond*. New York, Allen & Unwin, 1993.

Fanning, R. 'Playing it Cool: The Response of the British and Irish Governments to the Crisis in Northern Ireland, 1968–9', in *Irish Studies in International Affairs*, 12 (pp. 57–85). 2001.

Farouk, O. 'The Origins and Evolution of Malay-Muslim Ethnic Nationalism in Southern Thailand', in Abdullah and Siddique, 1986 (see above).

Farrell, M. *Northern Ireland: The Orange State* (2nd edn). London, Pluto Press, 1980 (originally 1976).

Fee, L. K. 'The Political and Economic Marginalisation of Tamils in Malaysia', in *Asian Studies Review*, Vol. 26, No. 3 (pp. 309–29). Sept. 2002.

Feeney, B. *Sinn Féin: A Hundred Turbulent Years*. Dublin, O'Brien Press, 2002.

Feeney, B. 'No time for "going back to the future"', in *The Irish News* of 30 Dec. 2004.

Ferguson, N. *The War of the World: History's Age of Hatred*. London, Penguin, 2007 (originally London, Allen Lane, 2006).

Ferrer, M. C. 'The Moro and the Cordillera Conflicts in the Philippines and the Struggle for Autonomy', in Snitwongse and Thompson, 2005 (see below).

Finer, H. *Dulles over Suez: The Theory and Practice of his Diplomacy*. London, Heinemann, 1964.

Fischbach, M. R. *Records of Dispossession: Palestinian Refugee Property and the Arab-Israeli Conflict*. New York, Columbia University Press, 2003.

Fisher, R. 'US and Iran Pause at the Brink', in *Asia Times* of April 2006.

Fisk, R. *The Point of No Return: The Strike Which Broke the British in Ulster*. London, Andre Deutsch, 1975.

FitzGerald, G. *All in a Life: An Autobiography*. Dublin, Gill & Macmillan, and Basingstoke, Macmillan, 1991.

FitzGerald, G. 'What happened to Good Friday?' in *London Review of Books*, Vol. 21, No. 17. 2 Sept. 1999.

Fizpatrick, D. 'Chinese Family Firms in Indonesia and the Question of "Confucian Corporatism"', in Hooker, 2002 (see below).

Fleshman, M. 'Counting the Cost of Gun Violence', in *Africa Recovery*, Vol. 15, No. 4 (at www.un.org/ecosocdev/geninfo/afrec/vol15no4/154arms.htm). Dec. 2001.

Foster, J. W. (ed.). *The Idea of the Union: Statements and Critiques in Support of the Union of Great Britain and Northern Ireland.* Vancouver, BC, Belcouver Press, 1995.

Fouskas, V. K., and Gökay, B. *The New American Imperialism.* Westport, CT, Praeger, 2005.

Foucault, M. *Surveiller et punir.* Paris, Harmattan, 1975.

Francis, D. J., et al. *Dangers of Co-deployment: UN Co-operative Peacekeeping in Africa.* Aldershot, Ashgate, 2005.

Frankfurter, D. *Evil Incarnate: Rumors of Demonic Conspiracy and Satanic Abuse in History.* Princeton, NJ, Princeton University Press, 2006.

Fraser, T. G. *The Arab–Israeli Conflict.* London, Macmillan, 1995.

Freedman, A. 'Political Institutions and Ethnic Chinese Identity in Indonesia', in *Asian Ethnicity*, Vol. 4, No. 3 (pp. 439–52). 2003.

Freedman, L., and Karsh, E. *The Gulf Conflict, 1990–1991.* London and Boston, MA, Faber & Faber, 1993.

Freedman, R. O. (ed.). *The Middle East Since Camp David.* Boulder, CO, Westview Press, 1984.

Friedman, I. *The Question of Palestine: British-Jewish-Arab Relations, 1914–1918.* New Brunswick, NJ, and London, Transaction, 1992.

Fukuyama, F. *State Building: Governance and World Order in the Twenty-first Century.* London, Profile Books, 2005.

Fuller, G. A., Murphy, A. B., Ridgley, M. A., and Ulack, R. 'Measuring Potential Ethnic Conflict', in *Growth and Change*, Vol. 31, No. 2 (pp. 305–31). 2000.

Funston, J. 'Challenges Facing ASEAN in a More Complex Age', in *Contemporary Southeast Asia*, Vol. 21, No. 2. Aug. 1999.

Furley, O. 'Conflict Prevention and Conflict Resolution: Interventions and Results', in Belshaw and Livingstone, 2002 (see above).

Furley, O. (ed.). *Conflict in Africa.* London, Tauris, 1995.

Galnoor, I. *The Partition of Palestine: Decision Crossroads in the Zionist Movement.* Albany, NY, State University of New York Press, 1995.

Gammer, M. *Muslim Resistance to the Tsar: Shamil and the Conquest of Chechnia and Daghestan.* London and Portland, OR, Frank Cass, 1994.

Ganesan, N. 'ASEAN's Relations with Major External Powers', in *Contemporary Southeast Asia*, Vol. 22, No. 1. 2000.

Ganguly, R., and Macduff, I. (eds). *Ethnic Conflict and Secessionism in South and Southeast Asia: Causes, Dynamics, Solutions.* London, New Delhi and Thousand Oaks, CA, Sage Publs, 2003.

Ganguly, S. *The Crisis in Kashmir: Portents of War, Hopes of Peace.* Washington, DC, Woodrow Wilson Center Press, and New York, Cambridge University Press, 1997.

Ganguly, S. 'Ethnic Policies and Political Quiescence in Malaysia and Singapore', in Brown and Ganguly, 1997 (see below).

Ganguly, S. *Conflict Unending: India-Pakistan Tensions since 1947.* New York, Columbia University Press, and Washington, DC, Woodrow Wilson Center Press, 2001.

Gat, M. *Britain and the Conflict in the Middle East, 1964–1967: The Coming of the Six-Day War.* Westport, CT, and London, Praeger, 2003.

Gates, C. L., and Than, M. (eds). *ASEAN Enlargement: Impacts and Implications.* Singapore, Institute of Southeast Asian Studies, 2001.

Gelber, Y. *Palestine 1948: War, Escape and the Emergence of the Palestinian Refugee Problem.* Brighton and Portland, OR, Sussex Academic Press, 2001.

Gershman, J. 'U.S. and Malaysia now Best Friends in War on Terrorism', in *Foreign Policy in Focus* (www.fpif.org—International Relations Center, Silver City, NM). 10 May 2002.

Giblin, S. 'Civil Society Groups Overcoming Stereotypes? Chinese Indonesian Civil Society Groups in Post-Suharto Indonesia', in *Asian Ethnicity*, Vol. 4, No. 3 (pp. 353–68). 2003.

GlobalSecurity.org. 'Military' (The Karen), at www.globalsecurity.org/military/world/para/karen.htm.

Godson, D. *Himself Alone: David Trimble and the Ordeal of Unionism.* London, HarperCollins, 2004.

Gökay, B. (ed.). *The Politics of Oil.* London, Routledge, 2006.

Golan, G. *Soviet Policies in the Middle East: From World War II to Gorbachev.* Cambridge, Cambridge University Press, 1990.

Goldenberg, S. *Pride of Small Nations: The Caucasus and Post-Soviet Disorder.* London, Zed Books, 1994.

Goulding, M. 'The United Nations and Conflict in Africa since the Cold War', in *African Affairs*, Vol. 98 (No. 391). 1999.

Govrin, Y. *Israeli-Soviet Relations, 1953–1967: From Confrontation to Disruption.* London and Portland, OR, Frank Cass, 1998.

Gowan, P. 'The Post-Communist Socialists in Eastern and Central Europe', in Sassoon, D. (ed.). *Looking Left: European Socialism after the Cold War.* New York, New Press, 1997.

Gowan, P. 'The NATO Powers and the Balkan Tragedy', in *New Left Review*, No. 234. March–April 1999.

Gowan, P. 'The Twisted Road to Kosovo: The Political Origins of the NATO Attack on Yugoslavia', in *Labour Focus on Eastern Europe*, No. 62. Spring 1999.

Grandvoinnet, H., and Schneider, H. (eds). *Conflict Management in Africa: A Permanent Challenge.* Paris, OECD, 1998.

Green, R. H. 'Planning for Post-Conflict Rehabilitation', in Belshaw and Livingstone, 2002 (see above).

Gregory, S. 'The French Military in Africa: Past and Present', in *African Affairs*, Vol. 99 (No. 396). 2000.

Grey, B. 'A Political Bombshell from Zbigniew Brzezinski', from World Socialist Website (www.wsws.org) of 2 Feb. 2007.

Guelke, A. *Northern Ireland: The International Perspective.* Dublin, Gill & Macmillan, 1988.

Gupta, S. *Kashmir: A Study in India-Pakistan Relations.* New Delhi, Asia Publishing House, 1966.

Haacke, J. *ASEAN's Diplomatic and Security Culture: Origins, Development and Prospects.* London, Routledge, 2002.

Hadiz, V. R. 'Mirroring the Past or Reflecting the Future? Class and Religious Pluralism in Indonesian Labor', in Hefner, 2001 (see below).

Hadiz, V. R. 'The Rise of neo-Third Worldism? The Indonesian Trajectory and the Consolidation of Illiberal Democracy', in *Third World Quarterly*, Vol. 25, No. 1. 2004.

Hagerty, D. T. 'Nuclear Deterrence in South Asia: The 1990 Indo-Pakistani Crisis', in *International Security*, Vol. 20, No. 3 (pp. 79–114). Winter 1995/96.

Halliday, F. *Nation and Religion in the Middle East.* London, Saqi Books, 2000.

Hammel, E. *Six Days in June: How Israel Won the 1967 Arab-Israeli War.* New York, Charles Scribner's Sons, 1992.

Harris, D. 'From "Warlord" to "Democratic" President: How Charles Taylor Won the 1997 Liberian Elections', in *Journal of Modern African Studies*, Vol. 37, No. 3 (pp. 431–55). 1999.

Hasan, N. 'Faith and Politics: The Rise of the Laskar Jihad in the Era of Transition in Indonesia', in *Indonesia*, 73 (pp. 145–69). April 2002.

Hefner, R. W. *Civil Islam: Muslims and Democratization in Indonesia*. Princeton, NJ, Princeton University Press, 2000.

Hefner, R. W. (ed.). *The Politics of Multiculturalism*. Honolulu, HI, University of Hawaii Press, 2001.

Heikal, M. *Sphinx and Commissar*. London, Collins, 1978.

Heiser, B. 'Laos Pages', at private.addcom.de/asiaphoto/laos/index.htm (Laos, www.asiaphoto.de). From 1998 and 2002.

Heller, J. *The Stern Gang: Ideology, Politics and Terror, 1940–1949*. London and Portland, OR, Frank Cass, 1995.

Henders, S. J. 'Debating Theories and Conceptions', in Henders, in Henders, S. J. (ed.). *Democratization and Identity: Regimes and Ethnicity in East and Southeast Asia*. Lanham, MD, Lexington Books, 2004.

Henley, D. *Nationalism and Regionalism in a Colonial Context*. Leiden, KITLV Press, 1996.

Henley, J. 'Thatcher "Threatened to Nuke Argentina"', in *The Guardian* (London) of 22 Nov. 2005.

Herring, G. C. *America's Longest War: The United States and Vietnam, 1950–1975* (2nd edn). Philadelphia, PA, Temple University Press, 1986 (originally 1979).

Herring, G. C. 'America and Vietnam: The Unending War', in *Foreign Affairs*, Vol. 70, No. 5. Winter 1991-92.

Herzog, C. *The War of Atonement*. London, Weidenfeld & Nicolson, 1975.

Herzog, C. *The Arab-Israeli Wars: War and Peace in the Middle East*. London, Book Club Associates, 1982.

Hewitt, V. *The New International Politics of South Asia*. Manchester and New York, Manchester University Press, 1997.

Hicks, D. 'Timor-Roti: Eastern Tetum, Atoni', in LeBar, F. (ed.). *Ethnic Groups of Insular Southeast Asia, Vol. 1: Indonesia, Andaman Islands, and Madagascar*. New Haven, CT, Human Relations Area Files Press, 1972.

Hintjens, H. M. 'Explaining the 1994 Genocide in Rwanda', in *Journal of Modern African Studies*, Vol. 37, No. 2 (pp. 241–86). 1996.

Hinton, A. L. 'Why Did You Kill? The Cambodian Genocide and the Dark Side of Face and Honor', in *Journal of Asian Studies*, Vol. 57, No. 1 (pp. 91–122). 1997.

Hirsch, P., and Wyatt, A. 'Negotiating Local Livelihoods: Scales of Conflict in the Se San River Basin', in *Asia Pacific Viewpoint*, Vol. 45, No. 1 (pp. 51–68). 2001.

Hitchcock, R. K. 'Human Rights and Indigenous Peoples in Africa and Asia', in Forsythe, D. P., and McMahon, P. C. (eds). *Human Rights and Diversity: Area Studies Revisited* (pp. 205–28). Lincoln, NE, University of Nebraska Press, 2003.

Hohe; T. 'The Clash of Paradigms: International Administration and Local Political Legitimacy in East Timor', in *Contemporary Southeast Asia*, Vol. 24, No. 3. 2002.

Hooker, M. B. (ed.). *Law and the Chinese in Southeast Asia.* Singapore, Institute of Southeast Asian Studies, 2002.

Hooker, M. B., and Dentan, R. K., et al. *Malaysia and the Original People: A Case Study of the Impact of Development on Indigenous Peoples.* Boston, MA, Allyn & Bacon, 1996.

Hourani, A. *A History of the Arab Peoples.* London, Faber & Faber, 1991.

Huang-Thio, S. M. 'Constitutional Discrimination under the Malaysian Constitution', in *Malaya Law Review*, 6. 1964.

Hughes, C., and Pupavac, V. 'Framing Post-conflict Societies: International Pathologisation of Cambodia and the post-Yugoslav States', in *Third World Quarterly*, Vol. 26, No. 6 (pp. 873–89). 2005.

Human Rights Watch (www.hrw.org). *Human Rights in Northern Ireland: A Helsinki Watch Report.* New York, Human Rights Watch, 1991.

Human Rights Watch. *The Ingush-Ossetian Conflict in the Prigorodnyi Region.* New York, Human Rights Watch, 1996.

Human Rights Watch. 'Nigeria: Crackdown in the Niger Delta', Human Rights Watch Report 11(2A). 1999.

Human Rights Watch. 'The Niger Delta: No Democratic Dividend', Human Rights Watch Reports 14(7A). 2002.

Human Rights Watch. '"They Came and Destroyed Our Village Again": The Plight of Internally Displaced Persons in Karen State', Human Rights Watch Reports 17(4C). 2005.

Human Rights Watch. 'No Sanctuary: Ongoing Threats to Indigenous Montagnards in Vietnam's Central Highlands', Human Rights Watch Reports 18(4C). 2006.

Human Rights Watch. 'Cambodia (Human Rights Development). Defending Human Rights: The Role of the International Community' in *World Report 2000* (at www.hrw.org/wr2k1/asia/cambodia.html). 2001.

Human Rights Watch. 'Burma—UN Must Act to End Attacks on Karen: Army uses Landmines to Prevent Civilians from Fleeting Conflicts', in *Human Rights News* (at hrw.org/english/docs/2006/05/03/burma13301.htm) of 3 May 2006.

Hupchick, P. D. *The Balkans.* New York, Palgrave, 2002.

Hussain, M., and Ghosh, L. (eds). *Religious Minorities in South Asia: Selected Essays on Post-Colonial Situations.* New Delhi, Manak Publs, 2002.

Hussin, M. April 2000. 'Illiberal Democracy and the Future of Opposition in Singapore', in *Third World Quarterly*, Vol. 21, No. 2 (pp. 313–42). April 2000.

Huxley, T. 'Singapore and Malaysia: A Precarious Balance?', in *Pacific Review*, Vol. 4, No. 1. 1991.

Ibingira, G. S. *African Upheavals since Independence.* Boulder, CO, Westview Press, 1980.

Ihonvbere, J. O. 'The "Irrelevant" State, Ethnicity, and the Quest for Nationhood in Africa', in *Ethnic and Racial Studies*, 17(1) (pp. 42–60). 1994.

Imperial and Royal Austro-Hungarian Marine Corps. *Fourth Generation War*, draft manual (FMFM 1-A) (www.sftt.us/HTML/article07072005a.html). 2005.

Institute for the Analysis of Global Security. 'Iraq Pipeline Watch', at http://iags.org. Washington, DC, IAGS, 2005.

International Crisis Group. 'Cambodia: The Elusive Peace Dividend', Asia Report No. 8 (www.crisgroup.org/home/index.cfm?id=1425&1). 11 Aug. 2000.

International Crisis Group. 'Burma/Myanmar: How Strong is the Military Regime?' Asia Report No. 11 (www.crisisgroup.org/home/index.cfm?l=1&id=1529). 21 Dec. 2000.

International Crisis Group. 'Jemaah Islamiyah in Southeast Asia: Damaged but Still Dangerous', Asia Report No. 63 (www.crisisgroup.org/home/index.cfm?l=1&id=1452). 26 Aug. 2003.

International Institute for Strategic Studies (www.iiss.org). Armed Conflict Database, at acd.iiss.org (subscription only).

International Law Commission of the UN. 'Principles of the Nuremberg Tribunal (1950)', at deoxy.org/wc/wc-nurem.htm.

Iraqi Government. 'The Constitution of Iraq', draft text (trans. from the Arabic by The Associated Press). 2005.

Isichei, E. *A History of the Igbo People.* Basingstoke, Macmillan, 1976.

Islam, S. S. 'Ethno-communal Conflict in the Philippines: The Case of Mindanao-Sulu Region', in Ganguly and Macduff, 2003 (see above).

Ismail, R., and Shaw, B. J. 'Singapore's Malay-Muslim Minority: Social Identification in a post-"9/11" World', in *Asian Ethnicity*, Vol. 7, No. 1 (pp. 37–53). 2006.

Israeli, R. *Islam in China: Religion, Ethnicity, Culture and Politics*. Lexington, MA, Lexington Books, 2002.

Jacobsen, M. 'Islam and the Process of Minorisation among Ethnic Chinese in Indonesia: Oscillating between Faith and Political Economic Expedience', in *Asian Ethnicity*, Vol. 6, No. 1 (pp. 71–88). 2005.

Jakobsen, M. 'Nation-making and the Politicisation of Ethnicity in Post-Suharto Indonesia', Working Papers Series 26 (www.cityu.edu.hk/searc/WP26_02_Jacobsen.pdf). Hong Kong:, City University of Hong Kong (Southeast Asia Research Centre), 2002.

Jalal, A. *Democracy and Authoritarianism in South Asia: A Comparative and Historical Perspective*. Cambridge, Cambridge University Press, 1995.

Jefferies, P. A. 'Human Rights, Foreign Policy and Religious Belief: An Asia/Pacific Perspective', in *Brigham Young University Law Review*, 885. 2000.

Jemadu, A. 'Democratisation and the Dilemma of Nation-Building in Post-Suharto Indonesia: The Case of Aceh', in *Asian Ethnicity*, Vol. 5, No. 3 (pp. 315–32). 2004.

Jeong, H.-W. *Peace and Conflict Studies: An Introduction*. Aldershot, Ashgate, 2000.

Johnston, D. *International Petroleum Fiscal Systems and Production Sharing Contracts*. Tulsa, OK, PennWell Books, 1994.

Johnson, D. H. *The Root Causes of Sudan's Civil Wars*. Oxford, James Currey, 2003.

Joffe, J. 'A World without Israel', in *Foreign Policy*, Jan./Feb. 2005.

Johnson, E. A., and Monkkonen, E. H. (eds). *The Civilization of Crime: Violence in Town and Country since the Middle Ages*. Urbana, IL, and Chicago, IL, University of Illinois Press, 1996.

Johnston, D. *International Petroleum Fiscal Systems and Production Sharing Contracts*. Tulsa, OK, PennWell, 1994.

Jones, D. M., and Smith, M. L. 'The Changing Security Agenda in Southeast Asia: Globalization, New Terror, and the Delusions of Regionalism', in *Studies in Conflict and Terrorism*, Vol. 24, No. 4 (pp. 271–88). 1 July 2001.

Jones, Martin. *Failure in Palestine: British and United States Policy after the Second World War*. London, Mansell, 1986.

Jones, Matthew. *Conflicts and Confrontation in Southeast Asia, 1961–1965: Britain, the United States and the Creation of Malaysia.* Cambridge, Cambridge University Press, 2002.

Jones, S. 'The changing nature of Jemaah Islamiyah', in *Australian Journal of International Affairs*, Vol. 29, No. 2 (pp. 169–78). June 2005.

Judah, T. *Kosovo: War and Revenge.* New Haven, CT, Yale University Press, 2000.

Just, P. *Dou Donggo Justice: Conflict and Morality in an Indonesian Society.* Lanham, MD, Rowman & Littlefield, 2001.

Kadian, R. *India's Sri Lanka Fiasco: Peace Keepers at War.* New Delhi, Vision Books, 1990.

Kahin, G. *Nationalism and Revolution in Indonesia.* Ithaca, NY, Cornell University Press, 1952.

Kalaw, M. M. *The Development of Philippine Politics, 1872-1920.* Manila, Oriental Commercial Co, 1926.

Kalis, M. A. 'Child Soldiers in Africa: Solutions to a Complex Dilemma', in *African Journal on Conflict Resolution*, Vol. 2, No. 2 (pp. 31–52). 2002.

Kambwa, A. E., et al. 'Angola', in Adedeji, 1999 (see above).

Kandeh, J. D. 'Sierra Leone's Post-Conflict Elections of 2002', in *Journal of Modern African Studies*, Vol. 41, No. 2 (pp. 189–216). 2003.

Kang, D. C. 'Getting Asia Wrong: The Need for New Analytical Frameworks', in *International Security*, Vol. 27, No. 4 (pp. 57–85). Spring 2003.

Karagiannis, E. *Energy and Security in the Caucasus.* London, RoutledgeCurzon, 2002.

Karnow, S. *In Our Image: America's Empire in the Philippines.* New York, Random House, 1989.

Karsh, E. (ed.). *From Rabin to Netanyahu: Israel's Troubled Agenda.* London and Portland, OR, Frank Cass, 1997.

Karsh, E. *The Arab-Israeli Conflict: The Palestine War 1948.* Oxford and London, Osprey, 2002.

Karsh, E. *Arafat's War.* New York, Grove Press, 2003.

Kartodirdjo, S. *Protest Movements in Rural Java: A Study of Agrarian Unrest in Rural Java in the Nineteenth and Early Twentieth Centuries.* Singapore, Oxford University Press, 1973.

Kastfelt, N. (ed.). *Religion and African Civil Wars.* London, Hurst & Co, 2005.

Kearney, R. *Communalism and Language in the Politics of Ceylon.* Durham, NC, Duke University Press, 1967.

Kemp, G. 'Iran and Iraq: The Shia Connection, Soft Power and the Nuclear Factor', at www.usip.org, Special Report No. 156 (www.usip.org/pubs/specialreports/sr156.html). United States Institute of Peace, Nov. 2005.

Kennedy, M. 'External Affairs Reaction to the Outbreak of the Troubles', in *Irish Studies in International Affairs*, 12 (pp. 87–96). 2001.

Kerr, M. *The Arab Cold War, Gamal 'Abd al-Nasir and His Rivals, 1958–1970* (3rd edn). Oxford, London and New York, Oxford University Press, 1971.

Kessler, R. J. *Rebellion and Repression in the Philippines.* New Haven, CT, Yale University Press, 1989.

Keyes, C. F. 'Cultural Diversity and National Identity in Thailand', in Brown and Ganguly, 1997 (see above).

Khouri, F. J. *The Arab-Israeli Dilemma.* Syracuse, NY, Syracuse University Press, 1968.

Kiernan, B. 'The Demography of Genocide in Southeast Asia: The Deaths Tolls in Cambodia, 1975–79, and East Timor, 1975–80', in *Critical Asian Studies*, Vol. 35, No. 4 (pp. 585–97). Dec. 2003.

Kimmerling, B., and Migdal, J. S. *Palestinians: The Making of a People.* New York, Free Press, 1993.

King, N., Jr, et al. 'Iraq War would Alter the Economies of Oil and Politics of OPEC', in *Wall Street Journal Europe* of 19 Sept. 2002.

Kinnvall, C., and Jonsson, K. (eds). *Globalization and Democratization in Asia: The Construction of Identity.* London, Routledge, 2002.

Kivimäki, T. (ed.). *Development Cooperation as an Instrument in the Prevention of Terrorism*, research report. Copenhagen, Ministry of Foreign Affairs, 2003.

Kivimäki, T. 'The Long Peace of ASEAN', in DANIDA *Journal of Peace Research*, Vol. 38, No. 1 (pp. 5–25). 2001.

Klaehn, J. 'Canadian Complicity in the East Timor Near-Genocide: A Case Study in the Sociology of Human Rights', in *Portuguese Studies Review*, Vol. 11, No. 1 (pp. 49–65). 2003.

Klare, M. 'More Blood, Less Oil', from TomDispach on Global Policy Forum of 21 September 2005.

Klemperer, V. *Language of the Third Reich—LTI: Lingua Tertii Imperii. A Philologist's Notebook* (trans. Brady, M.). London and New Brunswick, NJ, Athlone Press, 2000 (originally, in German, *LTI—Lingua Tertii Imperii: Notizbuch eines Philologen.* 1947).

van Klinken, G. 'What Caused the Ambon Violence? Perhaps Not Religious Hatred but a Corrupt Civil Service Sparked the Bloodletting', in *Inside Indonesia*, 60 (www.insideindonesia.org/edit60/ambon.htm). Oct.–Dec. 1999.

van Klinken, G. 'Ethnic Fascism in Borneo', in *Inside Indonesia*, 68 (www.insideindonesia.org/edit68/kalteng.htm). June–July 2000.

van Klinken, G. 'The Maluku Wars of 1999. Bringing Society Back', in *Indonesia*, 71. 2001.

van Klinken, G. 'Indonesia's New Ethnic Elites (Central and East Kalimantan)', in Nordholt, H. S., and Abdullah, I. (eds). *Indonesia: In Search of Transition.* Yogyakarta, Pustaka Pelajar, 2002.

Kodikara, S. U. *Foreign Policy of Sri Lanka: A Third World Perspective.* New Delhi, Chanakya Publs, 1982.

Korbel, J. *Danger in Kashmir* (revised edn). Princeton, NJ, Princeton University Press, 1966.

Kraft, H. J. S. 'The Autonomy Dilemma of Track Two Diplomacy in Southeast Asia', in *Security Dialogue*, Vol. 31, No. 3 (pp. 343–56). Sept. 2000.

Krag, H., and Funch, L. *The North Caucasus: Minorities at a Crossroads.* London, Minority Rights Group International, 1994.

Krishna, S. *Postcolonial Insecurities: India, Sri Lanka and the Question of Nationhood.* Minneapolis, MN, University of Minnesota Press, 1999.

Kumaraswamy, P. R. (ed.). *Revisiting the Yom Kippur War.* London and Portland, OR, Frank Cass, 1999.

Kumins, L. 'Iraq Oil: Reserves, Production and Potential Revenues', CRS Report for Congress (Order Code RS21626). Washington, DC, Library of Congress, 29 September 2003 and 13 April 2005.

Kuniholm, B. *The Origins of the Cold War in the Near East: Great Power Conflict and Diplomacy in Iran, Turkey and Greece.* Princeton, NJ, and London, Princeton University Press, 1980.

Kupchan, C. *The Vulnerability of Empire.* Ithaca, NY, Cornell University Press, 1994.

Kyle, K. *Suez.* London, Weidenfeld & Nicolson, 1991.

Laffin, J. *The War of Desperation: Lebanon, 1982–85.* London, Osprey, 1985.

Laío Hamutuk (Timor-Leste Institute for Reconstruction Monitoring Analysis). 'The UNMIT Mission in Timor-Leste', at www.laohamutuk.org/reports/UN/06UNMITcreation.html. August 2006.

Lall, A. *The UN and the Middle East Crisis, 1967.* New York, Columbia University Press, 1968.

Lamb, A. *The Kashmir Problem: A Historical Survey.* New York, Frederick A. Praeger, 1966.

Lamb, D. *The Africans: Encounters from the Sudan to the Cape.* London, Mandarin, 1990.

Lan, G. B. 'Rethinking Modernity: State, Ethnicity and Class in the Forging of a Modern Urban Malaysia', in Wee, C. J. W.-L. (ed.). *Local Cultures and the 'New Asia': The State, Culture, and Capitalism in Southeast Asia.* Singapore, Institute of Southeast Asian Studies, 2002.

Lapidoth, R. *Legal Aspects of the Palestinian Refugee Question.* Jerusalem, Jerusalem Centre for Public Affairs, 2002.

Laqueur, W. *Confrontation: The Middle East War and World Politics.* London, Abacus Books, 1974.

Layne, C. *A Peace of Illusions.* Ithaca, NY, Cornell University Press, 2006.

Lee, H. G. 'Malay Dominance and Opposition Politics in Malaysia', in Singh and Smith, 2002 (see below).

Lee, H. G. 'Malaysia: Re-examining Malay Special Rights', in Heng, R., and Hew, D. (eds). *Regional Outlook: Southeast Asia 2003–2004.* Singapore, Institute of Southeast Asian Studies, 2003.

Lee, R. L. M. 'The State, Religious Nationalism, and Ethnic Nationalization in Malaysia', in *Ethnic and Racial Studies*, Vol. 13, No. 4 (pp. 482–502). 1990.

Leifer, M. *Dictionary of the Politics of Southeast Asia* (3rd edn). London, Routledge, 2001.

Leifer, M., et al. *Michael Leifer: Selected Works on Southeast Asia.* Singapore, Institute of Southeast Asian Studies, 2005.

Lesch, D. W. *The Middle East and the United States.* Boulder, CO, Westview Press, 2002.

Levenberg, H. *The Military Preparations of the Arab Community in Palestine, 1945–1948.* London and Portland, OR, Frank Cass, 1993.

Levin, K. *The Oslo Syndrome: Delusions of a People Under Siege.* Hanover, NH, Smith & Kraus, 2005.

Levine, D. *Conflict and Political Change in Venezuela.* Princeton, NJ, Princeton University Press, 1973.

Levine, D. *Religion and Political Conflict in Latin America.* Chapel Hill, NC, University of North Carolina Press, 1986.

Levitt, M. *Hamas: Politics, Charity, and Terrorism in the Service of Jihad.* New Haven, CT, and London, Yale University Press, 2006.

Lewis, N. A., and Schmitt, E. 'Guantanamo Prisoners Could Be Held For Years, U.S. Officials Say', in *The New York Times* of 13 February 2004 (Vol. 124, No. 4).

LICADHO (Cambodian League for the Promotion and Defence of Human Rights). *Human Rights in Cambodia: The Façade of Stability*, a LICADHO Report (www.licadho.org/reports). Phnom Penh, LICADHO, 2005.

Liddle, W. 'Coercion, Co-optation, and the Management of Ethnic Relations in Indonesia', in Brown and Ganguly, 1997 (see above).

Lim, C. L. 'Race, Multi-Cultural Accommodation and the Constitutions of Singapore and Malaysia', in *Singapore Journal of Legal Studies*, 1 (pp. 117–49). 2004.

Lim, R. 'The ASEAN Regional Forum: Building on Sand', in *Contemporary Southeast Asia*, Vol. 20, No. 2 (pp. 115–36). Aug. 1988.

Lind, W. S. 'Understanding Fourth Generation War', at antiwar.com (antiwar.com/lind/index.php?articleid=1702) on 15 Jan. 2004.

Lind, W. S. *Fourth Generation War*—see Imperial and Royal Austro-Hungarian Marine Corps, 2005 (see above).

Lindblad, J. T.—Colombijn and Lindblad, 2002 (see above).

Lindgren, G. *The Role of External Factors in Economic Growth: A Comparative Study of Thailand and the Philippines, 1950–1990.* Uppsala, Uppsala University (Dept of Peace and Conflict Research), 1995.

Lindsey, T. 'Reconstituting the Ethnic Chinese in Post Soeharto Indonesia: Law, Racial Discrimination, and Reform', in Lindsey and Pausacker, 2005 (see below).

Lindsey, T., and Pausacker, H. (eds). *Chinese Indonesians: Remembering, Distorting, Forgetting.* Singapore, Institute of Southeast Asian Studies, 2005.

Lindstrom, L., and White, G. M. (eds). *Culture, Kastom, Tradition: Developing Cultural Policy in Melanesia.* Suva, University of the South Pacific (Institute of Pacific Studies), 1994.

Little, D. *Sri Lanka: The Invention of Enmity.* Washington, DC, US Institute of Peace Press, 1994.

Lloyd, S. *Suez, 1956: A Personal Account.* London, Jonathan Cape, 1978.

Loh Kok Wah, F. 'Where Has (Ethnic) Politics Gone? The Case of the BN non-Malay Politicians and Political Parties', in Hefner, 2001 (see above).

Loingsigh, G. *La estrategia integral del paramilitarismo en el Magdalena Medio de Colombia.* Bogotá, PDPMM, 2002.

Londoño, J., and Guerrero, R. *Violencia en América Latina: epidemiología y costos* (Documento de Trabajo R-375). Washington, DC, Inter-American Development Bank (Banco Interamericano de Desarrollo), 1999.

Lukacs, Y. (ed.). *The Israeli-Palestinian Conflict: A Documentary Record, 1967–1990.* Cambridge and New York, Cambridge University Press, 1992.

Lynch, D. *Russian Peacekeeping Strategies in the CIS: The Cases of Moldova, Georgia and Tajikistan.* New York, St. Martin's Press, 2000.

Ma, R.-W. 'Shifting Identities: Chinese Muslims in Malaysia', in *Asian Ethnicity,* Vol. 6 No. 2 (pp. 89–108). 2005.

MacFarlane, S. N. *Western Engagement in the Caucasus and Central Asia.* Washington, DC, Brookings Institution, 1999.

MacQueen, N. *United Nations Peacekeeping in Africa since 1960.* London, Longman, 2002.

Magallanes, C. J. I., Magallanes, C., and Holick, M. (eds). *Land Conflicts in Southeast Asia: Indigenous Peoples, Environment and International Law.* Bangkok, White Lotus, 1998.

Malley, M. 'Indonesia: Violence and Reform Beyond Jakarta', in *Southeast Asian Affairs 2001* (pp. 159–74). 2001.

Mallie, E., and McKittrick, D. *The Fight for Peace: The Secret Story behind the Irish Peace Process.* London, Heinemann, 1996.

Manning, C., and van Diermen, P. (eds). *Indonesia in Transition: Social Aspects of Reform and Crisis.* Singapore, Institute of Southeast Asian Studies, 2000.

Manogaran, C. *Ethnic Conflict and Reconciliation in Sri Lanka.* Honolulu, HI, University of Hawaii Press, 1987.

Manor, J. (ed.). *Sri Lanka in Change and Crises.* London, Croom Helm, 1984.

Mansergh, M. 'The Background to the Peace Process', in *Irish Studies in International Affairs,* 6 (pp. 145–58). 1995.

Mansfield, D. E., et al. *Economic Interdependence and International Conflict.* Ann Arbor, MI, University of Michigan Press, 2003.

Marshall, T., and Daragahi, B. 'Iraq Election Results Pose New Challenges for US Policy', in *Los Angeles Times* of 21 Dec. 2005

Martin, R. *Inter-Ethnic Conflict in Soviet Azerbaijan.* London, Thames Polytechnic, 1990.

Martinez, F. J. *Changes in Guerrilla Conflicts in Latin America after the Cold War.* Washington, DC, Storming Media, 2000.

Matveeva, A. *The North Caucasus: Russia's Fragile Borderland.* London, Royal Institute of International Affairs, 1999.

McFaul, M. *Post-Communist Politics: Democratic Prospects in Russian and Eastern Europe.* Washington, DC, Center for Security and International Studies, 1993.

McCann, E. *War and an Irish Town* (3rd edn). London, Pluto Press, 1993.

McCann, F. 'Argentina Talks Tough over New Claim to the Falkland Islands', in timesonline.co.uk (www.timesonline.co.uk/article/0,,3-2244476,00.html) of 27 June 2006.

McGarry, J. *Northern Ireland and the Divided World.* Oxford, Oxford University Press, 2002.

McGarry, J., and O'Leary, B. *Explaining Northern Ireland: Broken Images.* Oxford, Blackwell, 1995.

McInnes, C., and Rolls, M. G. (eds). 'Post-Cold War Security Issues in the Asia-Pacific Region', in *Contemporary Security Policy* (Special Issue), Vol. 15, No. 2 (August). London and Portland, OR, Frank Cass, 1994.

McIntyre, A. 'Modern Republicanism and the Belfast Agreement', in Wilford, R. (ed.). *Aspects of the Belfast Agreement.* Oxford, Oxford University Press, 2001.

Means, G. P. 'The Politics of Ethnicity in Malaysia', in *Current History,* Vol. 5, No. 19 (pp. 168–82). 1987.

Menon, R., and Ghia, N. (eds). *Russia, the Caucasus, and Central Asia: The 21st Century Security Environment.* New York, M. E. Sharpe, 1999.

Meyer, K. E., and Shareen, B. *Tournament of Shadows: The Great Game and the Race for Empire in Central Asia.* Washington, DC, Counterpoint Press, 1999.

Miall, H., et al. (eds). *Contemporary Conflict Resolution.* Cambridge, Polity Press, 1999.

Miller, C. T. 'Missteps Hamper Iraqi Oil Recovery', in *Los Angeles Times* of 26 September 2005.

Miller, M. A. 'The Nanggroe Aceh Darussalam Law: A Serious Response to Acehnese Separatism?', in *Asian Ethnicity,* Vol. 5, No. 3 (pp. 333–52). 2004.

Miller, S. C. *Benevolent Assimilation: The American Conquest of the Philippines, 1899–1903.* New Haven, CT, Yale University Press, 1982.

Minattur, J. 'The Nature of Malay Customary Law', in *Malaya Law Review,* 6. 1964.

Mishal, S. *The PLO under Arafat: Between Gun and Olive Branch.* New Haven, CT, and London, Yale University Press, 1986.

Mitchell, C. R. *The Structure of International Conflict.* London, Palgrave, 2001.

Mitchell, G. *Making Peace.* London, Heinemann, 1999.

Mohamad, M. 'The Unravelling of a "Malay Consensus"', in Singh and Smith, 2001 (see below).

Moloney, E. *A Secret History of the IRA.* London, Penguin, 2003.

Mommer, B. *Global Oil and the Nation-State.* Oxford, Oxford University Press, 2002.

Monroe, E. *Britain's Moment in the Middle East, 1914–71.* London, Chatto & Windus, 1981.

Morris, B. *The Birth of the Palestinian Refugee Problem Revisited.* Cambridge, Cambridge University Press, 2004.

Morris, E. D. *A Memoir of Ronald Reagan.* New York, Modern Library, 1999.

Morris, R. 'A Tyrant Forty Years in the Making', in *The New York Times* of 14 March 2003.

Munir. 'Indonesia, Violence and the Integration Problem', in Wessel and Wimhöfer, 2001 (see below).

Murray, G. *John Hume and the SDLP.* Dublin, Irish Academic Press, 1998.

Murray, G., and Tonge, J. *Sinn Fein and the SDLP: From Alienation to Participation.* Dublin, O'Brien Press, 2005.

Muslih, M. Y. *The Origins of Palestinian Nationalism.* New York, Columbia University Press, 1988.

Muttitt, G. *Crude Designs: The Rip-off of Iraq's Oil Wealth.* London, PLATFORM and Seacourt Press, 2005.

Nagazumi, A. *The Dawn of Indonesia Nationalism: The Early Years of Budi Utomo, 1908–1918*, Occasional Papers Series No. 10. Tokyo, Institute of Developing Economies, 1972.

Narin, S. 'ASEAN and the ARF: The Limits of the "ASEAN Way"', in *Asian Survey*, Vol. 37, No. 10 (pp. 961–78). Oct. 1997.

Narin, S. 'ASEAN and the Management of Regional Security', in *Pacific Affairs*, 71. 1998.

Narin, S. *Explaining ASEAN: Regionalism in Southeast Asia.* London, Lynne Rienner, 2002.

Ndikumana, L. 'Towards a Solution to Violence in Burundi: A Case for Political and Economic Liberalisation', in *Journal of Modern African Studies*, Vol. 38, No. 2 (pp. 431–59). 2000.

Negri, A., and Hardt, M. *Empire.* Cambridge, MA, Harvard University Press, 2000.

Nekrich, A. *The Punished Peoples.* New York, W. W. Norton & Co, 1978.

Newbury, C. 'States at War: Confronting Conflict in Africa', in *African Studies Review*, Vol. 45, No. 1. April 2002.

van Niel, R. *The Emergence of the Modern Indonesia Elite.* The Hague and Bandung, W. van Hoeve, and Chicago, IL, Quadrangle Books, 1960.

Nischalke; T. I. 'Insights from ASEAN's Foreign Policy Co-operation: The "ASEAN Way", a Real Spirit or a Phantom?', in *Contemporary Southeast Asia*, Vol. 22, No. 1. 2000.

Nonneman, G. (ed.). *Analyzing Middle East Foreign Policies.* London and New York, Routledge, 2005.

Nordstrom, C., and Martin, A. (eds). *The Paths to Domination, Resistance, and Terror.* Berkeley and Los Angeles, CA, University of California Press, 1991.

Northern Ireland Social and Political Archive—ARK (based in Queens University Belfast and University of Ulster), at www.ark.ac.uk.

Norton, A. R. *AMAL and the Shi'a: Struggle for the Soul of Lebanon.* Austin, TX, University of Texas Press, 1987.

Nye, J. S. *Understanding International Conflicts.* New York, Pearson, 2005.

O' Balance, E. *Wars in the Caucasus 1990–95.* London, Macmillan, 1997.

O'Brien, C. C. *The Siege: The Story of Israel and Zionism.* London, Paladin Books, 1988.

O'Cleary, C. *The Greening of the White House.* Dublin, Gill & Macmillan, 1996.

O'Grady, J. 'An Irish Policy Born in the USA', in *Foreign Affairs*, Vol. 75, No. 2. 1996.

O'Neill, K., and Munslow, B. 'Angola: Ending the Cold War in Southern Africa', in Furley, 1995 (see above).

O'Leary, B., and McGarry, J. *The Politics of Antagonism: Understanding Northern Ireland* (2nd edn). London, Athlone Press, 1993.

Ooi, G. L. 'The Role of the Developmental State and Interethnic Relations in Singapore', in *Asian Ethnicity*, Vol. 6, No. 2 (pp. 109–20). 2005.

Oren, M. B. *Six Days of War: June 1967 and the Making of the Modern Middle East.* Oxford and New York, Oxford University Press, 2002.

Oren, M. B. *The Origins of the Second Arab–Israeli War: Egypt, Israel and the Great Powers, 1952–56.* London and Portland, OR, Frank Cass, 1992.

O'Rourke, K. *Reformasi: The Struggle for Power in Post-Soeharto Indonesia.* Sydney, NSW, Allen & Unwin, 2002.

Orwell, G. *1984.* London, Penguin, 1990 (first Penguin edn 1956, originally 1949).

Ostrovsky, V., and Hoy, C. *By Way of Deception: The Making and Unmaking of a Mossad Officer.* New York, St Martin's Press, 1990.

Patočka, Jan. *Heretical Essays in the Philosophy of History* (trans. Kohak, E., ed. Dodd, J.). Chicago, IL, Open Court Publishing Co, 1996.

Paul, J. A. 'Oil in Iraq: The Heart of the Crisis', on Global Policy Forum, from Dec. 2002.

Pavel, B. *Russia's Policies in the Caucasus.* London, Royal Institute of International Affairs, 1997.

Pavlowitch S. K. *A History of the Balkans, 1804–1945.* London, Longman, 1999.

Pavlowitch, S. K. *Serbia.* London, Hurst & Co, 2002.

Peletz, M. G. *Islamic Modern: Religious Courts and Cultural Politics in Malaysia.* Princeton University Press, 2002.

Peluso, N. L., and Harwell, E. 'Territory, Custom, and the Cultural Politics of Ethnic War in West Kalimantan, Indonesia', in Peluso, N. L., and Watts, M. (eds). *Violent Environments.* Ithaca, NY, and London, Cornell University Press, 2001.

Peres, S. *The New Middle East.* Shaftesbury, Element Books, 1993.

Perkins, M. A. *Christendom and European Identity: The Legacy of a Grand Narrative since 1789.* Berlin, Walter de Gruyter, 2004.

Peters, J. *Pathways to Peace: The Multilateral Arab-Israeli Peace Talks.* London, Royal Institute of International Affairs, 1996.

Phadnis, U., and Ganguly, R. *Ethnicity and Nation-Building in South Asia* (revised edn). London, New Delhi and Thousand Oaks, CA, Sage Publs, 2001.

Philip, G. *Democracy in Latin America: Surviving Conflict and Crisis?* London, Polity Press, 2003.

Pilger, J. 'Blair's Meeting with Arafat Served to Disguise his Support for Sharon and the Zionist Project', in *New Statesman* of 14 Jan. 2002.

Ponnambalam, S. *Sri Lanka: The National Question and the Tamil Liberation Struggle.* London, Zed Books, 1983.

Pool, D. 'The Eritrean People's Liberation Front', in Clapham, C. (ed.). *African Guerrillas.* Oxford, James Currey, 1998.

Premdas, R. R., and Samarasinghe, S. W. R. de A. 'Sri Lanka's Ethnic Conflict: The Indo-Lankan Peace Accord', in *Asian Survey*, Vol. 28, No. 6. June 1988.

Quandt, W. B. *Decades of Decisions: American Policy toward the Arab-Israeli Conflict, 1967–1976.* Berkeley, CA, University of California Press, 1977.

Quandt, W. B. *Peace Process: American Diplomacy and the Arab-Israeli Conflict since 1967.* Washington, DC, Brookings Institution, 2005.

Rabinovich, I. *Waging Peace: Israel and the Arabs, 1948–2003.* Princeton, NJ, Princeton University Press, 2004.

Rajah, A. 'Ethnicity and Civil War in Burma: Where is the Rationality?', in Rotberg, R. I. (ed.). *Burma: Prospects for a Democratic Future.* Cambridge, MA, World Peace Foundation and Harvard Institute for International Development, 1998.

Ramage, D. *Politics in Indonesia: Democracy, Islam, and Ideology of Tolerance.* London, Routledge, 1995.

Ramaswamy, P. *New Delhi and Sri Lanka: Four Decades of Politics and Diplomacy.* New Delhi, Allied Publishers, 1987.

Ramcharan, R. 'ASEAN and Non-Interference: A Principle Maintained', in *Contemporary Southeast Asia*, Vol. 22, No. 1. 2000.

Rao, P. V. 'Ethnic Conflict in Sri Lanka: India's Role and Perception', in *Asian Survey*, Vol. 28, No. 4. April 1988.

Rashid, A. *Jihad: The Rise of Militant Islam in Central Asia.* London, Penguin, 2002.

Raum, T. 'Bush Rejects Lebanese Call for Cease-fire', from Associated Press on 14 July 2006.

Razvi, M. *The Frontiers of Pakistan: A Study of Frontier Problems in Pakistan's Foreign Policy.* Karachi, National Publishing House, 1971.

Reich, B. *Quest for Peace: United States-Israel Relations and the Arab Israeli Conflict.* New Brunswick, NJ, Transaction, 1977.

Reid, A. 'War, Peace and the Burden of History in Aceh', in *Asian Ethnicity*, Vol. 5, No. 3 (pp. 301–14). 2004.

Reyntjens, F. 'Briefing: The Democratic Republic of the Congo, from Kabila to Kabila', in *African Affairs*, Vol. 100 (No. 399). 2001.

Reyntjens, F. 'Briefing: Burundi, a Peaceful Transition after a Decade of War?', in *African Affairs*, Vol. 105 (No. 418). 2006.

Riad, M. *The Struggle for Peace in the Middle East.* London and New York, Quartet Books, 1981.

Riches, D. (ed.). *The Anthropology of Violence.* Oxford, Basil Blackwell, 1986.

Ricklefs, M. C. *War, Culture and Economy in Java, 1677–1726: Asian and European Imperialism in the Early Kartasura Period*, Southeast Asia Publications Series. Sydney, NSW, Allen & Unwin, 1993.

Riddell, P. G. 'Islamisation, Civil Society and Religious Minorities in Malaysia', in Nathan, K. S. (ed.). *Islam in Southeast Asia: Political, Social and Strategic*

Challenges for the 21st Century. Singapore, Institute of Southeast Asian Studies, 2004.

Riggs, F. W. 'Ethnonationalism, Industrialism, and the Modern State', in *Third World Quarterly*, Vol. 15, No. 4 (pp. 583–611). 1994.

Roberts, D. 'Sympathy with the Devil? The Khmer Rouge and the Politics of Consent in the Cambodian Peacekeeping Operation', in *Contemporary Security Policy*, Vol. 19, No. 2. Aug. 1998.

Roberts, M. (ed.). *Collective Identities, Nationalism and Protest in Modern Sri Lanka.* Colombo, Marga Institute, 1979.

Robertson-Snape, F. 'Corruption, Collusion and Nepotism in Indonesia', in *Third World Quarterly*, Vol. 20, No. 3 (pp. 589–602). 1999.

Robinson, G. B. *The Dark Side of Paradise: Political Violence in Bali.* Ithaca, NY, and London, Cornell University Press, 1995.

Robinson, G. B. 'Rawan is as Rawan Does: The Origins of Disorder in New Order Aceh', in *Indonesia*, 66. 1998.

Rodan, G. (ed.). *Singapore.* Aldershot, Ashgate, 2001.

Rohde, D. 'Indonesia Unravelling?', in *Foreign Affairs*, Vol. 80, No. 4. July–Aug. 2001.

Rolls, M. 'Indonesia's East Timor Experience', in Ganguly and Macduff, 2003 (see above).

Romano, L. 'Los costos de la violencia en El Salvador', Estudios Centroamericanos 52, in *Revista ECA*, No. 588. Oct. 1997.

Rose, R. *Governing without Consensus: An Irish Perspective.* London, Faber & Faber, 1971.

Ross, D. *The Missing Peace: The Inside Story of the Fight for Middle East Peace.* New York, St Martin's Press, 2004.

Ross, M. H. *The Management of Conflict: Interpretations and Interests in Comparative Perspective.* New Haven, CT, Yale University Press, 1993.

Ruane, J., and Todd, J. *The Dynamics of Conflict in Northern Ireland: Power, Conflict and Emancipation.* Cambridge, Cambridge University Press, 1996.

Rubin, B., and Colp Rubin, J. *Yasir Arafat: A Political Biography.* Oxford, Oxford University Press, 2003.

Ruhl, J. M. 'Civil-Military Relations in post-Sandinista Nicaragua', in *Armed Forces and Society*, Vol. 30. Fall 2003.

Rummel, R., and Zullo, C. (eds.). *Rethinking European Union Relations with the Caucasus.* Baden-Baden, Conflict Prevention Network, 1999.

Rupesinghe, K. 'Ethnic Conflicts in South Asia: The Case of Sri Lanka and the Indian Peace-keeping Force (IPKF)', in *Journal of Peace Research*, Vol. 25, No. 4. 1988.

Rupesinghe, K. (ed.). *Internal Conflict and Governance*. New York, St Martin's Press, 1992.

Rupesinghe, K. (ed.). *Conflict Transformation*. London, Macmillan, 1994.

Rutherford, D. 'Waiting for the End in Biak: Violence, Order, and a Flag Raising', in *Indonesia*, 67. 1999.

Sachar, H. M. *Israel and Europe: An Appraisal in History*. New York, Alfred A. Knopf, 1999.

el Sadat, A. *In Search of Identity: An Autobiography*. New York and London, Harper & Row, 1977.

Safran, N. *From War to War: The Arab-Israeli Confrontation, 1948–1967*. Indianapolis, IN, Pegasus, 1969.

Sahliyeh, E., Sinha, S., and Pillai, V. 'Modelling Ethnic Protest: The Case of the Middle East and Central Asia', in *African and Asian Studies*, Vol. 1, No. 1. 2002.

Sajoo, A. *Pluralism in 'Old Societies and New States': Emerging ASEAN Contexts*. Singapore, Institute of Southeast Asian Studies, 1994.

Sapir, E. *Selected Writing of Edward Sapir in Culture, Language and Personality* (ed. Mandelbaum, D. G.). Los Angeles, CA, University of California Press, 1986.

Sayigh, Y. *Armed Struggle and the Search for State: The Palestinian National Movement, 1949–1993*. Oxford, Oxford University Press, 1997.

Schellenberg, J. A. *Conflict Resolution: Theory, Research, and Practice*. Albany, NY, State University of New York Press, 1996.

Schexnayder, C. J. 'Watchdog Challenges US Drug War in Colombia' in *San Francisco Chronicle* of 7 Dec. 2005.

Schiff, Z., and Ya'ari, E. *Israel's Lebanon War*. London, George Allen & Unwin, 1984.

Schiller, A. *Small Sacrifices: Religious Change and Cultural Identity Among the Ngaju of Indonesia*. New York, Oxford University Press, 1997.

Schmidt, B., and Schröder, I. W. (eds). *Anthropology of Violence and Conflict*. London and New York, Routledge, 2001.

Schoenbaum, D. *The United States and the State of Israel*. Oxford, Oxford University Press, 1993.

Schulte Nordholt, H., and van Till, M. 'Colonial Criminals in Java, 1870–1910', in Rafael, V. (ed.). *Figures of Criminality in Indonesia, the Philippines, and*

Colonial Vietnam. Ithaca, NY, Cornell University (Southeast Asia Program), 1999.

Schwarz, A. *A Nation in Waiting: Indonesia's Search for Stability* (2nd edn). Boulder, CO, Westview Press, 2000.

Schwarz, A., and Paris, J. (eds). *The Politics of Post-Suharto Indonesia.* New York, Council on Foreign Relations, 1999.

Scott, J. C. *Weapons of the Weak: Everyday Forms of Peasant Resistance.* New Haven, CT, and London, Yale University Press, 1985.

Searle, P. 'Ethno-Religious Conflicts: Rise or Decline? Recent Developments in Southeast Asia', in *Contemporary Southeast Asia*, Vol. 24, No.1. 2002.

Sellato, B. *Nomads of the Borneo Rainforest. The Economics, Politics, and Ideology of Settling Down.* Honolulu, HI, University of Hawaii Press, 1994.

Shamir, S., and Maddy-Weitzman, B. (eds). *The Camp David Summit: What Went Wrong?* Brighton and Portland, OR, Sussex Academic Press, 2005.

Sharpe, S. 'An ASEAN Way to Security Cooperation in Southeast Asia?' in *The Pacific Review*, Vol. 16, No. 2 (pp. 231–50). June 2003.

Sheffer, G. (ed.). *US-Israeli Relations at the Crossroads.* London and Portland, OR, Frank Cass, 1997.

Shemesh, M. *The Palestinian Entity, 1959–1974: Arab Politics and the PLO.* London and Portland, OR, Frank Cass, 1988.

Sherman, A. J. *Mandate Days: British Lives in Palestine, 1918–1948.* London, Thames & Hudson, 1997.

Shirabi, H. *Palestine Guerrillas: Their Credibility and Effectiveness.* Beirut, Institute for Palestine Studies, 1970.

Shiraishi, T. *An Age in Motion: Popular Radicalism in Java, 1912–1926.* Ithaca, NY, Cornell University Press, 1990.

Shlaim, A. *The Iron Wall: Israel and the Arab World.* London and New York, W. W. Norton & Co, 2000.

Siddique, S. 'Corporate Pluralism: Singapore Inc. and the Association of Muslim Professionals', in Hefner, 2001 (see above).

Simmel, G. S. 'The Sociology of Conflict', in Ruitenbeek, H. M. *Varieties of Classic Social Theory.* New York, Dutton, 1963.

Singer, P. *The President of Good and Evil: The Convenient Ethics of George W. Bush.* New York, Dutton, 2004.

Singh, D., and Smith, A. L. (eds). *Southeast Asian Affairs 2001.* Singapore, Institute of Southeast Asian Studies, 2001.

Singh, D., and Smith, A. L. (eds). *Southeast Asian Affairs 2002*. Singapore, Institute of Southeast Asian Studies, 2002.

Singh, H. 'Tradition, UMNO and Political Succession in Malaysia', in *Third World Quarterly*, Vol. 19, No. 2. 1998.

Sloboda, J., et al. *Iraqi Liberation? Towards an Integrated Strategy*. Oxford, Oxford Research Group, 2005.

Smallman-Raynor, M., and Cliff, A. D. 'The Philippines Insurrection and the 1902–4 Cholera Epidemic, Part I: Epidemiological Diffusion Processes in War', in *Journal of Historical Geography*, Vol. 24, No. 1. Jan. 1998.

Smith, A. 'Indonesia's Role in ASEAN: The End of Leadership?', in *Contemporary Southeast Asia*, Vol. 21, No. 2. August 1999.

Smith, D., and Chambers, G. *Inequality in Northern Ireland*. Oxford, Clarendon Press, 1991.

Smith G. *The Nationalities Question in the Post-Soviet States*. London, Longman, 1996.

Smith, M. *The Soviet Fault Line: Ethnic Insecurity and Territorial Dispute in the Former Soviet Union*. London, Royal United Services Institute for Defence Studies, 1991.

Smith, M. L. R. *Fighting for Ireland? The Military Strategy of the Irish Republican Movement*. London, Routledge, 1995.

Snitwongse, K. 'ASEAN's Security Cooperation: Searching for a Regional Order', in *Pacific Review*, Vol. 8, No. 3 (pp. 274–94). Dec. 1995

Snitwongse, K., and Thompson, W. S. (eds). *Ethnic Conflicts in Southeast Asia*. Singapore, Institute of Southeast Asian Studies, 2005.

Solingen, E. 'ASEAN, Quo Vadis? Domestic Coalitions and Regional Co-operation', in *Contemporary Southeast Asia*, Vol. 21, No. 1. April 1999.

Spiegel, S. *The Other Arab-Israeli Conflict: Making America's Middle East Policy from Truman to Reagan*. Chicago, IL, University of Chicago Press, 1985.

Stein, K. W. *Heroic Diplomacy: Sadat, Kissinger, Carter, Begin and the Quest for Arab-Israeli Peace*. London and New York, Routledge, 1999.

Steinberg, D. J. 'An Ambiguous Legacy: Years at War in the Philippines', in *Pacific Affairs*, Vol. 45, No. 2. Summer 1972.

Storey, I. J. 'Living with the Colossus: How Southeast Asian Countries Cope with China', in *Parameters*, Vol. XXIX, No. 4 (pp. 111–25). Winter 1999/2000.

Sturm, A. . 'Democratization and Identity: Regimes and Ethnicity in East and Southeast Asia', in *Nations and Nationalism*, Vol. 12, No. 1. Jan. 2005

Sukama, R. 'Ethnic Conflict in Indonesia: Causes and the Quest for Solution', in Snitwongse and Thompson, 2005 (see above).

Sulistiyo, H. 'Greens in the Rainbow: Ethnoreligious Issues and the Indonesian Armed Forces', in Hefner, 2001 (see above).

Suny, R. G. *Looking Toward Ararat: Armenia in Modern History.* Bloomington, IN, Indiana University Press, 1993.

Suny, R. G. *The Making of the Georgian Nation.* Bloomington, IN, Indiana University Press, 1994.

Suryadinata, L. 'Governments' Policies Towards Ethnic Chinese: A Comparison Between Indonesia and Malaysia and Government Policy and National Integration in Indonesia', in Suryadinata, L. (ed.). *Chinese and Nation-Building in Southeast Asia: The Case of the Ethnic Chinese.* Singapore, Singapore Society of Asian Studies, 1997.

Suryadinata, L. 'China's Citizenship Law and the Chinese in Southeast Asia' a symposium paper for *The Law and the Chinese Outside China Conference.* Canberra, ACT, Australian National University, 1998.

Suryadinata, L. (ed.). *Ethnic Chinese as Southeast Asians.* Singapore, Institute of Southeast Asian Studies, 1997.

Swietochowski, T. *Russia and Azerbaijan: A Borderland in Transition.* New York, Columbia University Press, 1995.

Symonds, P. 'British Newspaper Alleges Israel is Planning a Military Strike on Iran', from World Socialist Website (www.wsws.org) of 15 Dec. 2005.

Symonds, P. 'Iraqi Oil Minister Resigns amid Protests and Economic Chaos', from World Socialist Website (www.wsws.org) of 9 Jan. 2006.

Tal, D. *War in Palestine, 1948: Strategy and Diplomacy.* London and New York, Routledge, 2004.

Tambiah, S. J. *Leveling Crowds: Ethnonationalist Conflicts and Collective Violence in South Asia.* Berkeley, CA, University of California Press, 1996.

Tambiah, S. J. *Sri Lanka: Ethnic Fratricide and the Dismantling of Democracy.* Chicago, IL, University of Chicago Press, 1986.

Tan, A. 'Armed Muslim Separatist Rebellion in Southeast Asia: Persistence, Prospects, and Implications', in *Studies in Conflict and Terrorism*, Vol. 23, No. 4 (pp. 267–88). 1 Oct. 2000.

Tan, A.. 'Terrorism in Singapore: Threat and Implications', in *Contemporary Security Policy*, Vol. 23. Dec. 2002.

Tannous, I. *The Palestinians: A Detailed, Documented Eye-Witness History of Palestine under the Mandate.* New York, IGT Publrs, 1988.

Taylor, K. W. *The Birth of Vietnam*. Berkeley, CA, University of California Press, 1983.

Tessler, M. *A History of the Israeli-Palestinian Conflict*. Bloomington, IN, and Indianapolis, IN, Indiana University Press, 1994.

Teveth, S. *The Tanks of Tammuz*. London, Sphere Books, 1969.

Than, M. *Myanmar in ASEAN: Regional Co-operation Experience*. Singapore, Institute of Southeast Asian Studies, 2005.

Than, M., and Gates, C. L. (eds), see Gates and Than, 2001 above.

Thatcher, M. *The Downing Street Years*. London, HarperCollins, 1995.

Thom, W. G. 'Sub-Saharan Africa's Changing Military Environment', in *Armed Forces and Societies*, Vol. 11, No. 1. 1984.

Thompson, M. R. 'Pacific Asia after "Asia Values": Authoritarianism, Democracy, and "Good Governance"', in *Third World Quarterly*, Vol. 25, No. 6. 2004.

Todd, J. 'Nationalism, Republicanism and the Good Friday Agreement', in Todd, J., and Ruane, J. (eds). *After the Good Friday Agreement*. Dublin, UCD Press, 1999.

van Tongeren, P., et al. (eds). *Searching for Peace in Europe and Eurasia*. London, Lynne Rienner, 2002.

Traas, A. G. *A Select Bibliography of Department of Defense Publications of the Southeast Asia Conflict*. Washington, DC, Army Center of Military History, 1983.

United Nations. *Conflict Diamonds: Sanctions and War* (www.un.org/peace/Africa/Diamonds.html). New York, UN, 2001.

UN. *Political Violence and Economic Development in Latin America: Issues and Evidence*. New York, UN, 2005.

UN Development Programme. *Tajikistan Human Development Report 1998*. Dushanbe, UNDP, 1998.

UNDP. *Abkhazia Briefing Note*. Tbilisi, UNDP, 2005.

UN High Commissioner for Refugees. *Population Movements as a Consequence of the Georgian–South Ossetian Conflict*. Geneva, UNHCR, Sept. 2004.

UN Security Council. *The Causes of Conflict and the Promotion of Durable Peace and Sustainable Development in Africa*, Report of the Secretary-General to the UN Security Council on 16 April 1998. New York, UN, 1998.

UN Security Council. 'Update Report No. 6: Myanmar', in *Security Council Report* (www.securitycouncilreport.org/site/c.glKWLeMTIsG/b.1715687/

k.BEA0/Update_Report_No_6BRMyanmarBR26_May_2006.htm) of 26 May 2006.

UN Security Council. 'Resolution 1704 (2006)' (www.un.org/News/Press/docs/2006/sc8817.doc.htm), of 25 August 2006.

United States Government (US Air Force). *Intelligence Targeting Guide*, pamphlet 14- 210. USAF, 1 Feb. 1998.

US Government (State Department). *National Strategy for Combating Terrorism*. Washington, DC, State Dept, 2003.

US Government (White House), see White House below.

Van Acker, F. 'Uganda and the Lord's Resistance Army: The New Order that No One Ordered', in *African Affairs*, Vol. 103 (No. 412). 2004.

Vanolli, H., Ruid, D., and Wallace, A. *Demobilizing and Integrating the Nicaraguan Resistance 1990–1997*. Managua, OAS International Commission for Support and Verification (CIAV-OAS), 1998.

Vieth, W., and Rubin, A. J. 'Iraq Pipelines Easy Targets for a Saboteur', at commondreams.org on 14 Dec. 2005.

Vital, D. *Zionism: The Crucial Phase*. Oxford and New York, Oxford University Press, 1987.

Waldman, A. *Arbitrating Armed Conflict: Decisions of the Israel-Lebanon Monitoring Group*. Huntington, NY, Juris Publishing, 2003.

Ward, J. *Latin America: Development and Conflict since 1945*. London, Routledge, 1997.

Watson, G. R. *The Oslo Accords: International Law and the Israeli Palestinian Peace Agreements*. Oxford, Oxford University Press, 2000.

Weekley, K. 'The Nation or the Social? Problems of Nation-Building in post-World War II Philippines', in *Third World Quarterly*, Vol. 27, No. 1. 2006.

Wessel, I., and Wimhöfer, G. (eds). *Violence in Indonesia* (pp. 82–98). Hamburg, Abera Verlag, 2001.

White House. 'President Bush Reaffirms Resolve to War on Terror, Iraq and Afghanistan. Remarks by the President on Operation Iraqi Freedom and Operation Enduring Freedom', press release (www.whitehouse.gov/news/releases/2004/03/20040319-3.html) of 19 March 2004.

Wierzbicka, A. *Understanding Cultures through their Key Words: English, Russian, Polish, German, and Japanese*. New York, Oxford University Press, 1997.

Williams, S. 'Review of Land Issues Literature', Cambodia Land Study Project, at www.ngoforum.org.kh/Land/Docs/draftlandlaw/ Review_of_land_issues_literature.htm. May 1999.

Wilson, M. C. *King Abdullah, Britain and the Making of Jordan.* Cambridge, Cambridge University Press, 1990.

Winichakul, T. *Siam Mapped: A History of the Geo-Body of a Nation.* Honolulu, HI, University of Hawaii Press, 1994.

Wirsing, R. G. *India, Pakistan and the Kashmir Dispute: On Regional Conflict and its Resolution.* New York, St Martin's Press, 1994.

Wistrich, R. S. (ed.). *The Left against Zion.* London, Vallentine Mitchell, 1979.

Wistrich, R. S. (ed.). *Anti-Zionism and Anti-Semitism in the Contemporary World.* New York, New York University Press, 1990.

Woodward, S. *The Balkan Tragedy.* Washington, DC, Brookings Institution, 1995.

Worth, R. F., and O'Neil, J. 'Iraq's Shiites Fall Short of Majority', in *International Herald Tribune* of 21–22 January 2006.

Yahuda, M. B. *The International Politics of the Asia-Pacific, 1945–1995* (2nd and revised edn), Politics in Asia Series. London and New York, Routledge, 2004.

Yodfat, A. Y., and Arnon-Ohanna, Y. (eds). *PLO Strategy and Tactics.* New York, St Martins Press, 1981.

Zartman, W. I. 'Bordering on War', in *Foreign Policy*, 124 (pp. 66–67). 2001.

Zartman, W. I. *Cowardly Lions: Missed Opportunities to Prevent Deadly Conflict and State Collapse.* Boulder, CO, Lynne Rienner, 2005.

Zasloff, J. A. 'Laos 1972: The War, Politics and Peace Negotiations', in *Asian Survey*, Vol. 13, No. 1. Jan. 1973.